Extending the Rafters

A book in the Williams Press, Inc., Series

A grant from the E. A. Barvoets Fund assisted
in paying the costs of publishing this book.

Extending the Rafters

Interdisciplinary Approaches to Iroquoian Studies

Edited by
MICHAEL K. FOSTER
JACK CAMPISI
MARIANNE MITHUN

A Publication of the Center for the History of the American Indian of the Newberry Library

State University of New York Press   ALBANY

Published by
State University of New York Press, Albany

© 1984 State University of New York

For information, address State University of New York
Press, State University Plaza, Albany, N.Y., 12246

Library of Congress Cataloging in Publication Data

Main entry under title:

Extending the rafters.

  Includes bibliographies and index.
  1. Iroquoian Indians—Addresses, essays, lectures.
2. Fenton, William Nelson, 1908–   —Addresses,
essays, lectures. I. Foster, Michael K. II. Compisi, Jack. III. Mithun, Marianne.
E99.I69E97 1984   973′.0497   83–5031
ISBN 0-87395-780-6
ISBN 0-87395-781-4 (pbk.)

10 9 8 7 6 5 4 3 2 1

Contents

List of Illustrations

Acknowledgments

Several people have assisted us in bringing this volume to completion. Sally M. Weaver provided valuable planning and editorial help, particularly in the early stages. Francis Jennings expressed continuing interest in the volume, and helped to arrange a publication grant from the Newberry Library Center for the History of the American Indian. We are grateful to the Center for this assistance, and to David R. Miller for attending to administrative details. William N. Fenton patiently assisted in the compiling of his bibliography, and Doris E. Foster played a vital role in its completion. Lise Lachance and Margery E. Toner at the National Museum of Man provided indispensable secretarial assistance. To all these people we express our thanks and appreciation.

The Editors

William N. Fenton, 1979

Preface

William N. Fenton, as many of his friends know, grew up in western New York State, the homeland of the Seneca. His early experiences with Indian families influenced his choice of a career in anthropology and left a distinctive mark on his thinking and style of writing about the Iroquois. In turn, his influence has been felt by virtually every student of the Iroquois over the past four decades. Anthony Wallace has stated the essence of the matter in the Overview by likening Fenton's role as dean of Iroquoian studies to the role of the ideal Iroquois sachem who tirelessly seeks consensus without, at the same time, discouraging diversity. Through the manifold directions that Iroquoian research has taken over the years—including studies of social, political, legal and economic organization, of myth, ritual, prehistory, personality-and-culture, language, material culture, ethnohistory, dance, and song—Fenton almost alone has maintained the stance of a synthesizer, steadfastly but gently urging others, many of whom have become very caught up with the pieces of the puzzle, to place their work in a context, to keep reaching for the broader sweep of Iroquoian culture history.

No doubt an integrated culture history of the Iroquois would have seemed more attainable in the mid-1940s, when Fenton established the Conference on Iroquois Research, than it does today. The early meetings at Red House, New York, were smaller and less formal than the bustling affairs held at Albany and Rensselaerville today. Indeed, Iroquoian studies have flourished into such a rich and diversified field that at times they threaten to break apart at the seams along disciplinary lines. The conference is, in many respects, a microcosm of North American anthropology with its numerous specializations: there are now prearranged sessions—once unheard of—sometimes with rather narrow foci of interest and attended by groups of enthusiastic partisans who use these occasions to exchange recent findings and who worry about shared problems. Yet the conference is unusual for the degree of interest in, and tolerance of, differing and sometimes novel approaches to Iroquoian problems. Most of the regular attenders go to all of the sessions, enriching them from a diversity of points of view.

There is no question that the present collection of papers reflects the considerable diversity of Iroquoian studies today. Many of the topics form nuclei of ongoing research projects, and some have a strong disciplinary orientation. At the same time there are significant tendencies toward convergence—at least a groping toward the broader culture-historical view which Fenton has been urging all along. We sense this, for example, when archeologists lament the inadequacies of single trait distributions, or small sets of trait distributions (once the *sine qua non* of interpretation), as the basis for drawing inferences about prehistoric migrations and time depth, and cast their nets far wider than before to take in factors such as climatic shifts, geography, linguistic distributions, and the perspectives gained from ethnology and ethnohistory; or when linguists turn from a preoccupation with synchronic description of linguistic structure to problems of historical relationship and time depth, or the drawing of inferences about prehistoric Iroquois culture from vocabulary; or when ethnologists place their conclusions about social and cultural patterns in an historic or even prehistoric context.

To the Iroquois, "extending the rafters" meant adding onto the longhouse, both in the literal sense of making room for new families and in the figurative sense of adding adopted individuals or nations to the Confederacy. By using this metaphor as the title of the volume we want to call attention to the fact that while the contributors are unquestionably breaking new ground in the areas of Iroquoian pre-history, linguistics, ethnology and ethnohistory, they also share a number of more general concerns which crosscut discipline lines. We decided early on that an organizational plan for the volume reflecting these concerns would be most in keeping with the spirit of inter-disciplinary cooperation which Fenton has tried to foster at Iroquois conferences and elsewhere.

In the first section, "Changing Perspectives in the Writing of Iroquoian History," a mix of ethnologists and historians explores a wide range of problems of the post-Contact period. Diverse though the topics of these papers are, we believe that all the writers share a special concern for the way Indian history has been—and ought to be—written. Of course, the historian, and now the ethnohistorian, have always had to deal with the problem of evaluating written records: this is particularly the case with efforts to piece together

Indian history from accounts made by white men, where a degree of bias must always be assumed. But what we think is reflected in these papers goes beyond the problem of evaluating primary sources to a rethinking of the historian's interpretive frame of reference, as the Indian point of view is better understood from ethnology. No other individual in Iroquoian studies has been more responsible for adapting the perspective gained from ethnology to problems of interpreting historical sources than Fenton himself, we might add.

The papers in the second section, "Aspects of Iroquoian World View," also represent a disciplinary mix, this time primarily in the fields of ethnology and linguistics. There is a continuation of the ethnohistoric interest of the first section, though there is a further focus in the concern for the past and present intellectual life of the Iroquois: their ceremonialism, their political institutions, and their mythology. Several of the papers are avowedly ethnolinguistic in that the writers find they must draw on the methods and data of both fields to define their problems.

The papers in the third section, "Iroquoian Origins: Problems in Reconstruction," are evenly divided between those by three archeologists and those by three linguists who bring varying perspectives, and entirely different sets of data, to bear on the question of Iroquoian origins and movements, on the one hand, and the question of prehistoric Iroquoian culture and society, on the other. (One paper in this section, a study of Mohawk dialectology, uses linguistic data as the basis for inferences about post-Contact movements of Mohawk speakers.) In recent years there has been a stepped-up interest in coordinating the results from historical linguistics and archeology to resolve the many outstanding questions of Iroquoian prehistory.

Three other papers fall somewhat outside this arrangement of sections, serving, as it were, to frame them. The first is Anthony Wallace's overview of Fenton's career and the development of Iroquoian studies. While this is not intended specifically as an introduction to the papers which follow, it provides a point of departure for the volume generally: it is clear to those who know Fenton's work that a recounting of the development of his career amounts to a recounting of the development of Iroquoian studies as a whole. This is, in fact, one of the themes developed by Fred Voget in one of two papers which form the concluding section, "The Fenton Tradition and Fenton as Applied Anthropologist." The other paper, by Laurence Hauptman, considers a little-known phase of Fenton's early career, his two years in the Indian Service.

Taken together, the papers constitute an interdisciplinary reader on a single people whose rich traditions have long made them a source of fascination to students of the history, cultures, and languages of the Northeast. The contributors all join in dedicating the volume to William N. Fenton who has done so much to demonstrate the value of a cooperative approach to the writing of Iroquoian culture history.

A bibliography of Fenton's works from 1935 to 1982 is included at the end of the volume.

The Editors

The Career of William N. Fenton and the Development of Iroquoian Studies

ANTHONY F. C. WALLACE

When the twenty-four-year-old graduate student from Yale, William N. Fenton, pitched his tent behind Jonas Snow's house in the summer of 1933, Iroquoian studies were in a very different condition than they are today, half a century later. Then, the Iroquois were indeed widely known among ethnologists as the subject of the great Lewis Henry Morgan's classic early ethnography, *The League of the Ho-De'-No-Sau-Nee, or Iroquois*, first published in 1851 and thereafter continuously in print in a series of new editions. And a number of English translations of major Iroquoian political, mythological, and religious documents had appeared, edited by such eminent scholars as Arthur Parker, Horatio Hale, and Duncan Campbell Scott. But little analytical ethnology had been published beyond the relatively slender contributions of Arthur Parker, J. N. B. Hewitt, F. W. Waugh, and Alexander Goldenweiser. Frank Speck, experienced in Algonkian studies, was just beginning his inquiries into Cayuga ceremonialism. Parker's student, William A. Ritchie, was starting his careful archaeological researches in upstate New York; Fenton's mentors at Yale, including Clark Wissler, Edward Sapir, Leslie Spier, and George Herzog, were not Iroquoianists at all. The intellectual ambiance was still "Boasian," both in the United States and Canada, calling for the recovery of aboriginal cultural remains and the carrying out of coordinated research programs designed to determine the typological and historical relationship of tribes. The new doctrines of functionalism, of acculturation studies, of culture-and-personality were in the air but not yet compelling. Thus the intellectual temper of the time demanded that the Iroquois be investigated thoroughly in more or less the Boasian way, with extensive ethnographic description, careful

1

classification, and historical reconstruction from primary documentary and archeological sources. This program has remained, for the most part, Fenton's personal "set" toward Iroquois research, although he has warmly encouraged the most diversified kinds of approaches among his students and colleagues.

Since Fenton's student days, the Iroquois have become one of the most extensively studied of the American Indian tribes; two generations of archeologists, linguists, ethnographers, and historians, have devoted a great deal of attention to them; the Iroquois bibliography has expanded enormously. And in this development, Fenton has been preeminent, both by virtue of his own scholarly contributions, and also through his influence on others. He is universally recognized as the dean of Iroquoian studies. There are implications in this use of the term "dean" that need to be made explicit in order to convey adequately the nature and extent of Fenton's contribution. The term implies that there exists a community of scholars, among whom the "dean" holds his place as a productive member and at the same time serves as the leader, organizing the education of the newcomers and facilitating the research of his mature colleagues. In this sense, Fenton fully deserves the title.

Fenton's career also can serve as the epitome of a certain kind of professional life in anthropology. He is and has always been an Iroquoianist, allowing himself only so much time with other subjects (Taos, Klamath, Blackfoot, Maori) as to give some added perspective to his view of Iroquois. This single-minded devotion to one group, and the emphasis on ethnographic and historical description and classification (although always illumined by, and illuminating, theory) makes Fenton's role unique among American anthropoligists of my acquaintance. Also noteworthy has been the closeness of personal and professional camaraderie with his Indian friends and his internalization of Iroquois traditions, as witnessed by his constant use of the Iroquois ritual language of metaphor in his own writing and conversation. The product of this intensity of investigation is also unique: an incomparable richness of detailed information on all aspects of a people's language, archeology, history, and ethnology is provided by Fenton and his collaborators. Few small populations anywhere in the world have been favored with such intense scholarly scrutiny. It is something of a model for the anthropological study of an ethnic group or culture area.

Fenton's interest in the Iroquois began earlier than his commitment to anthropology. The family farm in the Conewango Valley in western New York State lay midway between the Allegany and Cattaraugus Seneca reservations and for generations the Fentons had been patrons and hosts to Indian families who passed through on hunting excursions. There was even a small family museum of Seneca memorabilia that Fenton enjoyed as a child. This early exposure to the Iroquois as neighbors made anthropology a natural choice for a profession. After graduating from Dartmouth in 1931, he did a summer of archeology on the Great Plains, under the aegis of the Laboratory of Anthropology at Santa Fe, and then went on to Yale as a graduate student in anthropology. Oriented to Iroquoian studies from the first, he read the available published and manuscript sources, was sent by Sapir to consult with Frank Speck at the University of Pennsylvania on the conduct of field work among the Iroquois, and then began to study ceremonialism and herbalism among the Seneca on the Allegheny ox-bow, on Cornplanter Reserve and the Allegany Reservation above it. From 1935 to 1937 he served as a community worker for the Indian Service on Tonawanda Reservation, the seat of religious conservatism among the Seneca, thus gaining further acquaintance with Seneca ritual and religious belief.* The product of these first seven years of exposure to Seneca communities was a thorough knowledge of the language, a doctorate, and a series of publications that extended from his early (1936), and now classic, paper, "An Outline of Seneca Ceremonies at Coldspring Longhouse," to later papers through the 1940s. After teaching for two years at St. Lawrence University, he joined the staff of ethnologists at the Bureau of American Ethnology of the Smithsonian Institution, where he remained until 1951, pursuing Iroquoian studies. My first acquaintance with Fenton came in his office at the top of the tower of the old red sandstone castle overlooking Constitution Avenue and the mall.

During the war Fenton worked, along with other Smithsonian scientists, on the Ethnogeographic Board, assembling information on the South Pacific for Naval Intelligence, and served as Secretary of the Smithsonian's War Committee. In the latter capacity he also served on committees of the National Research Council that were providing anthropological and psychological advice to various federal agencies. These experiences, combining scientific and administrative skills, led to his appointment in 1951 as executive secretary to the Division of Anthropology and Psychology in the National Research Council. Here, he was involved in such matters as disaster studies, a field of intense concern to the federal Civil Defense Administration and the National Security Council, for at that time the merits of urban evacuation and deep shelter construction were being weighed as alternative defenses against the atomic bomb. (I was one of the

---

* Fenton's work at Tonawanda during these two years is the subject of Laurence Hauptman's paper in the present volume.—Eds.

disaster researchers whom Fenton recruited and used to meet with other colleagues in his office in the National Academy building on the other side of Constitution Avenue.)

A combination of administration and research activity was congenial to Fenton, but the interests of the National Research Council did not lie in the direction of encouraging Iroquoian studies. And so in 1954 he gladly accepted appointment as Assistant Commissioner of the New York State Museum and Science Service in Albany, where he assumed the duties of Director of the State Museum with its fine collection of Iroquoian archeological and ethnological specimens, and the leadership of the staff of resident Iroquoian researchers, headed by William A. Ritchie. Here Fenton remained until 1968, when he moved across town to become Research Professor of Anthropology at the new Albany campus of the State University of New York (and where he was in 1974 appointed Distinguished Professor of Anthropology). Thus from 1954 to the present, he has been able to focus a combined administrative, teaching, and research attention on the Iroquois, and to return, again and again, to the field and the archives.

Fenton's own published contributions to Iroquoian studies, both ethnographic and ethnohistorical, are guided by a very consistent set of theoretical interests and methodological principles. Pervasive in all his work is a concern with the problem of cultural "stability." Any ethnologist approaching the Iroquois has available not merely recent observations in the field, spanning perhaps three or four decades, but over four hundred years of historical records concerning their location, language, customs, and political and military entanglements with other Indian tribes and with Europeans. Iroquois today still speak the same languages, perform the same ceremonies, and use the same medicines as did their ancestors in early historic and proto-historic times. What is the mechanism by which so much of the Iroquois culture has been able to survive in the midst of the turmoil of an alien and changing world? The Iroquois are, as Fenton has been at pains to show, a kinship-based society (despite the importance of locality as a source both of internal village solidarity and inter-village cultural diversity). Beset by recurrent factionalism so deep that only unanimity can guarantee political cooperation, dependent on a simple moiety system to organize public ceremonials, and so acculturated in technology as to be in some households indistinguishable from their white neighbors, how could the heart of a kin-based culture live on?

Fenton's approaches to these problems have been by way of both the field and the library. In a remarkable series of major articles and monographs published between 1936 and 1953, based on field work among the Allegany and Tonawanda Seneca and on the Six Nations Reserve at Grand River, conducted both as a graduate student and as a Smithsonian ethnologist, Fenton took up the problem of stability-in-the-midst-of-change from both the ethnographic and the ethno-historical directions. Perhaps most widely known to his colleagues in cultural anthropology are the studies of Iroquois ceremonialism. The first of these, "An Outline of Seneca Ceremonies at Coldspring Longhouse," published in 1936, is a fundamental work, laying out the basic anatomy and one local variant of the annual ritual calendar. This was followed in 1941 by two major papers, "Tonawanda Long-house Ceremonies, Ninety Years after Lewis Henry Morgan," and, "Masked Medicine Societies of the Iroquois." In 1942 appeared the "program notes" of "Songs from the Iroquois Longhouse," and the album of the recordings themselves was issued by the Library of Congress in 1947. The best existing account of the Condolence ceremony of the League of the Iroquois, "An Iroquois Condolence Council for Installing Cayuga Chiefs," based on what he describes as "my best field work," appeared in 1946. The monograph of ceremonial practices associated with another aspect of the League, "The Roll Call of the Iroquois Chiefs: A Study of a Mnemonic Cane from the Six Nations Reserve," appeared in 1950. And in 1953 another monograph, "The Iroquois Eagle Dance: An Offshoot of the Calumet Dance," came out as Bulletin 156 of the Bureau of American Ethnology.

Another series of studies, less well known and more local in focus, must also be mentioned. These were short pieces, published in less widely distributed journals, that described in detail various aspects of the ethnobotany and ethnozoology of the few remaining Corn-planter Seneca who lived on the Old Cornplanter Grant in Penn-sylvania, just south of the Allegany Reservation. Beginning in 1940 with "An Herbarium from the Allegheny Senecas," the series added "Fish Drives among the Cornplanter Senecas" in 1942, "The Last Passenger Pigeon Hunts of the Cornplanter Senecas" in 1943, and concluded in 1945–46, with a five-part set of essentially ecological gleanings, collectively titled "Place Names and Related Activities of the Cornplanter Senecas," published in the *Pennsylvania Archaeologist*.

And finally, among publications of an essentially ethnographic character, mention must be made of the obituaries that Fenton wrote of some of his Indian friends and informants—Simeon Gibson (1944), Henry Redeye (1946), and Howard Sky (1972). For Fenton, field work has always been an intensely personal experience, a type of bond that fellow workers share in a valued common undertaking, and he gave his Indian collaborators the traditional Western scholar's farewell to a departed colleague.

These publications do not exhaust the list of Fenton's ethnographic contributions but they are, to my mind, the most noteworthy. With regard to ceremonial behavior, they cover most of the major Iroquoian categories: the annual calendar of subsistence festivals, the condolence ceremony of the League, the secret medicine societies and the eagle dance—all old traditional rituals that go back to pre-Columbian times. Absent is any treatment of the more recent Code of Handsome Lake, and the ceremonies associated with its recitation. (But his historical and editorial research did include a republication of Arthur Parker's *Code of Handsome Lake* and a first printing of Ely Parker's notes on an early version of the code that he sent to Morgan.) The Cornplanter Seneca papers are likewise a study of stability, in this case of the extremely detailed knowledge of a local habitat by a small kin-based community that has continuously occupied the site for over two hundred years.

His ethnohistorical contributions began slightly later than the ethnographic studies and are continuing today. The first (1940) was the classic paper on early historic Iroquois locality and population, *Problems Arising from the Historic Northeastern Position of the Iroquois*. It took up the question that has intrigued Iroquoianists for many years: how does one explain the apparently intrusive position of the Iroquois among the Algonkian tribes that surround them? Next year appeared "Iroquois Suicide: A Study in the Stability of a Culture Pattern" and in 1942 "Contacts between Iroquois Herbalism and Colonial Medicine." These ethnohistorical interests were gradually consolidated into a personal program of research that was intended to lead to a comprehensive political history of the Six Nations, particularly in the eighteenth century. Such work, though still in progress, has not yet appeared, for Fenton is as thorough a scholar as he is a field worker, and the archives that he has combed in Europe and America contain enormous quantities of information in rare book and manuscript collections that require careful transcription, editing, and in some cases, translation. A good part of Fenton's publication on the ethnohistorical side has been bibliographic and editorial, making available to other scholars carefully evaluated materials until now relatively inaccessible and difficult to use. Among these valuable editorial contributions must be mentioned the republication, with indispensible introductions by Fenton, of Horatio Hale's *Iroquois Book of Rites* (1963), of *Parker on the Iroquois* (1968), and of the recent (1974) translation (with Elizabeth Moore) of J. F. Lafitau's *Moeurs des sauvages amériquains* (1724). He has placed in print a number of unpublished works by early observers of the Iroquois like the missionary Asher Wright (1956 and 1957), sketch artist Baroness Hyde de Neuville (1954), James Emlen as delegate to the Canandaigua treaty (1965), and Ely Parker as informant to Lewis Henry Morgan (1951), to mention only a few. Of a more strictly bibliographical nature are the books prepared for the Institute of Early American History and Culture at Williamsburg, particularly the indispensable *American Indian and White Relations to 1830: Needs and Opportunities for Study* (1957), and the earlier (1953–1954) "Calendar of Manuscript Materials Relating to the History of the Six Nations of Iroquois Indians in Depositories Outside of Philadelphia." All of this scholarly editorial and bibliographic work not only increases the availability of primary sources to other scholars but also makes a substantial contribution to the history of anthropology.

In all of these works the problem of cultural stability has remained the guiding theoretical issue. In the early 1950s, prompted by an interest in factionalism among the Iroquois (in itself an old problem), Fenton visited the Taos Pueblo, and the Klamath and the Blackfoot on reservations, to gain a comparative perspective on the Iroquois; and these experiences in turn prompted a set of three theoretical papers in which he articulated the problem more abstractly than it was possible to do in the closer examinations of Iroquois materials. In "Factionalism in American Indian Society" (1952), he noted that native custom in self-government invariably "shines through" imposed European political systems. And again in 1953, in "Cultural Stability and Change in American Indian Societies," he pointed out that in an era of acculturation studies, the problem of stability was receiving too little attention. He characterized his own orientation as "historical functionalism" (meaning a "strain toward internal consistency" recognizable through time), and said of his own research strategy, "my purpose was to understand contemporary Iroquois society in order to comprehend the past." And in 1957, in a paper on "Long-term Trends of Change among the Iroquois," he noted that ethnographic "recovery" was his objective, and declared, "Why Iroquois culture has survived at all is a question that has plagued me since the first day of my field work a generation ago."

The other aspect of Fenton's contribution is, in the broadest sense of the word, administrative—the "deanship" referred to earlier. His first major contributions, on the Coldspring Longhouse ceremonial cycle (1936) and the study of the "historic northeastern position of the Iroquois" (1940), were both consciously programmatic, clearly articulating a set of problems that could only be solved by a cooperative program of research. This program was broadly conceived to include not only historical and ethnographic work, in which he himself was the leader, but also archeology and linguistics, fields in which he was knowledgeable but deferred to others for definitive research. Furthermore, it was articulated with Algonkian and Siouan studies in a grand scheme of research on the anthropology of north-eastern North America. This scheme had been formulated by Edward Sapir and others in Canada at that time and by Speck at Pennsylvania and was thus explicitly a part of the larger enterprise of world ethnography launched by Boas and his immediate students.

James Pilling (1888) had long before compiled a survey of the available works in Iroquoian linguistics, and Sapir was interested in the problems of the relationship of Iroquoian to other stocks, but it remained for younger linguists to carry forward the study of Iroquoian languages in the field. Most noteworthy, of course, are Floyd Louns-bury and Wallace Chafe, as well as a still more recent generation of linguists including Nancy Bonvillain, Michael Foster, Marianne Mithun, and Hanni Woodbury who among them have contributed to all Six Nations languages and have received guidance and en-couragement from Fenton.

In archeology, a host of professionals and qualified amateurs has worked at various sites under Fenton's helpful eye. Some have moved to other areas, like Richard MacNeish, who early developed the persuasive formulation of the *"in situ* hypothesis" of Iroquoian cul-tural origins, and James B. Griffin, whose surveys of the archeology of eastern North America brought Iroquoian sites into the broader framework of classification. But others have remained with the Ir-oquois, particularly William A. Ritchie, working out of the Museum at Albany, and James Wright and others excavating the Huron sites in Ontario.

In ethnography a host of younger anthropologists have been brought up in Iroquoian studies, the writer for one, who was encouraged to undertake his doctoral research at Tuscarora by Fenton's review of Frederick Johnson's symposium *Man in Northeastern North America,* in which Hallowell, the writer's mentor at Pennsylvania, had outlined the problem of the historical persistence of Algonquian personality styles. Fenton, in the review, had raised the question of the appli-cability of Hallowell's model to Iroquois, and Hallowell in response sent several students into the field to find the answer. Many other men and women have worked with Fenton's encouragement and guidance in Iroquoian ethnography; they are too numerous to attempt a complete list, but one cannot fail to mention Annemarie Shimony, whose monograph *Conservatism among the Iroquois at the Six Nations Reserve* (1961) complements Fenton's own work by suggesting an additional mechanism, namely the value placed on an Indian identity and thus on conservatism itself. Other names now familiar to Amer-ican ethnology include William B. Sturtevant, Elisabeth Tooker, Cara B. Richards, Barbara Graymont, Morris Freilich, Gertrude Kurath (a collaborator of Fenton's in the Eagle Dance study), John Witthoft, and David Landy—to mention only a few.

And finally, in the ethnohistorical field (where again the writer was aided by Fenton in his study of the origin of the Handsome Lake Religion), Fenton gave aid and direction to both professionals and capable amateurs. In the latter category must be included the late Merle Deardorff of Warren, Pennsylvania, and the late Charles Congdon of Salamanca, ethnohistorians, casual ethnographers, and patrons of an Indian clientele on the upper Allegheny in an almost Indian-agent style, who contributed largely to the discovery of valuable manuscript materials, as well as to the success of the Iroquois conferences (of which more will be said below). Fenton also has inspired and guided many other ethnohistorians, young and old, including a number already mentioned, and perhaps most notably Bruce Trigger, whose noteworthy history of the Huron up to 1660, *The Children of Aataentsic* (1976), was reviewed by Fenton himself (1978).

The effectiveness of Fenton's influence in guiding and encouraging Iroquoian studies depended, in its early years, not on the management of large amounts of federal or foundation grant funds (the one effort to set up a well-funded center for Iroquoian studies was abortive), but on a network of informal collegial relations among northeastern scholars and on his own teaching abilities. From the eyrie of the Smithsonian, and then from the Albany State Museum, by dint of publication, reviews, lectures, seminars, and personal visits, Fenton became the person to whom later these scholars sent their manuscripts for review. Furthermore, Fenton, with the help of Deardorff and Congdon, set up the Conference on Iroquois Research, which from 1945 to the present has met annually (with a few intermissions) at various locations for the informal reading and discussion of a few papers by young contributors, and, on a few occasions, for more formal symposia later to be published (see Fenton 1951; Fenton and Gulick 1961; and Tooker 1967). In the friendly and noncontentious atmosphere of the Iroquois conference, by firelight if possible, the Iroquoianists have lounged about, listened for new ideas, and laid plans for continuing research. In my opinion, the unfunded and informal convocations of the Iroquois conference achieved a success in inspiring Iroquoianists to continue and improve their work, with each other as a primary reference group, that more ambitious, expensive, and elaborately planned conferences could never have achieved. Perhaps more than any other single thing, Fenton's annual lighting of the council fire gave spirit to Iroquoian researchers.

In all of this, Fenton has always encouraged and facilitated, but has never assumed an intellectually dictatorial role. His method-

ological papers, particularly the 1952 "Training of Historical Ethnologists in America," are positive and encouraging rather than
critical. Consciously emulating the ideal Iroquois sachem, he has
been able to elicit consensus without discouraging diversity. This has
been a profoundly important factor in the success of the program,
for it has allowed Fenton himself to develop the essentially culture-
historical part of the research while others have been actively encouraged to study acculturation, revitalization, personality processes,
symbol systems, and various other topics. This division of labor,
made possible by Fenton's unique combination of administrative
flexibility and personal single-mindedness, had made Iroquoian studies a field of perennial freshness. But in the introduction to a work
such as this, celebrating the contributions of a scholar who has not
stopped contributing, an effort at definitive assessment of Fenton's
program of Iroquoian studies would be premature. Furthermore, the
only Iroquoianist with sufficient breadth and detail of knowledge to
measure progress in the solution of the host of particular scientific
problems is Fenton himself.

Before concluding this review of Fenton's contributions to anthropology, a few words are called for to discuss the current relations
between this discipline and the Iroquois themselves. The old patterns
of relationship between anthropologists and "their" tribes have come
into question in recent years in many parts of the world. Some
Iroquois communities have been loath to encourage ethnographic
and linguistic field workers in their midst, have complained about
archeologists' desecration of ancient villages and graveyards, and
have demanded the return of cultural treasures, like the Iroquois
wampum. Fenton himself describes the grilling he received in 1968
from young conservative activists at Coldspring Longhouse in a
moving personal document contrasting his first days of field work
with present conditions (1972). And later, in his capacity as Director
of the State Museum, he was criticized by some Indian friends for
being less than eager to return to Onondaga claimants the council
wampum long held by the Museum.

In "the good old days" before 1950—some of the best of which
I remember from accompanying Frank Speck on a visit to Alexander
General at Grand River in the winter of 1948—the enterprise of
ethnographic recovery was typically a collaborative patron-client relationship between a reasonably well-read and well-traveled ethnologist, with a broad comparative knowledge of the distribution of
culture traits in the general area, and an elderly chief or religious
leader who was anxious to have the old ways of his people per-
manently and accurately recorded before they were forgotten by an
apparently indifferent younger generation. Franz Boas's relationship

with his Kwakiutl informant, George Hunt, was a model of this kind of collaboration, and Fenton worked in a similar way with a number of Iroquois holders of traditional knowledge. The "informant" worked for years with the ethnologist, teaching him the language, dictating and translating texts, sponsoring his presence at ceremonies, legally adopting him by Indian custom, and serving as informant—and teacher—to his students and younger colleagues. The ethnologist's expertise lay in recognizing problems of local diversity and diffusion and in stimulating the informant by asking intelligent questions and jogging his memory by such devices as showing him pictures and artifacts of this and that and asking if he had ever heard of the old people doing such and such. The culture-historical orientation of an ethnologist like Fenton, interested in the problems of the survival of Indian custom, fitted precisely the motivation of the informant, which was to ensure the preservation of the knowledge of Indian custom in every way possible including ethnography.

In this kind of collaborative enterprise, the ethnohistorical methodology commonly called "upstreaming" fits perfectly. This method is sometimes misunderstood by horrified graduate students as leading to a Whiggish interpretation of a past seen as a sequence of efforts by one's ancestors to realize the values of their descendants (i.e., of the historian), or, even worse, as simply projecting the present upon the past. But, in Fenton's usage, upstreaming is neither of these but a technique for maximizing the recovery of information from broken, terse, incomplete historical and archeological remains. Starting with a relatively "complete" description, provided either by field ethnography or museum specimen, it becomes possible to jog the informant's memory, or to recognize in historical accounts the probable occurrence of a complete event from a partial description. Thus knowing, from ethnography, what the "three rare words of requickening" are, and their use in the Condolence Council, gives meaning to laconic notations by the secretaries who recorded colonial treaties. But this method obviously has its risk, not so much the projection of the present upon the past, but the possibility of selecting for attention in the present only that which can be recognized as having existence in the past.

The culture-historical approach thus is open to two criticisms. The informant—or, more likely in an Indian setting, his younger kinsmen—may feel that the agreement to undertake a collaborative effort to recover the past has been violated by the ethnologist (or by the white establishment of which he is a part), who has allegedly "taken away" the information and placed it in an inaccessible place like an expensive book or technical monograph, or has buried it in a file cabinet somewhere, or has even exposed it to ridicule. This can hardly be said of Fenton's work, which is published in a language readily accessible to the Iroquois, almost all of whom read English, and who can readily secure copies of the work in addition to those supplied them by Fenton himself. But the problem of upstreaming is more difficult. Although it is an essential technique for ethnographic reconstruction, it does permit the unwary to indulge in a kind of selective perception which subtly emphasizes those things that "survive" as being the interesting things about Indian culture. Such a selectivity of emphasis in ethnology has, of course, led Vine Deloria to criticize anthropologists for being unable to see present-day Indians as they really are and for perpetuating a kind of racist myth of the Indians as primitive, incapable of participating on equal terms in contemporary American civilization. But it is not clear that upstreaming or culture-historical interests always have this effect, or that they necessarily lead to a lack of attention to the identity dynamics that perpetuate old customs. As Fenton was well aware, and as Annemarie Shimony and I have both pointed out (1961 and 1961), the conservative people value Indianness itself highly and thus perpetuate not only the ancient calendar of increase rites but also the relatively recent "old way" of Handsome Lake. The ceremonies do not merely survive out of cultural inertia or by reason of functional fit; their survival is part of a conscious and essentially political policy. And, of course, these views of Shimony's and mine, and others like them, do grow out of Fenton's program of Iroquois studies (in my case, the paper was even published in a symposium edited by Fenton).

We hope the lessons of the recent past will not be lost upon us. Younger anthropologists, including the Iroquoianists, whether the research problem is historical or linguistic or functional, are being careful to ensure that the *quid pro quo* between anthropologist and community is clearly understood on both sides and that the anthropologist scrupulously observes the agreement. (And in this connection, it may be recalled that Fenton's *first* publication in 1935 was both culture-historical and applied, was jointly authored with a member of the Coldspring community, Cephas Hill, and bore the title "Reviving Indian Arts Among the Senecas.") As the Iroquois origin myth tells us, in the *really* good old days, when the world on the turtle's back was young and still had no form given to it by the Good Twin, the rivers flowed both ways. For Bill Fenton, the river of knowledge between anthropologist and community has always flowed both ways.

I

Changing Perspectives in the Writing of Iroquoian History

INTRODUCTION

A quarter of a century ago William Fenton (1957: 3) invited an audience of historians to consider a rapprochement between their discipline and ethnology, an approach which he felt would be highly beneficial to both, particularly in regional studies of Indian-white relations. In his appeal he borrowed from the pungent forest metaphor of the Iroquois Condolence Ceremony:

> It is in the spirit of Dekanisora, speaker of the Five Nations, who called on Governor Spotswood here at Williamsburg supposedly before 1720, that I have come to your fire to polish the "Chain of Friendship" between the ethnologists and the historians. I stand here therefore with the white wampum of friendship in my hands and address to you three words only of requickening—first, to wipe away your tears for those who have gone the long trail since our last meeting, second, to remove the obstructions from your ears so that you may hear my message, and third, to clear your throats of any bitterness that may subsist between us that you may reply later with a clear mind. One by one my words will pass across the fire to you—a string of wampum to attest each word, which you may grasp firmly and rack up on a pole to remind you of what I have said, that you may also put my words under your heads as a pillow and sleep on them before you answer another day. Now my message is on its way to you.

The field of ethnohistory has made considerable strides since 1957, so much so that historians and ethnologists now fraternize quite unabashedly at meetings such as the Conference on Iroquois Research.

What has been the result of these exchanges across the fire at scholarly meetings? On the ethnologists' side there has been an injection of greater time depth into descriptive studies which in an earlier period all too often seemed to present Iroquois society as though it existed in a timeless present. The effect on the historians' side has been somewhat different. Within Iroquoian studies, as Wallace mentions in his Overview, Fenton has been instrumental in developing the technique of "upstreaming" by which a perspective gained from ethnographic sources is used to evaluate documentary sources. So long as the historian confines himself to the records kept by white men, he is bound—even in the most conscientious interpretation of Indian-white relations—to miss something of the Indian point of view. The historians' primary materials are already one stage removed from native realities; indeed, they are often badly distorted representations of those realities. An ethnological perspective, then, provides a backdrop against which to view and test historical hypotheses, particularly as to *why* Indians did what they did. (*What* they did has been extensively documented in the source literature of the Northeast.) Ignorance of real Indian intentions and strategies has often resulted, even among the most respected historians such as Francis Parkman and George T. Hunt, in imputing far-fetched, and usually rather unflattering—not to say senseless—motives to the Indians, as Bruce Trigger shows in the opening paper.

All the papers show in one way or another a concern for the way Indian history has been written, a position which is informed from familiarity with the Iroquoian ethnographic literature. Trigger provides the most general statement about the need for a new Indian history, one that is not a mere "appendage" to white history. Hence, Indian warfare, which Trigger elsewhere argues was an activity permeated with ritual meaning for the Iroquois, was not the product of innate Indian "treachery" and "perfidy," as sometimes claimed, but rather a matter of calculated policy shaped by the competition for trade and by political rivalries. This approach forces us to take a completely new look at such figures as Champlain, Brûlé and Brébeuf of the first half of the seventeenth century, Canada's Heroic Age.

Gordon Day exposes another common fault of earlier historical writing, the tendency to repeat and pass along uncritically the conclusions of previous workers. The notion of Iroquois invincibility in the Northeast, which can be traced to Cadwallader Colden and which has descended through several generations of historians, simply does not stand up to a careful analysis of the colonial records, at least before the mid-seventeenth century; and even after this time epidemics, encroachment by whites, and reforming alliances played as great a role in the depopulation of parts of New England as the threat of Iroquois raids, which in any case were often unsuccessful. Day illustrates his point by a detailed account of the little-known Ouragie war of the 1660s.

In James Axtell's tracing of the steps leading to the founding of the Dartmouth Indian School, Eleazor Wheelock's program of educating Indian youth is shown up as a thinly disguised racist effort whose Puritan purpose in saving Indian souls from damnation amounted to little more than saving the English from the Indians. Such accusations are not new, but what gives Axtell's paper its freshness is the statements he has been able to tease out of the records by Indian leaders who lamented the treatment of their young people at the school. These statements show that the Iroquois were not unaware of Wheelock's designs, or the effects of the civilizing (enculturation) process. Wheelock's program was not particularly successful, an outcome which he attributed to Iroquois intransigence, and ultimately to original sin.

Charles Johnston takes up concerns similar to those of Axtell and Trigger, detailing the career of the Anglican missionary Robert Lugger at Six Nations Reserve in the early nineteenth century. In view of the large number of churches at Six Nations representing a half dozen or so different sects, it is surprising that so little has been written about the impact of mission activity among Canada's largest group of surviving Iroquois, and this paper makes an important first step.

Thomas Abler describes a law suit over land assigned to the New York Iroquois in Kansas. He is interested in showing the adaptation of traditional Iroquoian political structure, as embodied in the principles of the League Confederacy, to nineteenth-century political realities. Hereditary chiefs of the League joined with elective officials from the Seneca Nation in an unusual cooperative effort to formulate the claim, but following its settlement, old factional divisions emerged once more. The case is noteworthy in that it shows a willingness by Iroquois leaders to bend ideology to meet challenges of the day. Abler's approach provides an interesting twist to the notion of upstreaming, since it draws upon the historical record to shed light on a phenomenon usually reserved for the ethnologist, the structure of the League Confederacy. The Confederacy is more often described in terms of its abstract principles than its practice. Abler relies heavily upon tribal council documents which he interprets against the background of American legislative and historical sources.

Jack Campisi examines the broader context of Iroquois-white relations as it emerges in U.S. legislative and judicial history. Much
of the confusion over the status of the Iroquois in the United States
has been the result of conflicts between the Federal and New York
State governments. The legal status of the Iroquois has changed from
time to time since the Revolutionary period to fit particular administrative and legislative ends. The Iroquois have by no means been
docile bystanders in this process, but have acted periodically to assert
their own claims of sovereignty which have at times been recognized
by one level of government or the other, but in general the litigation
has been confused and nondefinitive. Here the role of the anthropologist, as, for example, an expert witness in contemporary land
cases, becomes not only desirable but urgent in interpreting native
institutions.

Elisabeth Tooker writes from an ethnological perspective, not so
much to expose errors in the Iroquois historic record as to show
how certain popular misconceptions have arisen about Iroquois society
from the anthropological literature. Without denying the importance
of the role of women in traditional Iroquoian life, she argues that
the notion of the Iroquois matriarchate has been considerably overdrawn. The exaggeration of the role of women has arisen from a
misunderstanding of the basic structure and function of Iroquois
clans, principles of kinship, economic practices, and the nature of
ownership of property. Based partly on the popularity of Lewis Henry
Morgan's writings, the Iroquois became the type of a certain kind
of non-Western society at a time when anthropology was dominated
by evolutionistic thinking. When the true principles of Iroquois social
organization are understood, she contends, women are found to have
a far less exalted role than has often been attributed to them.

CHAPTER ONE

Indian and White History: Two Worlds or One?

BRUCE G. TRIGGER

ORIGINS OF AMERINDIAN HISTORY

William Fenton's career has witnessed the birth and development of ethnohistory as a recognized methodology, if not a discipline (Fenton 1962). Throughout his working life he has carried forward the interests of Frank Speck and John Swanton in utilizing historical records for ethnographic purposes and in his writings and contacts with students he has succeeded in communicating these interests to younger generations of Iroquoian scholars. He has thus played an important role in the development of Amerindian history.

Nineteenth-century historians in the United States generally viewed the Indians as a prologue to Euro-American history. Like that of the forests and the buffaloes, their fading from the scene was interpreted as an unambiguous manifestation of progress and of divine providence. Indeed, until recent census returns demonstrated squarely to the contrary, the imminent physical extinction of the American Indians was taken for granted by most scholars. The frontier ideology that had developed in America in the seventeenth century in order to justify the usurpation of Indian lands by Whites predisposed historians in varying degrees to regard the Indians as savages and to interpret their displacement by Whites as a triumph of civilization over barbarism (Pearce 1965; Jennings 1975: 9–14). It is regrettable, but perhaps not coincidental, that the most popular of nineteenth-century historians, Francis Parkman, was among the least sympathetic to the Indians.

This paper is based in part on a talk given at the University of New Brunswick, March 29, 1974. I wish to thank Professor A. G. Bailey for his comments on that talk and for encouraging me to write this paper.

Prior to modern times, the climate and geography of Canada precluded extensive White settlement and enhanced the economic importance of the fur trade. Moreover, for a long time Indians and Whites living in Canada were allies, against first British and then American aggressors. Beginning with Marc Lescarbot (1907–1914) and lasting through the French regime, educated Europeans meeting and interacting with the Indians of Canada collaborated with "armchair" savants in Europe to produce the "myth" of the Noble Savage. More recently, it was Canadian historians who first appreciated the role that the Indians had played in enabling the European colonization of North America. Harold Innis's (1956) "Laurentian hypothesis" viewed Canada as having been fashioned by the fur trade, as it penetrated the northern interior of the continent by way of the St. Lawrence Valley. Innis concluded that "the Indian and his culture were fundamental to the growth of Canadian institutions" (p. 392) and he and the like-minded anthropologist T. F. McIlwraith (1930: 132) were to inspire A. G. Bailey (1937) to write his now classic monograph on relations between Indians and Europeans in eastern Canada prior to 1700. Independently, Léo-Paul Desrosiers (1947) wrote his *Iroquoisie,* a major historical work attempting to describe and explain political relations between the French and the Indians during the seventeenth century. While these studies increased historians' awareness of the importance of Indians for understanding Canadian history, they did not have a significant impact on Canadian historiography, nor did they result in the development of Amerindian history.

The latter evolved in the United States, out of studies of acculturation, such as Ralph Linton's (1940) *Acculturation in Seven American Indian Tribes.* These studies of the relationship between dominant and subordinate cultures in colonial situations marked the beginning of a concern in anthropology with the use of history based on written documents. Early studies dealt with how whole peoples or cultures responded to European contact. What individuals or specific groups within a tribe did was of interest only in terms of the total process of adaptation. Nevertheless, under the general rubric of ethnohistory, this sort of approach was developed along more explicitly historical lines by such anthropologists as E. H. Spicer (1962), E. B. Leacock (1954), N. O. Lurie (Leacock and Lurie 1971), and H. Hickerson (1962; 1970). The aim of their work, at least in part, was to produce rounded accounts of Indian groups to counteract the European bias of traditional historiography.

The development of ethnohistory has also been encouraged by the experience that many anthropologists have gained from using archival materials while doing research for land claims suits and by a growing interest among Indians in their own history. Concurrently, the study of Indian history has been taken up by professional historians, such as Francis Jennings (1975: vii), who perceive the value of anthropological perspectives and utilize them in their work. These historians have brought to this research professional skills which complement those of anthropologists. So great has the interest in Indian history become that professional anthropologists and historians are no longer lonely pioneers, but stand in danger of being submerged in a burgeoning popular culture. All of these developments promote confidence that Indian history is possible and desirable.

Nevertheless, the development of ethnohistory has compelled its practitioners to confront a variety of conceptual and methodological issues, not all of which have been resolved to everyone's satisfaction. Awareness of these problems is, however, an indication of growing sophistication. It seems no accident that most of these problems stem from ethnohistory's original concern with acculturation.

SOME PROBLEMS OF ETHNOHISTORY

It is now evident that most Indian societies were radically altered as a result of the Indians' contact with Europeans. Population decline was universal and warfare related to European settlement or trade frequently shattered Indian groups and forced them to seek refuge in new ecological zones. Many traits that once were believed to have characterized Indian societies prior to European contact are now understood to have been introduced or evolved as a response to it. These include such diverse items as splint baskets, individual trapping territories, and religious institutions including the Delaware Big House and the Ojibwa Midewiwin. It is also likely that many tribal groupings extant in the early historic period had consolidated as a response to the penetration of European commerce inland. This suggests that most, if not all, Indian societies had been significantly transformed as a result of direct or indirect European contact prior to when Europeans recorded their first substantial descriptions of them. Because of this, our conventional assumptions about the pristine state of Indian societies, as embodied in the "ethnographic present" of traditional ethnographies, seem to be based upon unacceptable data (Brasser 1971).

The problem therefore remains as to how one may ascertain the state of such societies prior to the commencement of European influence. Archaeology and historical linguistics offer only weak palliatives, since their conclusions are almost invariably conjectural and concern isolated fragments of a cultural inventory. Because reliable data are scarce, it is possible that some anthropologists may be tempted into making doctrinaire pronouncements about what is and what is not aboriginal on the basis of erroneous general assumptions. For example, it is not at all evident to me that family-owned trade routes must have developed among the Huron as a response to European trade; while there is good evidence (Tooker 1960; Chafe 1964) to refute the suggestion that the Iroquoians' emphasis on curing rituals arose as a response to European diseases. Nor would it be prudent to believe that Indian confederacies did not develop except to cope with problems posed by Europeans.

Archaeological evidence makes it clear that Indian cultures were not static prior to European contact. This refutes the opinion of those who have conducted studies of cultural change as if change did not occur prior to the arrival of the Europeans (Gamst 1969: 6). The latter view has been popular both among racists, who maintained that native peoples lacked the intelligence to change, and with idealists, who believed that in their native state Indian cultures were in such perfect harmony, both internally and with their environment, as to preclude change. Archaeological evidence indicates that some Indian cultures had indeed been changing slowly in prehistoric times, but that others had been evolving very rapidly. The latter included the Iroquoian ones, which from about A.D. 500 had undergone massive changes, involving the transformation of their subsistence economy from a hunting and gathering base to a horticultural one. These sorts of observations indicate that the idea of an "ethnographic present" followed by a series of transformations resulting from European contact is in error. Instead, Indian cultures should be viewed in terms of a continuum of change, beginning before the arrival of the Europeans and extending to the present. Such change can be analyzed either as a continuum or more schematically in terms of successive periods linked by various transformations. While archaeological data address themselves to different problems and in terms of different perspectives from historical or ethnographic data, it is evident that whatever understanding of the late prehistory of Indian cultures can be obtained from them is essential if early Indian history is to be properly understood. This broader approach also helps to rescue Indian history from being nothing more than a study of the response of Indian cultures to the presence of Europeans. As such, the broader findings of archaeologists must be regarded as an integral part of Indian history.

From what has been stated above, it is clear that changes in Indian society were influenced rather than initiated by European contact. Most anthropologists would probably go further and assert that, in general, Indians "made their first adjustments to Europeans in terms of existing native conditions" (Lurie 1959: 37). This probably means that the adaptive strategies that had proved successful in prehistoric times provided groups with the models for their initial attempts to cope with the problems posed by European contact.

The idea that traditional Indian values and intertribal relationships existing from before the time of European contact played an important role in the development of Indian-White relations runs directly counter to George T. Hunt's (1940: 5) assumption that as soon as Indians began to seek European goods they became entangled in a network of trading relations and intertribal competition that was fashioned by economic self-interest rather than by their traditional modes of thought and behavior. According to Hunt, these new economic imperatives transformed the lives of the Indians so quickly and so thoroughly as to make any understanding of their previous behavior unnecessary. Much seems to have happened, however, that Hunt's hypothesis does not explain (Snyderman 1948; Trelease 1960). Indeed, few economic anthropologists would accept that either Indians or Whites were able to determine their economic self-interest independently from their broader cultural biases (Salisbury 1973). This conclusion reinforces the value of using archaeological data to determine to what degree early descriptions of Indian life reflect developments that occurred subsequent to European contact.

Another imponderable is the degree to which the ethnohistorian's reliance on White documents results in his placing excessive emphasis on Indian-White relations at the expense of those within or between Indian groups. It is acknowledged that Indian life was greatly altered, both deliberately and inadvertently, as a result of White contact. It is also generally agreed that the colonial history of Canada and the United States cannot be understood without detailed consideration of the role played by Indians. The reactions of ethnohistorians, however, to the more nuanced problem of bias in their sources of data vary considerably. Some argue that relations between Indians and Whites rapidly became the dominant factor in Indian life; hence the bias in sources of data is an accurate reflection of reality. In this view, Indian history becomes an extension or a part of colonial history (Jennings 1968). Other ethnohistorians assume that the largely unrecorded internal dynamics of Indian cultures and their longstanding relations with other tribes were also important determinants of their behavior. Little can be done to reconstruct such relationships, except to study all available sources carefully and cross-check them in the hope that this may yield fresh information about unexpected topics. In coping with this problem, as with the social anthropologists' allegation that archival material is no substitute for ethnographic data, the ethnohistorian has no choice but to work harder, hoping that in specific instances he may demonstrate the contrary.

INDIAN HISTORY—AN AUTONOMOUS STUDY?

While the development of ethnohistory has provided anthropology with a new dimension, the term itself has outgrown its usefulness. It can be argued that it is patronizing to draw a distinction between "regular" history and "native" history and that this practice should be avoided. The only valid counterargument seems to be that, from the point of view of methodology, it is valuable to distinguish conventional history, which is based largely on a culture's own written documents, from the history of nonliterate peoples, which perforce must be based on documents that have been recorded by representatives of an alien culture. Writing the latter requires an ethnological perspective and the ability to use information from various alternative sources, including archaeology, linguistics, and oral traditions. While this provides a useful operational definition of ethnohistory, it is by no means evident that the methodological niceties of this terminology outweigh its social disadvantages. While a change of name will involve little if any change in practice, ethnohistorians can express their aims and purposes more adequately by calling their work Indian history.

We have already suggested that some scholars view Indian history as a facet of colonial history, which implies that they may not view it as a rounded field worthy of study in its own right. Most ethnohistorians, however, tend to view it as a separate application of historical method to new material. No doubt, this partly reflects a still earlier view of acculturation as a holistic approach to analyzing certain phenomena within anthropology.

One of the concomitants of this assumption has been the belief that when relations between Indians and Whites are examined, the behavior and motivations of the Whites can be assumed to have been explained already by conventional historians. This suggests that while the findings of White history are likely to constitute an indispensable element of Indian history, Indian history is unlikely to reveal anything of importance for understanding White history. The flow of knowledge is therefore viewed as unidirectional, from the developed field of conventional history to its colonial satellite, ethnohistory. This view of conventional history was understandable when the new discipline had few resources to fall back on and its practitioners found it reassuring to believe that there was a solid body of data to build upon and extend. Ethnohistorians may therefore be forgiven for failing to observe that this position violated a major tenet of historical method: the need to consider the implications that every piece of available evidence may have for understanding any particular piece. Historians were implicitly functionalists long before ethnologists had heard of the term.

In his recent book, *The Invasion of America*, Francis Jennings (1975) recounts how an elementary knowledge of Amerindian ethnology made him keenly aware of the deficiencies in traditional White history. His realization of the discrepancy between how Francis Parkman portrayed the Indians of New England and how anthropology suggested they must have been led him to penetrate the mythology by which the Puritans had justified their conquest of these Indians and their dispossessing them of their lands. The effectiveness of this mythology, combined with the Puritans' "pervasive calculated deception of the official records" (p. ix) had permitted the Puritan version of history to flourish unchallenged for over three centuries. Here we have a striking example of how a consideration of Indian behavior has resulted in a more objective interpretation of White history.

My own experiences have been similar to those of Francis Jennings, although less dramatic. In 1968, I began work on a history of the Huron Indians prior to their dispersal in 1660 (Trigger 1976). My aim was to write an account of the Huron that was comprehensible in its own terms and not merely as an appendage to White history. Among the problems with which I hoped to deal were to trace continuities from prehistoric times into the historic period, to explain the tangle of motives that accounted for the Iroquois wars, and to explain why in their final years the Huron were overcome by a moral and political paralysis that left them unable to resist the Iroquois. French fur traders, government officials, and missionaries had to be considered, but I was determined to do so only in relationship to Huron problems. At the beginning, I accepted that the related White history was thoroughly understood and viewed myself as attempting to extend a similar understanding to the Huron.

In retrospect, I find my view of White history to have been extremely naive. This is so both in terms of the theoretical considerations outlined above and because of the specific nature of the evidence. The first half of the seventeenth century was Canada's "heroic age." Although only a handful of Europeans resided in Canada, many of them have come to be regarded as great historical figures, whose bravery and integrity are revered by French and English Canadians alike, as well as beyond the borders of Canada. In an age marked by religious bigotry, the personal qualities of the Jesuits elicited the admiration of the New England Protestant Francis Parkman (1867), while Samuel Morison (1972) is only the last of many historians to treat Champlain with a respect bordering on adulation. The magnanimity and heroism attributed to the leading

figures of this period contrast strikingly with the pettiness, factionalism, and quarreling that characterized the later history of New
France.
    Yet is this contrast real or apparent? There are relatively few
contemporary sources for the first half of the seventeenth century
and most were written for partisan purposes and are either auto-
biographical or adulatory. These sources represent only limited points
of view, particularly of the clergy and of some administrative officers.
Very few firsthand reports are available from fur traders, who were
relatively numerous and who had close and often good relations
with the Indians. It is significant that what is available from traders
provides a very different view of the period from the canonical one
(Adams 1961). Even controversial works that might assist in pene-
trating behind the mask of self-adulation that characterizes our sources
are rare. Marc Lescarbot (1907–1914) gently chides Champlain and
Sagard (1866) criticizes the Jesuits, but the blatantly polemical works
dealing with this period are of later date (Le Clercq 1691; Charlevoix
1866–1872). The latter are valuable mainly insofar as they preserve
documents or hearsay that otherwise would have been lost. The
limited and largely uncontroversial nature of the sources for this
period greatly increases the danger that the views which their major
protagonists committed to writing will be accepted at face value by
historians. It is therefore worth considering the possibility that the
"heroic age" of New France was produced by an uncritical reading
of its own propaganda.
    As I began to examine the data concerning the various Frenchmen
who had dealings with the Huron and their neighbors during the
first half of the seventeenth century, my first task was to make sense
of these dealings in terms of what was known about the concepts
and behavior of the Indians at this time. This exercise cast much
fresh light on the lives and motivations of these Frenchmen and
began to provide valuable insights into the reliability of the data
concerning them. Eventually this led me, as a separate enterprise,
to reexamine the careers of various key Frenchmen who had dealings
with the Huron, with the view of using what was known about the
Indians to expand and improve an understanding of these people
(Trigger 1971). Like Francis Jennings, I found that my work on Indian
history was resulting in significant revisions of White history. Some
indication of the nature of these revisions is best provided by sum-
marizing the salient findings concerning three individuals.

CHAMPLAIN

    Samuel de Champlain, often called the Father of New France, is
generally believed to have understood the Indians and to have been

skilled at getting along with them. His biographers invariably point out that he wished the French and Indians to become a single people; although by this he really meant that Indians should become Frenchmen. In recent years, even the charges that his accompanying Huron and Algonkian raids against the Iroquois was responsible for the latter's fateful hostility towards the French have been shown to be groundless (Trudel 1966: 190). As a result, Champlain's reputation as an Indian diplomat has been enhanced.

The fact remains, however, that prior to 1616 Champlain was employed by successive trading companies. He was charged with governing their trading post at Quebec, exploring the interior, and forging and maintaining alliances with the Indians. Yet general policies for dealing with the Indians had been formulated by these traders prior to Champlain's arrival in New France and it is these policies that Champlain was expected to execute (Trigger 1976: 229–31). It is uncertain whether the decision that Champlain should fight against the Iroquois in 1609 originated with him or with the trader François Gravé Du Pont. It is clear, however, that it was Gravé Du Pont who ordered Champlain to visit the Huron country in 1615— a trip that Champlain himself had not envisaged and did not relish (Champlain 1922–1936, 3: 28–32). Moreover, when Champlain went, it was not with the intention of spending the winter there (ibid., 32–33, 80). In spite of his sojourn among the Huron, he failed to understand something as elementary as their tribal structure (he still called all of them Attignawantan) and he interpreted their work habits, political organization, and religious beliefs with procrustean ethnocentrism. His summation of the Huron was that (unlike Europeans) they acted on the basis of passion rather than reason and that, not believing in any supernatural powers whatever, they lived like brute beasts (ibid., 142–43).

Not surprisingly under these circumstances, Champlain does not appear to have understood the significance that his own actions had for the Huron. Although the Huron viewed his visit to each of their villages as confirming a series of treaties with individual Huron headmen on which the French-Huron alliance was henceforth to be based, Champlain appears to have viewed it more as an accidental ramble. Nor did he seek to understand the nature of Iroquoian warfare, which was based upon concepts of blood feud and human sacrifice and therefore was totally different from European warfare. Because of this, he judged Indian wars by the same standards as he did European ones and concluded that his attack on an Oneida village in 1615 was a failure, whereas his Indian allies almost certainly viewed the expedition as a success. His lack of understanding of Indian customs seems to have resulted in his being misled by the

Indians on a number of occasions. One of these was in 1613, when the Algonkin headman Tessouat convinced Champlain that Nicolas de Vignau had lied to him concerning the Algonkin's knowledge of trade routes leading north to James Bay (Trudel 1963–1966: 200–201; Trigger 1976: 283–85). A quarrel between some Huron and Algonkin also seems to have been used in part to prevent Champlain from accepting a Nipissing invitation to accompany them into northern Ontario (Trigger 1976: 324).

As Champlain personally became more deeply involved in the campaign to restore a trading monopoly for New France, he came to view himself more as a colonizer and vice-regal official than as the employee of a trading company. His desire that the fur traders expend more money on colonization brought him into conflict with these traders, whom he was unable to control. As a result he was to remain the untitled governor of a colony that was nothing more than a trading post.

Among the ways in which Champlain sought to enhance his authority was by having the Montagnais headmen living in the St. Lawrence Valley recognize themselves as French subjects and hence bound to obey him. One of the rights that he sought to have the Indians recognize was to appoint new headmen to rule over them. Because Champlain conceived of all power as being delegated from above, he did not understand that Indians viewed authority as being based upon public opinion and that leaders were required to secure individual consent from their followers as each new issue arose. The Indians regarded him as the headman, and therefore only as the spokesman, for the French who were living at Quebec. When he was asked as a fellow headman to support the investiture of Miristou as head of the Tadoussac band, he falsely imagined that the Montagnais had recognized his right to invest headmen. Hence Champlain provided a feast at which he presented Miristou and his brother with swords and tried to explain that they were henceforth required to support the French with these arms (Champlain 1922–1936, 5: 60–70). The Montagnais probably viewed this as the normal sort of feast that was given by an ally to celebrate the installation of a headman. In 1629, when a British attack on Quebec was imminent, Champlain sought to establish a council of headmen that was henceforth to regulate affairs between the French and their Algonkian-speaking allies. He insisted that a drunken and obsequious Indian named Chomina be appointed head of this council and made acceptance of the council and of his nominee a condition for the release of an imprisoned Montagnais who was dying at Quebec. The Montagnais nominally agreed to this proposal in order to save the prisoner's life, but Champlain's demands hardened their support for the English (ibid., 6: 7–25). Champlain's desire to have Montagnais settle near Quebec and become farmers foundered from his lack of adequate inducements or coercive power, and on the inveterate hostility of the French traders, who exerted much more influence over the Indians than Champlain did (ibid., 5: 60–62).

Champlain, who had executed the locksmith Jean Duval at Quebec in 1608, was repelled by the Indian custom of settling charges of murder by means of reparations payments. In 1617 and again in 1628 he refused to accept such payments for the murder of Frenchmen, also fearing that to do so would be construed as weakness. The result in both cases was growing hostility among the Montagnais, which ultimately forced the French to grant humiliating "pardons" that weakened Champlain's position (Trigger 1971: 94–100). By 1623, Champlain found himself calling the Montagnais his "worst enemies." When he returned from France in 1633 he hoped to lead an army to conquer the Iroquois and to "impose our laws on them, giving them what laws and customs we should desire" (Bishop 1948: 330–31). The failure of similar plans when New France was far more populous than in 1633 shows how unrealistic was Champlain's understanding of the enemy he was preparing to fight.

We may continue to admire Champlain's courage and tenacity, but his dealings with the Indians are revealed to be of far from heroic stature. Like many French officials (Naroll 1969), Champlain was unwilling to make the effort to understand Indian ways. Because of this, he frequently erred in his interpretation of Indian behavior and formulated policies that were unrealistic and self-defeating. At all times, Champlain viewed the Indians as a means to an end and in later years his dealings with them became increasingly callous. Champlain was firmly convinced of the superiority of all aspects of European civilization and believed that he had the right and duty to render the Indians subject to French control and to impose European culture on them. He was frustrated in his dealings with the Indians by his chronic military and financial weakness, which made it impossible to impose his policies on them by force.

An ethnographically informed reexamination of Champlain's career shows that the popular image of him as a man who understood the Indians and knew how to get along with them is in error. His increasingly ruthless attitude towards the Indians seems to parallel his growingly desperate, and ultimately frustrated, struggle to become the governor of a thriving colony. What this may imply in terms of reconsidering Champlain's dealings with his White associates constitutes what Ives Zoltvany (1973: 100) describes as a "starting point for a general re-evaluation of Champlain's life and works."

ETIENNE BRÛLÉ

In the spring of 1633, the Huron murdered the French trader and interpreter Etienne Brûlé after he had lived in their midst since 1610. On the basis of indirect reports, Sagard (1866: 431) stated that Brûlé had been condemned to death by the Huron and eaten by them, but no specific reason was given for his death. This has produced feverish speculation about why a man who had apparently lived amicably among the Huron for twenty-three years suddenly should have been murdered by them. The most popular fantasy is that he had committed some sexual indiscretion (Cranston 1949: 137–44), although because of Huron liberality in sexual matters nothing seems less likely. Nevertheless, a few relevant facts about his life are clear. In 1616, when he was captured by the Seneca, he befriended them and promised to promote good relations, and no doubt trade, between them and the French (Champlain 1922–36, 3: 224). As a Frenchman living in the Huron country, Brûlé was free to visit the Neutral and to trade with them. There he would have been able to maintain his contacts with the Seneca, who also visited the Neutral. In 1625, Brûlé was detained at Quebec by the Jesuits who had secured authorization to suppress traders who were antagonistic to their work. The next year he was sent back to France and it is uncertain whether or not he returned to the Huron country before 1629, when he turned up in the service of the English at Tadoussac (Trigger 1976: 404–5). During the British occupation of Quebec, he continued to work as a trading agent among the Huron. In 1632, the Huron who came to Quebec to trade ascertained that Champlain regarded Brûlé as a traitor and that his life was no longer protected by the French-Huron trading alliance. The following spring he was murdered because, as the Jesuits were later informed, of "such journeys [to the Neutral] which made the [Huron] country uneasy and fearful of a transference of trade" (Thwaites 1896–1901, 21: 211).

At that time the French traders not only were trying to promote indirect trade with distant groups such as the Winnebago, but also were seeking direct trading partnerships with the Oneida and Onondaga (at the same time that Champlain was hoping to wage war against them). Brûlé might have hoped that, if he could promote trade between the French and the Seneca, the French would pardon him for his treasonable relations with the English. Alternatively, he may have learned that Champlain was determined to punish him and had decided to seek Dutch sponsorship to work among the Iroquois. Either decision would have outraged the Huron, who were fearful of any Frenchmen living among the Iroquois lest trade and friendly relations might develop between the Iroquois and the French.

The decision to kill Brûlé appears to have been taken by Aenons, an Attignawantan headman who was an active participant in the fur trade. Brûlé was not eaten but instead his body was interred in the traditional manner for one who had died a violent death (Thwaites 1896–1901, 10: 305). His murder caused the Huron to abandon Aenons's village of Toanché. Toanché split to form two communities, one occupied by Aenons and his supporters and the other by clan segments that objected to the murder because they feared that it would endanger relations with the French. The killing also produced quarrels between the northern and southern Attignawantan that went on for several years. In spite of Champlain's assurances that Brûlé's death meant nothing to the French, the Huron continued to fear their reprisals for many years.

An ethnographically informed reexamination of Brûlé's murder removes it from its popular status as an example of barbarian treachery and perfidiousness. Instead, it was a political assassination which illustrates the lengths to which some Huron were prepared to go to prevent alliances between the French and the Iroquois which they feared would harm their own relationship with the French. That Brûlé was murdered only after he had been abandoned by his own people and that the Huron murdered no other Frenchmen before 1649 demonstrate the degree to which the trading alliance between the French and the Huron protected French residents, such as the Jesuits, even when they were held guilty of gravely injuring the Huron. The reexamination also suggests that there is much that we do not know about the activities of French fur traders at this period. Much of their activity fell outside the interests, purview, or control of Champlain and our missionary sources.

JEAN DE BRÉBEUF

Jean de Brébeuf was the first Jesuit to work effectively among the Huron and from 1634 to 1638 he was superior of the Huron mission. Even after he was replaced as superior by Jérôme Lalemant, the Huron continued to regard him as the true leader of the Jesuit missionaries in their country. Historians have depicted Brébeuf as a missionary *par excellence*, skilled at learning the Huron language and customs and toiling to the end of his days to convert them. Yet, in 1641 Brébeuf was ordered to return to Quebec and he remained there until 1644. Thereafter, he was stationed at Sainte-Marie, the headquarters of the Huron mission, where he tended to the needs of this settlement and of a few nearby Huron villages (Thwaites 1896–1901, 34: 169–71). It was in one of these villages, only about three miles from Sainte-Marie, that he was captured by the Iroquois who tortured him to death. A striking feature of every biography of Brébeuf is the abundance of data concerning his mission work prior to 1640 and the scarcity of references to such activities between 1644 and 1649. No explanation for this emerges from a study of European sources but a highly probable explanation emerges when the latter are examined in the context of Huron culture.

The epidemics that had decimated the Huron between 1634 and 1640 resulted in numerous charges of sorcery being leveled against the Jesuits, whose reasons for wishing to remain among the Huron were incomprehensible to the Indians. Brébeuf, as the leader of the Jesuits, was viewed as their principal sorcerer and hence was held personally responsible for the deaths of many Huron. Although the Huron did not kill the Jesuits, because they feared losing their trade with the French, many Huron continued to hate and fear Brébeuf long after the epidemics were over. More than twenty years later, Huron captives who were living among the Iroquois remembered him as a malevolent sorcerer who killed people with spells (Thwaites 1896–1901, 52: 187).

In the autumn of 1640, Jérôme Lalemant decided to begin a mission to the Neutral and sent Fathers Brébeuf and Pierre Chaumonot to spend the winter there. Lalemant knew that the Huron were jealous of their control over trading European goods with the neighboring Neutral and Tionnontaté. While they allowed Frenchmen to visit these groups briefly, they did not allow the French to pass an entire winter with them lest the French encourage these groups to go to trade at the French settlements (Sagard 1866: 809–10). Moreover, Brébeuf personally had observed the trouble that had arisen when the Recollet missionary Joseph de La Roche Daillon had attempted to conclude an alliance with the Neutral in 1627. Nevertheless, he and Chaumonot set off for the Neutral country, attempting to give the impression that they were part of a brief and regular trading expedition. The Huron were suspicious of this journey from the start and their headmen refused to provide the Jesuits with guides. The Neutral were reluctant to allow the Jesuits to remain in their midst over the winter and, when in spite of this the Jesuits stayed, the Huron offered them presents to murder the missionaries. The Huron also warned the Neutral that the Jesuits were visiting them in order to use sorcery to spread disease among the neighboring Seneca. Were the Seneca to learn of such rumors and believe them, they might attack the Neutral for exposing them to such danger. The Neutral's access to trade goods would not have been impaired if they had killed the Jesuits, but their action would have pleased the Huron not only because they hated the Jesuits but also because they believed that it would wipe out any chance of a future trading alliance between the Neutral and the French. Finally, Huron objections and Neutral harassment caused Jérôme Lalemant to recall the mission early in 1641.

Huron anger arising from this mission compelled the Jesuits to cease further missionary activities among both the Neutral and the Tionnontaté. Soon after, Chaumonot narrowly escaped being hatcheted by a Huron youth and early the following summer Brébeuf was ordered to return to Quebec. Most of his biographers suggest that this was to receive medical treatment for a clavicle broken while crossing the ice on Lake Simcoe on his return from the Neutral country (Jones 1909: 324; Talbot 1956: 241–42; Latourelle 1966: 123). It is hard to believe, however, that a man with a disabled shoulder would have left the relative comfort of Sainte-Marie to undertake an excruciating month-long journey to Quebec. Even more significantly, it was two years before Brébeuf disclosed the nature of his injury to a surgeon there.

A more convincing explanation seems to be that the Huron believed that Brébeuf, like La Roche Daillon, had attempted to conclude a trading alliance with the Neutral and because of this his life was in great danger. Although the trading alliance between the French and the Huron had sufficed to save Brébeuf's life when he was accused of witchcraft during the epidemics, the belief that he transgressed this alliance by attempting to subvert Huron trading rights may have rendered it ineffectual to do so at this time. It suggests great concern for Brébeuf's safety that the convoy which took him to Quebec set out ahead of the other Huron traders and was manned by four presumably armed Frenchmen and six Huron, all of whom were Christians or converts undergoing intensive instruction (Thwaites 1896–1901, 23: 35). When the Huron who followed Brébeuf's group were attacked by the Iroquois, it was rumored that Brébeuf had not been attacked because he had a secret understanding with them. A Huron who had escaped from the enemy alleged that Brébeuf had conspired with the Seneca while visiting the Neutral the previous winter. He also claimed that when Brébeuf traveled down the Ottawa River, he had met with the Mohawk, given them presents, and told them where they might ambush the Huron who were following him (ibid., 21: 75–77; 23: 35–37). All of these charges that Brébeuf was seeking to exterminate the Huron, either through witchcraft or by conspiring with the Iroquois, indicate how deeply the Huron had come to mistrust and fear Brébeuf as a result of the epidemics.

Brébeuf worked as a procurator and teacher at Quebec and Three Rivers until 1644, when it appears that Huron anger had cooled sufficiently to allow him to return to the Huron mission. Even then, it may have been considered dangerous to let Brébeuf resume work in the larger Huron settlements, which contained strong anti-Jesuit factions. This, as much as age or physical handicaps, may explain why he passed the last years of his life in and near the mission headquarters of Sainte-Marie.

Once again, a consideration of ethnographic data forces a reconsideration of the career of a prominent European. Throughout the course of the Huron mission, Brébeuf showed himself to be a brave and devout man whose desire to save souls led him to risk his life on many occasions. Like most of his fellow missionaries, he actively courted martyrdom in order to win supernatural aid to help convert the Huron. On the other hand, Brébeuf does not appear to have had as deep an understanding of Huron ways as he has been credited with and his missionary zeal often led him to discount what he did know. As a result of this, many of his actions were counterproductive for the Huron mission and his superiors may well have acted wisely in replacing him as head of that mission. Lalemant's apparently unopposed desire to establish a permanent mission to the Neutral was no less imprudent. The combined result of it, and of Brébeuf's previous injudicious conduct, was not martyrdom, but the end of Brébeuf's career as a front-line missionary. The Jesuits veiled this setback with a discreet silence and ultimately it was expunged for them by a glorious, if somewhat accidental, martyrdom.

Conclusion

Recent developments have proved that Indian history is both possible and worthwhile. It also has been recognized that colonial history cannot be understood without fully considering the role that Indians have played in it. While there may be much merit in stressing the "symbiotic interdependence that prevailed between [Indian and White] societies in America for well over two centuries" and in viewing modern American society as "evolved from that web of interrelationships" (Jennings 1975: ix), I would argue that Indian history need not for that reason be regarded as being merely an appendage of colonial history. That Indian societies had their own internal dynamics and that intertribal relations and those between Indians and Whites were determined by more than the colonial situation, make the histories of Indian groups independent foci of study.

The present study illustrates that while an understanding of Indian activities requires an adequate knowledge of related White history, White history cannot be fully understood without an understanding of Indian history. Nevertheless, Indian history and European colonial history bear the same relationship to each other as do any histories of distinct but interacting peoples. This observation reinforces the suggestion that the name ethnohistory has outlived its usefulness. We have reached the point at which we ought to regard Indian history in the same manner as we do European history; and Huron, Iroquois, or Montagnais history as we do French, English, or Dutch history.

CHAPTER TWO

The Ouragie War: A Case History in Iroquois-New England Indian Relations

GORDON M. DAY

INTRODUCTION

Much has been written about the wars of the Iroquois. Writers have tended to focus on the wars with the French and on their dramatic destruction of the surrounding Iroquoian nations—the Hurons, Neutrals, Eries and Susquehannocks, seeing these are more central to the Iroquois story of the seventeenth century. Less has been said about their wars in New England, and their war with the Ouragies has been passed over almost unremarked. But the wars with the Eastern Indians shed significant light on Iroquois methods and motivation for war and should not be disregarded.

One reason for this neglect may lie in an impression which has grown up that the New England Indians were a negligible force and always lived in mortal terror of the Mohawks. This impression proves under examination to be an example of three errors in methodology—anachronism, historians copying other historians, and overgeneralizing from a particular. John DeForest (1851: 65–66), speaking of the early seventeenth century, thought that the very appearance of the Mohawks sent the Connecticut Indians flying for safety. Francis Parkman (1867:xxi) pictured the New England Indians at the time of white contact as having been driven eastward by the Iroquois and as flying in terror from the Mohawk war cry. John Fiske (1900, 1:46) claimed that by 1609 the sight of a single Mohawk would cause them to flee like sheep before wolves. William Beauchamp (1905: 180) asserted that a cry that the Mohawks were near always created a panic among the New England Indians. Walter D. Edmonds (1968: 198) said that the sight of a single Mohawk would send a whole

village fleeing. It is rather clear from the wording of these statements
that all were based on a sentence in Cadwallader Colden's *The
History of the Five Indian Nations of Canada* (1902,1: xviii). Since the
secondary historians added something or generalized from Colden,
it is worth quoting his original statement written in 1727:

> I have been told by old Men in New England, who
> remembred *(sic)* the Time when the Mohawks made War on
> their Indians, that as soon as a single Mohawk was discover'd
> in the Country, their Indians raised a Cry from Hill to Hill, a
> Mohawk! a Mohawk! upon which they all fled like Sheep
> before Wolves, without attempting to make the least
> Resistance, whatever Odds were on their Side.

Finally Hunt (1940: 23) pointed out the anachronism involved in
attributing Iroquois terror in New England to the early contact period.
All historical statements about the Iroquois terror in New England,
even Gookin's (1970: 34), refer to a period after plagues had decimated
the southern New England tribes. We find the contact situation
reflected in the words of William Wood (1634: 57). He said that the
Aberginians were at that time terrified of the Mohawks, but ". . .
before the sweeping Plague, were an Inhabitant not fearing, but
rather scorning the confrontments of such as now count them but
the scumme of the country. . . ."[1] Later events, however, proved
that even Wood's evaluation of 1634 underestimated the fighting
qualities of the New England Algonquians. This image of the New
England Indians as a negligible force may be the chief reason why
serious treatments of the Iroquois wars to the eastward have been
so long in appearing, but a sufficient reason has also existed in the
intractability of the source materials. Happily an insightful treatment
of the southern New England situation will soon be available (Thomas
1979). The war with the Ouragies remains the least known of the
eastern wars, and they are singled out here to bring them out of
obscurity.

Who were the Ouragies? Ouragie was the Mohawk name for some
group of Eastern Indians, but we should be ignorant of their further
identity were it not for a statement in the Livingston Papers (Leder
1956: 158) and one in Colden (1902, 1:124) which identify them as
the Penacooks.[2] The Penacooks were an Algonquian-speaking people
who lived at a place called *penŏkok* 'at the falling bank' (Day 1973:
34–35), the steep sandy bluffs on the east side of the Merrimack
River opposite present-day Concord, New Hampshire. Although it
seems likely that there was a chronological series of villages along
the top of these bluffs, the location of the historic village was on
the point of the bluff known as Sugar Ball Hill (Bouton 1856: 18).

We meet the Penacooks first on a map in William Wood's *New Englands Prospect* (1634), which shows a fortified village called "Pennacooke" on the east side of the Merrimack River under a sagamore named Mattacomen. Later writers tended to extend the name Penacook to all the tribes on the Merrimack River, but Daniel Gookin (1970: 10), who as Superintendent of the Indians for Massachusetts was in a position to know, carefully distinguished in his time (about 1670) the Penacook proper as one member of the great sachemship under Passaconaway at Pawtuckett Falls (Lowell, Massachusetts). The fact that Wood referred to both Mattacomen at Penacook and Passaconaway at Pawtuckett as sagamores may indicate an earlier coordinate status. We do not know just which peoples the Mohawks understood by the name Ouragie, but it seems likely that the Penacooks were the central and perhaps the only group meant.

From the Iroquois viewpoint, the war with the Penacooks was only one aspect of their wars with the Eastern Indians and it is best understood in this context. The Mohawks' nearest enemy to the east was the Mahicans in the valley of the Hudson River (See Fig. 2.1). Over the Berkshire Hills to the east in the valley of the Connecticut River lived several tribes. On the upper River were the Cowassucks; on the middle River with their villages and planting grounds near Northfield, Massachusetts, were the Sokwakis; near Deerfield were the Pocumtucks; the Norwottucks were at Hadley and Northampton; the Agawams at Springfield and the Woronocos lived up the Westfield River. The Iroquois were also aware of the tribes of the southern New England seacoast. Still farther eastward beyond the Sokwakis were the Penacooks, the subject of this paper and beyond them in the present-day state of Maine lived the Eastern Abenakis. There were hostilities in the historic period between the Mohawks and all these eastern Indians. The origins of these hostilities are obscure and probably had their beginnings in the prehistoric period. There is one scholarly inquiry into the causes of the Mohawk-Mahican wars (Trigger 1971a), but the origins of the New England wars are not to be found even in the earliest traditions

The Dutch witnessed the beginning of a war with the Mahicans which culminated in a Mohawk victory in 1628 (Wassenaer in Jameson 1909, 8:89). The consequences of this victory have been debated, but it apparently brought about the removal of the northernmost Mahican village and gave the Mohawks direct access to the Dutch trade at Fort Orange (Brasser 1974: 15–16). Few topics in northeastern ethnohistory have been more confused than the course of subsequent Mohawk-Mahican relations, this by reason of confusion in tribal names and extrapolation from the meager statements in the records. In a treatment of the subject, Brasser (1974: 19) points out that three

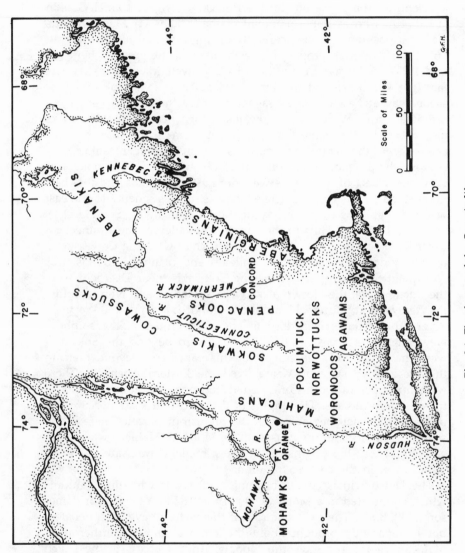

Fig. 2.1. The theatre of the Ouragie War

of the five Mahican villages remained in place near Fort Orange throughout the seventeenth century. Periods of hostility alternated with uneasy peace up through 1677 (NYCD 13:508–9, 513; Leder 1956: 40–42).

The Pocumtucks seem to have been involved on the side of the Mahicans in the war of 1628 (NYCD 13:381). The Sokwakis may have been involved also, since they had been conquered by 1646 (JR 28:275) and were still under tribute in 1651 (ibid., 36:105). However, their subjection may not have occurred at the time of the Mahican defeat but only in the early 1640s when the Mohawks were expanding their conquests after obtaining guns (O'Callaghan 4:8).

The Sokwakis, however, retained an enmity for the Mohawks. They were dissatisfied about the annual tribute, and an incident in 1643 certainly exacerbated their resentment. In October 1642, an Algonquin war party brought back to Three Rivers a prisoner whom they thought was a friend and neighbor of the Iroquois (JR 24:193). He was rescued by the French, identified as a Sokwaki, and sent back to his own country (ibid.: 183). This was Messabitout, an important man among the Sokwakis (ibid., 31:87; Druillettes 1933: 949). In gratitude for this act, the Sokwakis sent an ambassador to the Mohawks in April 1643 for the ransom of Father Isaac Jogues or one of his companions who were prisoners among the Mohawks. But in Jogues's words, "The Iroquois retained the presents, without setting one of them at liberty, which treachery is perhaps unexampled among these peoples,—for they inviolably observe this law, that whoever touches or accepts the present which is made to him, is bound to fulfill what is asked of him through that present" (ibid., 25:53; 31:85, 87). The estrangement widened two years later. In the summer of 1645 a Sokwaki embassy brought some scalps taken at Sillery and asked the Mohawks, since they claimed to be allies of the Sokwakis, to take up the hatchet against the Algonquins whom they had called their "enemies even beyond the grave." The Mohawks, who had hostages among the Algonquins and were profiting by a new peace to hunt freely on the edges of Algonquin territory, refused the Sokwaki request (ibid., 28:287), and it appears that Mohawk-Sokwaki relations broke down soon afterwards.

In 1650 the Mohawks petitioned the Dutch at Fort Orange for permission to cross their land in order to go against the Indians to the eastward (Beauchamp 1905: 198). That the expedition did take place and that the Sokwakis were one of the targets is fairly clear from a letter written the next year by the Council of Quebec urging that the Commissioners of New England check the Iroquois who were killing the Sokwakis and Abenakis (NYCD 9:5–6).

It is conceivable that the Eastern Abenakis in Maine had been drawn into war with the Iroquois by alliances with the Saint Lawrence Valley Algonquians, who had been at war with the Iroquois prior to recorded history (Biggar 5:78). Record of this continuing warfare was made in 1628, when the French were asked by the Abenakis for help and were told that the French decision would influence the Abenakis' arrangements for the war (ibid., 3:313). The war was still continuing in 1647 when an Iroquois war party returned after six months in the field with twenty Abenaki prisoners (JR 31:85).

THE OURAGIE WAR

Where did the Ouragies or Penacooks fit in this picture of wide-spread warfare? It appears unlikely that they could have stayed out of wars which involved their neighbors on all sides, but there is no record of any Mohawk-Penacook relations prior to 1650. The nearest we have to a pertinent statement seems to be that of Wood who wrote that the Mohawks "were wont to come down" on the Aberginians prior to his residence in Massachusetts (1634: 57), although Gookin wrote in 1672 that the Maquas "had for several years been in hostility with our neighbor Indians" and mentioned the Penacooks among others (1970: 34). His statement previously cited may imply that there had been hostilities before the onset of the plague in 1617. The event which introduced Mohawk-Penacook relations into the record was the political mission of Father Gabriel Druillettes to New England. His purpose was to enlist military aid by the New England colonies and the New England Indians against the Iroquois in return for trade with Quebec. In the autumn of 1650 Druillettes met with the Abenakis and a Sokwaki delegate on the Kennebec River and proposed to them an alliance with the French against the Iroquois. The Abenakis urged the plan with a present of fifteen wampum collars and a dozen bracelets (JR 36:103). They were perhaps the instigators of the plan, since they had lost thirty persons killed by the Iroquois who, they said, had violated the peace three or four times, and they expected the Iroquois to attack them during the coming winter or spring (Druillettes 1933: 944, 945).

During the ensuing winter, the Sokwakis held council with the Mahicans, the Pocumtucks, and the Penacooks, and in April 1651, a Sokwaki messenger brought word to Druillettes that the four villages had resolved to join the French and Montagnais against the Iroquois whether the English did or not (JR 36: 101-3). The Sokwaki messenger claimed that several other nations would join them and that one of them was very numerous and dreaded by the Iroquois. The identity of this nation is uncertain, but it may have been the Minsis.[3] Druillettes returned to New England in June 1651, but the New England colonies were not ready to pick up what they saw as an essentially French quarrel, and Druillettes's mission came to naught execept for perhaps strengthening the bonds between the Abenakis, Sokwakis, Penacooks, Pocumtucks, and Mahicans.

The several reasons of these tribes for desiring an alliance against the Iroquois can be glimpsed from the foregoing. The Mahicans were continually living next door to the Mohawks under an unsteady and uncertain truce. The Sokwakis were dissatisifed at having to make annual wampum payments and their supposed alliance with the Mohawks was working so poorly that they had been attacked by them that very year. The Abenakis had been at war with the Iroquois. The relations of the Pocumtucks with the Mohawks may well have been soured by the Mohawks' failure to help a Pocumtuck and Narragansett force against the Mohegans. But again we are left to infer the state of affairs between the Iroquois and Penacooks. It is likely that all the New England allies were uneasy with the thought that the Iroquois, having destroyed the Hurons and Lower Algonquins, might turn on them next, and in these circumstances were glad to have the French as allies. And the fact that the Penacooks were willing to align themselves against the Iroquois at this time suggests that there had already been hostile incidents which escaped the record (JR 26: 104–5; Hubbard 1848: 463).

Whatever their separate motivations, no united action seems to have resulted from the alliance. The Iroquois were at this time engaged in a war which dispersed the Neutral Nation. In 1654 they dispersed the Eries, and for the remainder of that decade they were occupied in attempting to stop the fur traffic on the Ottawa River. In 1660 they turned their attention again to the east, to the Abenakis in Maine. The reason they gave the Dutch for this action was that the Abenakis had twice helped the "Canada Indians" in engagements which cost the Mohawks one hundred men (NYCD 13:225), but we have seen that the underlying enmity was old. In any event, the Mohawks were planning an attack on the Abenakis on the Kennebec River in November 1660 (ibid., 13:169), and they definitely attacked the Abenakis on the Penobscot River in May of 1662 (ibid., 13:224). When the Governors of Nova Scotia and Massachusetts complained about this through the Dutch at Fort Orange, the Mohawks replied that they had good grounds for the war and cited their losses, but they agreed not to fight the Abenakis again until the next spring so that some Abenakis could be brought to make a peace (NYCD 13:225–26). The following summer, when the Council of New Netherland through the Fort Orange authorities urged the Mohawks to make peace, they rather surprisingly announced that they did not then consider themselves at war with the Abenakis (ibid., 13:257–58). But they asked to be allowed to make war on the Sokwakis without English interference. The reason was probably an attack by the Sokwakis apparently assisted by some Abenakis (ibid., 13:308).

By November 1663 a large war party, not only of Mohawks but also of Onondagas and Senecas were on their way against the Sokwakis. About December 1 they attacked and beseiged the strongly fortified town on Fort Hill near Hinsdale, New Hampshire, in an engagement which proved disastrous for both sides. On December 11 and 12 the Iroquois passed through Fort Orange in detachments, admitting important losses (ibid., 13:355). It was rumored to the Dutch that they had lost two or three hundred men and returned with only two captives (ibid., 13:356). Although suffering heavy losses themselves, the Sokwakis remained in their fort. The Coassucks from the upper Connecticut River condoled with them and sent forty men to help them hold the fort. The Penacooks did likewise, and the allies resolved to continue the war in the spring (David Wilton to J. Winthrop, Jr., 25 Dec. 1663, 28 Dec. 1663, Winthrop Papers).

The next May, however, a Mohawk delegation interested in re-covering some prisoners from the Pocumtucks, two Dutchmen interested in establishing peace for the sake of the fur trade, and three Mahicans probably as interpreters, traveled over the Berkshire Hills to Pocumtuck. The Mohawks and Pocumtucks came to an agreement and exchanged presents. Discussions were also held with some Sokwaki chiefs then present at Pocumtuck. The Dutch tried to persuade them to make peace, and the Mohawks told them they had been drawn into an unwise war by the Abenakis who were the Mohawks' real enemies, but there is no indication that any Mohawk-Sokwaki agreement was reached (ibid., 13:378–80). In June, Mohawk ambassadors passed through Fort Orange to confirm the treaty with the Pocumtucks, but they were murdered on their way (ibid., 2:371–72). Suspicion fell on the Mahicans, the Pocumtucks, and even the English, but the Sokwakis and Abenakis also had reason not to want the Mohawks to make a separate peace with the Pocumtucks. Judging by their reaction, however, the Mohawks seem to have blamed the Pocumtucks (J. Winthrop, Jr., to Thomas Willet, 27 July 1664; J. Pynchon to J. Winthrop, Jr., 25 July 1664; Thomas Willet to J. Winthrop Jr., 26 July 1664, Winthrop Papers).

Then in September of 1664 New Netherlands became the English colony of New York, and before the month was over, the English had made an agreement with the Iroquois—the English in order to protect their fur trade and the Iroquois in order to ensure that the English would not side with the New England Indians in the war. In the first article proposed by the Iroquois, they named the Penacooks as official enemies: "1. That the English do not assist the three nations of the Ondiakes (Sokwakis), Pennekooks, and Pacamtekookes, who murdered one of the Princes of the Maques, when he brought ransomes & Presents to them upon a treaty of peace," and their last proposal was "5. That if they be beaten by the three Nations above menconed, they may receive accomodacon from ye English" (NYCD 3:67–68). This does not sound like our modern stereotype of the Iroquois, the terror of the Eastern Indians.

Having secured English neutrality and a source of supplies at Fort Orange, now Fort Albany, the Iroquois did not long delay. A large party of Mohawk and Upper Iroquois warriors, said to number three thousand, assembled, threatened the English possibly as a feint, and moved against the Pocumtucks (Richard Nicolls to J. Winthrop Jr., 25 January 1665, Winthrop Papers). No account of this campaign has turned up, but it appears that the Pocumtuck fort had fallen by February 6 and that the surviving Pocumtucks, as well as their neighbors, the Sokwakis and Norwottucks, had mostly fled to two forts near Springfield (J. Winthrop Jr. to Roger Williams, 6 February 1665, Winthrop Papers). The Pocumtuck chief Onopequen was killed and his family captured. This accomplished, the Mohawks joined the Senecas on an expedition against the Susquehannocks, probably in return for Seneca aid given in their New England campaigns (Nicolls to J. Winthrop jr., 23 February 1665, MHSC 4:531–32).

In the summer of 1665 the Mohawks raided as far east as Boston (General Court of Massachusetts Bay to Mohawk Sagamores, 2 September 1665, Mass Archives 30, No. 127, 127a), and the Connecticut Valley Indians raided the three Mohawk villages in return (Winthrop Jr. to Nicolls, 27 August and *post* 4 November, 1665; Nicolls to Winthrop Jr., 28 September and 9 October 1665, Winthrop Papers). In January and February 1666, Sieur Rémy DeCourcelle led a French force against the Mohawk villages, and although he withdrew without doing any damage to them, the ability of the French to put such a force in their territory impressed the Mohawks sufficiently so that in April they asked the English at Albany to assist them. Governor Nicolls promised to ask the French for terms if the Mohawks would make peace with the Mahicans and the Northern Indians, that is the Sokwakis and their allies. Consequently, in May, Mohawk delegates went to Quebec and one went to Hartford, Connecticut to negotiate for peace (Winthrop Jr. to Nicolls, 13 June 1666, Winthrop Papers). While the latter was waiting for the eastern chiefs to assemble, his mission was aborted by the action of a Mohawk raiding party near Norwottuck (Wilton and Webb to Winthrop Jr., 16 June 1666, Winthrop Papers). Therefore, when the Mahican, Sokwaki, Pocumtuck, Norwottuck, and Podunk chiefs assembled at Hartford, they did not vote for peace. Rather raiding parties went out towards the Mohawk country. Moreover, a considerable company of Pascataways and Penacooks who "have been alwaies their confederates . . . of the extreme party" arrived and tried to persuade the Indians assembled at Hartford to go against the Mohawks (NYCD 3:117; Winthrop Jr. to Nicolls, *post* July 2, 1666, Winthrop Papers). This is noteworthy as testifying to an old alliance between the Penacooks and the Connecticut Valley tribes and to the Penacooks' steadfast hostility for the Iroquois. Winthrop was inclined to blame this on French influence, but there is little record of French contact after Druillettes's visit.

That summer, Captain Pierre de Sorel led another expedition against the Mohawk villages (ibid., 1:67–68) which, though abortive, nevertheless made an impression on both the Mohawks and the English. England ordered an attack on Canada, but the Connecticut Valley tribes were still strong and formidable enough so that the New England colonies did not dare to carry it out (Winthrop Jr. to Nicolls, *post* 2 July 1666, Winthrop Papers). There was raiding in both directions until early August when word reached John Pynchon in Springfield that a force of nine hundred Mohawks, Senecas, and "hoccogs" [4] had assembled and started to move eastward (Pynchon to Winthrop Jr., 7 August 1666, Winthrop Papers), but there is no record of this Iroquois army attacking any New England town.

In the summer of 1667, the Connecticut Valley tribes joined by Abenakis from the Kennebec River, resumed raiding of Mohawk villages. There was a lull in hostilities in 1668, perhaps brought on by the New England Indians' lack of confidence in French backing, since the French had made a peace with the Mohawks. Then in the summer of 1669, a force of six or seven hundred men from the allied New England tribes under the leadership of the Massachusetts sachem, Wampatuk, besieged the easternmost Mohawk town. When the siege proved ineffective they withdrew. The Mohawks ambushed them on their withdrawal route and a bloody battle took place. It has often been counted as a defeat for the New England allies because all their captains were killed, but the losses were heavy on both sides, and the New England accounts reported that the Mohawks were finally put to flight (JR 53:137–53; Gookin 1970: 40–42). Both sides needed time to recuperate. In December 1671, the English and Dutch brought together the Mohawks and some Connecticut Valley chiefs who were hunting in the vicinity of Albany. They mutually pledged to attempt a real peace, but there is no record of either a real treaty or of important hostilities before the outbreak of King Philip's War in 1675 (NYCD 13:458; Pynchon to Winthrop Jr., 11 December 1671; Pynchon to Winthrop Jr., 6 January 1672. Winthrop Papers). Small parties of Mohawks continued to harass the Praying Indian villages of Massachusetts right under the noses of the English, but the Mohawks' official posture was one of peace (Gookin 1970: 35 ff.; Leder 1956: 35–37).

THE BOUTON TRADITION

It would appear then that the contemporary records tell us very little about Iroquois-Penacook relations. They tell only of Penacook participation in an anti-Mohawk alliance in 1650, their coming to the support of the Sokwakis after the Mohawk attack of 1664, their attempts to incite the Connecticut Valley tribes to attack the Mohawks in 1666, and their participation in the unsuccessful attack on the Mohawk town in 1669. If this be the gist of the record it is small wonder that historians have not dwelt on the Ouragie War. There is, however, a tradition of two Iroquois attacks on the Penacooks' fortified village which should be considered. This tradition came down from the early settlers of Concord, New Hampshire, until it was written down by the town historian, Dr. Nathaniel Bouton (1856: 18–20). This tradition, if true, adds so much to our scanty knowledge of the war, that it is worth quoting verbatim.

> On the east side of the river, upon a bluff called "Sugar Ball," northeast of the main village (of Concord) and in full view, was an ancient Indian fort. Tradition has so preserved and fixed the identity of this location with Sugar Ball that it is presumption, at this time, to call it in question. Near the fort, a little to the north, is the spot which probably was their ancient burying-ground—as a considerable number of human skulls and bones have been dug and ploughed up, or washed away by the rains, and been picked up on the side or at the bottom of the bank . . .
>
> At this fort, according to tradition, there was once a terrible fight between the Penacooks and Mohawks. . . . The tradition of the bloody battle between the Penacooks and Mohawks is substantially this: The Mohawks, who had once been repulsed by the Penacooks, came with a strong force, and encamped at what is now Fort Eddy, opposite Sugar Ball, on the west side of the river. Thence they watched their prey, determined either to starve the Penacooks by siege, or to decoy them out and destroy them.
>
> Having gathered their corn for the season, and stored it in baskets around the walls of their fort, the Penacooks, with

their women and children, entered within and bid defiance to their foes.

Frequent skirmishes occurred between individuals of the parties. If the Penacooks went out of the fort, they were sure to be ambushed; if a canoe pushed off from one bank of the river, others from the opposite side started in pursuit. Some time had thus passed. and no decisive advantage was gained by either side. The Penacooks dared not adventure a fight on the field nor the Mohawks to attack the fort.

After a day or two of apparent cessation from hostilities, a solitary Mohawk was seen carelessly crossing Sugar Ball plain, south of the fort. Caught by the decoy, the Penacooks rushed out in pursuit. The Mohawk ran for the river. Band after band from the fort joined in the chase, till all were drawn out and scattered on the plain, when the Mohawks, who had secretly crossed the river above, and by a circuitous route approached in the rear, suddenly sprung from their hiding places and took possession of the fort. A shriller war-whoop than their own burst on the affrighted Penacooks: they turned from the chase of the solitary Mohawk, and long and bloody was the battle. The Penacooks fought for their wives and children—for their old men—for their corn—for life itself; the Mohawks for revenge and for plunder. On which side the victory turned, none can tell. Tradition says the Mohawks left their dead and wounded on the ground; and from that fatal day the already reduced force of the Penacooks was broken into fragments and scattered. A diversity in the skulls which have been dug up in the ancient burying-ground has induced the belief that in it the dead of both the savage tribes were promiscuously buried.

This tradition is not history. We must examine its credentials. We can dismiss at the outset any notion that Dr. Bouton was inventing or romancing. He was a reputable scholar and made conscientious use of his sources, and it is evident that he himself believed the tradition. It seems equally apparent that he embellished the story a bit in retelling.

It seems to me that the problem is to decide whether in the main it represents a plausible event, when it took place, and whether it could reasonably be transmitted by oral tradition from the time it occurred until it could be learned by the early settlers of Concord. There does not seem to be anything improbable about the Iroquois making one or more attacks on the Penacooks. Their longstanding enmity seems established, and Iroquois attacks on their neighbors and even on the Abenakis far beyond them is history.

We simply do not know when the attacks in the Bouton tradition took place, but we have the ingredients for fashioning an hypothesis. Since it may be assumed that Penacook like other Indian villages moved every few decades, and since the battle took place at Sugar Ball Hill, the location of Penacook which was known to the English, it must have taken place towards the end of the Indian occupation of Penacook. The latter part of the seventeenth century seems to be indicated, and, with less justification, I propose to narrow the date to the fall of 1666. For one thing, it appears that Iroquois campaigning in New England was greatly intensified during the 1660s with the massive attack on the Sokwakis in 1663 and the destruction of Pocumtuck in 1665. There are a number of indications that the Penacooks were an object of greater concern to the Iroquois during this decade than previously. Following the Iroquois attack on the Sokwakis in December 1663, the Penacooks condoled with the Sokwakis and sent them reinforcements. In 1664 they were named along with the Sokwaki and Pocumtucks as the Mohawks' formal enemy. In 1666 they were militantly urging the New England tribes gathered at Hartford to join them against the Mohawks. The Iroquois had already dealt a severe blow to the Sokwakis, the Pocumtuck fort had been destroyed the previous winter, and Penacook would have made a logical target for the next attack.

Coincident with this, in early August of 1666, an army of nine hundred men was assembling east of Albany, destination unknown. What more likely objective than Penacook? The lack of any record of this army attacking any Connecticut Valley town has led Thomas to surmise that the expedition may have been abandoned because of the threat of Chevalier de Tracy's gathering army. But de Tracy's army did not assemble at Fort Ste. Anne until September 28, and it was mid-October before it reached the Mohawk towns. The Iroquois force, half assembled on August 9, could have assembled, moved against Penacook in early September after the corn was harvested as the tradition states, returned to their own country and disbanded before Tracy's army even moved. (It is perhaps noteworthy that Tracy's army encountered no resistance in the Mohawk Valley. The nine hundred warriors from three nations had dispersed).

Considering the Western Abenaki tenaciousness of oral tradition, I should expect the Penacooks to remember such an important event in their history from the seventeenth century or even earlier until English settlement in 1726 (Day 1962, 1972). And there were many ways in which it could have been transmitted to the English who had known the Penacooks and Passaconaway, the principal sachem of the Merrimack River, since 1625 (Baxter 1893: 108–11; Winthrop 1826: 1.89; Wood, 1634, *map*). Richard Waldern of Dover, New Hampshire, and Peter Weare of York, Maine, were traveling and trading in the Merrimack River region as early as 1635 (Shurtleff, 1853–1854, 2:242–43). A surveying party reached Penacook in 1638 and another passed through it in 1652 (Shurtleff 1853–1854, 2:242; Winthrop, 1:303; Kimball 1878: 158; Day 1975: 376–77). Waldern established a trading post at Penacook in the spring of 1668, only two years after the suggested date of the battle, and it appears that the people of Salem established one there about 1674 (Shurtleff 1853–1854, 2:414–15; Bouton 1856: 53). A few Penacooks remained in place for several years after the English settlement of Concord in 1726 and were on generally amicable terms with them (Bouton 1856: 40, 48; Penacook Papers, 3:212; Moore 1824: 80). When Concord was first settled, Ebenezer Eastman became well acquainted with Chief Wattanummon (Bouton, 1856: 40, 48), and an important battle in the mid-1660s would surely have been remembered by Wattan-ummon. Moreover, Isaac Bradley, the great-uncle of Robert Bradley, one of Bouton's informants, was captured by the Penacooks in 1690 at the age of ten and spent twelve years with them, becoming acquainted with Wattanummon and many other Penacooks (Provincial Papers of New Hampshire, 19:319–20; Bouton 1856: 18, *note*).

Another local tradition seems to add to the probability that the Iroquois attack took place and that the traditional account has some substance. There is local knowledge of a fort having once existed at Fort Eddy, the low flat land directly across from Sugar Ball Hill on which, according to the first tradition, the Iroquois camped for the siege. Although this could have been a Penacook site, it would be a poor one for defense or even for year round occupation. I suggest that it was a temporary fort thrown up by the Iroquois for use during their siege. Making such a temporary fort to guard against surprise was a practice of woodland warfare documented in 1609 by Champlain. All in all, I incline to the opinion that since the main substance of the Bouton tradition is congruent with what we know from history and since there was no lack of channels for its preservation and transmission, it is easier to accept it as true than to reject it as whimsy or an invention. In any event, it can be accepted as a working hypothesis to stimulate research for documents which would shed more light on the matter.

CONCLUSION

Historians have often attributed the removal and even the destruction of the Penacooks to Iroquois pressure, even as Bouton did, but this is invention. Some Penacooks seem to have moved downriver about 1670 and built a fort at Wamesit closer to the English (Allen 1820: 144), but Penacook was not abandoned. About the time of King Philip's War (1675–1676), large numbers of Sokwakis and Penacooks removed to Lake Champlain, Saint Francis, and the Abenaki mission at Sillery. In spite of these emigrations, the band remaining at Penacook under Kankamagus was feared by the English whose recourse was to threaten them with Mohawk attack. The Mohawks obligingly made threats and even sent delegates to the English but apparently had no intention of assisting them. (Colden 1902, 1:119–25; Leder 1956: 154–58). The Penacooks, having moved to Canada, almost vanish under a set of new names. We must search for them in the French documents under the name Openengoes and try to pick them out from the conglomeration which the French created under the name Loup (Day 1973; 1975). The name Ouragie disappears and the Penacooks in Canada seem to have acquired from the Mission Iroquois a new name apparently derived from their own place name *penōkok*, namely, Cannogagehronoun (Day 1973; NYCD 9:261–62; Day 1975: 42).

The last confrontation in the field between the Mohawks and the Penacooks as Penacooks seems to have been the unsuccessful attack on Gandouagué in 1669. However, those Penacooks who, together with emigrant Sokwakis, moved northward into the French sphere of influence, still constituted as French allies a threat to Iroquois trade and polity until the great peace treaty of 1701.

In spite of Colden's underestimate of the fighting qualities of the New England Indians and the blows which they struck at the myth of Iroquois invincibility, the New England campaigns of the Iroquois partly confirm and partly query the conclusions drawn from their better known western and southern wars. They are again shown to have been relatively successful in bringing off effective aggressive action. An important reason for this seems to lie in their ability to mobilize large armies from the full breadth of the Confederacy. They appear to have had a greater ambition for conquest, for whatever reason, but Hunt's thesis of a life or death struggle to control the fur trade finds little support in New England. Mohawk desire to keep open a trade with the French may have been the underlying cause of their 1624 war with the Mahicans (Trigger 1971a; 277), and as we have seen, both Pocumtucks and Sokwakis were probably involved on the side of the Mahicans. I agree with Trigger that this war had other than simple economic motivation, and this must have been even more true of the New England wars because of their geographical position. We desperately need to know more about the sixteenth and perhaps even the fifteenth century to get at the roots of the wars between the Iroquois and the Indians to the eastward.

The role of the Iroquois in the destruction or removal of New England tribes should be reassessed in a broader perspective. The New England Indians, who had apparently held their own against the Iroquois in prehistoric times, were caught between the English competition for land, with the subsequent shortage of beaver to pay debts, and Iroquois aggression (Thomas 1979). This latter pressure may have been the decisive impetus for the northward movements to find better trapping grounds, fresh fields, and closer proximity to French trade goods with which they were already acquainted (Thomas 1973; 35; Hubbard 1865,1: 203).

NOTES

1. The denotation of the name Aberginian is nowhere stated, but the implication in the writings of Wood and of Christopher Levett in 1623 (Baxter 1893; 110) is that it was used for the Indians encountered by the English northward of Massachusetts Bay at least as far as York, Maine. We may surmise that it embraced the tribes of at least the lower Merrimack, of the Piscataqua and beyond.

2. The name has been variously spelled—Ouragies (Colden 1902: 112), Uragees (Colden: 122), Owaragees (Colden: 124–25), Aurages (Leder 1956, 154–58), Ouwerage (NYCD 4.758), and Aorage (NYCD 4.1164). The meaning of Ouragie is nowhere given. Mohawk *owerà:ke* 'windy place' has been suggested (Christine Shackleton, personal communication 29 July 1977).

3. It was called the Noutchihuict and Noutchihout in the Jesuit Relations (JR 36:103, 105) and Noutchikan and Nourchikan in the printed version of Druillettes's report (949, 947). He understood that they lived between the Mahicans and Manhattan and near the "Landastré" (Andastes?) (JR 36:103; Druillettes: 947). The Minsis seem to be indicated on geographical grounds, and there may be some confirmation of this identification in the name Noutchikan, which has a superficial resemblance to the Western Abenaki word *nodzõmbikat* 'bead maker'. This would be an appropriate name for the Minsis at that time, and they were probably included in the French term 'porcelain maker' (JR 50:135).

4. Possibly the Kahkwas, usually regarded as Eries or a subdivision of the Eries (Hodge 1907, 1.432, 2.1055, 1068; Wright 1974). The Eries had been dispersed before 1666, but it is possible that the "hoccogs" were an adopted village or a discrete component of a village in the Seneca country.

CHAPTER THREE

Dr. Wheelock and the Iroquois

JAMES AXTELL

If Eleazar Wheelock had had his way, Dartmouth College—Bill Fenton's alma mater—would have been seated in the heart of Iroquoia. From New York, not New Hampshire, Wheelock thought he heard most clearly the Indian's "voice crying in the wilderness" for the white man's brand of salvation. For ten years the forceful founder and master of Moor's Charity School in Lebanon, Connecticut, focused his educational and religious attentions upon the Iroquois before the other eastern tribes. And for the last eight of those years he tried to obtain land among the Iroquois to establish a missionary college and a large community of English Christians whose civil and pious example would reduce the natives from their "savage and sordid Practices" (Wheelock 1763:25). But his plans were checked by the Iroquois and their adopted kinsman, Sir William Johnson. So in 1769 he turned to Hanover for consolation, leaving the Iroquois to "go to Hell in their own Way" (WP 767558.1).

Yet even in his disappointment Wheelock never abandoned his "Grand Design" of rooting the college in the rich soil of the Iroquois. Even after Dartmouth had risen out of the New Hampshire forest, he petitioned King George III for twenty-five thousand acres in New York, and nursed the delusion that the college might inherit part of Sir William's vast estate and move to the Mohawk River. Whether it partook of land lust or of Christian challenge, Wheelock's obsession with the Iroquois—and his failure to "save" them—left an indelible mark not only on the microcosm of Moor's Charity School but on the larger course of Indian-white relations in colonial North America.

According to his own recollection, Eleazar Wheelock was no johnny-come-lately to Indian affairs. He told an Iroquois council in 1765 that he had had the Indians upon his heart "ever since I was a boy"—he had been born in Windham, Connecticut in 1711—and that he had prayed daily for their temporal and spiritual salvation for the past thirty years. But not until the Great Awakening did providence bring him his first native student.

After earning a bachelor's degree at Yale, Wheelock had been licensed to preach in 1734 and the following year called to the pulpit of the Second Congregational Church in Lebanon. When the Great Awakening of religious fervor broke over New England in 1740, Wheelock was its warmest supporter in Connecticut. He traveled extensively, preached persuasively, and served as the chief intelligencer of revival news. But the religious establishment of the colony, the so-called "Old Lights," did not appreciate his itinerary, the neglect of his own parish, or his promulgation of "a meer *passionate* Religion." So in 1743 he was deprived of his church salary (though not his office position) by the General Assembly act "for regulating abuses and correcting disorders in ecclesiastical affairs."

Although Wheelock owned considerable farmland, the loss of his salary prompted him to take a few English boys into his house for college preparation. They were soon joined by Samson Occom, a young Mohegan Indian from New London, Connecticut, who came to Wheelock with the hope of improving his self-taught literacy in three or four weeks of tuition. As a leading "New Light," Wheelock saw an opportunity to extend the divine hand to New England's nonwhite pagans, and invited the twenty-year-old Indian to join his small group of students. Occom stayed nearly five years, in which time he became a devoted Christian, an affecting public speaker, and a partial convert to the English way of life. Despite his unusual accomplishments, however, there was no place for a man of his color in English society. He returned to a wigwam and spent the next twelve years in poverty, teaching and preaching to the Montauk Indians on Long Island, binding books, and carving spoons, pails, and gunstocks for their white neighbors, most of whom were his spiritual and intellectual inferiors.

If Occom's postgraduate career did not speak well for the conceptual clarity of Wheelock's later design, the Doctor was unaware of it. In late 1754 he took two Delaware Indian boys under his wing, which prompted a charitable neighbor, Col. Joshua More, to endow the fledgling school with several buildings and two acres of land. By the summer of 1761 "Moor's Charity School" had accepted ten Indian students from the "remnant" tribes of the Northeastern seaboard. But with the fall of Canada a wide door was opened to the relatively uncontaminated "back nations" of America, and Wheelock entered it with a driving vision of tawny souls "washed white in the blood of the Lamb." General James Wolfe's victory on the Plains of Abraham was well timed, for Wheelock was becoming increasingly disenchanted with the "little Tribes" of New England. Schools set among them, he felt, had always failed because the natives placed no value on the white man's "Learning," led an unsettled, impoverished existence, lacked any social or familial authority, and resented the English masters who tried to impose a "good and necessary Government" over their children (O'Callaghan 1849–51, 4: 202). Most damning of all in Wheelock's eyes was their stubborn ingratitude for the inestimable benefits offered by Protestant saints such as himself. It was simply foolish to waste God's time and the public's money on ingrates while there were "such Vast Numbers intirely without Means of Knowledge and"—he was assured by friends— "continually suing and pleading for Missionaries and Schoolmasters to be sent among them" (WP 760628). Turning his back on too-familiar local tribes, Wheelock was quickly captured by the unknown challenge of the Six Nations.

He did not have long to wait before confronting the challenge he had so blindly and blithely accepted. On August 1, 1761 three Mohawk boys sent by Sir William Johnson, the British superintendent of Indian affairs, arrived in Lebanon with "great Caution and Fear." Each brought a horse, "prepared to return in haste, if there should be occasion" (Wheelock 1765:22). One, Joseph Brant, understood a little English and, being the son of a "Family of Distinction," was "considerably cloathed" (Wheelock 1763:40). But his teen-aged companions, Negyes and Center, were nearly naked and "very lousey" (WP 762113). Neither could "speak a word of English" (WP 761625.1). Center was visibly ill, his "blood spoiled" according to the local physician, so he was sent home to die. But not before swallowing the bitter pill of white prejudice. "I was very sorry," Wheelock wrote Johnson, "for the Jealousies which the [English] Schollars conceived concerning the Nature of Center's Disorder while I was gone to Boston, and that there was that said or done which gave him a Disgust" (WP 761602.3). Negyes too was soon lost to the cause, for when he accompanied Center home he was "captivated by a young Female and married" (Wheelock 1763:42).

Less than four months later two Mohawk boys arrived to take their places, "direct from the wigwams." One had learned "4 or 5 letters in the Alphabet, the other knew not one, nor could either of them Speak a Word of English." Excepting "two old Blankets & Indian Stockins," their clothing "was not worth Sixpence." And as Wheelock had come to expect of such "poor little Naked Creatures, . . . they were very lousey, which occasioned considerable Trouble." Yet they were hardly typical schoolboys. Johannes had "carried a Gun" in the army that captured Montreal the previous year—at the age of twelve (WP 761625.1, 762113).

A scant two weeks after their arrival, Wheelock penned a *cri de coeur* that might well stand as the motto of Moor's Charity School: "Few conceive aright of the Difficulty of Educating an Indian and turning him into an Englishman but those who undertake the Trial of it" (WP 761664.3). To the Rev. George Whitefield, who had the good sense not to try, he explained his predicament:

> They would soon kill themselves with Eating and Sloth, if constant care were not exercised for them at least the first year. They are used to set upon the Ground, and it is as natural for them as a seat to our Children. They are not wont to have any Cloaths but what they wear, nor will without much Pains be brought to take care of any. They are used to a Sordid Manner of Dress, and love it as well as our Children to be clean. They are not used to any Regular Government, the sad consequences of which you may a little guess at. They are used to live from Hand to Mouth (as we speak) and have no care for Futurity. They have never been used to the Furniture of an English House, and dont know but that a Wine-glass is as strong as an Hand Iron. Our Language when they seem to have got it is not their Mother Tongue and they cannot receive nor communicate in that as in their own . . . And they are as unpolished and uncultivated within as without. (WP 761404)

Predictably, time and experience brought little relief, and Wheelock's list of headaches only grew. Before he moved the school to Hanover in 1770, he tried to turn some sixty-seven native children—forty-nine boys and eighteen girls—into English men and women. Many came from the New England tribes with a helpful modicum of English language, dress, and religion, but the largest number—thirty—were Iroquois, tough adolescents like Johannes and Negyes with an ingrained suspicion of the English and their schemes for "reducing" them to "civility." In his *Narrative* of the school of 1771, Wheelock boasted that he had produced forty "good readers, and writers," all sufficiently masters of English grammar and arithmetic and some advanced in Latin and Greek, who had behaved well in school and left with "fair and unblemished characters." But he also admitted that "I don't hear of more than half who have preserved their characters unstain'd either by a course of intemperance or uncleanness, or both; and some who on account of their parts, and learning, bid the fairest for usefulness, are sunk down into as low, savage, and brutish a manner of living as they were in before any endeavours were used with them to raise them up" (Wheelock 1771:19–20). Six of the best were already dead.

If these twenty apostates are added to the twenty-seven matri-
culants who dropped out prematurely (most of whom were Iroquois),
Moor's Charity School—on its own accounting—enjoyed a success
rate in the short run of something less than 30 percent. Perhaps this
figure fell within the range of Wheelock's expectations after his
introduction to the Iroquois. In 1763 he told his public benefactors
that "if one half of the Indian boys thus educated shall prove good
and useful men, there will be no reason to regret our toil and expence
for the whole . . . and if but one in ten does so, we shall have no
cause to think much of the expence" (Wheelock 1763:28–29). In all
likelihood the public had somewhat higher hopes for their benefac-
tions, as well they might at an annual cost of sixteen to twenty
pounds per boy, the equivalent, some critics said, of that for an
English boy at Harvard College (WP 762165).

A satisfactory explanation for this inauspicious record is not hard
to find. Colonial critics suggested that the native students came too
late and left too early, that the curriculum was inappropriate, and
that the goal of civilizing the Indians before Christianizing them was
unnecessary if not impossible in the first place. Wheelock's characteristic response was to lament the heartbreaking "Behavior of some
I have taken unwearied pains for" and to turn his energies toward
a less frustrating project (WP 772174.1). Rather than redefine his
objectives, he merely sought more malleable subjects. But of all
people, the Indians—his students and their parents—had the best
insights into the cause of Wheelock's failure, a failure magnified by
the boundless ambition and unblinking certitude of his goals.

Like those of his Puritan predecessors, Wheelock's missionary goals
were essentially two: to save the Indians from themselves and the
English from the Indians. The best way to accomplish both was, as
he stated so facilely, to turn the Indians into Englishmen. In religious
terms, one of the primary goals of nearly all the American colonies
was the "enlargement of Christian Religion" and the "propagating
of the gospel" (Protestant version) to the Western hemisphere (Farnham 1901:21; Morgan 1964:453). In Massachusetts, where Wheelock's
great-grandfather landed in 1637, the settlers were enjoined in the
royal charter to live such exemplary lives that their "orderlie conversation maie wynn and incite the natives of the country to the
knowledg and obedience of the onlie true God and Savior of man-
kinde, and the Christian fayth" (Morgan 1964:320). The key word
was obedience, as it was to be in all the English dealings with the
natives. Unlike the king's patent, most of the colonial plans for Indian
missions spoke of reducing rather than seducing Indians to "Civil
Societie and Christian Religion" (Farnham 1901:24; Morgan 1964:320).
The reason was simple—if you subscribed to the English cosmology.

In English eyes, the Indians were "savages," beings closer to "brutes" than to "men," and suffered from four vital deficiencies: civil and social order, a work ethic, modesty of manners and dress, and the Protestant version of Christianity. Their "savage" condition was equated with the "sinful liberty" of postlapsarian Adamism in which "overweening pride"—the original sin—marred all their thoughts and actions. As God's "chosen people," the missionaries of New England could do these "heady Creatures" no greater good than to "bridle" their lawless impulses and force their pagan necks into the "yoke of Christ."

From such premises it was obvious to "the most sensible Writers" of Wheelock's day that "it is necessary to civilize Savages before they can be converted to Christianity" (JP 7:506). With fitting medical metaphor, the Doctor said that his educational goal was to "cure the Natives . . . of their Savage Temper" and to "purge all the Indian out" of his students (WP 762521.1, 764560.1). Even a casual acquaintance with eighteenth-century medical practices will convey the full rigor of the treatment implied. Yet the medicine, however caustic, was administered in the patients' best interests. Without a strong purgative to rid the Indians of their "savage" disorders, their body politic would not absorb the "civilized" antidote to the white man's contaminants—alcohol and land greed. Only a settled agricultural life like that of the English colonists could guarantee the Indians' subsistence "when their Resources from the Wilderness fail, (as they certainly must do, when, and so fast, as the English extend their Settlements among them)" (WP 766504.4). And time was running out, especially for the obstinate Iroquois. "They evidently appear to be in, and very far gone already by, a quick consumption," wrote Wheelock in 1771, "they are wasting like a morning dew . . . before the rising sun" (Wheelock 1771:22; 1773:13).

If the "savages" could be saved from themselves, the English would also be saved from the "savages"—and could turn a pretty penny in the bargain. For Anglicised Indians would no longer threaten the English frontiers, which could then be greatly extended westward. Wheelock and his colleagues were convinced that missions and schools for the Indians were far more effective and far less expensive instruments of colonial policy than guns, armies, and gifts. If the missions had worked as well in practice as they did on paper, they would have been right. "Nothing can be more Agreeable to our Christian Character than to send the Gospel to the benighted Pagans," a like-minded friend wrote Wheelock, "Nothing more Conducive to our Civil Interests than to bring them to a Subjection to the Religion of Jesus" (WP 758618). "Civilizing the Indians" was tantamount to "reducing them to Peace and good Order," according to the mission litany, and only by "being civilized, and taught the Knowledge of the only true GOD and SAVIOR" could they be made "good Members of Society, and peaceable and quiet Neighbours" (Wheelock 1766:9, 21). But either way the English stood to gain. "For if [the Indians] receive the gospel," admitted Wheelock, "they will soon betake themselves to agriculture for their support, and so will need but a very small part, comparatively, of the lands which they now claim . . . ; and if they will not receive the gospel, they will, as they have done, waste away before it. . . ." (Wheelock 1773:12–13).

Wheelock's way of winning the Indians to Christian civility was to induce native children, usually aged eleven to fourteen, to come to his school in Connecticut, far removed from the "pernicious Influence of their Parents Example" (Wheelock 1763:25). There he proceeded to inure them to "Decency and Cleanliness" in the form of soap and water, English clothes, and, of course, the critical difference between hand irons and wine glasses (Wheelock 1775:11). In an atmosphere of beetle-browed piety, they were initiated into the arcana of the Westminster Assembly's *Shorter Catechism*, the English alphabet and grammar, arithmetic, and, in still more abstruse languages, the pastoral classics of ancient Greece and Rome. Since the plan was for them to return to their own villages as preachers, teachers, and interpreters of the English way, they were encouraged to retain their native languages and to teach them as well to their fellow students—Indians from other tribes and English boys preparing for Indian missions. Their spare time was "improved" by learning a trade, such as blacksmithing, from a local master or "husbandry" from the hands on Wheelock's farm. Native girls were apprenticed to local women to learn "the Female Part, as House-wives, School-mistresses, [and] Tayloresses" whereby they, as the helpmates of the native missionaries, would prevent "their turning savage in their Manner of Living, for want of those who may do those Offices for them" (Wheelock 1763: 15). Over all Wheelock sought to spread a benevolent but firm patriarchalism, to treat them as "My [own] Children" and to make them feel at home as "in a Father's House" (WP 767427.1; Wheelock 1763:40). What the Indians, especially the Iroquois, soon discovered, however, was that English children were treated much differently from children in the longhouse.

One of the reasons, perhaps the main reason, Wheelock preferred to locate his school among the English was that he knew the Indians' "great Fondness for their Children" was incompatible with the birchen "Government" necessary to "humble them, and reform their Manners" (Wheelock 1763:44; WP 762667.2). "Here," he admitted, "I can correct, & punish them as I please, . . . but there, it will not be born" (WP 762667.2). "And who does not know," he asked rhetorically, "that Evils so obstinate as those we may reasonably expect to find common in the Children of Savages, will require that which is severe? " (Wheelock 1763:26). When in 1772 the Onondaga council rejected for the last time Wheelock's offer to educate their children, they condemned ten years of hard usage of Iroquois children at the hands of his self-fulfilling prophecy. Grabbing Wheelock's high-handed son Ralph by the shoulder and shaking him, the council speaker replied with unaccustomed anger: "Brother, do you think we are altogether ignorant of your methods of instruction? . . . We understand not only your speech, but your *manner* of teaching Indian[s] . . . Brother, take care," he warned, "you were too hasty, & strong in your manner of speaking, before the children & boys have any knowledge of your language." And then in a verbal slap that must have stung the Wheelocks' Protestant souls to the quick, he concluded: "Brother, you must learn of the French ministers if you would understand, & know how to treat Indians. They don't speak roughly; nor do they for every little mistake take up a club & flog them" (McCallum 1932:287–88).

The sting of the rod was perhaps the sharpest indignity the Indians suffered but it was not the only one nor the worst. The school's work program, aimed at teaching the boys in play time to farm, seemed to the boys little more than an elaborate ruse for getting the master's chores done at no expense. Wheelock hoped that part-time farm work would "effectually remove the deep prejudices, so universally in the minds of the Indians, against their men's cultivating lands" (Wheelock 1771:5). Instead it seemed to confirm them and to create new ones against the Doctor for taking advantage of his students. Long was Wheelock's list of Indian students who were "reluctant to exercise [themselves] in, or learn any thing about Husbandry" (WP 774657). Only slightly shorter was the roster of complaining students and parents. John Daniel, a Narragansett parent, told Wheelock that "I always tho't Your School was free to the Natives; not to learn them how to Farm it, but to advance in Christian Knowledge, which wear the Chief motive that caus'd me to send my Son Charles to you; not that I'm anything against his Labouring some for You, when Business lies heavy on you," he allowed, "but to work two Years to learn to Farm it, is what I don't consent to . . ." (McCallum 1932:231). The Onondaga council simply made it clear that they expected their children to be treated "as *children* at your house, & not *servants*! " (McCallum 1932:287). But the last word came from Daniel Simon, a Narrangansett and later Dartmouth's first Indian graduate (1777): "if we poor Indians Shall work as much as to pay for our learning," he told Wheelock, "we Can go some other place as good as here for learning" (McCallum 1932:221).

When Hezekiah Calvin, a Delaware and one of Wheelock's former schoolmasters to the Iroquois, opted out of the Doctor's "Design" in 1768, he let it be known around New England that the inmates of Moor's School were not one big happy family. A Rhode Island correspondent told Wheelock that Calvin had "given the School a bad Charracter," complaining (among other things) that "you use the Indians very hard in keeping of them to work, & not allowing them a proper Privelidge in the School, that you . . . Diot & Cloath them with that that's mean, . . . That Mary [Secutor, a Narragansett] ask'd for a small piece of Cloth to make a p[ai]r of Slippers, which you would not allow her, [saying] twas to[o] good for Indians &c . . . [and] That you wont give no more of the Indians more learning than to Read, & Write—[alleging] 'twill make them Impudent; for which they are all about to leave you" (McCallum 1932:65).

Regardless of the accuracy of these criticisms, many of the Indians and their tribesmen *felt* them to be true. What was not in doubt, however, was that the Indian students were surrounded on every side by overt prejudice that often exceeded cultural arrogance and fell clearly into racism. Wheelock instinctively knew that native students could never be mixed with English (except those special few who were preparing for Indian missions), "for it hath been found by some few Instances of *Indians* educated elsewhere, that the *English* Students have been apt to look upon them with an Air of *disdain*, which these Sons of *ranging* Liberty cannot so well brook" (Wheelock 1766:6). For this reason even Yale, his alma mater, was inappropriate for his Indian graduates; too many sons of Eli would "disdain in their Hearts to be Associates and Companions with an Indian. And what the Consequences of such Contempt of them will be is not hard to guess" (WP 756615).

The problem could also be found closer to home. Wheelock had great difficulty in apprenticing his Indian boys because "their fellow Prentices viz. English Boys will dispise them & treat them as Slaves" (WP 764268.1). In 1765 David Fowler, an older Montauk student, received such an "injury" and "provocations" from the Lebanon townies in a sleighing incident that his mentor was somewhat surprised that his new "Christian forebearance" overcame his native spirit of revenge (WP 765164.1). Even a young minister turned down Wheelock's offer of an Indian mission because, he said, "[I] should be prodigiously apt to batter some of their Noses, or else Skulk and run for it" (WP 770367).

The pestilence of racism, however, infected all of New England, especially during the Seven Years' War and the Indian "rebellion" that concluded it. Wheelock could not raise funds for the school because his potential donors in the colonial legislatures and churches "breath[ed] forth nothing towards [the Indians] but Slaughter & destruction" (WP 758422). A collection plate passed in Windsor, Connecticut, in 1763 returned empty save for "a Bullet & Flynt," symbolizing an attitude that survived in Wheelock's own colony long after the frontier hostilities had ceased (WP 763581). Four years later the table conversation of several gentlemen in Middletown was reported to Wheelock and it cannot have pleased—or much surprised—him. They spoke frankly of the hopelessness of converting Indians by anything but "Powder & Ball." On the basis of a wide acquaintance with "human nature," at least as he knew it in New England, one of them declared the Doctor's scheme "absurd & fruitlis" because of "the ireconsilable avertion, that white people must ever have to black . . . So long as the Indians are dispised by the English we may never expect success in Christianizing of them." For their own parts, they confessed that "they could never respect an Indian, Christian or no Christian, so as to put him on a level with white people on any account, especially to eat at the same Table, no—not with Mr [Samson] Ocham himself, be he ever so much a Christian or ever so Learned" (WP 767604.1). As the cultural competition of the seventeenth century gave way to the racial antipathies of the eighteenth, popular support in America for "Grand Designs" such as Wheelock's evaporated.

There was a slim chance that the Indian students could have withstood the corrosive currents of popular prejudice that swirled about them if Wheelock had shown some sensitivity to their cultural dilemma and sustained his originally high sense of their purpose. Unfortunately he did not, for his cultural and theological assumptions were as ethnocentric and as racist as those of his neighbors, and the Indians were quickly reduced to a secondary role in their own salvation. If he was not before, the Great Awakening turned Wheelock into a seventeenth-century religious Puritan. For the misnamed "New Lights" of the revival, the religious premises of the old covenant theology acquired renewed relevance. Basic to that theology was a dim view of human nature, which had been corrupted at the source by Adam's fall, and a belief that the original sin, pride, must be constantly crushed in man to allow God's omnipotent will full sway. That in Wheelock's eyes the Indians were the proudest people on earth did nothing to make their life in Moor's School an easy one.

Of all the sins committed by his Indian students, none so angered Wheelock as "Insufferable pride," which he felt to be the foundation of their "Contempt of all Authority," particularly his own (WP 763666.2). When Jacob Woolley, a twenty-year-old Delaware, got drunk, threw a clench-fisted tantrum, cursed God, and tried to throw his bed out the window, Wheelock judged him not culturally disoriented or personally frustrated but simply guilty of "Pride of Heart," and administered several stripes to "humble & tame him" (McCallum 1932:255; WP 763666.2). When he ran away to the Mohegans five months later, Wheelock presented him with an "Indian Blanket" because he had renounced his "polite education" and "herded with Indians (little better than Savages)." A clerical correspondent agreed that this was a "mortification" more "humbling" than blows or stripes, and added his hope to Wheelock's that "God will yet humble him" (WP 763659, 763666.2). In such an atmosphere it was inevitable that Wheelock's need to dominate absolutely would collide with the sons of the Mohawks, who were, he complained, "proud and high in their own Esteem above any other Tribe, having long been reckon[e]d at the head of the Nations" (WP 767265.2). In 1767 he rusticated two Mohawk youths, though, understandably, not without some misgivings. "Great William," the natural son of Sir William Johnson by an Indian woman, had been "too proud, & litigious to consist with the Health & well being" of the school. His traveling companion, who had been at the school only a few months, was "so lifted up with his having been in the Wars, and sent to Hell one or two of the poor Savages with his own hand, that [Wheelock's] House was scarcely good enough for him to live in, or any of the School honourable enough to speak to him. . . . There is," the Doctor told Sir William, "& shall be Government in this School" (WP 767163).

At the root of Wheelock's unhappy relations with his Indian students was a racial attitude that placed Indians on a level with blacks—on the lowest shelf of humanity. Like many of his contemporaries, Wheelock frequently referred to his "Black" children, especially his "black Son," Samson Occom, and to the "Black Tribes" on the frontier who needed his help, a verbal preference that was not lost on his students (WP 762516, 761304.1; Wheelock 1769:16). Just the way they wrote to him, even as adults, betrays how they must have been treated and taught to think of themselves in his presence. Joseph Johnson must have been taught well. On one occasion he referred to himself as "a Despicable Lump of polluted Clay, as is inclosed in this tawny skin of mine," on another as "your Ignorant Pupil, and good for nothing Black Indian." "If I was an Englishman, & was thus Respected by you," he wrote, "I should be very thankful, but much more doth it now become me, being an Indian, to be humble & very thankfull in very deed." Though Johnson was a Mohegan, he sought temporary relief from his educated self-abasement among the Oneidas in 1768 when "he turn'd pagan for about a week—painted, sung, danc'd, drank & whor'd it, with some of the savage Indians he could find" (McCallum 1932:183, 131, 148,

141). Hezekiah Calvin, the Delaware drop-out, may have chosen an even apter symbol of protest; he is last seen in prison for "forging a pass for a Negro" (WP 769209.2). As an owner of black slaves for much of his life, Wheelock was perfectly capable of distinguishing the two races; that he did not suggests an unconscious reduction of the people he was consciously trying to elevate and a deep ambivalence about his "Grand Design."

Wheelock's innate distrust of the Indians worked to the surface during the course of the 1760s. Originally he felt that Indian missionaries were superior to Englishmen and gave a dozen reasons in his first *Narrative* (1763). Yet as early as 1760 he was planning to take "poor & promising [English] Youth" into the school "in case of a failure of Indians" (WP 760566). By the time the first Iroquois arrived he was no longer talking privately of Indians as schoolmasters, interpreters, *and* missionaries—only the first two. He was obviously lowering his sights. In 1762 he had his revised plans confirmed by the Boston Board of the Scottish Society that funded much of his work. "If the Design is to Educate only a few that shall be qualified, to be Missionaries, Schoolmasters &c," they wrote, "We Apprehend Indians will not be so proper for these Purposes, as Persons Selected from Among the English" (WP 762412.1). After several frustrating years with his Iroquois students, the Doctor needed only an excuse to complete his institutional shift to white missionaries.

In the winter of 1769 the Oneidas provided one by abruptly withdrawing their six children. They gave him an innocuous reason but Wheelock suspected two others: that "an ugly fellow" had spread "Slanders" that "their Children were not well treated" at school, and that, having heard a rumor of an impending Indian war with the colonies, they were "not willing their children should be with the English [as hostages] at such a time" (WP 769255; Wheelock 1771:16). Whatever their reasons, Wheelock considered their action providential; he sent the other Iroquois students home and prepared to move to Hanover to found a college for English missionaries. God, he told his English benefactors, had convinced him that "Indians may not have the lead in the Affair, 'till they are made new Creatures." Their "Sloth," "want of Stability," and "doleful Apostacy" disqualified them (WP 769255, 769274.2).

In the future, after the Indian school was transplanted in less fertile New Hampshire soil, Wheelock would prefer native students from the "praying towns" or Indian reserves of Canada—St. Francis, Lorette, Caughnawaga—who were descended from adopted English captives, even though most had been raised as Catholics. "Though they were born among the *Indians*," he wrote, "and have been exposed to partake of their national Vices . . . ; yet they appear to be as sprightly, active, enterprising, benevolent towards all, and sensible of Kindnesses done them, as English Children commonly are" (Wheelock 1775:11). His racial preference was unmistakable, as was his characteristic feeling that the "other" Indians, just over the horizon, were always more susceptible to his designs. These Anglo-Indians, he vowed, were "by far the most promising set of Youths, I have ever yet had from the Indian Country" (Wheelock 1775:14). How quickly he had forgotten his words to Sir William Johnson only a few years before: "The Boys I have from your parts behave very well, better than any I have had from any other Quarter, and it seems to me they are really a much better Breed" (WP 764574). Apparently the Doctor wished to begin his experiment in cultural transmogrification with subjects who resembled as nearly as possible his desired results. With the unpromising methods and attitudes he employed, that was perhaps the only way to ensure success.

Wheelock's self-confessed failure to produce a cadre of native missionaries made in his own image met with a timely remedy in 1767 upon the return of Samson Occom and the Rev. Nathaniel Whitaker from a fund-raising tour of England and Scotland. Sent by Wheelock to procure donations for his Indian school, the pair raised more than twelve thousand pounds during their two-year sojourn. This enormous windfall enabled him to sever all ties with the missionary societies upon which he had long depended and to begin a serious search for a way to subordinate his involvement in the unrewarding "Indian business" to a project that gave more scope to his energy, political acumen, and need to dominate. He found such an outlet in Dartmouth, a liberal arts *college* intended primarily for English missionaries that borrowed the name of the *school's* ranking English benefactor, the Earl of Dartmouth.

But the idea of founding such a college was not new to Wheelock; the British donations only made it possible for the first time. As early as 1761 Wheelock had begun to cast his eye around the Northeast for a college site. His heart was initially set on the rich farmlands of Iroquois country, "near the Bowells of the Pagan Settlements," where he thought fifteen to twenty square miles would suffice to plant a model Christian community, including a school for Indians and a college for English missionaries. When it became clear that the Iroquois and their Anglican protector, Sir William Johnson, would never countenance an invasion of grasping, grim-lipped New England Congregationalists, Wheelock considered other sites in Ohio, New York, Pennsylvania, and most of the New England colonies before accepting Hanover's offer of land and capital. In that day as in ours, colleges were economic boons to their towns, and Dartmouth simply went to the highest bidder. Wheelock now had the makings of an institution equal to his ambitions and the opportunity to delegate his waning interest in the schooling of Indians. Moor's Charity School continued to admit Indians after the move to New Hampshire, but with increasing admixtures of English students. The dilution of its original purpose and the lengthening shadow of the college finally closed its doors in 1829.

The subordination of the Indians in Wheelock's new design for Dartmouth College was symbolized nowhere better than in his first draft of its charter. Dartmouth was being founded, Wheelock wrote, to educate "Youths of *the English* and also of the Indian Tribes in this Land in reading, writing & all . . . liberal Arts and Sciences." Then he remembered that several thousand British benefactors had given thousands of pounds to a charity school primarily for Indians, not white colonists, and he scratched out the reference to English youth and added it at the end of the passage as if to indicate their subordinate position in his design. In its revised form the charter became New Hampshire law, and Doctor—now President—Wheelock proceeded to exhaust his ample treasury—over the protests of his English trustees—on a liberal arts college that graduated only three Indians in the eighteenth century and eight in the nineteenth.

But not everyone was fooled by the Doctor's legerdemain, least of all his "black son," Samson Occom. With the frank shrewdness he had shown all his troubled life in his dealings with the English, Occom told his mentor, "your having so many White Scholars and so few or no Indian Scholars, gives me great Discouragement . . . I am very jealous that instead of your Semenary Becoming alma Mater, she will be too alba mater [white mother] to Suckle the Tawnees, for She is already adorned up too much like the popish Virgin Mary." In short, he accused, "your present Plan is not calculated to benefit the poor Indians."

President Wheelock did not have to be told.

CHAPTER FOUR

To the Mohawk Station: The Making of a New England Company Missionary— the Rev. Robert Lugger

CHARLES M. JOHNSTON

When explaining his approach to ethnology, William N. Fenton likes to talk about "upstreaming," the exercise of proceeding from the known and observable present to the unknown historical past. (Fenton 1957: 21–22; 1969: 12). Some forty years ago, at about the time Fenton was embarking on his productive field work among the Iroquois of Ontario, A. G. Chisholm, a lawyer in London, was using a similar tactic to gather information on the validity of Six Nations Indians' land claims against the New England Company in that province. The company in question, founded in the seventeenth century to administer to the spiritual needs of New England's aborigines, had transferred its operations, first to New Brunswick and then to Upper Canada, in the years after the American Revolution (Kellaway 1961). In any case, the "upstreaming" which admirably serves the purposes of Fenton, the ethnologist, also benefited the efforts of Chisholm, the lawyer.

While searching out additional material for this essay, I followed a trail to the archives of the Six Nations Indian Office in Brantford where I discovered the voluminous documents that Chisholm had painstakingly compiled to buttress the Indians' case. Following its successful conclusion in 1934, he rejoiced with Six Nations' well-wishers that the action had resulted in "so much of your lands and money [being] retrieved out of the clutches of a despoiler . . ." (SNIO, Chisholm File, Accounts and Letters). Chisholm's opinion of the company graphically speaks for itself.

Obviously the "ancient friendship" which had supposedly characterized the relationship between company and Indians in Ontario had come under fire. But how had that friendship been struck up in the first place, roughly a century earlier? Whatever happened in the long interval to sour the association, to fuel the grievances of the Six Nations, and to arouse the wrath of A. G. Chisholm, however engrossing those events may be, will not be explored here. Rather the object will be to examine the background and career of the Rev. Robert Lugger whom the company appointed in 1827 to serve its newly established mission in the Grand River Valley of Upper Canada. This will amount, in other words, to an exercise in "downstreaming," to an examination of the past for its own sake, without explicit reference to the present.

To appreciate Lugger's role among the Six Nations one must pry into his earlier career and try to ascertain what went into the making of this missionary. To begin with, he was a West Countryman. As a native of a seafaring center—Plymouth Dock in Devon where he was born in 1793—he was well named, *lugger* meaning a small vessel with lug or square sails. His origins were respectably middle class, his father, a "Gentleman," having the means and the connections to educate his son at a reputable grammar school (Venn 1951: 232; Potts 1855: 403). When the young Lugger graduated, the Napoleonic War was in full swing so he set aside plans for holy orders and a possible missionary and teaching career and instead sought and obtained a commission in the Royal Artillery. Subsequently assigned to the Board of Ordnance, he was dispatched in 1817 to Barbados, where he was put to work on fortification schemes.

His penchant, however, for missionary work and teaching was not to be denied. Anticipating his later efforts among Upper Canadian Iroquois, he had, before his departure, laid plans to educate Barbadian blacks. To this end he solicited the aid of the recently formed Church Missionary Society, which, overwhelmed by his enthusiasm, readily complied and urged him to establish a school in Barbados under their auspices. Indeed his army career seemed to be given a distinctly subordinate place in his order of priorities (CMS, MR 18: 346–48).

His subsequent exertions as schoolmaster and school founder in Barbados and Upper Canada can only be appreciated, however, if the pedagogical innovations of that generation are taken into account. In many respects Lugger personified some of the major changes then unfolding on the educational front. His shipboard organization of an adults' school, for example, was doubtless inspired by the recent campaign aimed at instructing the working class population already spawned by the Industrial Revolution (Adamson 1930: 20). The latter, moreover, had been accompanied by a spiritual revival, one characteristic of which was the work of the Methodists in organizing class meetings and Sunday Schools. Taken together, these institutions provided not only the rudiments of religious and secular instruction but a form of social control deemed so essential in an age threatened by the unsettling ideology of the French Revolution. Judging from the words that he dropped and from the approach that he took to his chores, Lugger was patently in tune with these educational efforts to reach a population in the throes of dramatic social and economic changes.

Following his arrival in Barbados early in 1818, he speedily organized what he termed a "NATIONAL NEGRO SCHOOL." In so doing he publicly acknowledged his debt to another enterprise, the so-called "National System of Education" fashioned by the Scot, Andrew Bell (Bell 1807: 81–82). As a tactic to serve his strategy Bell had put together the "monitorial system," which made up for a notorious lack of teachers by using monitors as disciplinarians and teaching assistants. After being taught by a master, the monitor would then be expected to convey to his confrères whatever enlightenment he himself had received (Stewart 1972: 96). It was this ambitious program that Lugger would apply in Barbados to meet the needs of transplanted Africans and ultimately in a modified form those of the Six Nations. In spite of the formidable obstacles posed by the slave's "degradation" and "peculiar circumstances," his school seemed to prosper, show results, and impress those in authority (CMS CW 06, Thos. Harris Letters, 1820; PRO, CO 28, 86: 1817).

Recurring ill health and, perhaps more importantly, a desire to pursue studies toward a degree and holy orders, his original ambition, prompted Lugger's return to England in the spring of 1819. During a vigorously spent year and a half in Barbados he had learned much. The leitmotif of his West Indian efforts and of his future career in Upper Canada can best be traced in a letter he wrote after his return home. The twinning of education and evangelism, always his hallmark, came out in his comment that, "You know, *education alone will never do,* unless the ground be broken up and the *good seed* sown at the *same time* . . ." (CMS, G, AC3; 13 Apr. 1820). Lugger's simultaneous assault on two fronts—the tutorial and the spiritual—reflected his deep interest in what a later generation would call "cultural imperialism."

By the time Lugger was writing his reflections on the proper role of the missionary, he had already matriculated at Cambridge University. His admission to St. Catharine's College seemed appropriate enough, given its practice of enrolling so-called "military parsons" who wished to assume the studies deferred by wartime service. A classmate who may well have influenced Lugger's choices was the brother of Sir Peregrine Maitland, the then lieutenant-governor of Upper Canada who took a keen interest in the welfare of its Indian communities (Jones 1951: 106).

While a student at St. Catharine's, Lugger was doubtless exposed to the Evangelical movement within the Church of England, one which owed much to the initiative of Cambridge itself. A "species of Anglican Methodism" grew up within the so-called Low Church— to distinguish it from the High Church of orthodoxy and conformity— which sought to build a bridge to the Evangelicalism of the Methodists (Halévy 1961: 434). Years later, evidence that this influence had rubbed off on Lugger cropped up in his statement before the Commissioners of the New England Company that he would be willing to work with missionaries of other "persuasions" (NEC, 7920, 2: 262). Following his ordination in 1823 and his graduation from Cambridge the following year, Lugger was appointed to livings in Wiltshire and Hampshire. But clearly he was anxious, now that his health was on the mend, to resume his overseas career (CMS, G, AC3, 30 Dec. 1824).

While he was keeping alive the "fire of missionary zeal," the New England Company, his future sponsor, was making its move in the valley of the Grand in Upper Canada. The people who would be entrusted to Lugger had been residing in the valley for some forty years, ever since Sir Frederick Haldimand, Governor of Québec, had granted them a tract of nearly 600,000 acres, "six miles deep from each side of the [Grand] river, beginning at Lake Erie, and extending to [its] head" (PAC, Haldimand Papers B222: 1061). This arrangement, made in 1784 to acknowledge the role played by the Mohawks and their confederates as Britain's allies during the American Revolution, had enabled approximately sixteen hundred Iroquois to decamp from their homeland in New York and settle on the tract that Haldimand sanguinely referred to as a "fertile and happy retreat." Over the years it proved to be fertile enough for those who wished to farm it but its happiness was periodically placed at risk. Disputes over land sales to whites, renewed hostilities with the United States in 1812, and recurring economic slumps that created deprivation and depopulation; all these had contributed to retarding the progress of the Confederacy on the Grand. Whitehall for its part, distracted by the drawn-out conflict with Napoleonic France, had apparently been unable to deploy the material assistance and spiritual guidance that the Six Nations had grown to expect. After the return of peace in 1815, however, there were soon straws in the wind indicating that more attention would be lavished by both public and private agencies on the Indians' needs, particularly on the educational side (Harlow and Madden 1953: 588–91; Wilson 1974: 297–98).

Thus in the fall of 1820 the New England Company received a letter from the Right Rev. John Stewart, Bishop of Quebec, giving them a comprehensive survey of the Six Nations' situation and urging them to assist those Indians. The letter arrived just when the company was deciding to wind up its work among the Indians at Sussex Vale in the colony of New Brunswick. From the beginning there, the local Indians' addiction to the "Wandering Life" and their aversion to the "habits of civilization" had frustrated the company's efforts (NEC 7956, 24 Feb. 1806). Consequently Stewart's letter of 1820, describing the state of affairs of a reasonably settled and agrarian community in Upper Canada, one, moreover, which was "generally Protestant," doubtless came as welcome news to company directors (NEC 7923: 146–49). In fact, the majority of the Mohawks, for whom a projected mission would primarily be planned, had long been adherents of the Church of England and cared for by the Society for the Propagation of the Gospel at their Fort Hunter church in the Mohawk Valley (Lydekker 1938).

The gist of Stewart's statement was that there was a genuine need for the services of a resident missionary on the Grand, the occasional visitations of an SPG missionary being dismissed as insufficient for the purpose. Mindful that the "effect of Education has been to civilize," he also asked that the two schoolmasters already at work in the Six Nations community be paid on a regular basis. Obviously he felt that the New England Company, with its enviable resources and long history of productive service, would be the most appropriate agency for achieving these objects and correcting a situation described in a report submitted a few years earlier. It had indicated that formal instruction, even among the more advanced Mohawks, was in a less than flourishing state. Thus the school in the Mohawk Village was often unattended during the "hunting season," and when children did go to it they were inadequately taught to write and read. Furthermore, it was said that education was discouraged by "many of the old men" who were convinced that learning turned people into idlers or worse and prevented them "from excelling in the hunt" (NYSL, MSS #13350–51). In spite of these discouraging accounts the company complied with the Bishop's requests and forwarded sixty pounds to pay the annual salary of one of the schoolmasters (NEC 7923: 150, 159). By this act they officially forged their connection with the Six Nations, organizing a beachhead of interest and commitment that Lugger would occupy in some six years' time.

It was at this juncture, in the early 1820s, that another personality entered the picture, one whose path would shortly cross the missionary's. John Brant (Takarehoga), the youngest son of the storied war chief, Joseph Brant, was as anxious as Stewart to promote an educational revival among his people. A full-blooded Mohawk and well-armed himself with educational credentials, he was invariably described by admiring whites as "very much the gentleman" (Landon 1922: 121). Like Indian leaders before him the young Brant journeyed to the center of Empire whenever he needed guidance and assistance. This he did in the spring of 1822 in order to inspect London's institutions of a "humane and benevolent Character," and in the process he visited the offices of the Commissioners of the New England Company (Stone, 1838, 2:527). Brant made a favorable impression on his hosts and, after acquainting them with the work that could be done by the company, particularly among such non-Christian Iroquois as the Cayugas and the Senecas, they responded by offering an additional two hundred pounds for schoolmasters' salaries (NEC 7920, 2: 75–76, 82). Over the next four years supplementary monies were earmarked not only for religious and secular instruction but for the erection of schoolhouses for the Mohawks and their kinsmen, the Oneidas (NEC 7913, 2: 166, 175). But judged equally desirable was the appointment of a resident missionary, one who could be the spiritual director of the educational program that Brant was seeking to expand and the company was apparently willing to finance.

To gather additional information before embarking on the step that would ultimately bring Lugger on to the scene the company commissioned the Rev. John West to undertake a survey of the Six Nations' needs. West was well qualified for the task, having been chaplain to the Hudson's Bay Company on the Red River and an astute observer of Indian customs in the Northwest. His report was all that Brant would have wished and helped to smooth the way for the appointment of a resident missionary to what would shortly be called the "Mohawk Station" (West 1827: 276–89). West's remarks provided an effective backup to Brant's comment that the Six Nations "would rejoice to have a . . . clergyman amongst us, who would not consider it too laborious . . . to travel frequently to our several hamlets, to preach the Gospel . . . , to visit the sick, and always to evince . . . his devotion . . . , not only by preaching *but by example*. . . ." (Stone, 1838, 2: 529–30).

The next move was up to the company. Late in 1826 its Court or general meeting approved the expenditure of over a thousand pounds on requisite buildings—a parsonage at the Mohawk Village and two schoolhouses—and half that sum again to meet the anticipated annual salaries of a missionary and two schoolmasters (NEC 7920, 2: 244–45, 251). In the following spring Lugger was summoned to London to attend a meeting of a "special committee" of the company charged with the task of selecting the sought-after missionary. At the interview

a hopeful Lugger furnished a brief autobiography, dwelling understandably on his educational career in Barbados, one that had, he
was careful to note, been pursued gratuitously. As well, he allowed
that while he was reluctant "to state any particular plan until I get
on the spot," he would expect to adopt "Dr. Bell's plan" so far as
circumstances in Upper Canada would permit.

The question, however, arises: what did Lugger know about those
circumstances and the habits of those among whom he hoped to
work? Hints and clues emerge from his responses to the committee's
queries. In one instance he referred to his conversations with William
Wilberforce, the indefatigable abolitionist, whom he had visited on
the eve of his departure for Barbados. Slavery had doubtless been
discussed but the humanitarian leader may also have alluded to
North America's aborigines. Wilberforce's knowledge of the subject
had been augmented through his association with John Norton, an
adopted Mohawk of mixed blood who had produced a lengthy and
perceptive journal on the customs of the Indians of the eastern
woodlands (Norton 1970). There are indications that the same Norton
had recommended the use of Bell's approach in the instruction of
the Six Nations and argued the need for manual training and a
school of industry. Wilberforce may well have brought Norton's work
to Lugger's attention.

Again, what about the possible impact on Lugger's generation of
the monumental treatise published a century earlier on the mores
of the Iroquois by the Jesuit missionary, Joseph François Lafitau (and
recently reissued by the Champlain Society under the skilful editorial
care of William Fenton and Elizabeth Moore) ? In part, Lafitau's study
was an attempt to discover the ancient state of man in the eighteenth-
century culture of the North American aborigine, a preoccupation as
well of contributors to the Scottish Enlightenment (Teggert 1960:
94–96; Bock 1956: 79–80). Some English writers of that earlier period—for example, Samuel Purchas—had also shown an interest in
"conferring earliness on contemporary savagery" (Lafitau, 1, 1974:
xlix).

Was all or some of this activity known to Lugger, had it been
debated while he was a student at Cambridge, and did it stimulate
the conversations of fellow missionaries or directors of the New
England Company? Perhaps it was so integral a part of the shared
assumptions and knowledge of that generation that it is pointless to
trace Lugger's own thinking on the problem to any particular source.
Or it may simply be a matter of his having already consulted the
considerable corpus of information that the company had collected
on the Iroquois (NEC 7956, 17 Jan. 1815).

Although Lugger was ill prepared to minister to the Six Nations in their own tongues, a shortcoming he would later seek to rectify, he had clearly done some kind of homework. Indeed it would have been strange had he not done so. Thus he had learned that the Iroquois "are attracted by the parabolical Language, the speeches of their Chiefs [being] highly figurative." He then conceded that he "should expect greater difficulty with Indians than with Negroes from the proud character of the Indians." The admission reflected a popular attitude once held by Europeans, and one assiduously promoted by eighteenth-century writers like Cadwallader Colden (Colden 1958). Lugger may well have been aware that the months he had spent caring for Barbadian slaves might not have been the best possible preparation for work among partially acculturated Indian bands who had rarely if ever regarded themselves as servants of the white man. In any case, he went on to assure committee members that he would endeavor to "deal with the Indians according to their customs and manners" and would never preach faith "without Works," a pledge that would have gone down well with John Brant (NEC 7920, 2: 265-67).

As to spiritual teaching, Lugger anticipated that the Indians "would understand the facts of the Gospel not the Doctrines of the Trinity or of Justification . . ."; he stated that, generally speaking, he would not bring before them "abstract points." These comments prompt the question: had Lugger at some stage flirted with Arianism, from which Unitarianism stemmed, a form of theological criticism that assaulted the doctrine of the Trinity and gained considerable strength after the turn of the century? (Hunt 1873, 3: 15–29; Warre Cornish, 1910, 1:40). Might these developments account for his downplaying of trinitarianism in the message he prepared for the Six Nations? Or was it because he had convinced himself that the Iroquoian mind would not readily comprehend the subtleties of such a concept? Answers to these questions are hard to come by. But so far as the presentation of "abstract points" are concerned, Lugger's reluctance to do so seemed fully in accord with established company policy, which had disavowed any "fanatical zeal to spread . . . peculiar or exclusive Doctrines" (SNIO, Six Nations vs. New England Co., J. M. Busk to Sir George Grey, 13 Dec. 1838).

In this connection Lugger, as already noted, had dwelt on the desirability of working with "other Missionaries of different persuasions." He had in mind here, among others, the so called "Moravians" or United Brethren who were active among the Delawares in western Upper Canada. He had familiarized himself years before with their educational exertions in the West Indies, particularly their blending of religious instruction with secular training in the mechanical arts (CMS Records, 21 Feb. 1821; Gollin 1967: 83).

Lugger had every intention of pursuing the same course: "I should consider civil and moral Improvement," he remarked, "very essential to religious improvement." This strongly echoed what he had had to say about his Barbadian experience, that secular and religious instruction ought to go hand in hand for best results. Lugger's stand seemed to be a compromise in the struggle then going on between those who pushed civilization as the vital prerequisite to conversion and others who just as vigorously maintained that the "power of the Gospel" would pave the road to material achievement and social refinement (BPP, Report from Select Committee on Aborigines, 1836: 49, 635). With respect to the secular instruction he planned to introduce, Lugger was anxious to establish a school of industry—"I am desirous of the assistance of Artisans"—and to promote a productive agriculture in the Grand River Valley. In the true spirit of Bell's teachings he had every expectation of "getting the Mohawk School as forward as possible in order to send out teachers to other parts. . . ."

Lugger, meanwhile, did not lack for enthusiastic referees. Typical was a prominent Barbadian planter, who testified that the would-be missionary was "peculiarly calculated to fill the situation of instructor to the Indians and . . . stated this from the opportunity he had of . . . assisting him in the formation of the schools in that Island . . ." (NEC 7920, 2: 265–67). In the end, on 15 June 1827, the examining committee, which apparently interviewed no other candidates, satisfied itself that Lugger was the right choice and named him the company's first resident missionary to the "Mohawk Station." He would embark on his new career with the aid of an annual salary of two hundred pounds, an expense account of fifty pounds, and a house, albeit an unfurnished one. He was also afforded a generous traveling grant and promised a supply of books, maps, and carpenters' tools (USPG, Upper Canada Box; NEC 7913, 2: 171).

Before taking up his new duties Lugger gained more firsthand information by "passing an evening" with the Rev. William Hough, who had briefly served the Mohawks as a missionary for the Society for the Propagation of the Gospel in Foreign Parts (SPG) until failing health forced his retirement in 1827. Hough told (or reminded) Lugger of Sir Peregrine Maitland's interest in the Confederacy's affairs and filled him in on the activities of John Brant, just recently named Superintendent of the Six Nations. Lugger was assured that Brant was "influential and had the cause of civilization much at heart" (NEC 7920, 2:273–74).

As it turned out, Lugger's appointment caused some unpleasantness in the company's dealings with Hough's employer, the SPG. The society had initially welcomed the company's interest in the Six Nations' welfare and hailed Lugger's appointment as "opportune," but they reacted sharply to his thinly veiled criticism of their past efforts on the Grand and to the prospect that they might be shoved out of the valley altogether (USPG, 39: 235; NEC 7920, 3: 39–40). Although the controversy simmered until 1831, the society ultimately withdrew from the Six Nations field as gracefully as it could, noting, by way of explanation, "the insufficiency of its . . . funds . . . and the pressing calls for new Missions [elsewhere]." All the same, the SPG offered to provide Lugger with its own Mohawk translation of the Gospel of St. Mark (USPG, 39: 239).

After all the interviews, the reflections, the reading, and the conversations with "old hands," what kind of community actually greeted Lugger on his arrival at the Mohawk Village in October 1827? Since he left no account of his own, a picture of sorts must be pieced together from those of others. Admittedly, these are colored by the varied perceptions and prejudices of their authors, but, even so, some plausible impression can be formed. On a purely statistical plane, to be sure, one can speak with greater confidence. A report prepared the year Lugger arrived in the valley revealed an Iroquois population of 2,223, of whom 66 were labeled "halfbreeds." The Mohawks, Lugger's principal charges, accounted for a quarter of the total (divided almost equally between the Upper and Lower Mohawks, so named after their original "castles" or villages in the Mohawk Valley). Of the some 355,000 acres still left to them from the original tract, fewer than 7,000 were actually being cultivated by the Grand River Iroquois in 1827 (SNIO, Statistical Report for 1827).

The appearance of the Mohawk Village has been variously described. An official who paid it a visit a year after Lugger's arrival took a jaundiced view of its "half dozen miserable and scattered huts and paltry church. . . . The town was formerly more respectable," he conceded, "but the increasing scarcity of fuel in its neighbourhood and the fine quality of the soil induced [the Indians] to . . . settle on the banks of the river, where they cultivate the ground in companies or bands. . . . Their knowledge of farming is exceedingly limited . . . but those of more industrious habits follow the example of their white neighbours, and have separate farms" (Johnston 1964: 292). One of the latter was Superintendent John Brant who would work closely with Lugger, at least in the early years of the missionary's regime. One fruit of their collaboration was the undertaking to produce a Mohawk grammar.

Although some visitors like John West were more complimentary when describing the Mohawk Village (West 1827: 266 ff.), many others deplored the "drunkenness" that stalked the community and the degree to which the Indians had succumbed to the "favourite vices" of the whites who lived in the nearby village of Brantford. None was more scathing in his criticism than the English tourist who wrote that the "habits of the [Six Nations] are . . . opposed to civilization . . . , and the failure of . . . various attempts to civilize [them] . . . proves that they are a people whose habits and characters are . . . not susceptible of amelioration. . . ." He added the lament that their contact with whites had served to divest them "of those rude virtues and barbarous qualities which alone give a sort of respectability to the savage" (Howison 1821: 161–64).

With these words he summed up the transformation wrought over half a century in the European's attitude toward the North American Indian. Respected earlier in the Rousseauan sense as one endowed with a simple though engaging nobility (Hatzan 1927: 122), the Indian was now denigrated as demoralized and depraved and hopelessly incapable of responding to the progressive world of the white man. This judgment missionaries like Lugger would understandably reject. Fresh to his assignment and imbued with the incurable optimism of the educational missionary, he was convinced that the religious commitment of the Christianized Mohawks could be revived. Again, through an ambitiously applied program of instruction much could be corrected and the Iroquois generally saved for a productive role in a civilized environment. These convictions he shared with a good many of his contemporaries in Upper Canada, including the Rev. John Strachan, the acknowledged leader of the Church of England in the colony and an avid supporter of educational schemes for its Indian population (PAO, Strachan Papers, 1823–12 Aug. 1834: Letters, 6 Nov. 1826; 27 Feb. 1827; Wilson 1974).

Meanwhile, what facilities were available to Lugger when he started his mission at the Mohawk Station? Thanks to the largesse of the New England Company and the efforts of Brant and Hough, the building of a parsonage had been started and two schools already constructed near the "Mohawk Chapel," or Church of St. Paul, the transplanted Mohawks' original place of worship in the valley. Much, however, remained to be done. Apart from completing the parsonage and making repairs to the church, Lugger had the task of building two additional schools along with dwellings to house their prospective teachers.

While this work was being launched Lugger, accompanied by John Brant, journeyed down the river and visited all the Six Nations bands in the hope of gaining their acceptance of his mission. But his efforts to convert the non-Christian Iroquois met with stiff opposition in some quarters. Particularly hostile were those Delawares and Cayugas who followed the teachings of Handsome Lake (Ga-ne-o-di-yo), the Seneca prophet who had sparked a puritanical campaign to revive the Iroquois people's traditional religion at the turn of the century (Shimony 1961: 203). The main objection of some Indian critics, however, appeared to be the "bad example" set by those Mohawks who had resorted not only to the white man's religion but to his vices. But other Iroquois were brought around by Lugger's persuasive talk, including a number of Onondagas, Oneidas, and Tuscaroras. Indeed the latter went so far as to request a resident missionary of their own; he shortly materialized as the Rev. Abraham Nelles, an SPG missionary who was permitted to transfer his responsibilities to the New England Company and serve as an assistant to Lugger.

In the meantime, the schools projected by Lugger were duly constructed on lands specially granted by the Six Nations on what appeared to be the clear understanding that they would be held in trust for the Confederacy. This state of affairs was challenged by the company a generation or more after Lugger's departure from the valley when they insisted that the original transfers had been effected "without any trust whatever." The company also contended that since their operations were "not limited to any one class of Indians," involved as they were elsewhere in Upper Canada, they were under no special obligation to the Six Nations (SNIO, Six Nations vs. New England Company; letter, 13 May 1874). Still later, the company claimed that a grant made by the Crown of the varied school lots in 1836 had been an "absolute" one and that the property in question could be disposed of at the company's discretion. It was against this claim that A. G. Chisholm successfully battled in the courts in the 1930s.

The question that is begged is, did Lugger subscribe to the company's interpretation of events while serving as its representative? According to his only surviving letter in the Six Nations Office in Brantford, he was just as anxious as company directors at home to formalize the surrender of the sought-after school lots and early in 1834 he complained about the delay in the execution of the deeds. Significantly, the recipient of his letter, an official of the Indian Department, assumed that the lands in question, when ultimately conveyed to the company, would be *"held in trust for the benefit of the Indians"* (SNIO, Six Nations vs. New England Co., Lugger to J. Winniett, 22 Jan. 1834). What was clear to the official about the trust involved must, it could be argued, have been equally clear to the missionary. And in view of his own deep commitment to the Mohawks and their confederates, it seems unlikely that Lugger would have been a party to the interpretation the company years later put on their relationship with the Six Nations. He was, after all, unlike his sponsors overseas, very much the "man on the spot," engrossed in his mission to the virtual exclusion of other interests, including perhaps the larger imperial ones of the enterprise to which he was responsible.

Whatever Lugger's views on the question of the trust may have been, it is a matter of record that some chiefs had unhesitatingly questioned the transfer of the school lots in the first place. They, in fact, asked for them back on the grounds that the schools built on them were not measuring up to expectations. "Our School Masters are too frequently changed," ran the complaint, " [while] those who taught [our] children in the early years never asked for Lands" (SNIO, Council Letter Book, 1832 to 1837). Tempers were not soothed by reports in the 1830s that the schools established for the Oneidas and Onondagas were frequently shut because of poor attendance and rented out to whites for other purposes.

Further trouble erupted over the Methodist presence in the valley. In spite of earlier assurances that he would readily work with opposite numbers of other denominations, Lugger was singularly reluctant to cooperate with the Methodists, who had staked out a respectable mission of their own among the Six Nations (NEC Report 1832: 4,8). Why was Lugger so uncooperative? Did his good intentions recoil in the face of Methodism's own aggressive campaign? Did the encounter erode away his Low Church sympathies and drive him into the ranks of High Church orthodoxy? Certainly a Presbyterian clergyman who visited him in 1832 seemed to think so. "His mode of doing good," he observed, "is in the style of the high churchman, consequently he is not a match for the Methodists who . . . work around him." Yet apparently Lugger was not averse to fighting his rivals with their own weapons, principally—to quote the Presbyterian again—"by giving the Indians . . . more say in the affairs of the church" and by "calling young communicants before the church before admitting them into its fellowship and speaking to them and praying for them" (Clark 1948: 121).

The confrontation with Methodism also helped to drive a wedge between Lugger and John Brant. Besides supporting the work of the Methodists, Brant accused the missionary of trying to undermine his authority. While Brant drew his support from the Upper Mohawks, Lugger could count on the backing of the Lower Mohawks, who called on the authorities to dismiss their Superintendent, a call that went unanswered (Graham 1975: 45). In turn charges were preferred by Brant against Lugger, but a report subsequently brought in by a board of enquiry appointed by the Bishop of Quebec dismissed them and upheld the missionary and his work (NEC 7920, 3: 69,95). The feud between the two men only ended with Brant's death in 1832.

These squabbles were largely sublimated, however, by the effort that Lugger put into the showpiece of his mission—the so-called Mohawk Institution, which was designed as an elaborate school of industry for teaching trades to the Indians. By the spring of 1831 Lugger could report that "there were then four large rooms, in two of which girls might be taught spinning and weaving and in the other two, the boys tailoring and carpentering, besides an additional building for the mechanics' shop" (NEC Report 1839: 4–5). Shortly thereafter the venture was duly launched.

Some three years later, however, Lugger, Nelles, his assistant, and William Richardson, recently appointed lay agent of the Six Nations, prepared a report calling for significant refinements in the Institution's operations. The report was heavily seasoned with equal portions of disappointment and hope. "In many instances," it read, "the Indians show themselves insensible to the advantages [offered them] and continue irresolute and suspicious, and look upon all whites as intruders." Then the report went on to stress that "no measures would tend so much to remove their prejudices as the instruction of a number of the youth of both sexes in the acts, habits and customs of civilized life, *who may hereafter act as instruments in the hands of the Company for the complete civilization of the Indians generally. . . .*" (NEC Report 1839, Appendix C, 8 Sept. 1834).

This object would be achieved by boarding, lodging, and teaching a select group of boys and girls in various trades—blacksmithing, carpentering, wagon and sleigh making, cabinet-making, and gardening. In keeping with established old country procedure in schools of industry, the varied articles manufactured in the Institution were to be sold to help defray the costs of the undertaking. At the same time an "agricultural system" was proposed whereby Indians would be taught current farming techniques on land leased by the Company from their own holdings at a nominal rent (SNIO, Six Nations *vs.* New England Co., J. Busk to Sir George Grey, 13 Dec. 1838). As for the decision to board students, it was taken in spite of earlier advice, offered by, among others, the Bishop of Quebec, that the practice "is a degree of civilization above [the Indians]" (NEC 7923: 148–49).

At any rate, early in 1835 the special Indian committee of the company agreed in principle with the plan although they suggested some minor revisions and alterations. When the boarding school opened later in the year, with fourteen children in attendance, a venture was born that survived for over a century and a quarter. In more recent times, appropriately enough, it was transformed into a cultural center for Woodland Indians, complete with a museum and a library.

Lugger, however, did not live to see the full fruition of the scheme. He died on a visit to England in 1837 and the work passed into Nelles's hands. But a significant commentary on the missionary's decade of activity among the Six Nations had been furnished him on the eve of his departure. After paying him their compliments, a delegation of Mohawks and Oneidas returned their "sincere thanks to your Reverence for all the good things you have done . . . as well as for our temporal as our Eternal interests . . ." (USPG, Upper Canada Box, after f. 485). The "temporal interests" had been cared for primarily by Lugger's enterprises in education. Yet others had not been ignored by the missionary and, it would appear, by his wife, who had labored "to promote good conduct among the children, as well as the grown people . . ." as a counterpoise in part to the "bad conduct" of those whites whose "vicious ways" had been noted by a host of travelers and against which Lugger had sought to shield the Indians. In an age too when the recruiting of qualified medical assistance for the Six Nations had been all but impossible (Weaver 1972: 39–41), Lugger had done what he could to procure medicines and alleviate suffering.

A moving though inarticulate letter that arrived one day at the parsonage may have been typical of the communications he received after he had tried to improve the physical well-being of his charges. "I want you to know," wrote a Tuscarora who signed himself "Your Affectionate Brother," "what trouble I have, I have great deal trouble in my heart, my child lays very low, I write to you what bad journey I have the reason to inform you, what you promise . . . medicine to help us . . . Indians . . . thirteen days that my child was sick, to day is the . . . last breath to fetch, that is the reason to tell you . . . for what pain in my heart . . ." (USPG, Upper Canada Box, after f. 485; John Obadiah to Lugger, n.d.). Kinsmen of the writer trusted, when Lugger departed for England in 1837, never to return, that "he would not forget us" and would "come over and help us," the entreaty spelled out on the seal of the New England Company.

A century later when A. G. Chisholm, the lawyer, repudiated the company as a "despoiler" he may have paused before applying that epithet to the likes of Robert Lugger. As a student of missionary activity in old Ontario has argued: "a case can be made that missionaries helped Indians to preserve the remnants of their culture. Without [their] intervention, the Indians might . . . have died out from disease, alcoholism . . ., poverty and malnutrition . . . or from breeding with whites' (Graham 1975: 91). Lugger appears to have made his own contribution to that "ameliorating" process, at a time too when Indians were losing much of their land and whatever autonomy they still enjoyed and becoming abjectly dependent on government. His efforts had invariably been lauded by visitors to the valley and by the church leadership in the colony (PAO, Strachan Papers: Journal of a Tour through Upper Canada, 1828).

Lugger's career from "palm to pine" reflected many of the forces at work in that pre-Victorian era that would help to foster Britain's cultural expansion in virtually every quarter of the globe in the nineteenth century. By his application of the educational formulas then flourishing in the Imperial metropolis to an island in the West Indies and a frontier in Upper Canada he personified one dimension of that lengthy process. His career also displayed his generation's concern with the plight of aboriginal peoples confronted by a dynamic and acquisitive civilization (Mellor 1951). This factor probably went unappreciated in the busy, twentieth-century law office of A. G. Chisholm, but has not assuredly in the thinking of scholars like William N. Fenton who have so skilfully quarried missionary accounts, among others, for the data to enrich their own invaluable reconstructions of aboriginal cultures in North America.

Chapter Five

The Kansas Connection:
The Seneca Nation and
the Iroquois Confederacy Council

Thomas S. Abler

M. J. Herskovits (1948:483) argued that continuity and change are but two sides of the same "shield." William N. Fenton has emphasized this in Iroquoian studies. One might well say that this theme forms the leitmotif of Fenton's extensive writings on the Iroquois. It is illustrated by a delightful passage in which Fenton describes Seneca False Faces racing down an Allegany Reservation road in a Model T Ford, the horsehair on their masks streaming in the wind while they banged their turtle-shell rattles against the side of the car (Fenton 1941:425).

Continuing in the tradition established by Fenton of documenting conservatism *and* change in Iroquois culture, this paper considers aspects of the actions of the New York Iroquois in securing compensation for lands in Kansas.[1] This activity involved the traditional confederacy council of the Iroquois. The New York Iroquois demonstrated continuity with the past through their utilization of the institution of the Confederacy Council to pursue the Kansas claim; however, tolerance for change was demonstrated by the willing cooperation of venerated old chiefs, whose titles dated back to the prehistoric founding of the Iroquois Confederacy, with modern political leaders of a new style.

An ethnohistorical investigation into the form and policy of the Six Nations Confederacy council in New York in the latter portion of the nineteenth century indicates the Confederacy council had firm roots in the past, yet proved itself to be viable in the realities of the nineteenth century. Indeed it was the political events of the nineteenth century which encouraged the Confederacy to remain as a useful political institution. One can see continuity but one can also see change.

It is not argued that the Confederacy council was of overwhelming political importance in the latter half of the nineteenth century. Indeed, Morgan (1877:139) wrote that it only met for ceremonial purposes. However, it did assemble, despite what Morgan said, to discuss strategies to achieve a common goal relative to the Kansas Land Claim. The presence of potential compensation for lost lands in Kansas led the New York Iroquois to perceive advantages in intercommunication and cooperation. The Six Nations council was viewed as the appropriate arena for this communication and cooperation. At this late date, however, internal political changes among the Seneca prevented the Six Nations council from assembling in its traditional form; the New York Six Nations councils of the late nineteenth century proved to be far removed in form and style from those described in the standard ethnographic works on the Iroquois.

The Traditional Confederacy Council

Few native North American political institutions have received the attention which has been given the fabled Council of the Iroquois Confederacy. As described by Lewis Henry Morgan (1851) and later authors (e.g., Parker 1916; Fenton 1949), the Confederacy council consisted of fifty chiefs each representing a matrilineage within one of the five founding nations (or tribes) of the Iroquois Confederacy. The sixth nation of the Iroquois, the Tuscarora, joined later and had no formal voice among these chiefs. These positions were hereditary within the matrilineage and each individual upon assuming office took the name or title associated with that office. Membership was unevenly distributed, with the most populous tribe in the confederacy, the Seneca, having the fewest chiefs, eight. The Mohawk and Oneida each had nine chiefs; the Cayuga had ten; the Onondaga as Fire-keepers for the Confederacy had fourteen chiefs.

The council sat on two "sides" forming moiety divisions, and this functioned in decision making. The three largest tribes constituted the elder brothers or three brothers side while the Oneida and Cayuga were the younger brothers or two brothers side (Noon 1949:39). In actual councils, the Onondaga did not sit with the other elder brothers but instead served as moderators (they were styled the firekeepers of the Confederacy) for the council. Unanimity was a strict require-ment, and the process of reaching unanimity was a slow one. Noon (1949:39) presents a succinct if simplified description of the decision-making process:

Counselling began with the Mohawk chiefs conferring together, and having reached a decision, their speaker announced it to the Seneca. If these tribes found they were in agreement, the speaker of the "Three Brothers," who was usually a Mohawk, announced the decision of the "Three Brothers" side to the chiefs of the opposite side. In like manner, the chiefs of the Oneida and Cayuga arrived at a decision, which was then announced by the speaker of the "Two Brothers" side to the Firekeepers. The decision of the Firekeepers was final unless they chose to resubmit the matter to the chiefs.

While details of the organizational structure of the Confederacy Council were not recorded until well after the American Revolution, the consistency of the ideal system as reported by both Canadian and New York Iroquois argues that the structure outlined above existed prior to the dispersal of the Iroquois following the Treaty of 1783. As Fenton (1960:312) has stated, "Aboriginal political systems like primitive languages are neither lost in two generations nor are they invented to amuse anthropologists."

THE CREATION OF TWO CONFEDERACY COUNCILS

The outbreak of the American Revolution led the Iroquois to cover the council fire of the Confederacy while Iroquois warriors participated in the conflict. Most sided with the British crown, but they found at the close of the American Revolution that Britain had surrendered all interests in their homeland to the new United States of America. The peace treaty in fact ignored completely the question of His Majesty's native allies and any claims they had to lands in North America. The attachment of some of the Iroquois to the crown (or possibly their hostility toward Americans) led a large number, under the leadership of the talented Mohawk chief Joseph Brant, to seek a new home in Canada. With the exception of a faction of Mohawks under John Deseronto who settled on the Bay of Quinte, these Iroquois settled a land grant on the Grand River, the remains of which constitute the present-day Six Nations Reserve. Here the council fire of the Confederacy was rekindled. Another portion of the Iroquois clung to their lands in New York State. These Iroquois also rekindled the Confederacy Council fire, initially on the Buffalo Creek Reservation, land that is now part of the city of Buffalo and its suburbs.

Differing circumstances on each side of the international border exerted unique pressures on each of the two confederacy councils. In Canada, for the Iroquois who settled on the Six Nations Reserve on the Grand River, the Confederacy Council served as the governing body of that reserve. Hence the Council itself had real political tasks and power. All of the Six Nations were represented on the Grand River, but the Mohawk and Cayuga were predominant (Johnston (1964:52). Some of the chieftaincy titles remained vacant because particular tribes (Seneca and Oneida especially) were underrepresented on the Six Nations Reserve, but a reasonable approximation of the fifty-member hereditary confederacy council could be established through assignment of chieftaincies to lineages (if possible, in the appropriate clan) which previously had possessed no titles.

There are a number of other reserves in Canada occupied by Iroquois groups. Most of these split from the Iroquois Confederacy long before the migration of the Six Nations to Canada (the "Mohawks" of Caughnawaga, St. Regis [Akwesasane], Oka, and Gibson). Another reserve, Tyendinaga, represents a group of Mohawk who, because of factional differences, refused to settle on the Grand River. They constitute a distinct political unit and have never acted with the Grand River Iroquois (Torok 1967:31–32). Oneida on the Thames was settled in the 1840s by a faction of New York State Oneida seeking new homes (Campisi 1974). While they have participated ritually with the Confederacy Council on the Grand River, to validate their own chiefs (Ricciardelli 1961), the Grand River Confederacy Council operated in a political sense completely separate from these Oneida.

The Canadian situation was such that: (1) the structure of the pre-reserve Confederacy Council, with representatives from all the Iroquois tribes could be approximated on the Six Nations Reserve; (2) there were no reserves other than that of Six Nations with strong claims for representation on the Confederacy Council (the Oneida being late arrivals in Ontario); and (3) the British and (later) Canadian governments recognized the Confederacy Council as the appropriate body to govern the Six Nations Reserve.

In the United States the situation was radically different. Following the American Revolution no single reservation was established providing land for all the Six Nations. Instead, each group attempted to retain lands in its traditional homeland. Moreover, only the Oneida, Onondaga, Tuscarora, and Seneca retained land after the peace treaties concluding the hostilities of the American Revolution were signed, and pressures put upon the Oneida soon led to the removal of many to either Canada or Wisconsin. In the case of the Tuscarora, Seneca, and Onondaga, some members of the other Iroquois tribes occupied their reservations, but in every case the vast majority of reservation residents was from a single tribe.

NEGOTIATIONS WITH THE UNITED STATES

The new United States government negotiated treaties both with the Iroquois as a whole and with the separate nations of the confederacy. The treaties of Ft. Stanwix (1784), Ft. Harmar (1789) and Canadaigua (1794) were all negotiated between the United States and the Six Nations. We will probably never be certain of the role played in these negotiations by the Confederacy Council whose structure has been described in the works of Morgan (1851) and later ethnographers (Parker 1916; Fenton 1949; Shimony 1961). There is strong evidence that all members of the Confederacy Council were absent from the Ft. Stanwix proceedings. The Mohawk Aaron Hill stated he presented "the words of the Warriors, for there are no Sachems amongst us" (quoted in Kent 1974:87). Kent (ibid.:113) concludes, "There were no sachems at Fort Stanwix, but these ceremonial officers of the League and its Nations had, as usual, faded from view during the war, in a period when the emphasis was on ability, strength, and leadership rather than rank and ceremonies." Few names affixed to these treaties can be assigned to the titles associated with chieftainships in the Confederacy Council (see Fenton 1951:302). However, this same situation prevailed prior to the American Revolution (Fenton 1971:148–50). Ethnographers and ethnohistorians have speculated on the absence of hereditary chieftain titles from the historic record. Hypotheses have suggested either that the hereditary chiefs were less able and therefore less important than the other, nonhereditary, chiefs and headmen or that the dignified hereditary peace chiefs naturally assumed a less prominent role vis-à-vis the whites. It appears unlikely that either new documentary evidence or reanalysis of documents already known will shed conclusive light on this preplexing question.

Whether or not the Confederacy council played a decisive role, the negotiations were with all the Six Nations resident in New York and were signed by Seneca, Onondaga, Cayuga, Oneida, Tuscarora, and assorted Algonquian speakers who happened to be present. These treaties marked the formal cession of Iroquois claims to most of western New York and adjacent regions and led to the settlement of the New York Iroquois on a relatively small number of reservations. After this time there was little need for the U.S. to interact with the New York State Iroquois as a unified body. Federal and State officials dealt with the "tribal" units and as a political body, the New York Six Nations Council fell into neglect.

THE BUFFALO CREEK TREATY AND THE KANSAS MIGRATION

The last treaty negotiated between the Iroquois as a whole and the federal government was signed in 1838. By this date there were eight Iroquois-speaking reservations in New York State. Four of these were occupied by Seneca—Buffalo Creek, Cattaraugus, Allegany, and Tonawanda. The Onondaga had a single reservation near Syracuse. The Tuscarora Reservation bordered Lewiston. The Oneida retained lands in their ancient territory. In addition, the St. Regis Mohawk, Catholics who had split from their Mohawk Valley brethren in the seventeenth century, occupied a reservation on the St. Lawrence River which straddled the U.S.-Canadian border.

Two not unrelated forces combined to place pressures on the Iroquois to sell their lands. First, land speculators looked hungrily at reservation lands with the prospect of buying cheap and selling dear. Of particular importance in this regard was the Buffalo Creek Reservation, in the path of the expanding city of Buffalo on Lake Erie. Secondly, as a general policy, the federal government had the intention of moving all Indians to the west side of the Mississippi.

The land picture in much of New York was complicated. Conflicting royal grants had allowed both Massachusetts and New York claim to what is now western New York. The dispute was settled by giving New York sovereignty or jurisdiction over the region but awarding to Massachusetts the "preemptive" right—that is the right to purchase if and when the Indians chose to sell. Massachusetts sold this right to land speculators, who purchased major tracts before selling the preemptive right to the lands remaining in native hands to still other land speculators. In 1838 the preemptive right lay with the Ogden Land Company.

The remaining Seneca reservations were purchased by the Ogden Land Company at the Treaty of Buffalo Creek in 1838. In addition, the New York Indians surrendered interests in a tract of land set aside for them in Wisconsin. New lands were set aside for the use of the New York Indians west of the Mississippi, however. The well-documented charges of corruption surrounding this treaty (see [Friends] 1840) need not concern us here. The United States Senate refused to ratify the treaty because of the charges. Later, in 1842, another treaty was negotiated with the Seneca alone who sold Buffalo Creek and Tonawanda but retained the Allegany and Cattaraugus Reservations. None of the Tonawanda chiefs signed either the 1838 or the 1842 Treaties, however, and the Seneca residents on this reservation managed to obtain an agreement in 1857 allowing them to retain their reservation, albeit reduced in size. The Ogden Company got what it really desired, however, and that was Buffalo Creek, for which they paid the Seneca 10 percent of its appraised value (Manley 1947).

These treaties are important in another way. They laid the basis for cooperation among the Indians resident in New York, in pursuit of a single goal. For the remainder of the nineteenth century the New York Indians pursued a single goal involving lands in far-away Kansas. These treaties not only provided monetary compensation for the concessions granted to the United States Government and the Ogden Company, they also established a new homeland in Kansas for the New York Indians.

This proved to be a homeland few of them wanted, however. After the Seneca and others living on Buffalo Creek moved, largely to Cattaraugus, an unscrupulous white, Abraham Hogeboom, set about to gather a group of Indians to transport them to Kansas. His motives appear to have been purely mercenary. While he went about preaching the glories of Kansas, the Federal Indian Agent, Stephen Osborn, firmly advised the Indians that there was no need to go. When Hogeboom finally gathered the requisite number of Indians in 1845, it was alleged that it was only by recruiting Canadian Indians that he obtained the number required before he would be allowed to set out.

The trip to Kansas was a tragic event, still bitterly recalled by Seneca Indians. A large percentage of those who set out on the journey died en route or shortly after arrival. I have been told by descendants that those who arrived in Kansas found a barren land without even a single tree. Most chose not to stay, but made the long trek back to New York State. A census of Seneca emigrants indicates that sixty-six went to Kansas, twenty-six died en route or after arrival, two remained in Kansas, and thirty-eight returned to New York State (Abler and Tooker 1978: 511). Hogeboom submitted his expenses, apparently inflating the numbers of Indians he took to Kansas.

The New York Indians did not occupy the Kansas lands. Pressure from white settlers, who were presumably less appalled than were the Iroquois by the absence of trees, led the Federal Government to open the lands to white occupation. The lands reserved for New York Indians in Kansas disappeared under the tide of White settlement.

SENECA POLITICAL UPHEAVAL

Internal political events on the New York Seneca reservations were to color the pursuit of compensation for the loss of these Kansas lands, as well as affect the form and composition of the Confederacy

Council. In 1848, the Seneca resident on Allegany and Cattaraugus abolished their hereditary chiefs' form of government and instituted an elected council (Wilson 1960). The power of all chiefs was repudiated, and they were replaced by an annually elected president, clerk, treasurer, and council of eighteen (later reduced to sixteen).[2]

The Tonawanda Seneca did not participate in this revolution because they viewed it as a threat to their campaign to retain their reservation. They continued to be governed by hereditary chiefs and eventually all eight hereditary Seneca chieftaincies in the Confederacy council were claimed by lineages on the Tonawanda Reservation.

The Tonawanda Seneca engaged in a long struggle, led by John Blacksmith, Jimmy Johnson, and Ely S. Parker, to retain the right to live on their lands. This right was finally secured in 1857, but the Tonawanda Seneca gave up claims to Kansas lands and monies set aside for removal to Kansas (Abler and Tooker 1978: 512).

The result, then, of the internal Seneca political struggles was that the Tonawanda reservation retained government by hereditary chiefs but had no legal claim to Kansas lands, while the Allegany and Cattaraugus Seneca (the Seneca Nation) had reason to cooperate with the hereditary chiefs of the other Six Nations in pursuit of a Kansas claim but were themselves governed by annually elected councilors.

At the time the Tonawanda Seneca established their right to retain their reservation, agitation began on the Seneca Nation reservations and elsewhere among the New York Iroquois to pursue the Kansas claim. The reservation inhabitants were far from unanimous in favor of pursuit of the claim, however. The fear was present that action on the Kansas claim would lead not to a cash settlement but instead to a loss of the New York reservation lands. The Seneca Nation council rejected claim to Kansas lands in August 1857, by a six to five vote (SNRC.I: 227–28). It was claimed that those in favor of acting upon the claim acted "in a corner under a cloak" (RIC: Edward Purse to P. E. Thomas 20-v-1858).

Opinions changed, however. The Seneca Nation, like other New York Indian groups, hired an agent to pursue the Kansas claim. The Seneca Nation agreed to pay this agent, George Barker, 25 percent of the claim, and it is reported "the other tribes made a like stipulation with their agents" (ABC: A. Wright to S.B. Treat 3-viii-1864). Prospects of a generous settlement, hence a generous fee to Mr. Barker, led some Seneca to agitate for repudiation of his contract. Their mechanism for doing this was to again agitate for government by chiefs.

The Kansas claim, then, had produced factions among the Seneca Nation in 1864. The same was true among other New York Indians

(ABC: A. Wright to S.B Treat 3-viii-1864). Charles E. Mix, the U.S. Commissioner of Indian Affairs, entered this conflict-ridden arena in May, hoping to personally negotiate settlement of the Kansas claim with the Six Nations assembled at Cattaraugus. The council was short. The terse telegram from Mix to Washington sums up the results of the discussion. "NO TREATY. COUNCIL DISRESPECTFUL. I LEFT AT ONCE" (NYA: C.E. Mix to J.P. Usher 12-v-1864). Mix had begun the meeting with a demand that the assembled Indians present their credentials, proving that they were empowered to represent the reservations that they claimed to represent. The response to Mix's request was a speech termed "extremely imprudent and abusive" in which Mix was asked to produce his credentials. A vote of the council endorsed this request and Mix left in a huff (ABC: A. Wright to S. B. Treat 3-viii-1864).

CONTINUITY AND CHANGE IN PURSUIT OF THE KANSAS CLAIM

It is not known what the formal composition and rules of procedure were in Six Nations councils in the 1850s and 1860s such as Mix's encounter on the Cattaraugus reservation. It is possible that the Seneca Nation was still formally represented by those individuals who were hereditary chiefs. Those elected Seneca Nation Councilors who had no chiefly title may have been allowed to sit with the Six Nations Council and to voice their opinions; wise and influential members of the community were traditionally accorded this privilege. Later, however, the elected Seneca Nation Council sat with the chiefs of the other New York State Iroquois as the New York Indians continued to press their Kansas claim.

This should not be taken as implying that the Six Nations Confederacy was suing the United States Government for compensation for the Kansas lands. The actual pursuit of the Kansas Claim through the U.S. courts was by individual tribes or nations, *not* by the Six Nations council. Individual actions were initiated by the Seneca Nation, the Onondaga tribe, etc. I would argue, however, that since the constituent members of the Six Nations were pursuing a common political goal independently in the courts, they found it useful to meet on occasion to coordinate their actions. My reading of Iroquois history suggests this is not in the least unusual; if the pre-reservation Confederacy Council ever served a political function, it was usually only to coordinate actions of its tribal members in pursuit of already determined policies.

The prospect of dollars for Kansas lands remained in the consciousness of the Six Nations through the years. It was perhaps kept alive by the several white agents who had been appointed to pursue the matter. Preserved among the records of the Seneca Nation Council are the minutes of several Six Nations Councils over the years 1876 to 1888. Each is dominated by a single issue. Indeed, most consider only one issue. In all cases that issue was the claim for Kansas lands and the tactics utilized in its pursuit.

The record books of the Seneca Nation Council present minutes of eight Six Nations councils from the years 1863 to 1888. Two 1876 councils were held in the "Court House" on the Cattaraugus Reservation, as were the October 1884, and June 1885 councils. The rest were held on the Allegany Reservation, in the longhouses at Red House or Coldspring.[3]

The minutes of these councils indicate an intriguing blend of old and new procedures. From these minutes it is clear that the councils did not strictly proceed under White rules of order, but it is also clear that white diplomats who had dealt with the Six Nations in the previous century would notice little that was familiar in the activities. In all of these councils it is the *elected* councilors of the Seneca Nation who represent the Allegany and Cattaraugus Reservations. No mention appears of Tonawanda; there seems to have been no suggestion that Tonawanda chiefs should be present. The council was assembled solely to discuss obtaining compensation for Kansas lands, and Tonawanda and its hereditary chiefs had abrogated any rights to Kansas lands in 1857.

It is not merely, though, the presence of elected Seneca officials that make these Six Nations councils unusual. The Seneca appear to have assumed the Onondaga role as chairman of the proceedings. The mintues of the 1863 council are quite fragmentary. In the remaining seven councils, it was viewed as the prerogative of the council to choose its chairman. In five of the seven cases the person chosen was a Seneca. In the remaining two it was Daniel LaFort, the most influential Onondaga chief of the time (U.S. Census Office 1892:v). LaFort was present at other councils when a Seneca sat in the chair, and this leading chief of the Confederacy's firekeepers still had to observe his being nominated, seconded, and voted upon before he was able to take the chair.

The whole procedure of the council reflected influence from White society. Motions were made and seconded and voted on. The proceedings were a bit unusual, compared to the minutes of the Seneca Council of the same period, in that the numbers voting "aye" and "nay" on an issue have not been recorded. Indeed, the vast majority of decisions received unanimous approval, possibly reflecting the old ideal that "all the sachems of the League . . . were required to be of 'one mind' to give efficacy to their legislation" (Morgan 1851:111).

The issue before council for this period was the pursuit of the Kansas claim. The council met primarily to enter into contracts with agents and to disengage from contracts with previous agents involved in lobbying for the Kansas claim. Ancillary to this was the appointment of delegates to go to Washington in the pursuit of the claim.

The council of April 1888, provides an interesting illustration of the fusion of old and new elements in the Six Nations Council. An Onondaga, Daniel LaFort, was in the chair, probably as a result of his appointment at the December 1885, council. A vote was taken on clerk or secretary for the Council, and two Seneca Indians, William Patterson and John C. Lay, were elected. The council was necessary because the previously appointed agent and attorney for the Six Nations, Francis Miller, had died. Various candidates addressed the Council. When a failure to reach a quick unanimous decision was apparent, the chairman, Daniel LaFort, sent each of the participating "Nations" (Seneca Nation, Oneidas with Onondagas, Onondagas, St. Regis, Tuscaroras, and Cayugas) to deliberate separately and report the result. This harkens back to the procedure in the traditional council whereby nations came to be of one mind, then moieties, then the council as a whole. However, the minutes fail to suggest that the results of this "national" or tribal deliberation were reported in the traditional sequence. Most notably the Onondaga, traditionally the final voice in the council, reported their choice as agent and attorney prior to the report of the Oneida, St. Regis, Tuscarora, Cayuga, and Seneca Nation. The six groups found themselves evenly divided and finally appointed all the proposed agents to act in concert in the pursuit of the claim. After this decision, the council formally adopted the St. Regis people into the Six Nations of New York Indians. Two of the attorneys hired by the council were adopted by the Seneca, one into the Snipe clan, the other into the Wolf clan. The chairman then declared the council, after four days activity, adjourned *sine die* (SNRC IX:1–20).

The Kansas Settlement

These activities proved to be fruitful. Congress first had to give the New York Indians permission to sue the U.S. government. This was granted under an act of January 28, 1893. The case, which was appealed to the Supreme Court, allowed the New York Indians the sum of $1,998,744.46 in a judgment rendered November 22, 1898. The Indian Department was directed to withhold $10,000 to cover the expenses of enrolling those eligible and distributing the money. Money was distributed in two batches, each approximately $100 per person (Campisi 1974a). I have been told by a contemporary resident of Cattaraugus that her mother kept this Kansas Land money on a shelf in the kitchen, for use whenever it was needed. The short-term effects of this per capita distribution must have been considerable. It would be difficult to prove that there have been any long-term effects.

With the conclusion of the Kansas land claim the need for the Six Nations council to function ceased. The Seneca Nation elective council continued to govern Allegany and Cattaraugus; the traditional chiefs continued to govern their respective reservations. There was no need to look outside the reservation boundaries.

The Kansas land claim episode demonstrates, however, a willingness of the nineteenth-century Iroquois to adapt ideology and political institutions to the needs of the day. Clearly individually and collectively they had a great deal to gain with a successful pursuit of the Kansas claim. In that pursuit the Seneca president or elected councilor was able to sit comfortably with the Onondaga hereditary chief in council and neither had a problem in reaching a satisfactory decision.

Continuity and change can be seen as a theme of Iroquoian studies in this century. The behavior of the Six Nations council is illustrative of the stresses toward continuity and change found in all aspects of Iroquois life on the reservation. Indeed, the case of the nineteenth-century Six Nations Council illustrates the often contradictory pressures toward innovative or conservative behavior. An artifact of contact with white society and government was the possession of lands in Kansas. Had the New York Indians failed to have the goal of Kansas land money before them, the Six Nations council would have ceased to exist as a political institution. With the prospect of the Kansas claim, the Six Nations Confederacy continued as a political reality, albeit in a greatly modified form, for a century after it had surrendered most of its land and power to the Americans and had seen its constituent parts settled on widely scattered reservations.

NOTES

1. Initial data for this paper were collected with the support of the American Philosophical Society and the New York State Museum and Science Service. This work included generous access given to me to the records of the Seneca Nation by the administrations of Martin Seneca and Calvin John. Numerous Seneca Nation politicians and people contributed to the education of this political anthropologist. To all I give my thanks. In addition, like so many Iroquois studies, this study owes a debt to William N. Fenton who encouraged my initial efforts, provided an entrée into the field, and has been free with advice and comments.

2. The Allegany and Cattaraugus Seneca (hereafter referred to as the Seneca Nation and distinct from the Tonawanda Seneca) were preoccupied by a factional fight over the form of their government for several years following the 1848 "revolution." A substantial number favored the government by hereditary chiefs. This faction found allies in the hereditary chiefs elsewhere. Two Onondaga Chiefs, S. George and David Smith, praised the attempt by the Old Chiefs party "to defend the rights of the system of our old Indian Government . . . so highly important to us all to maintain" (MBPP: S. George and David Smith to Cattaraugus Chiefs 8-vi-1850). In July of 1850 four nations were represented at a Six Nations Council of chiefs which was "strong and unanimous" in its support of the traditional form of government (MBPP: Draft of Petition to N.Y. State Legislature n.d.).

Both the federal and state governments recognized the new republican government of the Seneca Nation, and by 1855 the agitation by the Old Chiefs to reinstitute the old form of government had largely ceased.

3. The "Court House" is tied to the institution of the elected Seneca Nation Council, for it was constructed after the ouster of the chiefs to serve as a meeting place for the elected council. The longhouse, however, is both a community and a religious structure, serving the adherents of the traditional Iroquois faith as refined by the prophet, Handsome Lake. So complete was the acceptance of the Allegany Seneca of the elective principle, however, that even this building, which we could well expect to be associated with conservative ideas, was utilized as the polling station in the elections of the Seneca Nation.

CHAPTER SIX

National Policy, States' Rights, and Indian Sovereignty: The Case of the New York Iroquois

JACK CAMPISI

Since earliest contact by Europeans there has been a long and sustained interest in the political organizations of the Iroquoian-speaking peoples of New York and Ontario. The reports of their councils and treaties, and their diplomatic missions and alliances, fill the correspondences, communiqués, and journals of hundreds of Dutch, French, English, and American participants and observers. The magnitude of the fascination with what were thought to be pristine aboriginal political institutions by these observers and by later historians and anthropologists has all but obscured the complex interrelationships which shaped the evolving political forms of the Iroquois. With some notable exceptions (Hunt 1940; Fenton 1957; Trelease 1960; Trigger 1976; and Berkhofer 1978), little attention has been directed toward an understanding of the Iroquois interactions, first with imperial, and later with national and state governments.

In recent years interest in the complex relationships resulting from overlapping policies and conflicting jurisdictions has been whetted by a spate of land suits which have raised questions as to the legal status of the Iroquois groups, ownership of land and the legitimacy of its transfer, the exact boundaries of aboriginal title, and the limits of claims to sovereign control. The issues have been raised and argued in state and federal courts, in executive offices, and the halls of Congress with increasing acrimony, but without resolution. Judge Cutberth Pound of the New York Court of Appeals, more than half a century ago, pinpointed the dilemma of the New York Iroquois: "Three sovereignties," he wrote, "are thus contending for jurisdiction over the Indians—the Indian Nations, the United States and the State of New York—none of which exercises such jurisdiction in a full sense" (1922:99). Little has occurred in the intervening years to alter this appraisal; if anything, the confusion has been compounded.

From earliest times the Iroquois and other Indian groups have had to contend with a legal system which they did not fully understand, which they could not control, and which imposed definitions and rules on them, placing them at a continual disadvantage. Policies changed, were often in conflict, or contained parts and language from past policies redefined for new exigencies. Regardless of these inconsistencies and contradictions, Indian policy was founded on two pervasive concerns: how to get title to land occupied by Indian groups, and who should have jurisdiction in matters relating to Indian groups. By and large, Indian groups have been reluctant to relinquish their title to land and have opposed, sometimes with force, the demands for land concessions. Their opposition, and that of their supporters in and out of government, has added further complexity to the labyrinth that has become "Indian policy."

Iroquois relations with Euro-America can be divided into four periods: the emergence of tribal sovereignty, the rise of domestic dependent nations, the removal and assumption of control of the tribes by the State of New York, and the reassertion, finally, of full federal control. While such divisions are useful in describing major policy concerns, initiatives, and trends, I should emphasize that they are inherently arbitrary and do not fully reflect the complexity of the issues involved.

THE EMERGENCE OF TRIBAL SOVEREIGNTY

Colonial policy was generally founded on the premise that the land in the "New World" belonged to the sovereign whose explorers first laid claim to it. At best, the natives who occupied the land had a right of use only so long as they continued to occupy the land peaceably. By discovery and by "planting the flag," the sovereign gained the exclusive right to "extinguish" native title. This was the so-called "right of discovery."

Early in the development of Indian-White relations, European sovereigns imbued native populations with the trappings of nation-states, largely to facilitate the transfer of land and to provide means to gain native support in the struggles for empire that marked the seventeenth and eighteenth centuries. In short order the New World was festooned with kings, castles, and cantons, and the lordly manner displayed by European aristocrats became the expected mode of behavior for chiefs and sachems. Indian communities in time came to be treated as sovereign states. Capitalizing on an existing native ceremonial system—the Condolence Council—Europeans carried on extensive, if not always conclusive, negotiations with the Iroquois tribes to garner their trade and their support, or at least their neutrality, in the struggles between contending European powers. In addition, there were the disputes that arose from Iroquois-White contacts which required settlement and for which the Condolence councils provided an ideal way to "wipe dry the eyes, open the ears and clear the throat," for both sides.

Thus, at an early stage, Europeans had established a framework for their relations with native peoples in the New World. Their views were shaped by the realities of European life and precepts of law. These principles were supported by a combination of religious and jural arguments of considerable logic and clarity, but also with a cultural astigmatism that distorted Indian social and political systems to fit European institutional models. As God's creatures, Indians were to be treated fairly and humanely, but rarely were they treated as equals. They were, for instance, granted the right of possession, a right they could nevertheless relinquish as a collective act only to a sovereign. While they were defined politically as the equals of sovereigns, there was a clear implication that the chiefs and tribes were socially inferior, lacking as they did the benefits of Christian teaching and civilized mores.

THE RISE OF DOMESTIC DEPENDENT NATIONS

By the mid-eighteenth century three special interest groups brought new pressures on the Iroquois tribes. The British Crown sought to keep them friendly or at least neutral in the conflict with France. This objective was complicated and often thwarted by colonial leaders who desired personal title to Iroquois land and who were willing to adopt any artifice to secure it. While crown and colony disputed land policy, missionaries from a number of sects trekked through the forests in search of souls to save. The competition was keen, and it was not long before the missionaries became as disputatious among themselves as their secular counterparts, with each proffering his pet scheme for civilizing and saving the "heathen" natives. By the time of the Revolution secular and religious interests had been intertwined, with "New Light" Presbyterians supporting rebellious "Bostonians," and the more staid Anglicans siding with the Crown. The divisions extended into Iroquoia. The Anglican Mohawks, influenced by Sir William Johnson, joined the British, while their "brothers," the Oneidas and Tuscaroras, followed their Presbyterian father, Samuel Kirkland, in support of the American cause. The Seneca, Cayuga, and

Onondaga joined with the Mohawks, although less as a result of religious influence than out of loyalty to the Crown as represented by Johnson. Fear concerning colonial land interests was an added cause of divisions. The split among the tribes led, in 1779, to the covering of the council fire at Onondaga and a policy that each tribe should choose the path which best served its self-interest.

The Treaty of Paris (1783) acknowledging colonial independence ended a period of Iroquois history during which the five tribes had the power to choose their friends and name their enemies. The treaty ending the Revolution was silent on the position of Britain's Iroquois allies. The United States was left to establish a separate peace with the hostile tribes. The conditions of the treaty of Fort Stanwix (1784) were harsh. The four tribes—Seneca, Onondaga, Cayuga, and Mohawk—were forced to deliver hostages and surrender any claims to land north and west of the Ohio River. In addition, the Senecas lost a sizeable portion of their land in what is now western New York to federal authority, although most of this land was returned in 1794 (American State Papers 1832:544). These concessions were made a condition for the cessation of hostilities and the extension of United States' protection to the tribes (ibid.). In these and subsequent negotiations only the Oneidas and Tuscaroras were treated as allies of the United States and not as vanquished foes.

The net effect of the national policy in these early years of the Republic was to change the status of the Iroquois gradually to that of dependent nations. In large measure the independent status of the tribes had rested upon the competition between colonial powers and the ability of the five tribes to give an impression of political unity even when divided on issues. The Revolution removed the factor of competition, and this altered the political balance ever afterwards. The peace treaty gave the new nation the exclusive right to extinguish Indian title to all lands east of the Mississippi River. To be sure, British agents continued to influence tribal affairs for another decade, but even without British advice and support the tribes in the Ohio Valley would undoubtedly have fought to preserve their land, and the Iroquois of New York would probably still have vacillated in their support of their western brethren. The status of "domestic nation," with all its subsequent ambiguities, was established for the Iroquois by the post-Revolutionary policies of the new nation, although it would take another fifty years before Chief Justice John Marshall of the Supreme Court would give that status legal standing. The domestic nation policy did one other thing: it established the preeminence of federal authority in Indian affairs, including the Iroquois tribes, and extended federal protection.

Throughout the post-Revolutionary period, New York State's attitude toward Indian affairs was governed by its own self-interest and not be federal policies. The state sought by every artifice of law and language to secure title to the Iroquois lands. Governor Clinton ignored the federal prohibitions against unauthorized land negotiations and with a zeal inspired by greed, swindled and extorted large tracts of land from the Iroquois. The results were a rising hostility between Whites and Indians, reflected in the number of violent incidents in the Ohio border area, a growing Iroquois disaffection with the national government, the threat of a general Indian war, and a widening gulf between the State of New York and the federal government that threatened the fragile national unity. From a national perspective the situation demanded a definitive policy which would maintain Iroquois neutrality and, if possible, achieve a degree of amity, resolve disputes over the United States land claims in the Ohio Valley, and curb the ambitions of New York.

To accomplish these aims the United States government considered two alternatives. First, there was the possibility of taking the Ohio lands by force, driving the Indians west, and maintaining control of the territory by manning a line of forts. This choice would require the commitment of enormous resources with little certainty of success. The second, more expedient alternative, and the one eventually chosen, was to negotiate treaties which would guarantee peace in exchange for limited land concessions. According to Secretary of War Henry Knox, the advantage of such a policy was clear:

> As the settlements of whites shall approach near to the Indian
> boundaries established by treaties, the game will be
> diminished, and the lands being valuable to the Indians only
> as hunting grounds, they will be willing to sell further tracts
> for small considerations. By the expiration, therefore, of the
> above period, it is most probable that the Indians will, by the
> invariable operation of the causes which have hereto existed
> in their intercourse with the whites, be reduced to a very
> small number. (American State Papers 1832:13–14)

While awaiting the effects of settlement the national government had to assert its dominance in Indian affairs in a way that would both placate the tribes and protect their lands from state and private seizure.

The policy of federally guaranteeing Indian land was translated into law in 1790. In that year Congress passed the first of a series of laws called the "Trade and Intercourse Acts," designed, among other things, to prohibit land purchases by individuals or states without the express permission of the federal government. However,

New York officials ignored the act, causing serious jurisdictional conflicts with the government which threatened to disrupt the tenuous peace with the Iroquois. Between 1790 and 1794 federal officials courted and counseled Iroquois leaders, urging neutrality in the Ohio conflict as the pressures for Iroquois involvement against the United States grew.

The defeat of the tribes in the Ohio Valley in the summer of 1794, however, removed any immediate danger. For its part the United States resolved its outstanding differences with the New York Iroquois at Canandaigua in the fall of 1794, completing the policy objectives initiated at Fort Stanwix a decade earlier and ending any possibility of the tribes posing a threat to national security. As national interests moved west, concern for the Iroquois faded, and federal policy towards them became one of benign neglect.

REMOVAL AND THE ASSUMPTION OF STATE CONTROL

The decline in federal attention did not mean a renunciation of federal rights or sovereignty over the Iroquois, however. The federal government continued to assert its right to exercise control, and the State of New York continued to reject this position. The differences between national and state governments raised constitutional issues which could only be resolved in court. As a result the ambiguous legal status of the New York Iroquois became assured.

The principle that Indian land was inviolate received general if grudging acceptance from the founding fathers. However, from this principle derived a corollary that proved quite vexing. In assuring an extensive domain to the Indian tribes, was not the federal government in effect guaranteeing the perpetuation of a semi-nomadic lifestyle, a lifestyle which was inimical with God's will and the national destiny? This dilemma could best be resolved by convincing the tribes voluntarily to abandon their traditional ways and adopt a way of life that required less land. To encourage the transition, agricultural techniques were to be introduced, at federal expense, and in this way the Indian hunter would become an Indian "yeoman." With his need for land reduced, it was hoped that unused portions would become available to his White brethren.

By the 1790s, these ideas had become embodied in national policy. The federal government assumed responsibility for civilizing the tribes—a task which was thought to consist of converting them from semi-nomadic, warlike hunter-gatherers to sedentary, peaceful, Christian, agriculturists. The life of the hunter, according to Timothy Pickering, a principal exponent of the policy, was not God's final design for mankind. Pickering told the Iroquois that Whites too had once been at this primitive stage of development but had progressed up the ladder of civilization. People in other countries had also laid aside their hunting and warlike ways, ". . . and learned to be farmers, carpenters, smiths, spinners and weavers, and going from one step to another, they learned to do a multitude of other useful things . . ." (Pickering Papers, 1791, vol. 60).

While Pickering and others saw an urgent need to bring civilization to the Indians, they realized that this would be a gradual process which should occur under an umbrella of federal protection of tribal lands and tribal autonomy. Of course, as President Jefferson cynically noted, the process of extinguishment of Indian title could be hastened if the Indians were encouraged to go into debt to purchase those material benefits that marked civilized society (Malone 1970:274).

REMOVAL AND THE ASSUMPTION OF CONTROL BY NEW YORK

The policy of civilizing the tribes through the introduction of agriculture had scarcely begun before other changes were made. It required but a modest extrapolation of then current thinking to justify the removal of all Indians to the west side of the Mississippi River. Moving Indians west, the argument went, would afford them an opportunity to achieve a civilized state free from the influences of the majority of Whites, whose ideals of civilization, if not whose actual, sometimes rather sordid lifestyle, they were to emulate. To Jefferson the choices were clear:

> . . . our settlements will gradually circumscribe and approach the Indians, and they will in time either incorporate with us as citizens of the U.S. or remove beyond the Mississippi. (Jefferson to W.H. Harrison, Feb. 27, 1803 as quoted in Malone 1970:275)

In either event land in the east would be freed from Indian claim. Indian land rights would be preserved but the tribes would be encouraged to exchange their claims for land west of the Mississippi River. In some cases encouragement amounted to coercion.

By the 1820s the federal policy of removal brought new pressures on New York Iroquois communities. Government officials, church leaders, land speculators, and some Iroquois, notably the Oneidas, planned to exchange lands in New York for land in the Wisconsin Territory. Most Iroquois communities rejected the move, but state and federal officials persisted, and in the end induced a portion of the Oneidas to move to the Green Bay area of Wisconsin. Still, the other Iroquois showed no inclination to move. The failure of the Iroquois to embrace the opportunity to migrate west, and the pressure

to open Wisconsin for settlement eventually caused the federal government to offer the Iroquois a plan by which they could exchange
their claims in Wisconsin for land in Kansas. In 1838 federal ne-
gotiators completed a treaty at Buffalo Creek which set aside tracts
of land in Kansas for such of the "New York Indians" who chose
to move. The State of New York and private land speculators placed
great pressure of the tribes to agree, so much so that the Senate,
after amending and ratifying the treaty, repudiated those portions
which dealt with Seneca lands (see Abler in this volume).

The Treaty of Buffalo Creek (1838) was more than a federal attempt
to clear western land title and effect the removal of Indians from
the east. It represented a reassertion of federal supremacy over the
New York Iroquois after a fifty-year hiatus. But the treaty did little
to resolve the jurisdictional questions between the two governments.
The State of New York increasingly asserted its claim to sovereignty
over tribal lands. The uncertainty over constitutional authority and
over the assumption of previously defined federal responsibilities by
the state was not unique. Other states, from Georgia to Maine,
exercised authority over Indians within their boundaries. While Congress and the Executive were loath to resolve the problem, the federal
courts were not.

THE REEMERGENCE OF FULL FEDERAL CONTROL

The issues of Indian land and legal status first came to the Supreme
Court in the 1820s. Appropriately enough, the first question the court
was called upon to resolve related to the doctrine of the "Right of
Discovery." In *Johnson v. McIntosh*, the Supreme Court considered
the nature of Indian land title. Chief Justice John Marshall, speaking
for the court, stated the longstanding policy of the right of discovery
as law; namely, that the sovereign held the fee to the land subject
only to the natives' right of undisturbed use. But Marshall went
further. He accepted as axiomatic that native populations could not
easily be assimilated into white society, which had been the prevalent
view in the late eighteenth century. Nor, in his view, could the
Indian way of life be preserved, because it was based upon the
utilization of a vast wilderness. In the words of one legal scholar:

> The European's choice was, therefore, clear; conquer or
> abandon. By choosing the former, the surging white
> population inevitably and necesarily drove the Indians from
> their habitat. The theory of title vesting by discovery and
> conquest was but judicial rationalization of the way things
> were and supposedly had to be. (Kelly 1975:659)

As a result of the *Johnson* case only titles derived from federal grants were valid, and neither Indian tribes nor states had the right to change title without federal approval. While the issue of title may thus have been put to rest, the question of which political entity, federal or state, had jurisdiction over Indian territory within state boundaries remained open until the so-called Cherokee cases. In two decisions in 1831 and 1832 Marshall explored the nature of the federal-state-tribal triad. In 1831 he found in the case of the *Cherokee Nation v. Georgia* that while Indian tribes had ". . . an unquestioned right to the lands they occupy . . .," they could not be considered as foreign nations. In Marshall's words:

> They may, more correctly, perhaps, be denominated domestic dependent nations. They occupy a territory to which we assert a title independent of their will, which must take effect in point of possession when their right of possession ceases. Meanwhile they are in a state of pupilage. Their relation to the United States resembles that of a ward to his guardian. (Price 1973:34)

The following year, in the case of *Worcester v. Georgia.* Marshall found that "The Indian Nations had always been considered as distinct, independent political communities, retaining their original natural rights, as the undisputed possessors of the soil from time immemorial . . ." and were not subject to the laws of any state. Supremacy in Indian affairs was, therefore, clearly vested in the United States (ibid.:44).

According to these decisions, however, tribes were equivalent neither to domestic states nor to foreign governments. Their land was assured them until they chose to relinquish it, but the ultimate control over title rested with the federal government which also had sole jurisdiction within tribal boundaries. These encumbrances upon tribal independence made the federal government, in fact, responsible for protecting Indian rights; tribes were national wards until such time as they ceased to exist as separate political entities or until Congress ended their special status. While the government thus asserted its prerogatives vis-à-vis the states, it did not always meet its responsibilities to protect Indian interests, as we shall see.

Since these cases involved states with Indian problems similar to New York's, the decisions should have resolved any legal uncertainties of that state in relation to the Iroquois, but they did not. Georgia, with the tacit approval of the federal executive, ignored the Marshall decisions, as did New York, which continued to argue that it enjoyed a special status vis-à-vis Indians within its boundaries by virtue of having been one of the original thirteen states. As a result,

the issue of federal versus state jurisdiction came before the court
again, this time in the case of *Fellows v. Blacksmith* (1856). In this
case the court was asked to rule on a motion to evict a group of
Senecas from their land. The court held that only the United States
could extinguish Indian title and that therefore the ejectment motion
was void (60 U.S. 19 Howard:366).

As if unaware of these decisions, New York asserted the twice
discredited sovereignty argument once again, in 1891, when the
Senecas sought to void a land sale made in 1826 *(Christy v. New
York)*. For procedural reasons this case never reached the federal
courts, so the state's argument went unchallenged until 1920 when
it was rejected in another land claims case, *United States v. Boylan.*
Once more a federal court held that the United States had sole
jurisdiction over Iroquois land. This position has recently been re-
iterated in at least two decisions: the Tuscarora case in 1958 and
the Oneida case in 1974, to which we shall return shortly.

By the middle of the nineteenth century the state's interest had
turned from securing Iroquois land to extending its laws and control
over the remaining reservations. In spite of the dispute with the
federal government over jurisdiction, New York State policy often
mirrored federal policy. Thus, when the federal government advocated
Indian removal in the 1820s and 1830s, the state was an enthusiastic
supporter. Later, in the 1880s, when Congress enacted legislation
under the Dawes General Allotment Act which divided Indian lands
in severalty, the state held extensive hearings and proposed the same
policy for the New York Iroquois. Nearly every session of the state
legislature saw the enactment of legislation relating to Indians—laws
which extended educational, health, and social benefits to reservation
populations. The continuing jurisdictional confusion was largely the
product of New York's spurious claim to special status as a founding
state, abetted by a federal bureaucracy myopic in its view of the
issues, timid in its assertion of national rights, and callous in the
performance of its trust obligations. The nineteenth century ended
in a policy stalemate and a jurisdictional dilemma.

Various factors conspired to frustrate all efforts to resolve the status
question: a general sense of uncertainty about the limits of contending
sovereignties, as referred to earlier in connection with Judge Pound's
assessment; concern over the applicability of federal laws such as
the Major Crimes Acts to the Iroquois; and an unresolved conundrum
over title to the Seneca lands resulting from an agreement between
New York and Massachusetts in 1786, and the subsequent purchase
of the right of extinguishment by private speculators. Periodically,
issues arose to add to the controversy. The discovery of gas and oil
on Seneca land brought about intense efforts to remove the cloud

over Seneca title. The issue of leases in the city of Salamanca resulted in bitter lawsuits and a lingering uncertainty. The building of dams at Tuscarora and Kinzua on the Allegheny brought the problem of Iroquois status into focus, even if the proposed resolution was legally and socially unsatisfactory.

Four major concerns have dominated Iroquois-federal-state relations during the present century. First, there is the continuing issue of who has ultimate jurisdiction over Indian lands within New York State. If the authority is shared, what are the limits of each party? Second, there is the related question of whether New York State's criminal and civil laws are applicable to Indians on a reservation without express Congressional authorization. Third, there is the question of the meaning of the land guarantees embodied in the federal-Iroquois treaties of the eighteenth century. Fourth, in view of the constitutional and congressional prohibitions, there is the question of whether the state's early land transactions with the Iroquois can in any sense be considered valid. While these issues could have been resolved by congressional action, in the absence of such determination the courts were repeatedly called upon to adjudicate disputes.

It might seem as though the question of who held sovereignty over Indian land had been resolved in the 1830s in the Cherokee case, already discusssed. Nevertheless, New York continued to hold to the position that as one of the original states it had special rights over the Indians within its boundaries. The issue came before the federal court, for another hearing, in 1958. The New York State Power Authority sought to take land from the Tuscarora tribe in order to build a hydroelectric plant. The state resurrected its founding state argument and pointed out that the land in question had never been part of the federal domain; nor was it part of the aboriginal lands of the Tuscarora, whose legal title was based upon an early nineteenth-century purchase. The federal district court found in favor of the state, but its opinion was reversed by the Court of Appeals for the Second Circuit. The appeals court found that the state had no special rights and that it could take Indian land only with the express consent of Congress (*Tuscarora Nation of Indians v. Federal Power Authority* 257 F. 2d.:885). Not only did the state lack the power to take Indian land, but it had never had such power because New York Iroquois, like other Indian tribes, were wards of the federal government. It was the same story all over again; the state lost the argument and the Tuscaroras the land. For while the court denied state authority over the Iroquois land, it found that congressional consent had been given for the taking of the land. The hydroelectric project went ahead (O'Toole and Tureen 1971).

Interestingly, the question of the application of the criminal and civil codes to the Iroquois was settled before those of land title, jurisdiction, and wardship. New York State had always assumed it had power over the internal affairs of the tribes and, until 1942, the federal courts had been reluctant to challenge the state. A peculiar legalistic anachronism resulted. The Cherokee decisions prohibited the enforcement of state laws on Indian reservations without congressional consent. This, in turn, required the enactment and enforcement of federal criminal statutes or the passage of special legislation making state laws applicable. New York did not recognize the first alternative and Congress had not provided the second. The case of *United States v. Forness* gave the judiciary an opportunity to speak to this issue. The case involved an attempt by the Seneca nation to cancel a Salamanca lease for the nonpayment of eleven years of rent—a total of $44. The case reached the Court of Appeals for the Second Circuit which found that state law was not applicable to Iroquois tribes unless extended by Congress (125 F. 2d.:928). This decision, which the Supreme Court refused to review, caused great alarm in the state government because it tore away the legal underpinnings of the state's assertion of jurisdiction. The court urged the state to seek a congressional remedy, and, in 1948, Congress authorized the extension of the state's criminal laws to Indians on reservations. In 1950 Congress made the civil codes of the state applicable. In so doing, however, the courts had once again asserted federal supremacy.

Among the Iroquois there is an article of faith that the Treaty of Canandaigua (1794) extends to them a special relationship with the federal government, a relationship that can only be altered by mutual agreement. But this is at variance with American legal realities. The Supreme Court has held that an Indian treaty is no different from any other treaty *(Worcester v. Georgia)* and that Congress has the power unilaterally to do violence to any provision, or to abrogate an entire treaty, if it so desires (*Lone Wolf v. Hitchcock* 1903, 187 U.S.). Issues of unilateral change or abrogation are considered by the courts as political in nature and therefore as not subject to judicial review. However, this does not mean that treaties can be abrogated by mere inference or legislative accident. The question of legislative intent does fall within the realm of the court.

In the 1960s the U.S. Corps of Army Engineers proposed to build a series of flood control dams on the Allegheny River. To complete the project the Corps recommended that a dam be built at the Kinzua narrows below the Pennsylvania-New York State line. The effect would be to flood a sizeable portion of the Allegany Seneca reservation. The land had been assured to the Seneca in perpetuity by the treaty of Canandaigua, in which the United States agreed that

it would ". . . never claim the same, nor disturb the Seneca nation
. . . in the free use and enjoyment thereof; but it shall remain theirs,
until they choose to sell the same to the people of the United States
. . . (American State Papers 1832:545). Despite the fact that there
was no specific reference to the effects of the legislation on the
treaty, the District of Columbia Circuit Court found that there was
sufficient evidence that Congress intended to break the treaty when
it appropriated funds for the project (*Seneca Nation of Indians v.
Brucker* 1958, 262 F. 2d.). In a related case, the Second Circuit Court
supported the action of the Corps condemning some Seneca land to
widen a highway adjacent to the dam's reservoir, finding this to be
consistent with authority delegated to the Corps (*Seneca Nation of
Indians v. United States* 1964, 338 F. 2d.). While it can be argued
that the courts displayed questionable judgment in both cases, the
import of the decisions with regard to the issue of a special status
for early Iroquois treaties is painfully clear: Iroquois-federal treaties
are like all other Indian treaties, equally fragile and subject to the
plenary powers of Congress.

If the Iroquois are legal wards of the federal government and their
land is not subject to state control, then it is fair to ask how New
York State was able to secure title to their lands without federal
approval. The Oneidas, among others, have asked that question
repeatedly, but, as it turns out, to no avail. For example, in the
1960s they asserted that the state had violated the Trade and Intercourse Acts (1790–1834) when it purchased land from the tribe.
The difficulty faced by the Oneidas was not the logic of their argument
but their inability to have it heard in a federal or state court. The
federal court denied having jurisdiction and the state refused them
the right to sue. However, in 1974 the Supreme Court did finally
rule that the Oneidas were covered by the provisions of the Trade
and Intercourse Acts and were subject to federal court jurisdiction.
In 1977 a district court sustained the Oneida claim of a possessory
right to 110 thousand acres lost in a state treaty of 1795. The decision
did not challenge the preemption right of the state but it required
that in the exercise of that right the state meet the requirements of
federal law.

Stripped of all the rhetoric, the Iroquois of New York are, from a
legal standpoint, like any other Indian tribe in the United States.
This is not to say that they are not *culturally* unique, but, rather,
that their status as "tribes" is a function of their legal recognition
by the federal government, in the same manner that other tribes
have been granted the same status. At the same time, they possess
some autonomy over their own internal affairs, subject only to express
limitations placed over them by Congress. One such limitation is the

extension of the state's criminal and civil codes to reservation land. Because of their status as wards of the federal government, the state is prohibited from taking tribal land without federal authorization. Recently, the courts have gone so far as to find that federal protection has been continuous since the earliest days of the republic, thereby resolving the issue of state sovereignty over the Iroquois within its boundaries. Thus, there are no special prerogatives that flow from being among the original states in the Union, at least as far as Indians are concerned. By the same token, the Iroquois have no special rights arising from their participation in the oldest federal-Indian treaty in force today. For both state and tribe, Congress has sole jurisdiction over the New York Iroquois.

CHAPTER SEVEN

Women in Iroquois Society

ELISABETH TOOKER

For over a century, students of comparative social organization have pointed to the Iroquois as an illustration of the extent to which a society can be controlled by women. As a result, Iroquois women have gained an enviable reputation.[1] It is one that has led Judith K. Brown (1970: 156), for example, to remark that Iroquois matrons enjoyed perhaps more authority "than women have enjoyed anywhere at any time" and George Peter Murdock (1934: 302) to write, "of all the peoples of the earth, the Iroquois approach most closely to that hypothetical form of society known as the 'matriarchate'."

However, not all students of the matter have concurred with this appraisal.[2] The most noted student of Iroquois society, Lewis H. Morgan (1851: 324) observed that "The Indian regarded woman as the inferior, the dependent, and the servant of man, and from nature and habit, she actually considered herself to be so," adding that "This absence of equality in position, in addition to the force of custom, furnishes a satisfactory explanation of many of the peculiarities characteristic of Indian society." And the best Harriet Maxwell Converse (1908: 138) could write of woman's status in Iroquois society was that "She may seem to have been a creature only and not a companion of the red man, yet by comparison with the restrictions, to characterize it by no stronger term, obtaining among *civilized* people, the Iroquois woman had a superior position and superior rights."

These differences of opinion suggest that the place of women in Iroquois society is not well understood. But I believe some of the obscurity surrounding this subject can be dispelled through a consideration of the principles of Iroquois sociopolitical organization—for Iroquois society may well rest on principles quite unlike those to be found in modern industrial societies or for that matter, agrarian ones. At least, it is the intent of the following to suggest what these principles might be and how inattention has led to contradictory interpretations of the place of women in Iroquois society, as well as to suggest why Iroquois women—probably erroneously—have come to be regarded by so many as wielding exceptional power.

THE IROQUOIS CLAN AND POLITICAL SYSTEMS

A review of the theoretical literature indicates it is their matrilineal clan system that has given the Iroquois the reputation of being a matriarchy or gynecocracy. But matrilineal clan systems are found in a number of North American Indian societies, and the fame of the Iroquois system does not derive from any basic difference between it and those of other North American Indians. Rather its renown is largely the result of two accidents of history. First, the political system of the Iroquois was well described by Lewis H. Morgan in 1851 in what was the first ethnography in the modern sense of an Indian people and is still the best single description of Iroquois society. Morgan's study appeared a decade before studies of the evolution of human societies became popular and provided data for the proposition that became widely accepted: that matriarchal systems preceded the patriarchal ones familiar from Scripture. Comparison of American Indian societies to those more familiar to Europeans from their own, ancient, and Biblical history was not then new nor was the idea that human society had progressed. Rather interest in such studies increased in the latter half of the nineteenth century, as is indicated, for example, by the numerous editions of Sir John Lubbock's *The Origin of Civilization and the Primitive Condition of Man,* first published in 1870. To this body of literature Morgan himself contributed *Ancient Society* (1877), a work that attracted the notice of Karl Marx and achieved additional fame when Frederick Engels, carrying out Marx's intention, published a discussion and summary of it as *The Origin of the Family, Private Property, and the State* (1942). As a result, the Iroquois matrilineal system became widely known, and so a convenient example of a matriarchical society for those who wished to interpret it thus.

Second, in the mid-1800s when anthropology was developing as a discipline, the Indians west of the Mississippi—and thus the Indians living there who had matrilineal clan systems—were little known to Whites, and some of these Indians, such as those of the Southwest who also have such an organization, were not so prominent in history. In contrast, the Iroquois were famous. In the early decades of the seventeenth century, the Iroquois, through a combination of favorable geographic position and political skill, became the most warlike and powerful Indians in the region. They remained so for a century and a half, holding the balance of power in the Northeast.

(That England finally defeated France in their contest for control of this region and so control of the continent was due in some measure to the military and diplomatic aid the Iroquois gave the English.) To Americans in the nineteenth century, interested as they were in their own recent history, Morgan's account of the right of women to select and depose chiefs in the warlike Iroquois society was of more than passing interest.

But although the data collected since Morgan's time indicates that the clan system of the Iroquois does not differ in any fundamental respect from a number of such systems among other North American Indians (Tooker 1971), Iroquois clans do differ in several important respects from the usual textbook definition, indicating the principles on which they rest are not those usually presumed. In the anthropological literature, a "clan" [3] is most often defined as a group consisting of two or more lineages which are assumed to be descended from a common ancestor although the genealogical connection cannot be traced. Iroquois clans are exogamous (or, more properly, were exogamous, for the rule of clan exogamy is not now observed by all Iroquois), and this suggests that the Iroquois might believe that all members of a particular clan are descended from a common ancestor. However, such a presumption is not confirmed in Iroquois tradition. To the contrary, Iroquois tradition states that some personage (variously identified in different accounts) went about giving to groups who were camped together their clan names, naming each such group after an animal or bird he saw nearby (see, for example, Shimony 1961: 55–56; Stern 1933: 142–43; Hewitt 1928: 593–608; Henning 1898: 477–78). There is no tradition indicating that all members of each group were descended from a common ancestor, either human or animal. And, in fact, the relationship of the members of the clan to the "totemic animal" after which it is named more closely resembles the relationship between college students and their college mascot than any of the more exotic relationships mentioned in the anthropological literature. Among the Iroquois, then, clans were groups in which membership was ascribed at birth; they were not primarily a means of retaining knowledge of kinship relations that might otherwise be forgotten as is so often supposed.

Neither is the clan a local residential unit.[4] As in most other North American Indian societies that have clans, members of the same Iroquois clan lived in different villages. In fact, it is this dispersal of clan members that accounts for one of the principal functions of clan affiliation among the Iroquois as well as other North American Indians: the obligation of clan members to provide food and lodging to visitors from other villages who belong to their clan.

Nor did the clan own much property, either sacred or secular.[5] There were no ceremonies belonging to clans, at least none are mentioned in the literature, and those few references to ownership of property by clans are usually an Iroquois shorthand reference to ownership by a family or to ownership of things that may be inherited matrilineally.

However, among the Iroquois as among a number of other Indians, clans owned personal names, and it is this feature of Iroquois clanship that gave Iroquois women such prominence as they had in political affairs. By Iroquois custom, each clan holds a set of personal names. When a child is born, he or she is given a name "not in use." This "baby name" is usually later changed for an "adult name" that is not then "in use," that is, one belonging to someone now deceased or to someone whose name has been changed. Certain of these names are associated with particular obligations (in effect, roles) in the society. The evidence suggests that in the eighteenth and earlier centuries when trade and war were more important in the Iroquois economy, some names were associated with trading privileges and others with war (see, for example, Tooker 1964: 25–26, 44–45). Now, however, only those names designating particular chieftainships in the League and those names (the "Faithkeeper" names) associated with special religious obligations (obligations similar to deacons and deaconesses in some Protestant churches) have such specific associations.

The famed League of the Iroquois was established when the leading chiefs of the Mohawks, Oneidas, Onondagas, Cayugas, and Senecas met in council and decided to end the animosity between them. Just when this meeting was held and so the League founded is not known (it was probably sometime between A.D. 1400 and 1600). In succeeding years, this council of chiefs continued to meet to decide matters of concern to the Confederacy and the clan-naming practices provided the basis for the perpetuation of the original council of fifty chiefs.[6] When such a chief (variously called in English, League, federal, or sachem chief) died, the senior woman of the clan (termed in English, the clan mother) to which he belonged, in consultation with the other women of the clan, selected the man from her clan who was to be given the name of the deceased chief and so his position. The man who was given this name was then "raised up" and the deceased chief "resuscitated" at a convocation known as the Condolence Council, or Condolence Ceremony—in the past, the first order of business at the councils of the League chiefs. If subsequently he proved unsatisfactory in this office, his name could be taken away. By this action he was "dehorned," that is, his symbolic horns of office taken from him and so deposed by the clan mother.

The seeming prominence of women in Iroquois political affairs rests almost entirely on this practice. By Iroquois custom, women did not speak in council, at least not normally. Councils were meetings of men, and council decisions the work of men, not women—however interested women might be in them. Men were the orators, the masters of the art of finding consensus in the welter of differing opinions among them—for the decisions reached by councils had to be unanimous in order to be binding. It was the men, too, who negotiated the treaties with other tribes and with European nations, meeting with representatives of those powers who came to the Iroquois capitals on such missions and sending delegations themselves to the seats of government of other nations. Women could, of course, and did attempt to influence the opinion of men. (One suspects women have always and everywhere tried to defend their own interests in ways that they could, as men have also attempted to defend their own interests.) This is attested by occasional references in the literature to women advising chiefs and to particular men being asked to speak for women (see, for example, Lafitau 1974–1977,1: 295, 298–99; Stone 1841: 56–60, 154–56), references that have on occasion been taken to mean that women wielded considerable political power. Such an interpretation is usually not applied to comparable kinds of indirect influence women exerted in, say, nineteenth-century England or America. In Iroquois society, as in others, council affairs were the business firstly of men.

It should be further noted that in the councils of the League, men did not exercise this political power for the sole benefit of their clans. Although chosen by clan mothers, League chiefs were not properly representative of the various clans of the Confederacy. To suppose they were is to suppose the Iroquois form of governance was of the representational type familiar in Western society. It was not. By Iroquois custom all decisions had to be unanimous, and in decisions affecting the League, not only did all the League chiefs have to agree but also the people generally. The League chiefs had no police or other coercive power at their disposal to enforce the decisions they made. Their principal power was that of persuasion. If others disagreed with the chiefs' judgment, they could act contrary to the chiefs' decision and so abrogate it. In effect, then, the council of the Confederacy acted as a kind of committee appointed to discuss particular kinds of issues and charged with proposing to the people generally the most reasonable course of action they could find. If all the people generally did not agree with the chiefs' suggestion, they could overturn it by ignoring it.

Attention to this form of governance helps explain why the clans were not necessarily equally represented on the council of the League and why some clans had no representation. (For example, of the eight names belonging to the Seneca, three are held by one clan, two by another, one each by two other clans; three clans have no League chiefs.) It was not essential that they be; it was only essential that differing points of view be taken into consideration in reaching a decision. Neither was it necessary that all members of a clan agree as to the choice of the successor of a chief having a name that belonged to his clan. Although the clan mother was supposed to consult with the other women of her clan in choosing such a successor, the available evidence indicates that she often did not and that her choice was usually a close relative such as a brother or son. In practice, the seeming prerogatives of clans in the selection of chiefs were obligations of certain lineages to staff the League council, to secure its continued existence rather—it is tempting to suggest—as women by giving birth to children insure the perpetuation of the society as a whole. Neither the role of certain women in certain clans nor the clan system generally was primarily a method by which women exercised political power as has so often been supposed.

If, on examination, the political power exercised by Iroquois women proves to have been limited, the economic power wielded by Iroquois women might seem to have been considerable. A number have suggested it was, among them Brown who asserts that "The high status of Iroquois women was the result of their control of the economic organization of their tribe" (Brown 1970: 164).

Such statements as Brown's—that Iroquois women had dominant control of the Iroquois economy—usually rest on two contentions: (1) that Iroquois women by their labor contributed the major portion of subsistence and (2) that they owned much property, including that used in production. For example, in Iroquois society, the women were responsible for the planting, tending, harvesting, and storing of crops, that is, of corn, beans, and squash—called by the Iroquois either "the Three Sisters," for they were found together like sisters in the fields, or "Our Life Supporters," an indication of the important role of these foods in the economy. It is also reported that women owned the fields and that this property was inherited in the female line. Women also seem to have owned the houses and their stores. These longhouses were multifamily dwellings made of a framework of poles covered with bark sheets, approximately twenty feet wide and as long as required for the number of families who lived in the house. As residence was generally matrilocal,[7] the household was composed of a number of related women and their husbands. Marriages were apt to be brittle. Although monogamy was the rule, divorces were frequent, and consequently, women were the more permanent residents of the longhouse.

However, control by the women of the fields and houses was not the result of their labor in constructing them. Men both cleared the fields and built the houses. These were not inconsiderable tasks; as Trigger (1969: 27) has noted, perhaps "The most arduous agricultural work . . . that of clearing land . . . was men's work." Using stone axes, the men girdled the largest trees, cut down the smaller ones, and cleared the underbush—a process that had to be repeated often because after a few years the fields became exhausted and new ones had to be cleared. Similarly, as the village was moved every eight, twelve, or twenty-five years (when both the fields that could be cleared and the firewood that could be collected nearby became exhausted, and perhaps also when the houses had deteriorated), men had to construct new houses relatively frequently.

Further, the contribution of men in supplying food was not negligible. The economy of the Iroquois was a mixed one, based on hunting, fishing, and collecting in addition to agriculture. The collecting of wild fruits and plants seems to have been women's activity, but hunting and much of the fishing—more important in the Iroquois economy than has often been recognized—were the responsibility of men. Although it is impossible at this date to make more than an educated guess as to the amount of food men contributed, it should be noted that a diet of corn, beans, and squash—which, aside from sunflowers and tobacco, were the only plants cultivated by the Iroquois—is a monotonous though balanced one. Hence, the contribution of men to it would seem likely to have been of more than casual interest to the Iroquois themselves.

But if the contribution of Iroquois men to economic production was perhaps as significant or almost as significant as that of the women—and therefore Iroquois women cannot be said to have had economic control of the society by virtue of their greater contribution to economic production, it might seem that it was their ownership of agricultural land, houses, and other property that gave Iroquois women this supposed control. Such an interpretation, however, ignores certain characteristics of Iroquois property: much of it lacked durability and hence great economic worth. Agricultural fields quickly lost fertility, and new ones had to be cleared. Their value lasted only a few years, and there was no shortage of fertile land. Houses lasted only a little longer. In a few years, the bark covering dried out, making their destruction by fire an ever-constant danger. The poles may well have rotted in the ground causing some disintegration of the structure, and perhaps the general deterioration of the houses as well as the reported exhaustion of agricultural land and of the firewood supply were factors in the decision to move the village and so rebuild the houses every dozen or two dozen years.

Similarly the implements used in production did not involve great investment in time and labor, nor did they last long. For example, the principal agricultural implement was the digging stick, a straight stick pointed at one end used to plant corn and in weeding. It was easily made, and although a particularly useful tool, it is hard to imagine it was a particularly priceless one. Thus, the likelihood that women owned such agricultural implements rather than men (Brown 1970: 159) was probably of little economic consequence.

What seems to have been important in Iroquois society in establishing rights to what we term "property" was not that idea so central in Western society—namely, ownership of a transferable legal title—but rather use. Property was "owned" by those who used it. Thus, a man "owned" those implements he used; a woman, those she used. In fact, concern with "use" pervades Iroquois society and culture. For example, in the Iroquois view of things, animals, plants, water, and the like were put on this earth for "our use," that is, for the use of human beings. This is evident in the Thanksgiving Speech that begins and concludes most Iroquois ceremonies. Of the earth itself, this speech states:

> And now this is what Our Creator did: he decided, "I shall establish the earth, on which the people will move about. The new people, too, will be taking their places on the earth. And there will be a relationship when they want to refer to the earth: they will always say 'our mother, who supports our feet'." And it is true: we are using it every day and every night; we are moving about on the earth. And we are also obtaining from the earth the things that bring us happiness. And therefore let there be gratitude, for we believe that she has indeed done all that she was obligated to do, the responsibility that he assigned her, our mother, who supports our feet. And give it your thought, that we may do it properly: we now give thanks for that which supports our feet. And our minds will continue to do so. [Chafe 1961: 19][8]

This view of the world probably explains statements to the effect that women "owned the agricultural land." Women, not men used it, that is, women planted, tended the crops, and harvested them. Men "produced" the fields in the sense that they cleared them, but since they did not use them, they were not regarded as having rights to these fields. Similarly, since houses were used more by women than men in the sense that women spent more time in them than men, they were often regarded as being owned by women. The same principle applied to other kinds of property. Thus, if a piece of property was clearly not being used by someone, another could use it and could claim rights to it so long as he continued to use it. If he ceased to do so, another could use it. As Fey and McNickle (1970: 21) state, "the right was a right to use, not to transfer in the market place."

Property rights, then, were probably of little importance in Iroquois society and, in fact, there was relatively little in the economic organization to "control." What little there was was fairly equally apportioned among individuals in the society.

IROQUOIS KINSHIP TERMINOLOGIES

Some confirmation of the lack of importance of property in Iroquois society comes from an unexpected source: their kinship terminologies. It is often supposed that Iroquois kinship terminologies reflect their clan and moiety system. (Among the Iroquois, clans are grouped into moieties.) For example, in the Seneca system of kinship terminology (the other Iroquois kinship terminologies are similar, see Morgan 1871: 293–376), mother and mother's sister are called by the same term. As both belong to the same clan, it would seem that for this reason, the term "mother" is extended to "mother's sister." Similarly, father and father's brother are called by the same term and both also belong to the same clan. Further, parallel cousins are called by the same terms applied to siblings and cross-cousins by different terms—a practice which, as Tylor (1889) suggested, might reflect a moiety system. (By Iroquois custom, an individual calls members of his moiety "brothers" and "sisters," and members of the opposite moiety, "cousins.")

However, this hypothesis obtains only if the first collateral line is considered. The peculiarities of the Seneca system are such that it does not hold for the second and more distant collateral lines. As Lounsbury (1964: 1079n.) has noted, the now "classic theory" that characterizes the Seneca kinship system as classifying kin according to membership in unilineal descent groups, predicts correctly only terms for the closest relatives; beyond that, it predicts, at best, only half the terms correctly.

Morgan, who more than any other writer is responsible for anthropological interest in systems of kinship terminologies, was well aware that matrilineal descent could not account for the Seneca system and others like it (see, for example, Morgan 1871: 475). And it is evident that in the rush to find a better explanation than Morgan's for these systems which began when Morgan's great *Systems of Consanguinity and Affinity of the Human Family* was published, this observation as well as others made by Morgan were overlooked.

What Morgan noted about the Seneca system was that it ignored the distinction most basic in ours: the distinction between collateral and lineal lines. It is a difference, Morgan suggested, that reflects the importance or lack of importance of property in the society. In those societies where property is negligible, Morgan (1871: 14) suggested, "The wider the circle of kindred the greater assurance of safety." The Seneca system and others of the type Morgan termed "classificatory" do this by ignoring in whole or in part the distinction between collateral and lineal kin, seeming to treat collateral relatives as if they were lineal ones. However, Morgan suggested, in those societies in which property is important, ownership of property and succession of estates becomes important, and with "its possession sprang immediately the desire to transmit it to children. . . . [which] was realized by the lineal succession to estates" (Morgan 1871: 492). The "descriptive systems" as Morgan termed them reflect this concern by distinguishing lineal from collateral relatives.

It is inattention to this difference between Iroquois society and ours, I would suggest, that has led to the presumption that Iroquois society is organized on the same basic principles as ours. But Morgan (1871: 492) may have been correct when he noted:

> It is impossible to over-estimate the influence of property upon the civilization of mankind. It was the germ, and is still the evidence, of his progress from barbarism, and the ground of his claim of civilization. The master passion of the civilized mind is for its acquisition and enjoyment. In fact governments, institutions, and laws resolve themselves into so many agencies designed for the creation and protection of property.

It is as if many anthropologists since Morgan's time by dropping the word "barbarism" from their vocabulary have been led to the assumption that the political and social institutions of all societies "resolve themselves into so many agencies designed for the creation and protection of property."

RELATIONSHIPS BETWEEN MEN AND WOMEN

Social relationships, then, between various classes of people in Iroquois society, including men and women, were not grounded in control of political power or economic resources. Rather, the contingencies of life as the Iroquois had to live it led to dependence on other kinds of relationships, most notably, on reciprocal obligations, for the Iroquois perforce did not rely on ownership of property but on other individuals. There were reciprocal obligations between the old and the young, including those between older and younger generations and between older and younger siblings. Other reciprocal obligations, including that of burying the dead, were the responsibility of the moieties, and when the moieties were exogamous, as they are said once to have been, they provided spouses for each other. Still other reciprocal obligations obtained between the chiefs and the people generally. Others involved the supernatural. These beings have obligations to the people and the people to them—as the quote given above from the Thanksgiving Speech illustrates. And, as will be suggested, relationships between men and women also rested on maintenance of reciprocal obligations.

In Northern Iroquoian societies, including those of the Iroquois proper and the Iroquoian-speaking Hurons, men and women occupied different domains: the forest and the clearing. Their principal villages were sparsely populated, having perhaps a few hundred to a thousand inhabitants, and few in number. For example, in the seventeenth century, the Iroquois had only thirteen principal villages and some scattered smaller settlements consisting only of a few houses in the considerable territory they controlled in what is now upstate New York (a region some two hundred miles long that stretched from the Mohawk valley in the east to the Genesee in the west). Nonetheless, these villages, small as they were, constituted islands of human habitation in a forest sea and it may be for this reason that the clearing—the village and surrounding fields—had a special importance to the Iroquois. It was from the village that the Iroquois ventured out to fish, to hunt passenger pigeons in the spring and deer and other animals in the fall, to collect maple sap in the early spring and later greens, berries, and nuts of various kinds, and to trade and war, returning with the produce so obtained. Since it was the men who most often left on such expeditions, the village became more particularly the world of the women as well as that of the people generally. Further, as the women did all the agricultural work of planting, tending, and harvesting of crops, the whole clearing (village and fields) also was regarded as the domain of women. The land beyond the clearing, the forest, was the domain of men, the land into which they traveled to hunt, war, and trade and the land they cleared to make the fields and village.[9]

Rather similarly, each house was the domain of the women, a consequence of the general practice of matrilocal residence. Each longhouse was occupied by a number of nuclear families related in the matrilineal line. Women, then, remained part of the household they were born into although the rebuilding of the village every eight, dozen, or two dozen years meant that a woman lived in several different houses in the course of her lifetime. Men, however, were apt to live in a number of different households in the course of their lifetime (divorce was frequent) as they traveled in and out of the village over the course of a year. In fact, it may well have been that the hunting, war, and trading parties the men so avidly joined (on occasion older men had to restrain some of this enthusiasm to insure that an adequate number of warriors remained to defend the village in case of attack) served as a kind of men's club, an escape from the domination of women. Village and League councils also may have served the same purpose.

Property seems to have figured little in marriage arrangements, for there was little of value to own. Marriage involved not rights to property, but reciprocal obligations between a man and a woman. These obligations were of no small moment, and they proved to be a major obstacle to conversion to Christianity with its idea of the indissolubility of marriage. As one Huron put it, "If we take a wife, at the first whim that seizes her, she will at once leave us; and then we are reduced to a wretched life, seeing that it is the women in our country who sow, plant and cultivate the land, and prepare food for their husbands" (Thwaites 1896–1901, 14:235).

It was the obligation of a man to provide the household in which he was living with the products of his activities away from the village. For this reason, according to Lafitau (1974–1977, 1:340), a mother was in no hurry to have her son marry, for when he did the mother's household was deprived of his economic contribution. In compensation for this loss, a wife was obligated to help her husband's maternal household with their work in the fields and the collecting of firewood (ibid.:348), one of the most important tasks of women. The reported practice of Iroquois mothers' arranging marriages (ibid.:341; Fenton 1951: 43) would seem to have been an attempt to insure that the wife fulfill these obligations. The practice is not reported for the Hurons, and it may be that few Huron marriages were arranged as Huron men did not make as much of an economic contribution to the households in which they were living as did Iroquois men; Hurons seem to have been less dependent on hunting than the Iroquois were.

These reciprocal obligations between the sexes extended beyond the marriage relationship. Most important, the obligation of women to provide food for men extended to the clan when men were visiting in other villages. On arrival in a village, a man was asked what his clan was so he could be directed to a house where he might expect to be given food and shelter. As has been noted, one of the important functions of the clan was fulfillment of this obligation.

It was also the obligation of the women of the clan to see that important leadership positions were filled, especially those of the League council. But as customarily such positions went to men of the clan, fathers could not expect sons to inherit their position, perhaps adding to a man's sense of being a drifter between households run by women.

An Iroquois man's concern, then, seems to have been a constant search for a household that would provide him with food and shelter—a household of mother, wife, or clan member who might be induced to provide these necessities, perhaps in return for such goods and services as he could provide. Women's concerns would seem to have centered on keeping the household running. One task involved obtaining stores, the women of the household often working together to provide the basic provisions (the household held these in common). It was the women who planted, cultivated, and harvested the crops—corn, beans, and squash—that constituted the basic diet. Such food as was furnished by the men supplemented that provided by women. Nonetheless, the women needed the help of men, particularly in clearing the land for cultivation and in building the houses. Since such activities demanded the work of a group rather than a single individual, it was to a woman's advantage to increase the number of men—related by blood or marriage—on whom the household could call for such help, thus extending her kin relations.

But within the village, these kin relationships were extended bilaterally. The matrilineal clan system was not so much a means of distributing property or of organizing life in the village as it was a means of relating to people in other villages beyond the surrounding forest. Men typically dealt with matters beyond the clearing, including political affairs. Hence, the chiefs who did so were men, but their names indicated they had been designated by women as worthy to speak for them and the people generally. On the other hand, visitors to the village needed only to know the name associated with a particular role to be directed to the proper individual and the name of his own clan to be provided with food and shelter.

In summary, the problems that Iroquois women and men had to confront were not those of contemporary western society. They only appear to be when the underlying principles of Iroquois sociopolitical organization are ignored, and the separate elements that make it up pulled from their context and reinterpreted in familiar—to us—ways, with the result that matters of little consequence to the Iroquois are presumed to be of great moment and matters of crucial significance to them overlooked. Perhaps, then, Morgan's (1851: ix-x) admonition given over a century and a quarter ago is apt: "The time has come in which it is befitting to cast away all ancient antipathies, all inherited opinions; and having taken a nearer view of their social life, conditions and wants, to study anew our concerning them."

NOTES

1. An earlier version of this paper was given at the Conference on Women in the Era of the American Revolution held in July 1975 at George Washington University.

2. In addition to the discussion to be found in the general ethnographic literature on the Iroquois, the role of women in Iroquois society has been the subject of a number of papers. These include those by Carr (1884), Beauchamp (1900), Goldenweiser (1915), Hewitt (1933), Randle (1951), Richards (1957; 1974) and Brown (1970).

3. The term "clan" is used here in preference to sib, gens, tribe, nation, or any other term that has been applied to these social units because in the anthropological literature on North American Indians this is the term most commonly used.

4. A statement made by Johannes Megapolensis in 1644 (Jameson 1909: 178–79) has often been interpreted as meaning the Mohawks had clan villages. But this is the only such reference in the literature, and a contemporaneous remark by Father Isaac Jogues (Thwaites 1896–1901(29): 53, 293) seems to indicate that the Mohawks had multiclan villages at the time.

5. Morgan's (1877: 70–85) summary of the rights, privileges, and obligations of clans is somewhat overdrawn as a close reading of this passage will indicate. The workings of the Iroquois system is somewhat better described in his *League of the Iroquois* (1851). Nevertheless, Morgan was a more careful observer and more accurate writer than he is often given credit for. For example, if he seems to slight some aspect of Iroquois culture, it is usually because the matter is of little consequence to the Iroquois themselves and if he seems to dwell too long on other matters, it is because these are of importance to the Iroquois. Further, his theoretical concerns reflect this knowledge. Thus, it is of some interest that one of the first papers he wrote after he became interested in more general and comparative problems rather than in just the Iroquois was on "The Indian Method of Bestowing and Changing Names" (Morgan 1959), a subject that has attracted little attention since then.

6. The number of League chiefs is variously given as forty-eight, forty-nine, and fifty. The number of chiefly names is fifty. However, by custom, no one is given the name of Hiawatha, who with Deganawida founded the League. (Longfellow later gave this name further fame by appropriating it for his poem about Algonquians.) Also, some Iroquois regard two of the Onondaga chiefly names as belonging to one person, while others contend they belong to two different men. Hence, different individuals calculate the total number of League chiefs differently.

7. Richards (1967) has questioned this, but the available evidence seems to indicate that the customary (although not invariant) rule was that of matrilocal residence. For a somewhat similar conclusion, see Trigger (1978: 58).

8. The Thanksgiving Speech is not recited by rote and consequently no two repetitions of it are identical. Nevertheless, the same basic ideas are

evidenced in all performances. For other examples of this speech see Foster (1974) and the references listed in Chafe (1961: 301–2).

9. To the best of my knowledge this contrast between forest and clearing was first made by Wallace (1952: 24–28). The idea was further elaborated by Hertzberg (1966: 23–30). Part of the intent of the present discussion is to indicate its usefulness in clarifying certain matters not considered by either Wallace or Hertzberg.

II

Aspects of Iroquoian World View

INTRODUCTION

In terms of primary focus, the seven papers in this section represent something of a departure from those of the sections which precede and follow. We may introduce this shift with a remark by William Fenton taken from the foreword to a work on St. Lawrence prehistory: ". . . as Thoreau wrote in his *Journal* of arrowheads, 'They are . . . as it were, fossil thoughts, forever reminding me of the mind that shaped them.' Since cultures are a product of the mind, so the study of cultures is an affair of the mind" (1972a:xvi). The unraveling of the history of the Iroquois has been a major concern of Fenton's over the years, but so too has been the notion that culture is an "affair of the mind," a notion which runs like a refrain through his writings. The papers which follow all deal with some aspect of Iroquois intellectual life: the ritual practices of the Longhouse, political structure and symbolism (particularly with regard to councils), the special knowledge of the bilingual individual, and a problem in Iroquoian cosmology. The writers share some general concerns. Not surprisingly, several of the papers deal with some aspect of language use or borrow from linguistic methodology in sketching an aspect of Iroquoian world view. Because the Iroquois are among the earliest and most voluminously documented of any Amerindian people, they have also invited interest in the problems and processes of cultural persistence and change. Their long historical record provides a natural yardstick for measuring one factor against the other.

The first paper by William Sturtevant points to a new direction in the study of Iroquois ritual. Research in this area over the last several decades has been dominated by intensive ethnographic work in local communities. Only one attempt to compare Iroquois ritual across

125

communities has appeared in recent years (Tooker 1970), and this deals with but one segment of a single ritual complex, the Midwinter Ceremony. With so much material now available on the different communities, the time is ripe, Sturtevant argues, for a comparative study, and not only of one ritual complex (the greatest amount of attention having been devoted to the Calendrical ceremonies) but of all of them together. In the first place, the Iroquois themselves see the various ritual complexes, which Sturtevant labels the Confederacy ceremonies, the Code of Handsome Lake, the Calendrical ceremonies, the Curing ceremonies, the Death ceremonies, and the Personal ceremonies, as forming a single "overarching cultural system" in which they all participate despite a considerable amount of local variation. In the second place, there are interesting questions about history, structure and function that can only be dealt with in a broader comparative framework, e.g., the fact that there are reserves which have retained the Calendrical ceremonies but given up those revolving around the Confederacy, while there is at least one reserve which has done just the reverse. This raises interesting questions about variations in the underlying function of the complexes in different communities.

The method Sturtevant uses is essentially an ethnoscientific one, though he does not devote much attention to the question of whether his taxonomy of ritual closely matches the native one—the "God's truth or hocus-pocus" question or the matter of "cognitive saliency," as it has come to be known. Because of the breadth of the undertaking, he finds that he must limit himself to sketching a programmatic approach which will be carried out more exhaustively at a later time. Hence his material is presented in the form of a series of tables which indicate (with pluses and minuses) the presence or absence of the ritual complexes and the components which make them up in the fifteen Iroquois communities. One reason Sturtevant has for calling his discussion a "structural sketch" is that this term was sometimes used in the titles of pre-Transformational grammars where the writer reworked existing materials in a standardized format. Thus, he works from existing descriptions of Iroquois ceremonialism to make a structural restatement.

With Sturtevant's paper, the interest that has been directed at Iroquois ritual has, in a way, come full circle. Perhaps the best known of the early descriptions of the major ritual complexes are those in Morgan's *League* (Morgan 1851). Though Morgan tended to speak of the "Iroquois" generally, his observations were based mainly on the practices of the Tonawanda Seneca. If we compare Tonawanda with the other Iroquois communities in Sturtevant's tables we can see that this reserve cannot today be considered typical of all Iroquois reserves, and there is no reason to think that it was typical in the mid-nineteenth century when Morgan was collecting his material. Whether Morgan was aware of local variation or not, his classic study has been interpreted as applying to the Iroquois across the board, and it was in part to correct this tendency toward overgeneralization that Fenton in the late 1930s—at about the same time as Frank G. Speck—conceived of the "program of local research" in Iroquoian studies (see Fenton 1951a, and cf. Fenton 1941b:147–51). During subsequent decades a great deal of effort was devoted to close ethnographic description of the ritual complexes in the different communities. (Some interesting omissions are brought to light in Sturtevant's tables, a valuable spinoff of his approach.) The emphasis was on differences rather than similarities. As Sturtevant points out, Speck and Fenton both looked forward to a time when comparative studies of Iroquois ritual would become practicable, recognizing that some historical problems could best be dealt with from such a perspective. It now seems appropriate again to be thinking in terms of the general Iroquois ritual pattern rather than in terms of the Six Nations, or the Allegany, or whatever patterns, but from a more informed viewpoint ethnographically than existed a century ago.

Annemarie Shimony is also interested in Iroquois ritual, though not from a comparative point of view. She discusses just two of the ritual complexes identified by Sturtevant, the Confederacy and the curing complexes, and limits herself to a particular time and place, the movement on the part of supporters of the Confederacy in 1959 to reinstate the chiefs as the rightful leaders of the Six Nations Reserve. Her discussion brings home a point anticipated by Sturtevant about the ritual complexes: although they can be separated from one another for purposes of classification (and there is some reason to believe that the Iroquois so categorize them), in terms of the daily life of the Longhouse people they exist in a state of dynamic equilibrium. Far from being independent foci of activity, they are interrelated in such a way that a change of state in one may bring about a change of state in another. How is such an interplay of cultural segments shown by the 1959 uprising? The series of events of that year detailed by Shimony resulted in few real changes; the uprising was eventually put down and reserve life returned to relative stability. But the intense feelings it stirred up among the chiefs' supporters were transferred from the political arena to the "psychical plane" where they affected behavior in various ways. There was a marked increase in what were locally interpreted as mental and physical disorders which were attributed to witchcraft. This resulted in increased demand for Indian doctors who prescribed curing rituals. The curing complex was—ironically, as some would see it—thus considerably revivified by the sequence of events, and this carried over into other aspects of traditional culture which also underwent something of a revival. In short, suppression of change in one complex resulted indirectly in new life being given to another. Shimony's discussion raises significant issues for ethnohistoric research in the area of Iroquois ritual. As mentioned, Sturtevant's comparative tables show us that there are Iroquois communities where the Confederacy no longer operates but where the curing and other complexes are strong, e.g., at Cattaraugus and Allegany which have had a Western-type constitution since 1848. It would be interesting now to examine the records of the period leading up to the changes in 1848 to see if there are indications of intensified activity in the other complexes at this time. Such studies are logically the next step following the one taken by Sturtevant.

Shimony has had a longstanding interest in the mechanisms of cultural persistence among the Iroquois (e.g., Shimony 1961). While she confines her discussion to a single historical event, the case is suggestive of a more general kind of cyclical process which has probably arisen often in Amerindian communities in post-contact times. Such a process, it may be hypothesized, is one kind of response to a situation of prolonged contact, and it may usefully be compared to a revitalization movement of the classic type experienced by the Seneca at the turn of the nineteenth century with Handsome Lake. Perhaps the 1959 uprising contained the seeds of a full-fledged revitalization movement, but no more than this, since it failed to carry through. And the traditional patterns given renewed vigor were either ones directly proscribed by the Iroquois (witchcraft) or those whose purpose was to combat the effects of such patterns.

The papers by Sally Weaver and Michael Foster both deal with codifications of Iroquois political traditions, particularly as these relate to procedures of the Confederacy council. (They thus shed further light on one of the complexes discussed by Sturtevant and are linked to Thomas Abler's paper in the previous section.) Weaver takes as her point of departure an observation made by Fenton that the so-called Newhouse version of the Iroquois "Constitution," which appears in highly edited form in Arthur Parker's well-known work bearing that name (Parker 1916), "unwittingly" recorded historical changes taking place at the Six Nations Reserve during the second half of the nineteenth century, leading ultimately to the reform movement which swept the chiefs out of power in 1924. The Newhouse version reflects a number of political realities of the period, of which Weaver chooses to discuss three: the prominence of the Mohawks in council, the rising tide of political reform, and increasing difficulties in the decision-making process in the council resulting from factional splits. The council was divided between a Mohawk-dominated reformist element and an Onondaga-dominated tradition-alist element, and Newhouse seems to have been genuinely motivated by a desire to find compromise. He was above all, attempting to systematize council procedures in order to avoid political stalemates and to impress the Indian department in Ottawa of the council's ability to cope. He was a conservative but also a realist. Yet the manuscript he labored over was twice rejected by the Confederacy chiefs. It may, Weaver suggests, have gone too far for the Onondagas and not far enough for the Mohawks.

Foster's paper on eighteenth-century Iroquois-white councils is an exercise in the ethnohistorical method of upstreaming, developed by Fenton for a wide range of Iroquoian cultural patterns. This method, which Wallace critically assesses in the lead paper of the present volume, draws upon contemporary ethnographic findings as a per-spective for evaluating past cultural patterns, especially where the early reports are fragmentary. There are, in fact, a large number of recorded instances of the councils held between the Six Nations and their allies and various colonial governments. But because of the selective interests of the white secretaries and the circumstances under which the councils were held which prevented their witnessing all of the goings on, some phases of the event sequence, particularly those preceding the main public council, tended to be neglected in the written accounts, and finer points of Indian protocol were often simply missed. Foster is interested in the councils as communicative events involving contact between alien cultures. He approaches them from a viewpoint in anthropology which has come to be known as the "ethnography of speaking" (for a review of what the term embraces, see Bauman and Sherzer 1975). In reading through the voluminous literature of the council fire, he was struck by the smooth alternation between Indian and white "sides of the fire" in taking the floor in council. Decorum normally prevailed, though the pro-tagonists were fundamentally divided over many issues, and they came from alien cultural worlds. The orderly progression of sides suggested to Foster that the whites and Indians must be following an underlying protocol at least tacitly agreed upon by both. How, for instance, did the participants know which side should have the privilege of speaking first, a privilege which carried the right to name the council's agenda? The answer did not seem immediately forth-coming from an analysis of the historic councils alone. It was only after a knowledgeable native authority had been located that the relatively straightforward rules governing speaker precedence fell into place.

Foster's paper can be compared with Weaver's on grounds of method. Both are concerned with codifications of Iroquois council procedure, but whereas Weaver seeks an explanation of one man's systematization of Confederacy procedures in the context of historic events, Foster, somewhat reversing this approach, uses a modern authority's codification of council protocol as a perspective for analyzing historic events. These approaches are by no means mutually exclusive. It has already occurred to some Iroquoianists, for instance, that the two English versions of the laws of the Confederacy (Parker 1916) can be used to upstream toward pre-contact events such as the League's formation; and Foster plans in future work to *downstream* from the historic councils to contemporary oral tradition in order to deal with the problem of change over two centuries.

Two of the papers discussed so far (Sturtevant's and Foster's) employ linguistic methodology or draw upon a phenomenon of speech such as oral tradition in dealing with the Iroquois world view. The two remaining papers in this section are concerned even more explicitly with Iroquoian language problems, although it would be a mistake to leave the impression that the writers confine themselves to narrow structural concerns. Each explores some aspect of the relationship between language and culture: Hanni Woodbury, by analyzing categories of meaning in specified contexts of use, Ives Goddard by relating historical accounts about the name of a now extinct Iroquoian deity to all that can be inferred about this deity's identity.

Woodbury examines an aspect of a problem which arises naturally in the contact situation. It is a curious fact that although bilingual individuals have historically played a significant role in Indian-white relations (e.g., the interpreter in early councils), and anthropologists and linguists in the modern period have been totally dependent upon them, almost nothing has been written about the place of bilingualism in Iroquois communities or the bilingual individual's special abilities. We take the bilingual, bicultural individual's skills for granted—if he seems to be fluent. But are we not just a little blasé in our assumption that such individuals can move rapidly and effortlessly between different linguistic and cultural worlds? This question leads back to the problem of linguistic relativity. Unless the field worker has mastered the language of the people with whom he works, and can pose questions and interpret responses in it, he must resort to a "contact" language, most often English on Iroquois reservations today. But there is a danger in using a language not deeply associated with a culture as the "metalanguage" for discussing that culture: one has little or no way of gauging the extent to which an informant's paraphrases may be distorting concepts in the original language and/ or culture.

Woodbury deals with only one aspect of the general problem of refining and verifying translations. Her suggestion is methodologically practical and interesting: make greater and more systematic use of the bilingual informant himself and his special competence in controlling two language systems. Linguists term the translations bilingual speakers make "glosses" on the assumption that it is safer to consider them approximations to meanings in the target language than precise equivalents of meaning. Still, Woodbury argues, the relationship between a gloss and the original meaning is far from random even if it is not precise: there will be some degree of semantic overlap. The question in a given case is how much.

One way in which we can draw further on bilingual speakers' skills is by having them point out the ways in which the glosses they supply do or do not match terms in the target language. This process of fine-tuning translations is illustrated with a set of verbs and affixes which express directionality in Onondaga. Morphemes denoting directionality often do not have precise *single* morpheme equivalents in English—so much by way of a nod toward linguistic relativity! But quite exact English definitions of the Onondaga morphemes can be obtained by factoring out a common meaning, expressed in English, from a list of glosses produced by a bilingual speaker in which a given Onondaga morpheme occurs in a variety of constructions. For instance, the Onondaga verb root -v- occurs in a range of constructions in which an agent falls, or pulls or pushes someone or something down, or something alights or happens (i.e., "befalls"). From such a list supplied by the speaker, a core meaning is determined for the root. Departures from this core meaning in various constructions are then attributed to the prefixes and suffixes which occur with the root. The affixes themselves must be subjected to the same treatment. The implication is that after much painstaking work the semantic systems of the two languages can be "calibrated," and this can best—perhaps only—be accomplished through the offices of a speaker who controls both systems.

While the examples discussed by Woodbury involve semantic categories, there is no reason for restricting the notion of translation to a linguistic context alone. The ethnographer is also concerned about explicating native categories and must deal with much the same process of refinement from grosser first approximations to more precise later definitions. Among the Iroquois it is certainly appropriate to speak of the bicultural individual as well as the bilingual individual: indeed, they are often one and the same person.

Ives Goddard's discussion of the Iroquoian deity Agreskwe illustrates a different kind of ethnolinguistic problem from that dealt with
by Woodbury, who was able to proceed with living speakers to
collect a large corpus of data. Since Agreskwe is no longer a member
of the Iroquoian pantheon of spirit forces, everything we know about
him is based on historical (seventeenth-century) sources. Although
references to Agreskwe are fairly common in the sources, there are
interpretational difficulties concerning what his special functions and
powers were, and there are also difficulties surrounding the form
and meaning of his name. Goddard's approach, which argues for
the "importance of philological control of the data in ethnohistorical
research," is the model of a certain kind of historical-linguistic reconstruction where both the ethnographic and linguistic facts are
problematic, and one must be content, finally, with a partial explanation. A careful evaluation of the sources shows that Agreskwe was
associated primarily with war, though he may have had other functions as well; however, he was probably distinct from the sun deity,
though some early writers have confused them. On the linguistic
side nothing definite can be inferred about the meaning or morphology of the name, except to point to a clear separation of Huron
and Five Nations variants in spelling. In effect, everything that can
be said about Agreskwe's name and identity is presented, and the
data are then evaluated. While we might wish for more, accurate
partial explanations are obviously preferable to tidier less accurate
ones, such as the one furnished in the eighteenth century by Lafitau
who conveniently equated Agreskwe with the sun on the supposition
that all "Americans" worshipped the sun. Whatever may be one's
specific interest in Agreskwe himself, Goddard's philological approach
has wide application in ethnohistorical work.

Chapter Eight

A Structural Sketch of Iroquois Ritual[1]

William C. Sturtevant

The proper basic units for ethnographic study of the modern Iroquois are their fifteen communities (Figure 8.1)—largely reservations or reserves—not the old six nations, tribes, or languages. Seven of these communities are entirely Christian, while the remainder consist of a majority of Christians and a minority of non-Christians. The latter form the congregations of the twelve longhouses, of which four are on the Six Nations Reserve in Ontario and one each on the Oneida Reserve in Ontario and the Tonawanda, Cattaraugus, Allegany, Onondaga, and St. Regis reservations in New York, the Caughnawaga Reserve in Quebec, and among the Seneca-Cayuga in Oklahoma. These Longhouse people are the "conservatives," the "real Indians," among whom most of Iroquois ethnography has been conducted ever since 1844 when Lewis Henry Morgan began his studies at Tonawanda.

The "traditional" or "aboriginal" aspects of the societies and cultures of the modern Iroquois are almost entirely directly related to the ceremonial complexes that are the topic of this paper. Not all of these ceremonial complexes are limited to the Longhouse people. But even for the Christian Iroquois the Longhouse segments of many of these communities are very important as symbols and reference points for their own Indianness and for distinguishing their communities from their non-Indian neighbors.

Each modern Iroquois community is in many respects a distinct separate society. But in ritual they all (or perhaps all but four) participate in a shared overarching cultural system, a fact that is explicitly recognized by the Iroquois themselves.

The literature on Iroquois ritual is very large and complex, full of details, and by a good many authors. For the last forty-five years all anthropologists who have studied this topic have closely followed

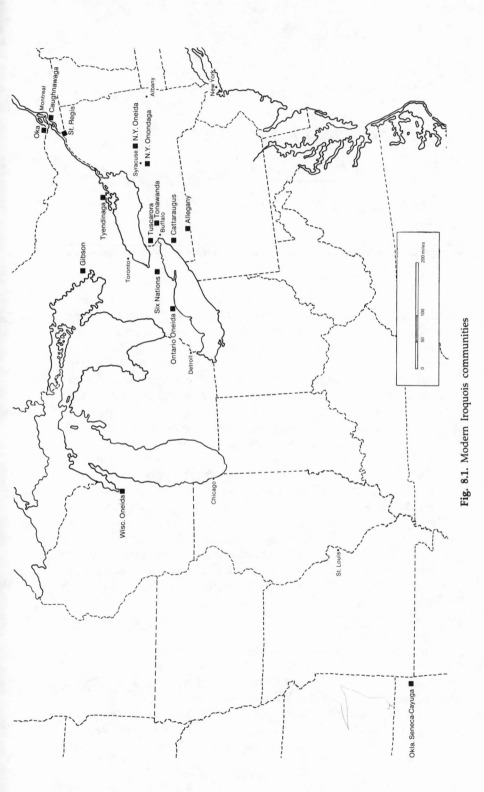

Fig. 8.1. Modern Iroquois communities

William N. Fenton's lead, reading his publications carefully, sending him manuscripts for comment, and consulting with him at the annual Iroquois conferences. We have also been in touch with each other, reading manuscripts and publications, listening to oral papers at the Iroquois conferences, and often exchanging letters and field notes. The usual pattern of Iroquois ethnography has involved repeated visits of varying duration, so that field work is interspersed with writing, reading, and, importantly, the Iroquois conferences. It seems from the published record that in the beginning of his research, Fenton collaborated with Frank G. Speck, who was then working on the Six Nations Reserve. They both were of course familiar with previous publications, beginning with Morgan's *League*, and with many of the manuscripts produced by earlier field workers. It is therefore often difficult to assign specific credit for ideas, methods, and even data that appear in the literature—and dates of publication are not necessarily indicative. The situation is made more complex by the justifiable tendency to depend heavily on a very few knowledgable, intellectual, and communicative ritual specialists. In any community there are always only a few outstanding men with this kind of knowledge and ability, and one inevitably finds or is sent to them, by both community members and other ethnographers, when one begins field research on ritual. One observes as much as possible, and gets explanations mainly from these specialists. They, in turn, have certainly been influenced to some degree by previous collaboration with ethnographers—at the least, in learning how to explain most effectively. Thus questions as to the cognitive status of the analysis here outlined are made even more difficult than is usual for ethnography. There is a tradition of analysis shared by ethnographers and by ritual specialists they work with. Because of the accidents of recent field work it is possible that this ethnographic tradition is biased towards Allegany, Tonawanda, and the Six Nations Reserve. My own initiation into Iroquois ethnography began at Allegany in 1952; my later experience at Cattaraugus and in Oklahoma, where no ethnographers of this tradition had recently worked, on the one hand was influenced by my earlier field work but on the other hand (especially in Oklahoma) indicated that the ethnographic tradition indeed was an accurate reflection of the pan-Iroquois situation.

What is attempted here, then, is an outline to serve as a framework for organizing and understanding the large, more specialized literature, and to indicate by implication some of the gaps in that literature.[2] What originality it has is chiefly, I think, that it attempts to present an overall pattern rather than to describe the ritual system of a single community. I hope to take one more step in the program

Speck (1949:2–4) attributed to Fenton: "comparative studies" to "show to what extent [Iroquois rituals] . . . are homogeneous," what are the "variations, additions, and omissions in the ceremonial procedures of [each] Long House"—"Dr. Fenton has sounded the marching orders for such undertakings." Fenton on the other hand (1941b: 143) gave Speck at least partial credit for this approach.

The analytical model I apply is heavily influenced by structuralist linguistics (and by an early version of ethnoscience). The parallels between ritual—at least the Iroquois ritual system—and language are not trivial, although there are many unsolved questions regarding the relevance of the idea (or ideas) of grammar, including the degree to which a poststructuralist generative approach would be feasible. This is a sketch in the sense that the outlines and general characteristics of the system are presented, but only a few examples are given of how the full system would appear.

The Iroquois ritual system can be described as a series of hierarchical levels or ranks—that is, as a taxonomy (Figure 8.2)—and there is reason to believe that this represents the way in which the Iroquois themselves conceive it, or at least the way their ritual specialists do. On each hierarchical level, each unit or taxon can be defined in terms of distinctive features that contrast it with other units or taxa on the same level under the shared superordinate taxon: each such set of taxa can be treated as a paradigm. Each taxon can also be described by specifying its constituents on the next lower rank. If one followed this procedure, by the time the lowest, most specific ranks were reached one would have a full description of the content and form of the ceremonies, which would amount to a very large monograph. Here I will focus on the fewer, higher-level taxa and on overt behavior rather than purposes or explanations, and give only a few examples of the manner in which a descriptive analysis might proceed through lower ranks.

Taking this approach may give the impression that these rituals are mere empty forms that are playacted as a demonstration of Indian identity. This is not the case, even though the Iroquois are highly Westernized and participation is in fact symbolic of Indianness. The participants are also mostly firm believers in the Longhouse religion, for whom these ceremonies are the main outward expression of a living religion, one which is deeply felt, which has an explicit ethical content, and which provides methods for coping with the difficulties of this life and offers to its followers a route to salvation in the next life. The ceremonies are also important means for affirming and strengthening the social life of the communities where they are

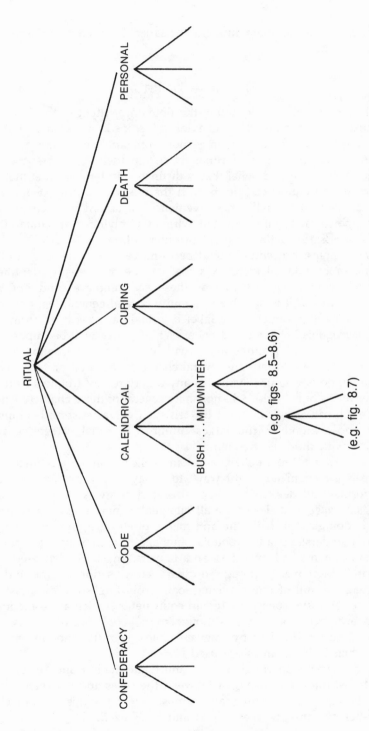

Fig. 8.2. Taxonomy of Iroquois ritual. In this diagram only the second level, with six ceremonial complexes, is fully charted. The lower levels often or always include more than the three taxa indicated (there are at least seventeen on the Bush. . . Midwinter level under the Calendrical complex), and further subdivisions, present everywhere, are only partly indicated under Midwinter.

practiced, and for maintaining boundaries between them and the outer world.

TAXONOMY OF RITUAL

The first problem is to define the domain of ritual in the Iroquois context, to determine what behavior is included and what excluded. The most useful solution comes not from applying some a priori cross-cultural definition of ritual, but from identifying a subset of Iroquois behavior and belief that is distinctive in terms of the internal structure of Iroquois culture itself. If there is such a distinct domain, we can label it "ritual" for convenience, in accord with customary anthropological terminology but without implying that similar features necessarily define "ritual" in other cultures.[3]

The simplest procedure would be to move down one level, to the six major ceremonial complexes that can be quite easily identified, and to define Iroquois ritual as these six complexes and nothing more. However, it is possible to identify several general features that characterize the domain here labeled "ritual" and set it off from the rest of Iroquois behavior and belief. While it may well be impossible to locate a set of features all of which occur in all Iroquois ritual and nowhere else, there are several characteristics that occur in most ritual yet do not occur together in any other areas of Iroquois culture. Other forms of behavior will not share several of these characteristics, while any ritual will do so. I list ten such characteristics, beginning with those found in the largest number of ritual categories and ending with the least frequent:

1. *Formality.* Ritual behavior has an explicit form and organization; there is a recognized "right way" to behave. Speeches and prayers are formal and delivered in special oratorical styles.

2. *Language used.* These are all bilingual communities, where English is dominant in daily life and many, often most, younger people do not understand any Iroquois language. But in rituals all public announcements, all speeches and prayers, must be delivered "in Indian." Moreover, although ordinary conversation in the Indian languages is full of unassimilated loans from English, these must be replaced in ritual speech by Indian equivalents (which are sometimes awkward circumlocutions). Although most people are ordinarily addressed and referred to by English names, in ritual announcements only their Indian names are used.

3. *Reciprocity.* In ritual there is much alternation and reciprocity in offices, roles, and behavior between the sexes and between moieties. Because of the latter, and almost solely for this reason, clan membership must be maintained and recognized.

4. *Feasting.* There are special foods for special purposes, and in most ceremonies food is distributed to the participants; it may be eaten during the ceremony or, more often, taken home.

5. *Song and dance.* These occur in great variety and are an important part of most rituals, enjoyed by both humans and supernatural beings. Song and dance usually go together, although there are occasional songs without dance.

6. *Tobacco.* "Indian tobacco" *(Nicotiana rustica)* is burned, usually in a stove or fireplace, to "carry the message" to the Creator and other spirit forces.

7. *Thanksgiving Address.* Almost every ceremony is opened and closed with a form of this standard speech or prayer, which gives thanks to the Creator for a conventional series of items, terrestrial and celestial, mentioned in a particular order (see Foster 1974; Chafe 1961).

8. *Dreams* are important, as is the necessity for interpreting them and acting out what they require.

9. *Confession* of sins is an important method for "clearing the mind" or purification.

10. *Special artifacts* accompany many rituals. Some, such as musical instruments (Conklin and Sturtevant 1953), "Indian costume," and some masks, have no particular power or sacredness as such, while others such as "medicine," many masks, and especially wampum require special handling because they are inherently powerful and carry heavy symbolic meanings.

The rank below "ritual" (the unique beginner of this taxonomy) is that of the six ceremonial complexes. Figure 8.3 demonstrates a prominent feature of the structure of Iroquois ritual: the taxa at each level may or may not occur in each of the fifteen communities. If they do occur, they are arranged and interrelated in a slightly different manner in each instance. In the table a plus or a minus indicates the presence or absence of a complex. Each plus can be understood as the tip of a pyramid of plusses and minuses, representing similar patterns of presence and absence of ritual taxa on lower levels. The arrangement of the columns from left to right reflects the co-occurrence of complexes and also the geographical and historical relations between the fifteen communities (one could plot ritual isolines on a map).

Each of these complexes is distinguished from the others by a set of features or attributes. These could no doubt be rigorously defined; here a rather unsystematic characterization and commentary is given.

	Six Nations Reserve	Ontario Oneida	Tonawanda	N.Y. Onondaga	St. Régis	Caughnawaga	Cattaraugus	Allegany	Okla. Seneca-Cayuga	Wisc. Oneida	Tyendinaga	Oka	N.Y. Oneida	Tuscarora	Gibson
Confederacy	+	+	+	+	+	+	−	−	−	−	(+)	−?	−	+	−
Code	+	+	+	+	+	+	+	+	−	−	−	−	−	−	−
Calendrical	+	+	+	+	+	+	+	+	+	−	−	−	−	−	−
Curing	+	+	+	+	+	+	+	+	+	(+)	−	−	−	−	−
Death	+	+?	+	+	+	+?	+	+	(+)	+	−?	−	−	−	−
Personal	+	+?	+	+	+	+?	+	+	+	(+)	?	+?	?	?	?

Fig. 8.3. The Six Ceremonial Complexes in the 15 Modern Iroquois Communities. Symbols: +, present; −, absent; (+), known to have once been present, but now absent; ?, doubtful, evidence lacking or inadequate.

Confederacy Ceremonies

These are ceremonies held by and for the hereditary chiefs of the League. There are fifty traditional titles, of which one (Hiawatha) has usually remained unfilled since the death of the original holder. These titles are allocated by tribe: eight Mohawk (plus Hiawatha), fourteen Onondaga, and eight Seneca, these forming the "Elder Brothers" side or political moiety; and nine Oneida and ten Cayuga, forming the "Younger Brothers" side. But the system is more complex than this idealized list. On the one hand, there are additional hereditary chiefs for the Tuscarora and other tribes that entered the Confederacy in a status subordinate to that of the original Five Nations. On the other hand, when the Iroquois divided after the American Revolution the titles were duplicated so that there have long been, in effect, two Iroquois Confederacies, one in Canada and one in the United States; that division is significant only for this "political" ceremonial complex. Within these two Confederacies there have been occasional duplications of titles, and also memberships across the international border, associated with factionalism in various communities (Ontario Oneida formerly, Caughnawaga presently). Furthermore some communities have or once had hereditary chiefs not affiliated with the Confederacy: Tyendinaga, Wisconsin Oneida, Oklahoma Seneca-Cayuga, probably Oka, perhaps Gibson.

Ideally, ignoring some of these complexities, the social units participating in Confederacy ceremonies are the ancient five tribes or nations, rather than (as for other ritual complexes) the modern communities or sections of these modern communities. For each of the two Confederacies, Onondaga is the capital or "central fire." The Canadian confederacy meets at the Onondaga Longhouse on the Six Nations Reserve, while the U.S. fire is on the Onondaga Reservation near Syracuse.

This complex differs from the next three (four in most communities) in that Christians may be full participants: the New York Oneida and Tuscarora are wholly Christian communities. Yet in some other communities, Christians cannot hold chiefs' titles. Patterning here provides opportunities for the method of controlled comparison. No functional explanation of the relations between hereditary chiefs and the calendrical ceremonies, for example, is likely to be valid unless it takes account of the communities where one complex occurs but not the other, and also includes an examination of the histories of communities where the hereditary chiefs have been eliminated or had their powers removed, and where the system of hereditary chiefs has been reinstalled.

The best described ceremony in the Confederacy complex is the Condolence Council, held to "raise up" a new chief and to condole those who have lost the previous holder of the title (see especially Fenton 1946a; 1950; Hewitt and Fenton 1944). We have very little information on the methods and procedures of Confederacy meetings held for other purposes. The outlines of the traditional committee system and the methods for reaching a conclusion have been described, but evidently not how (or whether) these are now carried out; nor is much known about the ceremonial format or religious aspects of such meetings.

Code

The 'good message' (Seneca káiwi·yo·h, and similar terms in the other languages) of the prophet Handsome Lake is a long text, orally transmitted, which is the formal charter of the Longhouse religion. It is an account of Handsome Lake's visions in 1799 and 1800 and of his subsequent ministry until his death in 1815, containing a collection of his ethical and ritual prescriptions, his answers to problems, and a description of the afterworld along with apocalyptic prophesies (Parker 1913; Deardorff 1951; Wallace 1969, 1978). The Code ceremonies are annual recitations of this message during four mornings, in a longhouse; the total time required for the recitation is about eight to ten hours.

The participating social units are eleven of the twelve Longhouse communities (excluding the Oklahoma Seneca-Cayuga), but for this complex the Tonawanda longhouse is the "central fire," where those qualified to recite the Code are ordained and where the annual schedule of the Code preaching is worked out. Each year the Code is first preached at Tonawanda, then in a circuit including about half the other longhouses; the next year, the circuit includes the remaining longhouses after starting again at Tonawanda. In most cases the preacher at a "Six Nations convention" (as the Code recitations are often called in English) is not from the community where he preaches, and many in his audience are also visitors from other longhouses. The afternoons and evenings are devoted to feasting, visiting, and social singing and dancing. Thus these "conventions" help unify the believers in and practitioners of the Longhouse religion, and must account for some of the similarities between the practices of the different longhouses.

The Iroquois in Canada and New York feel a very close connection between the Code and the Calendrical complex. Short versions of the Code are preached at the major calendrical ceremonies, and the Code itself refers to and supports these ceremonies, which are said to be an important part of the behavior the prophet required of his followers. Anthropological accounts have sometimes tended to merge these two complexes—and both are fully "longhouse ceremonies." But that they are distinct complexes is demonstrated by the example of the Oklahoma Seneca-Cayuga, who have the calendrical ceremonies but have never had the Code.

Calendrical Ceremonies

The ceremonies of this complex are always and primarily held in a longhouse. The participating social unit is the longhouse community, each one of which is independent and runs its own affairs without reference to what the other longhouses do. There is a set of longhouse officers, especially those designated "faithkeepers" or "deacons" in English, who organize and supervise these ceremonies for the community as a whole. The ceremonies are public, and all members of the community are supposed to attend (although in fact attendance varies quite widely, depending in part on the attractiveness of the ceremony or of the part of the ceremony). Rules regarding the admission of non-Longhouse people—especially non-Indians—vary between different longhouses and over time. Longhouse believers from other communities are always welcome. The explicit purpose of the ceremonies is to give thanks to the Creator for the natural processes of the weather, crops, and some wild foods (the Strawberry and Maple ceremonies can be called first-fruit rituals), and at the same time to ensure that these things continue. More details are given below.

Curing Ceremonies

These are not usually or primarily held in the longhouse. They were forbidden by Handsome Lake, but have continued because there was no method to forestall the serious consequences of cessation on their members and the descendants of members. They are associated with tutelary animals and supernatural beings, rather than with the Creator directly. In these respects, and as regards their functions or purposes for individuals' difficulties, the relation of the curing ceremonies to the Longhouse religion resembles that of animistic or local religious systems to the Great Religions in Southeast Asia. Curing ceremonies are performed by "private" medicine societies; they are not community wide. They are conducted by and for those who are or have been ill with the specific illness or illnesses which each society cures. Yet the label "secret medicine societies" sometimes found in the literature is misleading. Only the most powerful are secret in the sense of excluding all nonmembers from attendance;

for many, in fact, the ceremonies themselves, or parts of them, may be performed by skilled singers and speakers who happen not to belong. Most are hardly "societies" either, in that they are not tightly organized with one specific set of officers, and the full membership in any community fluctuates and is not generally known except that each person who has once been cured by that ceremony knows that he or she belongs to it. (The most detailed account of a curing society is Fenton 1953.)

Curing ceremonies are less structured and more varied than those in other major complexes. They differ from the calendrical ceremonies, for example, in occurring at irregular intervals with relatively few spectators and participants. The ritual conductors change more often and are more likely to be specialized, some knowing the proper songs, others certain types of more or less interchangeable speeches and prayers, others some of the ceremonial forms; some but not all know some of the origin myths, and others specialize in diagnosis ("fortune telling," dream interpretation). These ceremonies are more shamanistic or mediumistic, in contrast to the more priestly calendrical ceremonies. The overt functions and the forms of curing ceremonies vary considerably from occasion to occasion, depending partly on factors in the personal history of the sponsor. Differences here tend to be ascribed to this cause, a common response to questions being "It could be; I've never seen it that way, though," whereas in the case of calendrical ceremonies variations are more likely to be blamed on ignorance or forgetfulness on the part of the performers.

Curing ceremonies are usually held at night and in private houses (contrasting in these ways with the previous three complexes). However, commemorative repetitions, to prevent the recurrence of the illness, are often performed in brief in the longhouse during calendrical ceremonies; there are special periods set aside for this purpose during every Midwinter Ceremony. In the Six Nations Reserve longhouses, at least, it is also possible to perform an initial curing ceremony during these periods. But participants do not view these longhouse performances as equivalent to other longhouse ceremonies. In some cases Christians are members of medicine societies. The fact that they were once present, although now obsolete or obsolescent, among the Wisconsin Oneida and the Oklahoma Seneca-Cayuga demonstrates that they are not necessarily associated with any of the first three complexes. However, more complete understanding of this complex is hindered by a lack of data on the presence and the history of curing ceremonies in communities without longhouses or where longhouses have been introduced during the twentieth century.

The False Face society, the most prominent among the curing societies, has a somewhat ambiguous position. Masks are prominent at Midwinter, and not only for curing. Furthermore each spring or fall (or both) the False Faces go around the houses to protect the whole Longhouse community from affliction by disease and high winds (Fenton 1941; Sturtevant 1983).

Death Ceremonies

There are several ceremonies whose explicit purposes are associated with death. For each individual death there is a wake and funeral, a "ten day feast" ten days later, and a memorial feast one year later. There are no formal, permanent organizations that conduct these (in contrast to the first four complexes). They are largely held in private houses (with smaller sections also held in the longhouse).

In addition there is a ceremony (*ohki·we·h* in Seneca and similar terms in the other languages) for the dead of the whole community, conducted once or twice every year by a special society with special officers. This differs from a calendrical ceremony in its explicit purpose, in being held at night, and in having separate officers (see Fenton and Kurath 1951).

Personal Ceremonies

Finally, there are minor and mostly obsolete ceremonies which do not fit any of the above categories. This set includes rather disparate and poorly known items, and is difficult to define with distinctive features. Examples are ceremonies for marriage and adoption, establishing ritual friendship (these last share features with both adoption and curing ceremonies), and a few minor private rites performed in the fields at planting and harvesting. Witchcraft may be the exception to prove the rule: if more were known about its procedures, the distinctive features of the domain "ritual" might exclude witchcraft; if not, then it perhaps belongs here.

CALENDRICAL CEREMONIES

Patterning of rituals on the ranks below that of the six major complexes is best exemplified among the calendrical ceremonies— because they are better known, and perhaps because differentiation into hierarchical taxonomic levels is more explicit and probably of greater depth here than in the other complexes. The present analysis recognizes three paradigmatic levels below that of the complex as a whole. Certainly there are more, at still more explicit levels where elements of speeches and songs, dance steps and choreography, and yet more specific patterned elements can be recognized. It is likely that such an analysis carried out for the other complexes would contain fewer intermediate levels, so that the shapes of the taxonomic trees in each case would differ. There are two problems in this area of the analysis. The system is not rigidly taxonomic, because many of the taxa on these lower levels occur under several different higher-level taxa. Also, the manner in which the number and distinctness of the analytical levels reflect native ideas is unclear.

There are apparently seventeen different calendrical ceremonies, spread over the year in a more or less fixed order and held at approximately the same time each year. But no longhouse has all seventeen. Figure 8.4 shows the occurrences at all but the Caughnawaga longhouse (for which I have not located a reliable listing).

The same ceremony in different longhouses is recognizably similar, containing many or most of the same elements, but it is not identical. Figure 8.5 illustrates this by comparing the main elements (the next lower taxonomic level) of the main calendrical ceremony at two longhouses. Not every item is shared: Cattaraugus has an Inserted Message on the ninth day, whereas Sour Springs lacks it altogether (although from the Cattaraugus point of view this is an important element, being a long speech that recapitulates the events of the whole ceremonial year just ended); Sour Springs has a sermon on the fifth and seventh days, which Cattaraugus lacks (although this is important at Sour Springs, where it is an ethical and moral exhortation of the congregation).

These and others are paradigmatic differences. There are also syntagmatic differences—the order of elements differs, for example Sour Springs names children on the sixth day, when the Personal Chant also occurs, whereas Cattaraugus names children on the seventh and eighth days, and the Personal Chant occurs on the sixth. Figure 8.6 illustrates other syntagmatic variation, showing the four main components of the two main calendrical ceremonies (Midwinter and Green Corn)—the "Four Sacred Rituals" specified by Handsome Lake as especially important and pleasing to the Creator. They all occur wherever Midwinter occurs, in much the same form, but both the sequence and the assignment to subsequent days varies from longhouse to longhouse (cf. Tooker 1970).

When the same ceremony or rite occurs, it may differ in details on a still lower level of patterning—the appropriate song may be somewhat different, or the procedure slightly varied—but it is still readily recognizable to a visitor from another longhouse, who considers it to be the equivalent of what he or she knows at home. Figure 8.7 illustrates such a difference at a quite low level of the ritual taxonomy. In all longhouses, apparently, the seating of the congregation is according to both sex and moiety. The normal (unmarked) situation has men sitting in one end of the longhouse and

| | Six Nations Reserve | | | | | Seneca Nation | | | | | |
	Onondaga	Sour Springs	Seneca	Lower Cayuga	Tonawanda	Cattaraugus	Allegany	St. Regis	N.Y. Onondaga	Okla. Seneca-Cayuga	Ontario Oneida
Bush Dance	+	+	+	+	−	−	−	−	−	−	−
Maple	+	(+)	+	+?	+	+	(+)	+	+	−	−
Seed Planting	+	+	+	+	+	+	+	+	+	−	−
Moon	+	(+)	−(+?)	−(+?)	−	−	−	−	−	−	−
Sun	+	(+)	−(+?)	−(+?)	+	+	(+)	−	−	−	−
After Planting	+	(+)	+	−?	(+)	−	−	−	−	−	−
Strawberry	+	+	+	+	+	+	+	+	+	+	+
Raspberry	−	+	−	−	−	−	−	−	−	−	−
Blackberry (= Moon ceremony?)	−	−	−	−	−	−	−	−	−	+	−
Bean	+	+	+	+	−	−	−	+	+	−	−
Thunder	+	(+)	−	−	+	+	+	−	−	+	+
Little Corn	+	+	+	+	−	−	−	−	−	−	−
Green Corn	+	+	+	+	+	+	+	+	+	+	+
Our Sustenance	+	+	+	+	−	−	−	−	−	−	−
Harvest	+	+	+	+	+	+	+	+	+	−	+
End of Summer	−	−	−	−	−	−	−	+	−	−	−
Midwinter	+	+	+	+	+	+	+	+	+	−	+

Fig. 8.4. Calendrical Ceremonies at 11 of the 12 longhouses. Symbols: +, present; (+) recently obsolete; (+?), perhaps recently obsolete; −, absent; ?, doubtful.

Fig. 8.5. Major rituals in the Midwinter Ceremony at two longhouses.

Day	Sour Springs Longhouse	Cattaraugus Longhouse
1	"Our Uncles" (Bigheads) Circuit Stirring Ashes	Bigheads ("Our Uncles") Circuit
2	Stirring Ashes Curing Ceremonies, Dream Guessing	Stirring Ashes Circuit (Curing Ceremonies)
3	Curing Ceremonies, Dream Guessing	Feather Dance Circuit Curing Ceremonies, Social Dances
4	Nothing (formerly White Dog Sacrifice)	Dawn Song Skin Dance Circuit Curing Ceremonies, Social Dances
5	Feather Dance Sermon Feather Dance	Dawn Song Bowl Game Circuit Curing Ceremonies, Social Dances Hunters Husk Faces
6	Tobacco Invocation Personal Chant, Naming Children Skin Dance	Tobacco Invocation (formerly White Dog Sacrifice) Personal Chant
7	Bowl Game Feather Dance Sermon	Feather Dance Skin Dance Naming Children Social Dances
8		Bowl Game Naming Children Social Dances Husk Faces
9		Dances for Life Supporters Inserted Message Feather Dance Traditional Women's Dances

women in the other, each using the appropriate door (if there are two doors), with the moieties seated on opposite sides of the longhouse. This is the seating for all occasions but those when the moiety opposition is explicitly marked: during the Bowl Game at Midwinter and Green Corn (when the moieties play against each other) and, for some longhouses only, during the opening days of Midwinter. On these days the two moieties are seated in opposite ends of the longhouse, each using the appropriate door (if there are two), with

Fig. 8.6. Sequence of the Four Sacred Rituals at Midwinter in five longhouses. The day numbers are in the second half of Midwinter; they are actually days 6 through 8 at Cattaraugus and Onondaga, 7–9 at Allegany and 5–7 at Tonawanda and Sour Springs. The Onondaga column follows Tooker 1970:78, except for the last day where her "Bowl Game and Personal Chant" has been reversed. However, Foster (personal communication, 1980) has good evidence that the sequence at Onondaga is identical to that shown for Sour Springs.

Day	Seneca Nation		Tonawanda	Six Nations Reserve	
	Cattaraugus	*Allegany*		*Onondaga*	*Sour Springs*
1	Personal Chant		Feather Dance		
		Feather Dance	Skin Dance	Feather Dance	Feather Dance
2	Feather Dance	Personal Chant	Bowl Game begun	Skin dance	Personal Chant
	Skin Dance	Skin Dance	Personal Chant		Skin Dance
3	Bowl Game	Bowl Game	Bowl Game ended	Personal Chant	Bowl Game
				Bowl Game	

the sexes seated on opposite sides of the longhouse. These organizing principles are the same in all longhouses, but they are applied differently in each. At Six Nations Reserve one generalization is expressed: "The Wolf side is always the women's side," "No Wolf women move" (Shimony 1961: 68). But even this does not hold elsewhere: at Cattaraugus, Wolf women do move.

CONCLUSION

One of the difficulties in using a structuralist linguistics model for the analysis of other aspects of culture is that it is difficult to find comparable tests for the significance of differences. Even the simple question "Same or different?" is usually problematical. For phonology, the classical method for answering this question is to see whether a change makes a difference in meaning: if it does, the units are different; if not, they are the same. But no such (apparently) simple criterion can be found in most other areas of culture. In Iroquois ritual, comparison provides somewhat similar tests. The local manifestations of taxa at various levels are conceptually the same or equivalent to the Iroquois themselves (although they are of course aware of many differences between communities). A given ceremony or ritual element is usually called by the same term in different communities, or if the languages are different, by an exactly equivalent, directly translatable term. Also, different local forms are substitutable. It is quite common for a foreign form of a ceremony or rite to be substituted in the proper place in a local sequence; this is done if the local ritual specialist happens to be absent, and also as a compliment to a knowledgeable visitor. It happens on the specific

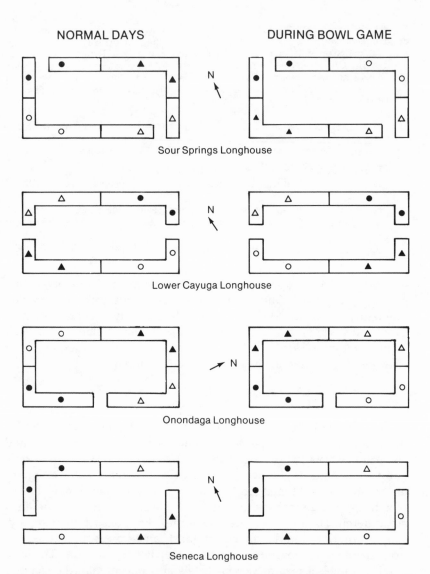

Fig. 8.7. Seating during the Midwinter Ceremony at the four longhouses on the Six Nations Reserve. Triangles indicate males, circles females, solid for the moiety that includes the Wolf clan, open for the moiety that includes the Deer clan.

level of a single dance, which may be sung or led by a visitor using the form of his home community, or a standard speech or prayer which may be delivered by a visiting speaker even in his own language when that is different from the language used in the longhouse he is visiting. Substitution may also occur on a higher level: it is built into the Code complex, in that the preacher is almost always an outsider and a different one each year; in the Calendrical and Curing ceremonies a ritualist from another community is sometimes called on to organize and supervise a whole ceremony (as happened at Cattaraugus in 1957, for example, when the entire Sun ceremony was run by Gus Williams from the Seneca Longhouse on the Six Nations Reserve). When different forms are seen to be "the same" by such tests, we can then search for the distinctive features they share, and these features are structurally more important than are other features that may be distinctive for a given ritual in a given community, but not distinctive for the same ritual elsewhere.

It is instructive to compare the Iroquois ritual system with a language with constituent local dialects. Each community has a distinct local variant, but this is mutually intelligible to members of other communities. There is a general grammar that applies to all, with special rules to account for minor local differences. Innovations may arise and persist in one community, as for example the Dawn Song on the fourth and fifth days of Midwinter (Figure 8.5) is unique to Cattaraugus, where it was introduced before 1900 in response to a dream. Borrowings between communities occur: some ritualists supposed the whole Bean ceremony had been borrowed by Tonawanda from the New York Onondaga (Fenton 1941b:149); the entire Calendrical complex was introduced at Caughnawaga and St. Regis in this century; the Cherokee dance was imported from Oklahoma to the Six Nations Reserve in 1936 (Speck 1949:158) and spread from there to other longhouses; the Rabbit dance was learned from northern Plains singers in the mid-1950s by Chancey Isaac and Percy Smoke of Six Nations Reserve, modified to fit Iroquois musical and dance styles, then diffused to other longhouses. There are of course many other examples, readily accounting for the greater resemblance between the various communities than would be expected from the time depth of the divergence among the northern Iroquoian languages and from the geographical and historical separation of the modern communities. Communication between communities, in part required by the ritual system, has prevented their rituals from diverging past the point of mutual intelligibility. That they are both similar and different has also been a factor in the persistence, increase, and importance of the ethnographic literature.

NOTES

1. An earlier version of this paper was delivered orally (with the Figures distributed on a handout) in 1967–1968 at several universities in England and Scandinavia and before the Philadelphia Anthropological Society, and in 1969 at the University of Arizona, Southern Illinois University, and the

annual Iroquois Conference. For helpful comments on the present version
I thank Michael K. Foster, Annemarie Shimony, and Harold C. Conklin.

2. Rather than document each point with references, I list my principal
sources here. *Six Nations Reserve:* Shimony 1961; Foster 1974; Speck 1949;
Weaver 1978. *Ontario and N.Y. Oneida:* Campisi 1978. *Tonawanda:* Fenton
1941b; Tooker 1970; Abler and Tooker 1978. *N.Y.Onondaga:* Blau 1969; Blau,
Campisi, and Tooker 1978. *St. Regis:* Frisch 1970; Fenton and Tooker 1978.
Caughnawaga: Fenton and Tooker 1978; Voget 1951. *Cattaraugus:* Sturtevant
1952–1961. *Allegany:* Fenton 1936; Sturtevant 1952–1961. *Oklahoma Seneca-
Cayuga:* Sturtevant 1961–1962; Sturtevant 1978. *Wisconsin Oneida:* Ritzenthaler 1950; Campisi 1978. *Tyendinaga:* Torok 1967; Fenton and Tooker 1978.
Oka and Gibson: Fenton and Tooker 1978. *Tuscarora:* Wallace 1952; Landy
1978. The most important general sources on Iroquois ritual are Shimony
1961; Tooker 1970; and Foster 1974. On Handsome Lake and his Code, see
Deardorff 1951; Wallace 1969; Wallace 1978. Comments here on the Code
recitation are based in part on Sturtevant 1962. For the names of the
calendrical ceremonies, the Four Sacred Rituals, and the main curing and
death ceremonies in the various Iroquois languages, see Tooker 1978a: 457,
460 (in a chapter that is otherwise useful, as is Tooker 1978).

3. Binns (1979:586–87) has recently discussed and illustrated some of the
problems of selecting appropriate terms for cross-cultural use in domains
resembling this one. An additional consideration is the need for different
terms in the analytical language as labels for different ranks or levels of
inclusiveness in a specific system. In the Iroquois case, it seems most
convenient to use "ritual" as the label for the whole domain, and terms
such as "ceremonial complex," "ceremony," and perhaps "rite," "festival,"
and others, to distinguish taxa on lower ranks. The labels required will differ
from society to society, from analysis to analysis, and even—for example in
the number of levels—as between different areas of the ritual structure of
a single society. According to Binns, "except for . . . the short-lived exper-
iments of the French Revolution, the Soviet system of non-religious ceremonies is unique in modern European societies." Presumably what is unique
is the relative lack or unimportance of religious ceremonies, rather than the
existence of a system of ceremonies that are ideologically nonreligious. In
many modern North American Indian societies there is a distinction between
religious and secular ceremonies: "powwows" are nearly always "not religious," although of great symbolic importance and in other respects clearly
ritualized. The Iroquois do not (yet) have such a distinction, although there
are many secular aspects of the existing Iroquois rituals and their sacredness
varies among different participants.

CHAPTER NINE

Conflict and Continuity: An Analysis of an Iroquois Uprising

ANNEMARIE SHIMONY

This paper is an exercise in ethnohistory, since it is my intention to show how the Iroquois uprising of 1959 is to be understood in the light both of persistent characteristics of Iroquois society and of a sequence of historical events which affected that society. It is particularly appropriate to dedicate such an inquiry to Professor W. N. Fenton, since he has contributed much to our knowledge of the connection between Iroquois history and Iroquois culture, and has brought the very field of ethnohistory into prominence.

One feature of the Iroquois which makes them interesting to social scientists is their development of an elaborate political system, which Morgan considered to be the most sophisticated in North America. Morgan (1877) himself, and later Beauchamp (1905), Parker (1916), and Hewitt (1920) gave excellent accounts of the ideal functioning of these political institutions, but it was Fenton (1955) who indicated that despite the celebrated requirements of unanimity and reciprocity there existed areas of tension which were never satisfactorily resolved. In particular, Fenton noted that from Jesuit times jealousy among rival chiefs had produced schisms and also that the three types of chiefs—sachems or peace chiefs, war chiefs, and pine tree chiefs— were often engaged in struggles.

Contributing to the jealousy of particular chiefs are the indefinite distribution of power and the indeterminate ranking of the peace chiefs in the laws of the Confederacy. Iroquois doctrine holds that "all trees are of equal height," i.e., that all the chiefs have equal powers, but Thadodaho *(thatótà:ho?)* and Hononwirehdonh *(honō-wiyèhti)* claim special prerogatives.[1] Thadodaho, legendarily snake-crowned and difficult to persuade, was promised the position of leadership if he brought his tribe into the League. As a consequence, the Onondaga became the keepers of the fire for the League as a whole, and Thadodaho became the first chief of the leading Onondaga phratry. Fenton terms this phratry of six chiefs the "executive committee" of the Confederacy, and there is no doubt that a special attitude is appropriate toward this chief and his group. But the Great Wolf, Hononwirehdonh, the seventh Onondaga chief, is often deemed even more important, for he is the arbiter of disputes and the tie-breaker in voting. To him are left decisions of referral back to the individual phratries, and to him accrues the task of "cooling down the fire" when arguments break out. He is, furthermore, the wampum keeper of the League, and the only chief to constitute a phratry all by himself. Consequently, it is not surprising that a contest between these two chiefs and their respective followers might occur, especially during a time of general political unrest.

The rivalry between the peace chiefs as a body and other men of status among the Iroquois may have several causes. Fenton (1955:335) feels that the peace and war chiefs may reflect age-grading, for the war chiefs tended to be younger men while the peace chiefs graduated from their ranks (though strictly speaking no man was eligible to be a sachem who had shed blood). Furthermore, there exists the class of Iroquois chiefs who attain their position through merit rather than inheritance. This group is known as pine tree chiefs, or simply "chiefs" by Morgan. The pine tree chiefs and to a lesser extent the war chiefs were allowed some influence in civil councils, but according to present native theory they ought to be subordinate to the peace chiefs in the governance of state. Fenton put forward the hypothesis that the Iroquois may have developed the institution of pine tree chief as a safety valve for the ambitions of young leaders whose potential competition for the limited number of hereditary peace chieftainships might have wrecked the League. Peace chiefs, who were ideally characterized as men of forbearance (with skins traditionally "seven spans thick"), patience, judiciousness, and conciliation, would be at a disadvantage if they were forced to compete with a group of men known for their charisma, daring, and flamboyance. Further, the many talented Iroquois, who would be denied positions of prominence, could be utilized for the well-being of the League. Of course, an outstanding individual might be borrowed for a chief's position if the matron holding the validating wampum had no eligible heir in her own matrilineage and "hung the title around the neck" of a nonlineage individual for his lifetime, but here also difficulties arose, for a borrowed chief often attempted to pass his title on to his own lineage.

Yet, in spite of these institutional accommodations to different human traits and abilities, it remains a fact that each situation which calls for action mobilizes the actors not only according to the ideal constructs of the culture, but also in terms of strong personalities and various idiosyncratic factors operative at the moment. Consequently, one is not astonished to learn that the wishes of the peace chiefs did not always prevail, and that either an amalgam of the desires of the various factions occurred, or one faction precipitated actions not necessarily approved by the others. In this context also, Fenton has been in the forefront of scholars pointing to the very prevalent factionalism among Native Americans and among the Iroquois. The reasons for splitting into competing groups are many, but surely one of the most prominent today is, and most likely in the past was, the allegiance of the population to one or another of the pine tree chiefs or warriors and his group rather than to the council of the peace chiefs as a whole. Speakers were obviously admired in the past; and today, as well, a persuasive orator can carry a meeting. But it is also quite characteristic for various factions to meet in private and determine a course of behavior, which they then attempt to have legitimized by forcing the action and confronting the other factions with a *fait accompli*. Especially today, with an active group of young progressives who do not have traditional chieftainships, but who consider themselves the contemporary counterparts of the war leaders and pine tree chiefs, there is apt to emerge an attitude of impatience with the leadership of the more traditional peace chiefs. These young activists may call themselves today either "warriors" or "chiefs," and assume roles they believe to have been appropriate to such persons in the past. On the other hand, there are some peace chiefs who also believe in much of the program of the modern "warriors," and who therefore are willing to go along with their planning, particularly at Six Nations Reserve, where the hereditary chiefs have been displaced by an elected council since 1924 and consequently are deeply aggrieved at their loss of legal power.

A dramatic modern illustration of the complex political accommodations among peace chiefs and chiefs and warriors occurred on March 5, 1959, at Six Nations Reserve near Brantford, Ontario, when a coalition of the more conservative factions staged an uprising against the elected and government-sanctioned council. One can profitably examine the details of this uprising, as well as its consequences, following Fenton's suggestion that a good technique for ethnohistory is the examination of modern events in order to help explain similar situations in the culture in the past, a process he termed "upstreaming."

On that day, a faction of the Iroquois, who represented themselves sometimes as "the Longhouse People," and sometimes as "the hereditaries" (because they wished the reinstatement of the hereditary peace chiefs), or "the conservatives," and who consciously attempted to perpetuate what they believed to have been old Iroquois Culture, marched some thirteen hundred strong to the council house in Ohsweken, where the elected council was in session. Upon their arrival at the scene, however, the front council door was locked, and the councillors, upon the advice of the Indian Department, escaped via the rear door. Baffled, yet determined, the insurgents removed the door from its hinges, surged into the council house, and declared themselves in sovereign command of the Iroquois Nation.

A proclamation announced the nullification of the Indian Act. The Iroquois would be a nation within a nation—Iroquoia within Canada—and they would not be ruled by the dictates of an oppressive usurper any more, but by the principles of their forebears. The abolition of the elected council was the first order of business. Hereditary chiefs would once again be the *de jure* and *de facto* rulers. It is not surprising that the uprising, which had long been desired by this coalition, was primarily conceived, planned, and executed by the hereditary chiefs in cooperation with some warriors.

The uprising was precipitated by a conversation between representatives of the hereditary chiefs—mainly warriors and clan mothers—and the Canadian Minister of Citizenship and Immigration, who at that time had jurisdiction over Indian affairs. The mothers explained the existing factions on the Reserve, particularly describing those who followed the elected council and those who favored the traditional system. The details were complex, the discussion was probably not absolutely clear, and the Minister is reported to have commented, "you'll have to settle that by yourselves." Thereupon, the clan mothers returned to the Onondaga Longhouse (where the hereditary chiefs had been holding their usual monthly council in exile since their deposition in 1924) and reported their conversation, as well as the Minister's remark, to the council. The peace chiefs were impressed by the action of the clan mothers and the warriors, and they also took the Minister's comment to be a mandate. Thereupon, they decided that settling the matter among themselves meant combining forces and taking over the functions of the elected council once more and establishing themselves as the legitimate government. The uprising was planned and followed shortly thereafter.

Upon the initial success of the uprising, the hereditary chiefs assembled in council in the traditional fashion and, adhering to the traditional procedures which aimed at a unanimous decision, they began to discuss further measures. One of their first moves was to establish their own law enforcement apparatus to replace the R.C.M.P., who had been residing on the Reserve and had long been taken as a symbol of Indian subjugation. One hundred and thirty-three "Iroquois Police," many of them belonging to that group who styled themselves as warriors, were appointed. They were not only to maintain order but also to administer a kind of popular justice as well. It was perhaps this decision, more than any other, which transferred the real power of the peace chiefs to the individual warriors, who then acted on their own and refused to be ruled by the more cautious decisions of the Confederate council. Furthermore, a general program of economic affairs, designed to make the Reserve self-sufficient and independent, was announced. It had a rather communal emphasis (which later helped to discredit it), involving the pooling of farm and other equipment for the use of all Iroquois in need, which to some looked akin to clan cooperation and to others akin to socialism.

Nor did the insurgents neglect what they considered to be traditional religious practices, and though some of them were Christian rather than Longhouse people, the speeches and prayers in the council house were directed to the Great Creator, in the traditional Longhouse manner, for he was believed instrumental in the success of the venture.

Beyond the measures mentioned above, and perhaps the expressed desire for the recovery of confiscated lands, there was no clear program of action. One had the feeling that the uprising, though long desired and often envisaged, actually took its partisans somewhat by surprise. The culturally prescribed deliberations by the council, with unanimous plans of action, had not taken place, and, of course, the emotionalism of the occasion and the disposition of some of the younger warriors made careful planning difficult. Uprisings in general take their participants by storm, and it would not be quite fair to expect more of the Confederate council than of any other political committee after a sudden change of government.

The conservatives and their followers inhabited the council house day and night, partly for fear of ejection, and partly to symbolize their sovereignty. However, on March 12, at 3 A.M., the Canadian government sent in a contingent of the R.C.M.P., and after some scuffling, especially with the women, they terminated the uprising. The elected council was reestablished and returned to normal deliberations in the Ohsweken council house.

Perhaps even more interesting than the uprising itself, and more symptomatic of the content of Iroquois culture, were the repercussions of its inevitable collapse. As an analysis of factionalism might well predict, the accusations and recriminations concerning the responsibility for the failure of the insurgency gave rise to an even more intense partisanship than had existed before the event. For the uprising forced many to acknowledge an open allegiance not only to the hereditary council or to the elected council, but also to certain chiefs and warriors. Over the objection of many, during the brief tenure of the supporters of the Confederate council, an attempt was made to poll all those loyal to the uprising, and the warriors in particular threatened that nonsigners would be the first to be exiled from the Reserve. However, even under duress, half the members of the Reserve failed to sign, and in actual fact, fewer than half the adults signed, since a large percentage of the signatures collected in favor of the new government were those of minors. This failure to present a solid front to the Canadian government was thereafter adduced as a major cause of the swift return to the *status quo ante.* In view of the traditional Iroquois theme that unanimity alone can bring satisfactory results, there developed the distinct belief among the conservatives that treachery by their own people had been responsible for their failure. Under ordinary conditions the Iroquois leaders at Six Nations are not naive in matters of relative power, but the intense involvement of the groups in this particular uprising seems to have blurred their political realism. That the Canadian government would not possibly allow a native minority group within its boundaries to abrogate the Indian Act and to declare itself a sovereign state, and that the government would inevitably suppress a separatist movement, did not fully register with all those involved. Instead, the tensions which existed between the members of the coalition, and which had been submerged in their common struggle, now found a focus of expression. The failure of the uprising spawned a more intense factionalism, at least for a time, than had existed previously, and the rivalries displayed were more varied than the predictable competition between the "hereditaries" and the "loyalists" (the faction loyal to the Candadian government and the elected council).

Not surprisingly, the undefined position of the "leader" of the Confederate chiefs or of the uprising was one of the causes of factionalism. Nominally, the Confederate chiefs at that time recognized Thadodaho as the moving force of the uprising, for they invoked the rule that as the first Onondaga chief he was traditionally the *ex officio* leader in matters of state. In addition, the incumbent in that position happened to have a very forceful personality and was highly respected by the entire community, although due to his advanced age, the actual control of affairs fell to his son and grandson—peace chiefs as well, but borrowed into matrilineages other than their own, so that there was a hint that they were "exceptions" in their positions.

All three chiefs were members of the Onondaga Longhouse religious community at Six Nations, and Thadodaho and his son were noted ritualists there too. Naturally, they were instrumental in persuading that Longhouse congregation to follow their leadership and support the uprising.

Many members at Six Nations Reserve (including at the time the influential peace chief Deskahe *(teskáhe:?)* and the activist group known as the Mohawk Workers) believed that church and state were separate institutions, meaning that adherents to the Longhouse religion did not necessarily have to support the council of chiefs—a secular organ of government—nor did adherents to the Confederate council necessarily have to practice the Longhouse religion. The latter proposition has long been true at Six Nations, where Christians have held hereditary chieftainships along with their Longhouse colleagues.

After the chiefs lost their secular power in 1924, however, many of them, especially those who were followers of the code of Handsome Lake and who had been invested in the traditional manner "with an ox" at a Condolence Ceremony, retreated into the Longhouse, where they claimed important leadership roles. At Onondaga Longhouse, where Thadodaho and his family were members, acting both as peace chiefs and as Longhouse deacons, the integration of the two institutions was particularly marked. As was to be expected, the original religious personnel and their adherents resented the assumption of religious functions by the chiefs. Consequently, after the Longhouse had been persuaded to support the uprising, only to have it fail, many Longhouse members felt that their religious community had lost ground and had become discredited because of the meddlesome activity of the chiefs. As a result, an active faction formed against these chiefs and their followers within Onondaga Longhouse and also within some of the other Longhouses. General sentiment against chiefs in the Longhouse was not an innovation at Six Nations Reserve, for Lower Cayuga Longhouse had long been known for sentiments of this sort; in fact, any chief entering the Longhouse is said symbolically to catch his antlers on the lintel of the doorway and to enter to worship without his title. But what was remarkable and rather unexpected after the uprising was that Onondaga Longhouse, known for its tolerance of chiefs and for their relative power in that congregation, should take on some of the ideology of Lower Cayuga. Processes of this nature, quite unique to a specific setting, yet not completely arbitrary, were also brought to the attention of researchers by Fenton (1951a) in his comments on local diversity among the Iroquois. Here was a specific instance of a locally accepted cultural pattern spreading to other communities on the Reserve.

Another focus of leadership in the uprising, aside from the group around Thadodaho, was Chief Deskahe, in the League roster the last Cayuga chief. Deskahe had been prominently associated with nativistic groups, who were most similar to the traditional "warriors" and who considered themselves as such, even if they were not formally recognized by all of the conservative community. Such organizations as the Mohawk Workers and the Indian Defense League professed aims identical to those of the Confederate chiefs (particularly the recovery of power by the Confederate council), yet many of the members were Christian. Deskahe, feeling that the revival of the Confederate council was the primary condition for the reestablishment of Indian freedom, openly sanctioned the participation of Christian chiefs and Christian sympathizers in the uprising, even though he personally was one of the most prominent Longhouse personalities at Six Nations. Despite the separation of church and state accepted by many of the conservatives, there were and still are others who feel that Christianity ought to disqualify a man from Confederate chieftainship, and that if a matrilineal family owning a chief's title converts from the traditional religion, the title should be transferred to a Longhouse family. The existence of Christian chiefs in the Confederate council, according to the beliefs of a large number of traditionalists, invalidates the legitimacy of the council. When Deskahe then sponsored the Christian activists, he was blamed for willfully thwarting the true nature of a genuine "Iroquois" uprising, and a large faction formed to oppose him and his followers.

Finally, a third issue which came to the fore and split the conservatives was a difference in the interpretation of the roles of the peace chiefs, who should represent the Reserve in dealing with the Canadian government. Deskahe and Thadodaho claimed it should be Thadodaho, and they were supported in this claim by the bilaterally extended family of the latter (an instance of modern family solidarity, which has partly supplanted the aboriginal matrilineal family ties). However, several of the Longhouse families, especially at Onondaga Longhouse, claimed it should be Hononwirehdonh, for he is considered to "direct the minds of all the nations." Had Hononwirehdonh appealed to the Canadian government, they argued, that government would surely have realized the legality of the Iroquois position and would have reestablished the League. A faction favoring Hononwirehdonh bitterly opposed both Thadodaho's and Deskahe's groups.

Interestingly, in these factional quarrels the failure of the uprising was blamed largely upon procedural errors rather than upon substantive factors. Such a reaction is not at all surprising in view of the traditional Iroquois emphasis upon procedure, not only in the political but also in the religious, medical, and occult aspects of the culture. Nor is the phenomenon of blaming failure upon incidental factors unusual in the history of nativistic movements or in other occurrences of extreme factionalism. It is manifestly a technique for saving face.

Significantly, at Six Nations, when the direct political agitation against the Canadian government ceased and the Iroquois realized that they had lost this particular conflict, much of the struggle was transferred and continued on the psychical plane. Blaming their failure on each other, every group felt that its purpose had been vitiated by every other group, and each group felt that its failure was the result of deliberate and willful actions. Consequently, one of the main weapons which members of the various factions used against their opponents was gossip. Another weapon was attempted ostracism from the Longhouse, usually by letting a person know, if only indirectly, that he was not welcome there. Onondaga Longhouse experienced the greatest disruption by attempts of this sort, which is understandable, since it was the center of two of the main factional disagreements within the conservative community.

The ensuing suspicion, gossip, derogation, and attempted ostracism caused great psychical tensions among the conservative Iroquois; and, indeed, some of the most dramatic consequences of the uprising were the psychical disturbances, including paranoia and fear of witchcraft, which pervaded the Reserve. Many of the participants in the uprising experienced repetitive and ominous dreams, suffered accidents, or felt ill, complaining either of lack of strength ("just going down") or of specific symptoms such as pains, rashes, convulsions, and paralysis, all of which appear to have been psychosomatic. Both white doctors and herbalists were frequently consulted, but their prescriptions, if indeed they found an organic cause or saw a symptom they might treat, were useless. The patients' luck and health did not improve. Suspecting, therefore, a typically "Indian" ailment, which is one caused either by a violation of traditional rules or by witchcraft, the patients consulted fortunetellers, as is proper in such circumstances. (These specialists diagnose or "see" in tea or cards, by scrying, or by use of special medicines, the cause of the ailment, and they usually prescribe a procedure for the cure.) Immediately upon the suppression of the uprising and for some considerable time afterwards, the fortunetellers "saw" witchcraft as the cause of the trouble, and they usually identified the witch—by indirection, to be sure—as a well-known member of a faction in opposition to the one to which the patient belonged. A typical diagnosis was: "I see two men, chiefs at that, at your Longhouse (Onondaga) who burned tobacco and who want you to die. Your grave is all dug and waiting."

The patient, a prominent member of the Hononwirehdonh faction, immediately identified the two chiefs as the leaders of the Thadodaho faction. He was ordered to "pass" a dance as a cure and recovered from a completely debilitating back ailment. He felt that he had only narrowly escaped death.

Never could anyone remember so many "doings" (curing rituals) to have been "passed" in a year as occurred in the winter after the uprising. One of the principal speakers who communicated the patients' desires to the appropriate Spirit Forces by burning Indian tobacco said that he "must have thrown one hundred pounds of tobacco into the stove," and though this is doubtless an exaggeration since only a pinch of tobacco is burned at a time, it does convey the sense of the large number of events which impressed the ritualist.

Another example of the fear of witchcraft after the uprising was the organization by one of the chiefs of a posse of his followers and family to guard their homes and lives. Since Iroquois witches assume the shapes of animals and travel to the houses of their victims at night, the men were instructed to fire at moving animals, for shooting witches is an accepted form of overcoming witchcraft. The next morning one of the hunting dogs of a member of the family was found shot to death, and on the following night the same fate was suffered by their other dog. These events were not deemed accidents; rather, the dogs had sacrificed themselves by giving warning of approaching evil, or perhaps even by absorbing the spirit of the witch. A reverent burial was advised for the dogs. And, soon afterwards, two members of the family had violent convulsive seizures, requiring several men to subdue them. No physiological cause could be discerned, and a fortuneteller was immediately consulted. As expected, he diagnosed witchcraft on the part of one of the factions opposed to the family of this chief, and prescribed one of his own medicines, which alone would protect the family from further witching. Medication had to continue until the fortuneteller released the family. The victims drank two to three gallons of medicine per week for a year, and only when their fortuneteller died did the prescription die with him. But quite aside from medication, many "doings" had been prescribed and performed.

Such case histories were not uncommon, and they point to the interesting conclusion that ritual activity in the Iroquois medical complex (which includes counter-witchcraft) increased markedly after the uprising. This reaction was not fortuitous, since the most deeply sanctioned values in the modern Iroquois community at Six Nations are values concerning the medical complex. To an average Iroquois, the numerous rituals and beliefs associated with his health are of paramount importance, and it must be said that health means not only bodily well-being, but also good luck and freedom from witchcraft. The political turmoil, and in particular the emotional strains of the uprising, were reflected in the state of health of the participating groups, which on the whole gave rise to a higher degree of ritual activity.

Since there is no institution which so consistently displays native Iroquois traits and complexes as do the institutions dealing with health, the resurgence of medical rituals after the uprising had a general tendency to revitalize the traditional culture as a whole. Therefore, the disruption of the personal relationships, which was the inevitable consequence of the bitter factional feelings within the conservative community, could to some extent be repaired by ritual activity which drew together the ritualists involved. The medical rituals involved peculiarly Iroquois features: the music, the dance, the False Faces, the prayers which embody Iroquois cosmology, and the beliefs which are recognizable as Iroquois from the earliest documents. Thus the medical activity of the insurgents perpetuated and even revitalized some of the traditional culture. A summary of the happenings might be as follows: the uprising caused an increase in factionalism; the factionalism caused, in an already suspicious society, a fear of witchcraft; the fear of witchcraft caused ill health; ill health elicited the curative rituals; these rituals acted as conservative agents, and traditional values were given new life.

What does this process imply for the future? First of all, none of the inherent problems were solved by the uprising. Neither the ambiguous relations among the chiefs nor the relations between peace chiefs and warriors and pine tree chiefs changed in any way, nor was the discontent with the elected council and the Canadian government removed. At the end of the uprising the recriminations were even more bitter than at the beginning, and they were finally smoothed over only in the realm of personal relations. People regained their composure by interacting with ritualists and with members of the various secret societies who came to cure them, and they renewed their belief in the efficacy of "old" Iroquois medicines. If anything, they felt more loyal to Iroquoia than before the uprising, and they wished fervently to preserve their distinctive culture. Does this portend another uprising? Can one "downstream" into the future? Let the reader conjecture.

NOTE

1. There is considerable variation in the spellings of the chiefs' titles, partly because these titles occur in all the Northern Iroquoian languages and partly because they have been represented traditionally in different ways in

these languages. I have chosen one traditional spelling for each title throughout. The first time a title appears I have given the phonemic spelling in the
appropriate language as this appears in Volume 15 of the *Handbook of North
American Indians,* (Tooker 1978:424–25).

Chapter Ten

Seth Newhouse and the Grand River Confederacy at Mid-Nineteenth Century

Sally M. Weaver

Introduction[1]

Throughout his careeer Bill Fenton has had a continuing curiosity about the traditions of the Iroquois Confederacy, the federal council of fifty hereditary chiefs created by the legendary Deganawidah in the mid-sixteenth century. In studying the Confederacy, Fenton used the standard ethnographic and ethnohistorical approaches (Fenton 1946a, 1949), but he also used what might be called the *Indian history* method, the subject of this paper. Here Fenton examined the manuscripts and mnemonic devices of native Iroquoian authorities who, working independently or with ethnologists, tried to record and preserve their own political traditions (Fenton 1944, 1950, 1972). Fenton's esteem for native authorities, and his respect for their own perspective of their traditions, is nowhere more evident than in his treatment of a remarkable manuscript on the Confederacy dated at Ohsweken, Ontario, 1885. Although the manuscript had come from the Grand River Reserve in Ontario where the traditions of the Confederacy have been best preserved, its author, Da-yo-de-ka-ne, remained a mystery at the time the manuscript was deposited in the American Philosophical Society Library in Philadelphia during the 1940s.

The manuscript, some 312 pages written in "Indian English," contained accounts of the Deganawidah legend of the founding of the League, as well as lists of clan names and some later correspondence from the 1890s. Although the author, Da-yo-de-ka-ne, had gone to great lengths to sytematize the rules governing the deliberations of the chiefs in council, his stated purpose for undertaking the work was to reduce the confusion surrounding the appointment of hereditary chiefs. Whether these confusions were recognized by others in the author's community in 1885, however, was unclear from the manuscript.

On learning of the manuscript in 1948, Fenton set out to determine who Da-yo-de-ka-ne was and why he had spent countless hours carefully recording the lore of the Confederacy (Fenton 1949a). Through careful comparison with other manuscripts in Philadelphia and in the Smithsonian Institution, Fenton attributed the authorship to Seth Newhouse, a Mohawk-Onondaga (1842–1921) of the Grand River Reserve (Fig. 10.1). Newhouse was the most productive Iroquoian scribe of the nineteenth century and during the late 1890s he worked with J.N.B. Hewitt translating his manuscript (Newhouse 1885) and other Iroquoian myths into Mohawk, the language in which he excelled (Fenton 1968:38–47). Although his manuscript remains unpublished, a heavily edited version was printed in Parker's *Constitution of the Five Nations* (Parker 1916; Fenton 1968:38–47).

In recounting the fate of the manuscript, Fenton suggested (1949a:145) that Newhouse's failure to receive official endorsement of his work from the Grand River council may well have been due to the prominent role Newhouse gave the Mohawk tribe in the history and ritual of the Confederacy. This prominence was absent in the council's later approved official version of its history (Scott 1912) which came from the memory of Chief John Arthur Gibson, an eminent authority on the Confederacy at Grand River (Fenton 1949a:145). Hewitt, less generous with his views, claimed the council's rejection was due to Newhouse's failure to appreciate the basic structure of the Confederacy (1917:430). Like Hewitt, Goldenweiser also noted several differences between the Newhouse and Gibson versions, among them Newhouse's concern over disagreements within the council and a general lack of loyalty to the Confederacy (1916:435).

In assessing the utility of Newhouse's manuscript for Iroquoian research, Fenton departed from Hewitt's approach which assumed there was a single correct version of the League's history and structure. Instead, Fenton argued that the manuscript should be considered in its proper historical context at Grand River, suggesting that Newhouse had "unwittingly" recorded Grand River history in the late nineteenth century (1949a:158). Although no historical research had been done on the Grand River council at the time he was writing, Fenton speculated that Newhouse's text reflected conditions of political uncertainty on the reserve in the early 1880s when Newhouse was preparing the manuscript. He went on to suggest that Newhouse had recorded the history in an attempt to justify the retention of the

Fig. 10.1. Seth Newhouse and two daughters, Six Nations Reserve, Ontario. Photo by F. W. Waugh, 1912. Courtesy the National Museum of Man, Ottawa, Neg. no. 14714

Confederacy whose future was endangered by reformers wanting to replace it with an elected municipal government.

This paper substantiates Fenton's suspicions that Newhouse's work reflected the political conditions at Grand River in the mid-nineteenth century. In a more general way it confirms Fenton's point that understanding such documents requires a knowledge of the historical context in which they originated. Having completed an historical analysis of the council's records for the period it governed the reserve (1847–1924), I can now link major historical developments in the Grand River council to Newhouse's version of the constitution, much as Fenton suspected. Although many linkages could be demonstrated, three examples will suffice to confirm Fenton's contentions: (1) the Mohawk prominence in the council, (2) the early origin of a reform movement to establish an elected local government, and (3) the existence of difficulties in the council over its decision-making procedures.

SETH NEWHOUSE

By placing Newhouse's manuscript in its historical context at Grand River, we can also shed further light on Newhouse's personal career and possibly on the conditions which prompted him to undertake the work initially.

Born in 1842 to an Onondaga mother, Kate, and an Upper Mohawk father, Nicholas Newhouse, he was raised in the Christian tradition and well educated for his day by the New England Company (Angelican Church), probably at the Mohawk Institute on the outskirts of Brantford (see Johnston in this volume). Through his mother he was a member of the Grey Swift Hawk clan (Fenton 1949a:153), but there is no evidence that he was in line for a hereditary chieftain title. He was bright, spoke Mohawk more fluently than Onondaga, and from his youth had a keen interest in political affairs on the reserve. He farmed for a living but, unlike his brothers and sister, he did not play an active role in the Grand River Methodist Church where he was finally buried in 1921. Throughout most of his adult life he traveled extensively to the Iroquoian reserves in Ontario, Quebec and New York State, collecting information on the history of the Confederacy. As a self-appointed historian, Seth Newhouse's basic ambition was to record and preserve the traditions of the League, and indeed to correct what he considered to be the erring ways of the Grand River council. Being as much Mohawk as Onondaga in his upbringing, Newhouse was well acquainted with the political prominence of the Mohawks at Grand River, a prominence that was clearly reflected in his manuscript where, among other things, he overemphasized the importance of the Mohawks being the first tribe to accept confederation and gave the Mohawks an explicit veto power in the council's deliberations (Newhouse 1885:18).

MOHAWK PROMINENCE AND THE GRAND RIVER CONFEDERACY

The Mohawks, the most populous of the Six Nations tribes in the valley, have always had a preeminent position in Grand River politics. They have taken great pride in the fact that the vast tract of Grand Valley land, which the Six Nations received in 1784 following the American Revolution, was specifically granted to the Mohawks and "such others of the Six Nations Indians" who sought continued protection of the Crown (Canada 1891(1):251–52). Despite Joseph Brant's actions in disposing of over two-thirds of the tract by the 1790s (Johnston 1964), it is also known that the land, and indeed their reserve, existed because of Joseph Brant's leadership in originally settling the bands along the river in 1784. After resettlement Brant retained powerful political control as Indian Superintendent to the Six Nations, and the influence of the Brant family and the Mohawks in general persisted in the council and the community long after Brant's death in 1807. Even though the Confederacy council became the major Iroquois vehicle for dealing with the Indian Department in managing the Six Nations affairs, the Mohawk chiefs continued to be extremely influential figures both inside and outside the council. Their influence was especially pronounced after 1847 when the tribes were consolidated on the reserve near Brantford and the hereditary council began a lengthy process of adapting its procedures and jurisdiction to meet the demands placed upon it as a local government under the aegis of the Indian Department.

During the 1850s and 1860s, the Grand River Confederacy council contained anywhere from forty-seven to sixty-seven chiefs, depending on the number of vacancies to be filled at any one time. The total number of chiefs included the possible fifty principal hereditary chiefs, their assistant chiefs who were equally active in council affairs, and the self-made chiefs (pine tree chiefs) who were appointed because of their outstanding leadership abilities. In addition there was a handful of war chiefs from the War of 1812.

Deliberations among the chiefs were conducted in Mohawk, the official language of the council, and mainly according to the traditional form of debate—beginning with the Mohawk-Seneca side of council, moving across the council house to the side of the Cayuga-Oneida and dependent nations (Tuscarora, Delaware, Nanticoke and Tutelo), then coming back to the Mohawk Speaker of the Council for announcement to the Onondagas. If the decision was unanimous and judged by the Onondagas to be beneficial to the Confederacy, the Onondaga chiefs endorsed it, but if they felt it endangered the Confederacy, the decision was returned for reconsideration. Unanimity among the regularly attending twenty to thirty chiefs required lengthy deliberations. The importance of ensuring that the final decisions were correctly summarized and translated for the government Superintendent fell to the council's Speaker and Interpreter. Both these offices were powerful positions in the routine management of the council's affairs, and both were held by a succession of well respected Mohawk chiefs from Joseph Brant's time until after the turn of the twentieth century. Through these offices the Mohawks could exert persuasive influence, although not control, on the council's deliberations and final decisions. The additional fact that most of the Mohawk chiefs also spoke English, and some of them could read and write it, gave them even greater power, allowing them to debate issues directly with the Superintendent, to defend their positions in a forthright manner, and to read legislation and government reports for their own information without having to depend on interpreters whom they might not trust. Thus although the Mohawks did not numerically dominate the council, they held powerful advantages over the other chiefs and in controversial issues often managed to get their own way.

This was clearly illustrated in 1863, for example, when the council decided to move its meetings from the old Onondaga council house (and Longhouse) in Middleport, on the north side of the Grand River, to the new village of Ohsweken in the center of the reserve where a new council house was to be built. The move was made against the heated objections of the Onondaga chiefs whose traditional right to determine the seat of the council was well known. Indeed, in the face of Onondaga opposition, the powerful Speaker of Council, Mohawk Chief John Smoke Johnson, announced that the Firekeepers had no right "to dictate" to the council when the other tribes had agreed on the decision (SNAM 1862:369).

Furthermore, outside the council, the Mohawk influence in the community was largely uncontested by any other tribe. The Mohawks had adopted Christianity and agriculture more readily than the other tribes, and beginning in 1830, they had taken greater advantage of the superior education offered by the New England Company. By the 1860s the Mohawks, Oneidas, Tuscaroras and, to a lesser extent, the Upper Cayugas—known collectively as the upper tribes because of their initial residence up river—contained the vast majority of Christians. The religious division of 20 percent Longhouse and 80 percent Christian became fixed at this time and has remained the pattern to the present day. Being better educated, the men of the upper tribes became candidates for the highly prized jobs with the council and, given their stronger farming skills, they became wealthier than others by reserve standards. Being more acculturated than the lower tribes, they were willing to promote and accept reforms in many areas of community life including the council.

Throughout the nineteenth century, but with certain notable exceptions, the Mohawks persistently defended the continuity of the Confederacy at Grand River but, unlike the lower tribes (Onondaga, Lower Cayuga and Seneca), they did not believe the Longhouse religious tradition was a necessary precondition for maintaining the Confederacy council. Led politically by the powerful Onondaga chiefs, the lower tribes were increasingly disturbed by the tendencies of the upper tribal chiefs to accept modifications in the council's procedures. In short, the Onondagas were traditionalists who firmly believed that the conventional procedures of the council were both adequate and appropriate for the purposes of local government. They adamantly opposed federal legislation in principle although in practice they had fought hard in the 1850s to keep legislation which protected reserve lands from taxation. In contrast, the Mohawks were experimenters and sometimes innovators. They were willing to try new procedures and adopt new policies in council as long as their control over local affairs was not endangered. The Mohawks increasingly assumed the role of middleman in the council between the Onondagas and the Superintendent, holding a more moderate position on government regulations than the Onondagas, but defending local autonomy very forcefully against the Superintendent's encroachments. When legislation threatened to diminish their power, the Mohawks were even more vociferous than the Onondagas in asserting their objections and often more successful.

As a young man growing up on the reserve Seth Newhouse was familiar with the two political traditions of the progressive Mohawks and conventional Onondagas. He also experienced the widespread political unrest caused by the first attempt in the community to replace the Confederacy with an elected council. The concern in his manuscript for remaining loyal to the Confederacy by honoring its rules and rituals is undoubtedly a response to these early reform pressures.

THE FIRST MOVEMENT FOR AN ELECTED LOCAL GOVERNMENT

In late 1861 and early 1862 a young Upper Mohawk warrior, Isaac Powless, circulated a petition on the reserve promoting the establishment of an elected local government. Powless was an Anglican and, like Newhouse, well educated for his day. He gained most of his support from the Upper Mohawks although predictably not from their chiefs. Both Powless and his supporters were heavily influenced by the widespread movement for responsible or elected government that swept the province in the 1850s. But they were equally influenced by the final bankruptcy of the Grand River Navigation Company in which the Six Nations, as major stockholders, lost their entire investment. As a result the reformers argued for an elected form of reserve government in which the council would be directly responsible to the electorate, and for educational qualifications for councillors which would better equip them to protect the property and rights of the Six Nations against white incursions.

The council's response to Powless's petition clearly illustrates the tendency for confederacies to splinter under severe stress (Fenton 1975:144). Even though the council unanimously opposed Powless's reforms, it became hopelessly divided over what strategy to adopt. In the end two separate delegations of chiefs visited the Superintendent to try to dissuade him from accepting Powless's proposals. The first delegation consisted of Onondaga chiefs, led by the newly appointed chiefs John and George Buck who jointly carried the functions of Wampum Keeper for the Confederacy. Although arguing against the need for reform, they took a *laissez faire* approach to the problem, claiming that if the Mohawks and upper tribesmen wanted to follow the ways of the white man they were free to do so. The second delegation was of Mohawk chiefs headed by the Speaker of Council, John Smoke Johnson, and his son G. H. M. Johnson, the Interpreter for council. The Mohawks were annoyed that the Onondagas had acted without official council approval in visiting the Superintendent. They felt that the Onondagas' independent action had demonstrated the council's inability to manage its own affairs, thus making it especially vulnerable to the charges of the reformers. But the Mohawks were even more displeased at the Onondagas' willingness to consider dividing the reserve under separate forms of government (SNAM 1862:206–9). The incident had demonstrated yet another difference between the Mohawks and Onondagas: the Onondagas tended to disengage and withdraw from the Confederacy in times of stress, while the Mohawks tended to confront issues and oppose any fragmentation in the council.

When the Indian Department took little interest in the petition, the issue subsided, but not before the dissension had deepened the cleavage between the Mohawks and Onondagas in the council.

Although pressures for an elected government did not disappear during the 1870s, they diminished after the chiefs rejected a later petition from the reformers requesting formal representation in the council. But some of the chiefs clearly felt that changes were needed within the council and the community. As a result, pressures for change shifted from external critics, like Powless, to the upper tribal chiefs within the council, particularly the Mohawks who sought to expand the council's jurisdiction in the fields of social welfare, education, and farming. Because the lower tribal chiefs considered these changes unwarranted, the strains within the council became severe. Heated debates and lengthy deliberations often failed to produce decisions, or, more frequently, produced a series of decisions, each reversing the former. Predictably, the chiefs began to focus attention on the form of their deliberations and consider ways in which they might streamline the council's operations.

It is not surprising that Seth Newhouse's manuscript reflected the preoccupation with procedures in the council, especially those for handling disagreements, for he was directly party to some of these discussions in the 1870s.

Strains Within the Council

Amendments to the Indian Act, the federal legislation governing Indian Affairs in Canada, invariably raised excited debate among the chiefs over whether they should "accept" its application to their reserve, or remain under their "ancient rules and laws." The 1869 Indian Act (Canada 1869), which gave the government the power to impose elected band councils on reserves, was no exception. In many cases, but certainly not all, the debate was academic, for the Indian Department had the authority to implement the legislation and to limit the actions of the chiefs in any matters requiring financial commitments. But the debates were important because they served to reaffirm the principle of the chiefs' authority and their determination to administer the reserve as they, not the Indian Department, preferred.

Unrest in the council over the 1869 Indian Act began as soon as the Act was passed because the Onondaga chiefs were particularly unhappy with some of its provisions. But they were even more upset at the government's contentious timber regulations of 1873 (Canada 1874) which prohibited the commercial sale of lumber from the reserve. Both of these edicts so angered the Onondagas that Chief George Buck, an able spokesman for the lower tribes, eventually demanded, although unsuccessfully, that the lower tribes be given a separate part of the reserve for their own where government regulations would presumably not apply. The upper tribal chiefs, being equally wary about legislative infringments on their authority, took a more selective view of the Act, finding some of its provisions and the timber regulations acceptable. The deep feelings generated by this issue became the source of a bitter confrontation between the upper and lower chiefs to the point where, in January of 1875, the Onondaga chiefs again acted independently of the council, sending a petition to Ottawa protesting the imposition of the laws. The petition, signed by Seth Newhouse, informed the government that the chiefs were badly divided over the 1869 law, claiming that the division could have been avoided if the proper deliberative procedures were used in the council. These procedures gave the Onondagas the right to reject decisions—such as those supporting the Indian Act— that endangered the Confederacy. After criticizing the upper chiefs for an alleged failure to grant their longhouse funds for repair, the petitioners pointed out that the Mohawks had refused to sanction their newly appointed chiefs, Seth Newhouse being among them. But the purpose of the petition was to reaffirm their loyalty to the Confederacy. To ensure the continuity of their traditions they intended "to draw up a plan or scheme of our ancient Rule [sic] to be passed in the Dominion Parliament" (PAC, RG 10, Red Series, Vol. 1949, File 4355).

In the end the petition was repudiated in full council, a fate befalling all such independent actions of chiefs acting outside the council's authority. It was also firmly rejected by the government on the grounds that the Indian Act applied to the reserve regardless of the chiefs' opinions. But the petition is significant because it sheds light on the possible origin of the Newhouse manuscript. It is highly likely that the decision of the lower tribal chiefs to seek parliamentary approval for the Confederacy's procedures was prompted by Newhouse because this strategy was completely foreign to the Onondagas. Traditionally, the Onondagas at Grand River had not sought government validation for their actions or beliefs, and in time of stress their standard reaction was to withdraw, either by suggesting that a reserve of their own be established or simply by boycotting council meetings for a while. Furthermore, even if the notion of codifying the Confederacy's procedures (which Newhouse did in his manuscript 1885) originated with the lower tribal chiefs, the petition is still important in understanding Seth Newhouse's political career because he was one of the new chiefs the Mohawks declared "illegal" and refused to confirm.

Newhouse's appointment appears to have been that of a "self-made" chief, the term used at Grand River for a pinetree chief, for Newhouse was not in line for a hereditary title. His signature on the repudiated petition would not have inspired the Mohawk chiefs to confirm his title even at a later date as the practice of the council required. Nevertheless, after his rejection, Newhouse attended council as a chief, even signing requisitions for band funds. But his position remained ambiguous and his participation lasted for only part of 1875, possibly because of his traveling to other reserves where he collected information on the Confederacy's history.

During the next few years (1876–80) when Newhouse was preparing an early version of his manuscript (Newhouse 1880), the council experienced a very innovative period in which the chiefs expanded their jurisdiction into several new fields. They experimented with ad hoc committees for the sick and needy and readily granted the use of the council house for any fund-raising activities believed to "advance" the Six Nations people. They provided small grants to longhouses and churches for repairs as they did in 1881 when the Seneca members split off from the Onondaga longhouse to form their own longhouse. A more major change in council policy came with a decision to systematically improve the roads and bridges on the reserve, a program which occupied much of the council's time. But the most dramatic departure came in 1878 when the council voted $1,500 from its own funds to match the New England Company's annual school grant, and embarked on a program of renovating the schools and improving the standard of education on the reserve. The following year, again under the persistent efforts of the upper tribal chiefs, they supported the construction of an agricultural exhibition hall in Ohsweken to house the increasingly popular fall fairs of the Six Nations Agricultural Society, founded in 1868 by Mohawk Chief William Smith and other upper tribesmen.

Although some lower tribal chiefs supported these policies, on the whole the Onondagas and Lower Cayugas were unhappy with the decisions to subsidize schools and the agricultural hall, arguing that the general band funds were being used to benefit a few tribes because their own members were unlikely to use these facilities. Since these issues brought into the open the basic differences in values and philosophies on culture change between the upper and lower tribes, they were extremely sensitive and difficult matters for the chiefs to handle. In trying to reach some agreement, procedural problems predictably arose in the council. A single issue, such as the agricultural hall, would be debated for months at a time, often producing a series of conflicting decisions and heated discourse in which each side occasionally ridiculed the other. The traditional right of the Onondaga chiefs to withhold confirmation on a decision they felt harmful to the Confederacy was frequently challenged by the upper tribal chiefs who failed to see how activities like the fall fair and education endangered either the council or the community. Understandably frustrated at being pressed by both the Mohawks and the Superintendent to adopt "progressive" measures, the Onondagas occasionally resorted to petitioning the government with their grievances but these protests only increased the dissension in the council. In an effort to deter the chiefs from petitioning the government, the Superintendent proposed that all chiefs speak their opinions openly in the council during the debate. The chiefs readily complied with this suggestion at first, but this created further problems. It turned the deliberations into an open forum in which individual chiefs continued to voice their views after the council had finalized its decision. This, in turn, sometimes led to a total reconsideration of the issue which usually annoyed the Superintendent who had already sent the initial decision off to Ottawa, and displeased the chiefs who had supported the decision in the first place. These situations, which were increasingly common in the early 1880s, often prompted the Superintendent to threaten the chiefs with the prospect of an elected system if they did not proceed more quickly with council business. The upper tribal chiefs, anxious to tend their farms and businesses, wanted the "tedious" deliberations shortened and council affairs run in a more efficient fashion.

The upper tribal chiefs, who were much more conscious of how the council was viewed by the Indian Department and anxious that it remain the vehicle for local government, felt that the council's procedures should be streamlined by establishing committees and a firmer control on the lengthy debates. They wanted the council to adopt a policy of individual voting for taking decisions, a procedure they were well acquainted with in the agricultural society and their church groups. Despite its radical departure from traditional council practice, this method was adopted in the spring of 1880 when the council was debating if it should accept the 1880 Indian Act amendments. The vote, surprisingly, went in favor of the Act, but immediately after this was realized the council reverted to its traditional procedures and reaffirmed its intent to honor the ancient rules of the Confederacy (SNCM 1880:37-38).

This same type of voting exercise was repeated in 1881, after Seth Newhouse resumed his seat in the council. The chiefs were being held progressively more accountable to the Indian Department for their decisions and, consequently, they were becoming more aware of the need to prove to its officials that the council could function as a proper forum for local government. In an effort to dissuade the Indian Department from implementing the legislation for elected band councils, the chiefs decided to reduce their numbers. The rationale behind the move was that with fewer chiefs the decisions would be taken more rapidly and the board money paid the chiefs during council sessions would be reduced. In a hasty move, the council "deposed" eleven chiefs on the grounds that they had not been appointed by the proper clan and condoled in the customary fashion

(SNCM 1881:125–26). It is unclear if Newhouse was instrumental in producing this decision, but the move was highly compatible with his attempts in his manuscript to correct the irregularities he saw in the practice of selecting chiefs (Newhouse 1885:3). It was also consistent with his tendency to grant the council, rather than the matrons, greater authority in deposing chiefs. But it was not a satisfactory approach to the upper tribal chiefs who wanted to speed up the business of council. So the next day they again proposed that a voting procedure be adopted by the council in cases of deadlocked decisions. Although the motion was supported by the most influential chiefs from the upper tribes, it failed to pass and at the end of the debate the Firekeepers announced new rules designed to reduce the confusions in council deliberations. Henceforth no chiefs would be allowed to speak after the council's final decision was reported, and assistant chiefs could not speak in council unless given permission by their "head Chief" (SNCM 1881:130–31). Both these rulings sharply contradicted established practices in the council, as did the action of deposing the chiefs. Assistant chiefs as well as self-made chiefs had always played full roles in the Grant River council, speaking directly on issues in council, accompanying official delegations, holding powerful offices, and receiving board money. As with most decisions that disregarded established conventions, the decision to depose the eleven chiefs was immediately ineffective. The next day in council the deposed chiefs were performing their duties as if the decision had never been taken.

After this unsuccessful attempt to change the procedures of the council Seth Newhouse's career encountered difficulties, suggesting that he may have been influential in persuading the council to adopt these measures. Although he was shortly added to the chiefs' list for board money, a move which indicated some degree of council recognition, he was publicly reprimanded in council for "using unbecoming language or written disrespectful language" on a notice published by the Indian Department (SNCM 1882:237). This was a unique and obviously frivolous charge and even though some chiefs thought he should publicly apologize for his behavior, as was customary at Grand River in such cases, others felt differently and the issue was dropped.

For the next two years (1882–83) Newhouse continued in council, on one occasion speaking out against the council's granting any further funds for education. But in January 1884 he was abruptly "deposed on account of dishonesty and emigrating to the States" (SNCM 1884:364). Newhouse's position had been contentious from the outset and the charges of dishonesty seem highly questionable. It appears that Newhouse's travels to the New York reservations

were finally seized by his critics in council as a basis for removing
his title. Prolonged absence from the reserve had been used by the
council in the past for removing chiefs' titles until they resumed
permanent residence on the reserve, but this ruling had been clearly
stretched to cover his temporary absences in an effort to rationalize
his removal.

That year (1884) apprehension increased among the chiefs as they
feared that the new Indian Advancement Act (Canada 1884), whose
main purpose was to encourage elected band councils, might be
applied to the reserve. The council's reaction to the legislation was
to examine its established operations and reaffirm its traditions.
Consequently, in the summer of 1885, the council scrutinized the
basis upon which its hereditary and self-made chiefs were appointed.
Newhouse's role in this examination is unclear although some of
the chiefs' appointments that he contests in his manuscript (1885:236)
were also contested in council. In the end, however, the exercise
was not taken very seriously by the chiefs. The council reconfirmed
all appointments, although not Newhouse's, concluding that "only
those Chieftainships that are vacant may be interfered with by filling
the vacancies or not as may seem proper to the parties concerned"
(SNCM 1885:172). It was in this context of self-examination and
confirmation that Newhouse approached the council for its endorsement of his manuscript.

Given his recent removal from council it is perhaps understandable
that Newhouse was not sympathetically received by the council. The
original plan for presenting his work called for the Interpreter to
read and translate it to the council. But it was soon evident that
Nanticoke Chief Josiah Hill, the powerful Secretary to the council,
thought otherwise. He suggested that a few chiefs who could read
and write English sit down with "two or three of the old men who
are well versed of the ancient confederation" and prepare a report
for the council's consideration (SNCM 1885:177). Newhouse's work
had been bluntly rejected. The council, despite its resolution, was
not interested in recording its traditions, and there was no follow
through on Josiah Hill's suggestion.

Many reasons lay behind the council's reaction to Newhouse's
work beyond the fact that his views differed substantially from those
of Seneca Chief John A. Gibson, whose version would eventually
receive official endorsement. Because Newhouse's ideas on the Confederacy were apparently well known to the council, it is fair to
assume that the chiefs were aware of the manuscript's contents. They
would also have been aware of the fact that if his strong ideas about
the minimal role of assistant chiefs (Newhouse 1885:129) had been
implemented, it would have silenced almost half the chiefs in council,

including the influential William Smith and A. G. Smith, both being Mohawk assistant chiefs. Furthermore, Newhouse's strictures against the participation of chiefs from the dependent nations (1885:176) would have eliminated Nanticoke Chief Josiah Hill, the council's Secretary, who clearly opposed Newhouse's efforts to get council approval. These men comprised the core of the progressive upper tribal chiefs; they were the ones who had opposed Newhouse's appointment as a chief initially and who supported measures for streamlining the council's procedures.

During the decade following the council's rejection of his work (1885–95) Newhouse did not play an active part in Six Nations politics. He married Lucy Sero, a young Mohawk woman from the Tyendinaga reserve near Desoronto, Ontario, and settled down to farm his forty-five acres west of Ohsweken and raise a family of three daughters and a son. He continued to travel to other reserves where he had friends and relatives who were as keenly interested in the Confederacy's history as he was. His nights at home, where he left his family when he traveled, were spent recording the personal names held by the Iroquois clans (1885:242–289) and, although he did not finish the task, his grandchildren recall friends and relatives coming to the house to consult the lists when an infant was to be given an Indian name. He was a disciplined and determined person, and most of his free time was devoted to his writing, working at nights under the light of his coal oil lamp and using special ink he made himself. The household was expected to respect his efforts and the children were often reminded that they were to remain quiet and not disturb him.

In the mid-1890s, when the movement for an elected system of local government surfaced once more on the reserve, Newhouse became more active in political affairs. He worked with some of the lower tribal chiefs to combat the reform pressures of the "progressive warriors," the well-educated and affluent men of the upper tribes who were increasing their agitation for an elected band council. The correspondence inserted at a later date in Newhouse's manuscript (1885:181–99) indicates his involvement.

A few years later, in the fall of 1899, Newhouse made his final attempt to secure the council's approval of his manuscript. By this time, however, the council was at the height of its development as a local government and the procedural preoccupations in Newhouse's manuscript no longer reflected its usually smooth operations. The council had become highly bureaucratized, conducting much of its business through a large number of standing committees. It had adopted a series of bylaws to promote farming and public health through the persistent efforts of the Mohawk and other upper tribal chiefs who held even greater influence in the daily management of Six Nations affairs. These chiefs had become the main brokers between the conservative Onondagas and the radical "progressive warriors" who were determined to establish elected government on the reserve. It was in this context of a secure but buffeted council that Newhouse made his last appeal for council endorsement of his manuscript.

On October 24, 1899, Newhouse began by reading the first passage in his work, "the article" giving the Mohawk chiefs veto power over all council decisions (1885:18). After council approved the article he was asked by Josiah Hill, the council's still powerful Secretary, if he would leave the material with the council as the property of the Six Nations after the entire work was confirmed by the chiefs. While granting that the history was Six Nations property, Newhouse said the labor put into the work was his own. He wanted some material reward from the council but when asked to specify the nature of the consideration, he "refused to do so and quietly retired from the Council and went home" (SNCM 1899:364). At that point the council appointed its own committee to record "the Constitution and Rules and Regulations of the six confederate Nations" (ibid.). Newhouse's effort proved to be an important stimulus for, from the dictation of Seneca Chief John A. Gibson, the official version of the Confederacy's lore was recorded and later published by Duncan C. Scott, the Superintendent General of Indian Affairs (Scott 1912), and still later by Parker (1916).

Following the council's rejection of his manuscript, Newhouse continued working with J. N. B. Hewitt, translating his manuscript into the Mohawk language (Hewitt 1917:430). The translation remains in unpublished form in the archives of the Smithsonian Institution (Fenton 1949a:158), but Hewitt did publish Newhouse's version of the Iroquois creation myth in his *Iroquoian Cosmology* (Hewitt 1903:255ff.). In later years Newhouse worked with various ethnologists from the National Museum of Canada—A. A. Goldenweiser, E. Sapir, and F. W. Waugh (Fenton 1949a:156). In 1910 he began correspondence with A. C. Parker, sending him a copy of his manuscript which Parker later published, in heavily edited form, with inconspicuous reference to Newhouse (Fenton 1968:38–47).

After the turn of the century Newhouse's political activities decreased. He appeared before the council in 1906, at the age of sixty-four, asking that his Onondaga title be restored because it had been improperly removed when he was absent in the United States, but the council postponed any action and failed to bring the issue forward again (SNCM 1906:259). On several other occasions he appeared before the chiefs to speak in favor of retaining the Confederacy, these reaffirmations becoming more frequent as the activities of the "progressive warriors" increased before the first World War. In 1921, at the age of seventy-nine, Seth Newhouse died and was buried in an unmarked grave in the Methodist Church cemetary along the Grand River. Three years after his death, the Confederacy was supplanted by an elected system of government, but the council, in its last years of operation, bore little resemblance to the "traditional" system either Newhouse or the Onondagas had hoped to preserve.

CONCLUSION

Although not a history of Six Nations politics, Newhouse's manuscript was, as Fenton suggested, a reflection of political uncertainty in the Confederacy council and on the Grand River reserve at mid-nineteenth century. It mirrored several significant developments at Grand River: (1) the continuing political prominence of the Mohawk tribe and its chiefs in the council, (2) the council's efforts to make its traditional rules of deliberation workable in the context of the federal government's system of indirect rule of reserves, (3) the attempts by council to exert greater influence over the appointments and deposition of chiefs, and (4) the increasing concern with loyalty to the Confederacy in response to the early (1860–1870) reform efforts to establish an elected system of local government. Thus, seen in this historical context, Newhouse's work becomes a remarkable document which echoed the strains of the tribal confederacy as it was being pressed into the mold of a reserve government under the increasingly powerful and centralized Indian administration.

As a reaction to political conditions, Newhouse's work was an obvious attempt to justify the continuance of the Confederacy to senior government officials and local reformers. He did this by recording and rationalizing its procedures in a systematic fashion, much like the articles of bylaws which the progressive farmers were promoting at the same time to the council. Newhouse's ultimate aim was to demonstrate that the Confederacy was a time-honored and workable system of government, as ordered and rational as those the reformers were proposing. Implicit in his work was the argument that if the traditional rules were reestablished there would be no need for the voting and committee procedures which the progressive Mohawks were promoting. As a reaction to political unrest, Newhouse's manuscript was a conservative statement reflecting an unmistakable preference for retaining Iroquois traditions rather than adopting Euro-Canadian models for local government.

In its entirety, Newhouse's manuscript was an unusual blend of traditional rules and contemporary procedures of the Confederacy council. For reasons which are now apparent, it is not surprising that the council withheld its official endorsement. To the powerful and progressive upper tribal chiefs, particularly the Mohawks, certain traditional practices of the council were outmoded, especially the deliberative procedures which required days of "tedious" debate. Newhouse's efforts to reaffirm and clarify these rules were seen as counterproductive to their attempts to streamline decision-making, thereby making the council more credible in the eyes of their more acculturated community members and the Indian administration. To the traditional lower tribal chiefs, especially the Onondagas, Newhouse's version of the League departed in many respects from the accepted one as known by Chief John A. Gibson (Scott 1912).

Newhouse's work is best understood as an attempt by a disciplined personality to reconcile the ideal traditions advocated by the Onondagas with some of the actual practices of the council at mid-nineteenth century. In the council's collective view Newhouse's work was neither a proper "history" of the Confederacy, nor an adequate depiction of its current form and operations. Its rejection, in light of this context, is understandable, but it does not make Newhouse's work any less valid an historical document. Indeed, it makes it a more interesting document, for it represents one man's serious attempt to resolve the differences between these two political traditions at Grand River—the conservative Onondaga and the innovative Mohawk traditions—and to bring some order to a period of intense political change.

NOTE

1. The research for this study was supported by a grant from the Canada Council. I am particularly grateful to Mrs. Della Henhawk and Mr. Raymond Reid, Seth Newhouse's grandchildren, and to Mrs. Georgina Reid for their kind assistance. Additional thanks must go to Tom Abler whose comments and criticisms on the first draft were extremely valuable.

CHAPTER ELEVEN

On Who Spoke First at Iroquois-White Councils: An Exercise in the Method of Upstreaming

MICHAEL K. FOSTER

During the seventeenth and eighteenth centuries the Iroquois held hundreds of councils with French and British colonial officials at designated "fires" *(katsihstakéhõ?)* burning at Montreal, Albany, Philadelphia and Onondaga, the capital of the League.[1] At these locations, plumed and painted Indian chiefs met frocked and bewigged white men in what must count as one of the most colorful developments of the colonial period and one of the most interesting examples of a contact phenomenon in the early history of Indian-white relations. Classic acculturation studies accustom us to thinking of the direction of influence as being from white to Indian culture; here, at least, is a striking instance—and one of considerable importance in shaping events of the colonial period—of the reverse situation. For, as Professor Fenton has explained in several papers, the roots of forest diplomacy can be traced to an entrenched piece of Iroquoian political ritual, the Condolence Ceremony for the mourning of dead chiefs and the installation of successors; and white government officials found it necessary to learn the native system in order to do business with the Indians (Fenton 1949: 235; 1957: 22–24; 1961: 272; 1971a: 446).[2]

What we are calling a council—*hotíhahshê?* 'they [masc.] are holding a council'[3]—consisted of a series of morning and afternoon sessions at which the Indian and white delegations addressed each other through specially appointed speakers *(hahthá:ha?)*. These sessions were conducted at a leisurely pace by today's standards and might extend over several weeks or even months. As in the Condolence Ceremony the participants divided themselves into two "sides of the fire," though along Indian-white (international) lines, rather than along intranational lines of divisions within the League.[4] More often than not, colonial councils were attended by more than one recognized political entity on each side. For example, at eighteenth-century Pennsylvania-Iroquois councils the Governor and Council of Pennsylvania were frequently joined by a governor or two—or some of their commissioners or agents—from New York, Maryland, Virginia or New Jersey, while the Six Nations might be joined by delegations of Delaware, Miami, Wyandot, or Shawnee. Public sessions ranged from smaller meetings of single groups on issues concerning them alone to large plenary sessions with all of the Indian delegations arranged on one side of the fire and the white groups on the other. Whatever their composition, these public sessions were interspersed with "private conferences" during which the groups on each side attempted to concert their positions in order to present at least the appearance of a common front to the opposite side. The agreements finally achieved were termed "treaties" in the written records kept by the colonial secretaries, or *watrihwiHs?óhsra?* 'the completed matter', in native parlance. The latter term contrasts with *hotíhahshē?* on a semantic dimension of *product* vs. *process*, more or less as English 'treaty' contrasts with 'council'.

The event sequence of an Indian-white council can be thought of as a kind of formal dialogue between the speakers appointed on each side. The speaker for one side stood up and presented a set of proposals, each marked by a string or belt of wampum, which an "interpreter" *(hatewēnaká:tas* 'he puts up the word(s)') then translated into the language of the opposite side.[5] When he was finished and had sat down the speaker for the opposite side took the floor, but at this point only to announce briefly through an interpreter that his side would withdraw to consider an answer, a process which usually took the remainder of the day. The form of the answer was closely tied to the form of the original proposals. Each point was first "repeated"—this consisted of a summary rather than verbatim recall—and then answered. During the repetition phase the speaker pointed to or occasionally held the wampum originally given; during the answering phase he pointed to or took up a wampum of comparable type from his own side (a string for a string, a belt for a belt). By thus linking proposals to answers wampum functioned to regulate the ongoing speech event, and, in the end, to leave each side with a mnemonic record of the proceedings.

When all of side A's proposals had been answered, side B might introduce proposals of its own which were then, of course, answered in like fashion after a private conference by side A. Yet the point remains that even though side B could in due course raise business of its own, it must dispose of A's business to the latter's satisfaction first; and indeed many historic councils consisted of only a single "cycle" of A's proposals followed by B's answers. It is obvious that the party in the position of side A enjoyed a certain advantage in the proceedings, not only having the privilege of naming the council's principal agenda but of setting the *form* of the answers given by side B. It would not be an exaggeration to say that side A determined the council's basic direction. Under such circumstances one might expect to find frequent references in the colonial accounts to an initial jockeying between the sides for the privilege of speaking first. Surprisingly, there is very little indication of any such activity, and with some rare and interesting exceptions—one of which we shall mention in a note at the end of this paper—the event sequences of most councils unfolded remarkably smoothly, with one side leading off and then speaker after speaker taking his turn at the floor. The question of speaker precedence only infrequently obtruded itself into the public sessions, let alone did it become a bone of contention. The "decorum" of the Indian-white councils is legendary, having been noted by white observers at the time as well as by later writers. The conclusion seems inevitable that there must have been some tacit rule or set of rules by which the participants on both sides of the fire knew, automatically, which of them should speak first. It is our purpose in this paper to formulate such a rule or set of rules.

Whatever the basis for the ordering of sides at a council, it was not predictable from any *single* factor such as the council's location, or the identity of the participating groups. If we examine a sample of historic councils we will find that the group in the position of side A—the group naming the council's agenda—was sometimes the host and sometimes the visitor; and this group was sometimes Indian and sometimes white. Moreover, in the absolute sequence of events, the group naming the council's agenda might actually speak *second*. Thus, the question "Who spoke first at councils?" turns out to be a complex matter, apparently involving the interaction of several factors. Our approach will be, first, to present thumbnail sketches of four historic councils in order to show the range of variation in speaker precedence, given the fact that there were two sides of the fire, two principal identities (Indian and white), and a choice of Indian and white territories in which the council could be scheduled. While this sample of four councils is but a fraction of the total council fire literature, we will argue that, as a selective sample, it illustrates all the *logically* possible combinations of factors involved and therefore describes a much larger segment of that literature. Our second step will be to jump forward two centuries in time to the ethnographic present to examine a piece of Iroquois oral tradition which still preserves the essential attributes of the tradition of council oratory. From an analysis of speeches accompanying two old wampum belts, the logic of the ordering of sides of the fire eventually emerges.[6] This affords us the opportunity to apply Professor Fenton's method of upstreaming, using the modern material as a perspective for evaluating historic materials.

The Historic Sample

The literature of the council fire, which Fenton has annotated and reviewed in several papers (1949; 1953a; 1957) is enormous, occupying a large part of the colonial records of Pennsylvania, New York, the New England colonies and New France. We will make no effort to survey this literature, instead referring the interested reader to Fenton's work. The four councils we will be drawing on to illustrate certain general points all come from a set of twenty or so major councils conducted between the Six Nations and the government of Pennsylvania during the final three tumultuous decades of the Anglo-French struggle for North America.[7] For purposes of this exercise we will rely primarily on two published sources which contain some of the most detailed accounts of council proceedings in all the colonial records: the Indian treaties printed by Benjamin Franklin (Boyd 1938), and the lengthy verbatim extracts from the journals of Conrad Weiser, Pennsylvania's "ambassador" to the Six Nations, published by Paul A. W. Wallace in his biography of Weiser (Wallace 1945). At most of these and the remaining councils in this group the Pennsylvania government and the Six Nations were the backbone of the two sides of the fire, though other white and Indian governments attended as well. In one case, the Delaware were the principal interlocutors to Pennsylvania, though the Six Nations were present.

Case 1: Onondaga, 1737

After a harrowing six-week trek up the Susquehanna Valley in the early spring, Conrad Weiser and his exhausted party reached an outlying southern Onondaga village where they encamped to rest up and, in the language of council oratory, to await "at the wood's edge" a formal invitation to the capital town, Sagogsaanagechtheyky (the place of the Name Carriers, as the Onondaga were termed in council), five miles away. The visitors were warmly welcomed by the local chiefs, shown a place to stay, and provided with abundant food—all normal Iroquoian etiquette for foreign emissaries. Some highlights of Weiser's arrival bear close examination. Almost immediately Weiser sent a message by way of the local chiefs to the capital in order ". . . to kindle their ffire with all Speed," signifying "the Earnestness of the Message" by enclosing a string of wampum (Wallace 1945: 90). The next day the chiefs returned to say that the great fire of the League "was kindled and a burning (that is) that some of the Chiefs of every of the Six Nations were there and that I should be welcome to deliver to them what I had from their Brethren of Philadelphia [and the governor of Virginia]." Weiser's party proceeded that same day to the capital where they were given an official welcome at the League's central "ffire with a string of Wampum" and told that they might speak "at such time or Day [as] I should appoint." Weiser pleaded urgency, which meant that he would address the Council of Chiefs the next day. In the morning the chiefs immediately turned the floor over to him and he delivered a formal invitation from the governor of Virginia, conveyed by way of the Pennsylvania government, asking the chiefs to attend a peace conference at Williamsburg, and a request from the governor of Pennsylvania to cease hostilities with the Southern Indians until a general peace could be concluded. Each proposal was marked by wampum. The chiefs withdrew to consider a response. Because Weiser was in a hurry the chiefs agreed to reconvene the council the same day. When the events got under way in the evening at the council house, Weiser's two wampums were "hung up in the middle of the House for every Body to see" (p. 91). The speaker for the Six Nations first repeated the substance of each proposal and then answered it. As each wampum was spoken to it was removed "and put by," another being presented in its place to "confirm" the answer. They agreed to meet the governor of Virgina, but suggested Albany rather than Williamsburg as the location ("we have no ffire at Williamsburg"); they agreed without reservation to Pennsylvania's request to take hold of the hatchet. At this council Weiser stated the main business and set the course of the exchanges between sides of the fire.

Perhaps the most striking thing about the event sequence is the fact that a *white man*—one who was unquestionably highly respected by the Iroquois but who still enjoyed no legal rights at the great Council of Chiefs—could "kindle" the central fire of the League, and not only that but name the "time or Day" when the council should convene. Yet these procedures, outlined routinely if in considerable detail in Weiser's journal, raised no one's eyebrows, least of all the chiefs': the sequence unfolded along even and, one cannot help feeling, entirely expected lines. Later, when we have had a chance to consider the modern data on council protocol, we will see that Weiser's apparent assumption of extraordinary powers, far from being exceptional, was entirely consistent with council protocol.

Case 2: Philadelphia, 1747

While he was at Lancaster in November on other business, Weiser encountered a party of Iroquois warriors from the Ohio country on their way to Philadelphia. From the fact that Weiser was surprised by this encounter (see Wallace 1945: 259–60) we conclude that the Iroquois were not responding to an earlier invitation from Pennsylvania which Weiser would certainly have known about. For all intents and purposes, the 1747 council was the mirror image of the 1737 Onondaga council, with the roles of the Indians and whites reversed at a *white* council fire: the Indians arrived unexpectedly, just as Weiser had arrived unexpectedly at Onondaga, and it was they rather than he who had important business to transact. From the council minutes we learn that Anthony Palmer, President of the Provincial Council, opened the proceedings in Philadelphia on November 13, immediately turning the floor over to the Iroquois warriors whose speaker explained: "You will, perhaps, be surprized at this unexpected Visit; but we cou'd not avoid coming to see you, the Times are become so critical and dangerous" (Boyd 1938: 103). He went on to name the council's agenda: a request for a greater show of resolve on Pennsylvania's part against the French presence in the Ohio Valley coupled with a request for material support. The white delegation withdrew to consider an answer which they returned point for point (wampum for wampum) three days later, agreeing to most of the terms. Thus, although the term does not appear in the minutes of this council, it was the Indians on this occasion who, as visitors, were "kindling" the fire at Philadelphia, the seat of the Pennsylvania government, just as Weiser had kindled the fire of Onondaga, the seat of the Confederacy government, in 1737. At both councils, however, the party in the position of stating the main business actually spoke *second*, i.e., after certain welcoming ceremonies had been given by the hosts.

Case 3: Philadelphia, 1736

In early September 1736, Weiser learned of the approach of a large delegation from the Six Nations, and traveled up the Susquehanna to Shamokin to meet them. Here, at a considerable distance from Philadelphia, Weiser formally welcomed the Iroquois chiefs into the Pennsylvania country and, on orders from the Provincial Council, presented them with a wampum to invite them to Philadelphia. Weiser withdrew to allow the chiefs to deliberate among themselves. The next morning "before Sun ris" they sent for him to give notice of their acceptance of the invitation (see Wallace 1945: 66–67). Weiser escorted the chiefs and their followers to President James Logan's suburban home Stenton, still some distance from the Great Meeting House in town (i.e., in present-day Germantown), where they were treated to the same kind of hospitality Weiser had enjoyed at Onondaga in 1737. Following a day of rest, Thomas Penn welcomed the Indian delegation with three "small Strings of *Wampum*" to brighten their eyes, open their hearts and offer them shelter, to which the speaker for the Indians answered "with three like Strings in his Hand," returning thanks for each "Article" of the welcome (Boyd 1938: 4). This phase of the council was followed by an additional period of rest, and seems clearly separable from the next phase which got under way after the Six Nations delegation had been escorted to the Great Meeting House in town. The activities at Stenton centered on the ceremonial welcome. This location bore the same relation to the "principal place" in Philadelphia (the Great Meeting House) that the first Onondaga village did to the League capital Sagogsaanagechtheyky: both served on a number of occasions as stopping-off points for visitors on their way to designated central fires.

The order between the sides at Stenton was, of course, Pennsylvania first and the Six Nations second. The order followed when the main council opened at the Great Meeting House is of particular interest. We will recall that Weiser had traveled to Shamokin to greet the Six Nations delegation *after receiving word of their approach*. On the basis of the two cases discussed earlier we might assume that the Indians would speak first and state the council's business. Instead, we find the following entry in the minutes for October 2, the opening session:

> The President, before proceeding to hear them, thought proper to inform the Audience, that in *August* 1732, a great Treaty having been held in this Place with several Chiefs of the Six Nations, they had made report thereof on their Return to their Great Council, where the several Propositions that had been made to them on the Part of this Government, had been fully considered; and that these Chiefs now present, of whom there never at any time before had been so great a Number met in this Province, were now come to return their Answer.
>
> The *Indians* being made acquainted [through the interpreter] with what the President had said, were told, that we were ready to hear them. (Boyd 1938: 6)

It was thus Logan who spoke first and who named the council's agenda, even though this amounted to little more than a yielding of the floor to the Six Nations. However brief his remarks, the phrase "now come to return their Answer" set a frame around anything the chiefs should say, and clarifies for us the role relationships between the sides. It was, in fact, the chiefs who had the most to say on this occasion: their answers to the proposals made by Pennsylvania in 1732 occupy nearly three text pages of the minutes as opposed to the summary of Logan's short speech. Nevertheless, the form and content of their speeches were fixed by the proposals made by Pennsylvania at an earlier time and recalled on the present occasion. The 1736 council thus differs from the two councils previously discussed in that it was the host group, not the visitors, that named the agenda. As in the previous cases, however, the hosts led off in the preliminary ceremonial phase of the council.

Case 4: Easton, November, 1756

Just as the Philadelphia council of 1747 (Case 2) represents a mirror image of the Onondaga council of 1737 (Case 1) as far as participant roles are concerned, so there is a logical opposite to the council just described. As it happens there is only one possible candidate in the Pennsylvania sample of councils that fits this category, and this case is not entirely unambiguous—though the ambiguities are quite interesting in themselves, and arose because of the location of the council and the unusual mix of personalities on this occasion.

At least five major councils took place at Easton (the "Forks" of the Delaware and Lehigh rivers) in the late 1750s. It was a period when the Iroquois were wavering in their loyalties as the Anglo-French conflict drew to a head and the English seemed unable to coordinate military and political policies. A delicate overall situation was further complicated locally by the sudden coming into prominence of Teedyuscung, the irrepressible and bibulous Delaware "King" (see Wallace 1949). Teedyuscung took every possible advantage of a faltering Iroquois-Pennsylvania alliance to press Delaware land claims against Pennsylvania. The dingy town of Easton was located in the heart of a disputed territory which was claimed by the Delawares by right of original ownership and present occupancy and by Pennsylvania on the basis of a dubious series of earlier treaties. Teedyuscung's approach was to stir up violence along the frontier and then, appointing himself plenipotentiary for "ten nations" (including, unbeknownst to them, the Six Nations of the Iroquois), to offer to treat with Pennsylvania for peace and the return of captives in exchange for guarantees of a permanent home on the Delaware. It was a desperate and ugly situation, a far cry from the harmonious dealings between Pennsylvania and the Iroquois.

In the early fall of 1756 a new and inexperienced Governor William Denny received peace overtures from Teedyuscung by messenger. Denny, who had just received an order from the new commander of the English colonial armies to relinquish all dealings with Indians to Sir William Johnson, and who did not like Indians very much anyway, balked at this overture, but sent Teedyuscung word to proceed to Easton to await further instructions (Wallace 1945: 457 ff.). Under pressure from the Provincial Council, Denny finally agreed to a meeting, but named Philadelphia as the location. Weiser was dispatched with an invitation string to bring Teedyuscung down. But Teedyuscung was a step ahead of Denny and sent a curt message from Easton that he would await the governor there. Although reluctant, Denny eventually agreed.

The problem posed by Easton was which party was the rightful host. Easton was not a recognized fire and the territory was disputed. Teedyuscung's intransigence can be seen as a shrewd move to bolster the legitimacy of the Delaware claim. At this council, protocol was to serve the interests of deeper political motives. When we turn to the minutes of the council (Boyd 1938: 150 ff.), we find Teedyuscung *assuming* the role of host, taking the initiative to clear the governor's eyes, ears and throat, and urging him to overlook any recent possibly unflattering reports as the mere "Whistling of Birds." The governor could do little but fall in with this gambit, returning each word and adding the sardonic comment that he was particularly opening a passage from Teedyuscung's heart to his mouth. Like it or not, Denny was now a *de facto* visitor at Teedyuscung's fire.

The next day when the council got down to business it was again Teedyuscung who seized the initiative, rising first to state his proposals of peace. Denny withdrew to consider an answer which was delivered three days later. Teedyuscung thus set the course for the council which consisted of several more exchanges between the two sides of the fire. As events developed this council represents a reversal of roles between the Indian and white participants from the 1736 Philadelphia council, though in both cases the party in the position of *host* also set the council's agenda. The council is different from those previously discussed, however, in that the circumstances allowed for certain initiatives to be taken which would not have been possible in the other cases where the allocation of roles was, as it were, given automatically by the surrounding circumstances including unambiguous locations. Compared with the accounts of the other councils, the minutes of the 1756 Easton council have a distinctly strained quality. Perhaps this was owing at least in part to the fact that the masters of forest diplomacy, the Six Nations, were represented on this occasion by only a few token observers.

A Contemporary Source on the Council Pattern

The four councils we have discussed show, I believe, the full range of variation in the allocation of speaking roles between the Indian and white sides of the fire in the Pennsylvania sample, and possibly in all of the council fire literature. At least two things now seem clear: there was no necessary relationship between a council's location and which side of the fire introduced the principal agenda: in two instances (cases 1 and 2) the party in the position of visitors did so, while in the remaining instances (cases 3 and 4) the party in the position of hosts did so; and there was no necessary relationship between a side's identity as Indian or white and the privilege of naming the council's agenda: at two councils the whites had this privilege (cases 1 and 3) and at two councils the Indians did (cases 2 and 4). The partners on the two sides of the fire were thus not arbitrarily ranked in council protocol but were full equals.

Although these four councils may represent the range of variation in speaker precedence found historically, we still have not explained the systematic basis for this variation. A good deal of light has been shed on this question, rather unexpectedly, from a contemporary ethnographic source. I say unexpectedly since it has often been assumed that with the splitting up of the League after the American Revolution and the efforts of private land speculators and the State of New York to extinguish Iroquois claims in New York during the nineteenth century, the system of forest diplomacy gradually fell into disuse, eventually dying out altogether. But it turns out that a handful of Iroquois living today know how to "read" some of the old wampum belts signifying ancient agreements between the Six Nations and various successive white governments, and this knowledge extends beyond recall of the provisions symbolized by the belts (no mean feat of memory in itself) to include a detailed grasp of council protocol—in short, a knowledge of how to actually conduct a council as opposed to merely remembering events gone by, or what we shall call an *active* knowledge of forest diplomacy.[8] In the course of recent field work I was surprised to learn that at least one, and possibly several councils of the "renewal" type where the ancient Chain of Friendship was brightened have occurred between the chiefs of the Confederacy and officials of the U.S. government in the present century, and the same belts may have been brought before Canadian and European audiences as well.[9]

One of the Iroquois retaining an active knowledge of council protocol is Chief Jacob E. Thomas, a gifted orator, a widely recognized authority on the traditional culture, an eloquent apologist for the Confederacy, and a fluent speaker of three Iroquoian languages.[10] In

1976 Mr. Thomas agreed to read two belts, the so-called Friendship Belt and the Two Rows (or Paths) Belt, into a tape recorder as part of an ongoing project to document the recent history of the League. At first I thought these readings would consist solely of the lengthy speeches accompanying the two belts, but it soon became apparent that Mr. Thomas was thinking in far larger terms of staging an entire council sequence involving two sides of the fire at which agreements of the kind symbolized by the belts would be renewed. Included in such a staging would be the numerous shorter and longer speeches preceding and following the readings proper at a major council, as well as the speeches and procedures comprising an invitation. In this way, almost by accident, I stumbled across a living vestige of a proud tradition that once shaped the course of empire in colonial America.

Mr. Thomas explained that in order to stage a council for taping it would be necessary to imagine a situation today in which Indian and white officials might actually meet at a designated fire. He suggested that the council could be set either at Onondaga (Syracuse, New York) or Washington, and—even more interesting—that *either* the chiefs *or* the U.S. officials could assume responsibility for the readings. This would place the opposite side of the fire in the position of answering the readings. Once these basic decisions had been made, the sequence of events would follow more or less automatically, and he would be able to speak the parts of both sides into a microphone. We note that Mr. Thomas was here assuming equal facility in the idiom and procedures of council on the part of the Indian and white participants—an unusually sanguine view in terms of present-day realities, as he himself admitted. But, he explained, either side *should* be able to call and conduct a renewal council since both had equal responsibility for guaranteeing the integrity of the alliance chain. We decided to stage a sequence with Onondaga as the location and the chiefs conducting the readings, and prepared an outline of the exchanges between the two sides of the fire on this basis. Then, following the outline, Mr. Thomas spoke all the appropriate speeches for the two sides into a microphone *as though the sequence were actually taking place.* The result was approximately 7½ hours of speeches recorded entirely in Cayuga.[11]

Although the sequence we chose is one of the more likely ones to occur should a renewal council be scheduled today, it is important to underscore the fact that it is not the only one Mr. Thomas could have staged or that might actually occur. For example, it would have been possible, as suggested above, to set the council at Onondaga but have the *white officials* read the belts and the chiefs answer them, or at Washington with either side assuming responsibility for the readings.[12] Mr. Thomas's apparent indifference to the allocation of basic roles between the Indian and white sides, and the ease with which he was able to assume the parts of the speakers for both sides at any chosen staging, attest, I believe, to his extraordinary mastery of council protocol, and to the relative "abstractness" of his grasp of its underlying pattern. (This is just the sort of flexibility, in fact, that we might expect of speakers in the historic period who were called upon on different occasions to play various different roles.) Since the knowledge of council protocol remains active for a few living Iroquois we must consider the tradition still viable, even though this is no longer the principal way business is conducted between Indian and white governments. Certain other implications of Mr. Thomas's active knowledge of the tradition will be mentioned later in the discussion.

According to Mr. Thomas, the ideal council sequence—the one chosen for taping or any other—should consist of four distinct stages, each of them constituting a council in its own right. Only during the last of these, the main, or, as we shall call it, the "scheduled" council, are substantive proposals exchanged; the first three councils are concerned with the process of invitation. These preliminary stages are more or less detectable in historic sequences (as at the Onondaga council of 1737), depending on the quality and length of the records kept. It is just here, however, that the modern version has proven to be so useful in attempting to reconstruct the underlying pattern of forest diplomacy, since the white colonial secretaries were generally more concerned with a council's outcome—the product ("treaty") rather than the process ("holding a council") as we earlier termed it—than with the lengthy events leading up to the scheduled council. Yet, as we shall see, *it was during the invitation phase that crucial decisions about a council's location and agenda were made.* Since the greater portion of Mr. Thomas's recorded material falls within the invitation phase of the sequence, his version assumes special importance for the problem at hand.

The first stage of that version consists of a council held by the group wishing to approach another on the question of renewing the old agreements ("polishing the Chain of Friendship"). It involves, of course, only one side of the fire. In the sequence chosen for staging this is the Iroquois chiefs who, following prescribed procedures for intra-Confederacy decision-making (see Morgan 1901, I: 105–7, Parker 1916: 30–34, 97–100), reach consensus that a renewal council with the U.S. government is due. During the planning council the chiefs appoint two messengers (*hatínha?thra?* 'they [who] are hired') to carry the invitation to the foreign council fire—in the Thomas version to the U.S. President or his stand-in in Washington. The invitation is then "read" into a string of wampum (historically, belts were more often used for this purpose) which will later be carried by the messengers over the "long forest path" (niwa-thahín'óthri:s).

The second stage of the sequence commences with the arrival of the messengers at a point where tradition prescribes that the cleared land around the foreign village meets the forest. The messengers pause at this point to await a formal invitation into the village by the host group, a phase we will recall from the historic cases. In the staged version a committee of U.S. officials proceeds to the outskirts of Washington to perform a ceremony called kaĕhawahḗ:tõh, an archaic term of uncertain meaning often glossed as the At the Wood's Edge Ceremony. It is perhaps here, more than in any other aspect of council protocol, that the debt to the procedures of the Condolence Ceremony becomes clear.[13] The hosts have prepared a small fire about which the two groups arrange themselves: structurally, the kaĕhawahḗ:tõh ceremony is a council in molecular form. A speaker for the white hosts leads off with the Rubbing Down of Bodies rite (aetshiya'totrő:ko' 'they rub your bodies down'), sometimes referred to in the secondary literature as the Three Rare Words rite. In words only and on behalf of the hosts, he wipes the eyes of the weary travelers with a soft white buckskin (their eyes are full of the things they have seen on their journey) so that their sight will be fully restored during coming events; he clears out their ears (they have heard many things along the way, some of which may be harmful to the present proceedings) so that their hearing will be fully restored; he clears their throats of all obstructions so that they will be able to breathe and speak properly at council; finally, he removes the briars from their tired legs and offers them a soothing "walking medicine" (tsyawekahő'tĕh). The first three "words" of the wood's edge welcome (Eyes, Ears and Throats), which we will recall specifically being mentioned as part of the opening of the 1736 Philadelphia and 1756 Easton councils, of course concern the principal organs for the perception and production of speech, and it is fitting— though nonetheless noteworthy—that these organs should receive such elaborate ritual attention before the council's main phase gets under way. This is only one of several ways in which council protocol shows an explicit concern for the contact or channel function of speech.[14]

In the Thomas version the messengers do not reply at ths point but are escorted "by the arm" (ĕyetshinĕtshí:neht 'they will lead you by the arm') to the place of council in town (the White House or the office of the Commissioner of Indian Affairs), where the greeting sequence continues.[15] Eventually the hosts yield the floor to the messengers. The messengers begin by returning thanks for each item in the Rubbing Down of Bodies rite (Eyes, Ears, Throats, Briars, Walking Medicine): they are now ready, they say, to deal with the business they have brought from Onondaga. After explaining the chiefs' decision to invite their white brothers to renew the old agreements, a decision reached at the stage 1 council, the messengers produce the invitation string and in a dramatic move pass it across the fire to the white officials, saying as they do, "They [now] take you by the arm!" (aetshinẽ:tsha:?). The chiefs have, as it were, reached across the miles to take the white officials by the arm to lead them to Onondaga.[16] The hosts announce that they will consider the matter in private conference and politely ask the messengers to withdraw, just as Weiser had been requested to do during the invitation phase of the 1736 Philadelphia council, but to be ready to return soon. After they have reached a consensus and have invited the messengers back they return their answer which in the staged version is an acceptance of the invitation. The speaker follows prescribed form by first repeating the highlights of the invitation speech as given by the messengers (specification of date, place and topic) and then indicating his side's concurrence on each point. The hosts keep the invitation wampum which in time will "lead them by the arm" to the Central Fire at Onondaga. The hosts offer entertainment (a festive meal followed by social dancing) and eventually declare to the messengers that they will "launch their canoe." Summing up the stage 2 council, we see that it is the white hosts who speak first at the wood's edge welcome and the Indian visitors who speak second after being led by the arm to the council house. But it is the latter who introduce the council's business which in turn is answered by the white government officials. The situation is identical to that of the 1737 invitation council at Onondaga—except, of course, that the roles between the Indian and white sides are reversed.

After the messengers return to Syracuse the chiefs call a League council (the third council in the sequence overall) to hear the results. This council follows the same plan as the stage 2 council, although the wood's edge welcome is somewhat more abbreviated and takes place at the main council fire rather than outside the village.[17] The messengers announce that they have returned owẽnoskõh ' [with] the word alone', i.e., without the invitation wampum. This is good news since the immediate return of a wampum would signify rejection of the proposal. The home council concludes the invitation phase of the overall sequence.

On the day of the scheduled council (stage 4), the white officials arrive at the outskirts of Onondaga where they pause to receive the wood's edge greeting. This is virtually identical to that described earlier in stage 2, except that the visitors, who may be a large

delegation and who are persons empowered to renew the old agreements, are offered a pipe after they have been led to the council
house. The allocation of roles between the Indian and white sides
is the reverse of the earlier council: the Indians are now hosts and
speak first in the Rubbing Down of Bodies rite; the white officials
return the compliment in the council house. They also return the
wampum string, whose "power" has led them to the place of council.
At this point *the white officials turn the floor back to the Indians:* it
is the latter who will do the reading of the two belts, as agreed at
the invitation council in Washington. Up to this point the second
and fourth councils have been, in all essentials, identical; but here
the significant difference between them emerges. During the invitation
council the messengers simply passed, i.e., without yielding the floor,
from their return of the opening welcome to their substantive proposals (details about the invitation). At Onondaga the white visitors
turn the floor back to the Indian hosts who lead off with the council's
business, the reading of the two belts. The white officials are asked
if they still "respect" the old agreements. They retire to consider an
answer which they return (positively) in due course. Their answer
consists of a summary ("repetition") of the readings and a reaffir-
mation of their commitment to the alliance. The Chain is bright and
shiny once more.

Summing up, if we compare the event sequences of the second
and fourth councils in the Thomas version—the two occasions when
foreign delegations come face to face across the council fire, we find
that it is the Indians who introduce the main business and the whites
who respond to them on both occasions, but that the Indians only
speak first in the absolute sequence of things when they are also
hosts. For purposes of what we shall be undertaking in the next
section the important point is that *petitioners may sometimes be in
the position of visitors and sometimes in the position of hosts.* From
this fact we can explain the sequencing of sides at the historic
councils—perhaps all of them, although we will limit our remarks
to the four mentioned earlier.

Upstreaming to the Historic Councils

To avoid some quaint misunderstandings that have arisen in discussions of upstreaming, I want particularly to emphasize that the
sense of the term I have in mind is the one consistently espoused
by Fenton himself (not the one conjured up by horrified graduate
students according to Wallace [see the Overview of the present
volume]), namely that modern ethnographic sources can be drawn
on to afford a *perspective* for *evaluating* earlier written sources. The

italicized terms appear in Fenton's own definitions of the method (see, e.g., 1949: 233; 1951: 39) and should caution us against a too literal approach, a slavish and mechanical reading of the past against the present or the present against the past. Such an approach, Fenton suggests, soon comes up against the "fallacy of uniformitarianism," which falsely assumes that cultural processes, like the physical laws of geology, say, remain immutable over time (Fenton 1957: 22; 1962: 12).[18] Manifestly it is unnecessary to exclude the factor of change to apply the method of upstreaming usefully as a heuristic guide to problems of reconstructing earlier patterns which may be detectable in only fragmentary form in earlier sources. Indeed, the method can be used precisely to trace the evolution of a pattern over time.

Earlier we pointed out that one aspect of Mr. Thomas's active knowledge of the council pattern was his relative indifference as to the allocation of basic roles among the Indian and white participants at a council sequence staged for taping. The U.S. government could have initiated the sequence and conducted the readings, making the white officials the petitioners. But it would also be perfectly "legal," according to Mr. Thomas, for the petitioner—be he white or Indian— to propose at the invitation council that the scheduled council take place at the fire of the *respondents* rather than at his own fire. I would argue that this information, obtained from a contemporary master of council oratory, is all we need to know to understand the sequencing of speakers at (possibly all) the historic councils. Let us now take another look at our four cases.

Case 1: Onondaga, 1737

The pause by the visiting petitioners at the wood's edge was closely described by Weiser in his journal. His party was warmly greeted and shown traditional hospitality. After they had been escorted to the Onondaga capital they were welcomed by a string of wampum to the League's fire. While this is all we are told—and many accounts are even more fragmentary than this—we would probably not be making an unwarranted leap to assume that the welcome followed the lines of the Rubbing Down of Bodies rite described earlier; the notion of clearing eyes, ears and throats constantly recurs in the historic literature, and is described more graphically by Weiser himself on another visit to Onondaga on behalf of Virginia and Pennsylvania.[19] Weiser "returned them thanks" (Wallace 1945: 90) and this concluded the first day's activities. Since Weiser was, of course, the petitioner on this occasion, he introduced the council's business the next day, and his two belts were then answered by the Six Nations' chiefs after a period of separate consultation. Earlier we noted the apparently remarkable language of Weiser's journal account: he was responsible for "kindling" the great fire of the League and for naming the "time or Day" when the august body of the Confederacy Council should convene. We now see that this was nothing more than a recounting of the petitioner's normal right to speak first during the business phase of the council; the journal gives no impression that Weiser was doing anything more than following well-established protocol. We should thus read the phrase "kindling the fire" as merely an elaborate figure of speech encapsulating the petitioner's prerogatives. The 1737 council follows the identical plan of Mr. Thomas's stage 2 invitation council, except that the roles between the Indian and white sides of the fire have been reversed.

Case 2: Philadelphia, 1747

Earlier we called this council the mirror image of Onondaga, 1737, in that the visitor-petitioners were Indian rather than white. Pennsylvania opened the proceedings with a welcome speech and then yielded the floor to Iroquois warriors from the Ohio country who stated propsals which were answered a few days later by Pennsylvania. Now the allocation of roles on this occasion was, in fact, identical to the allocation of roles in stage 2 of the modern version: in both cases the visitor-petitioners are Indian and the host-respondents are white. From this we see that it is possible for councils to have an identical pattern regarding the precedence of speakers but have quite different *purposes*. We shall call any council where the petitioner is in the position of visitor a "Type I" council. Of the three instances of this type discussed so far, two are invitation councils and one is a scheduled council; and two show the Indians in the role of visitor-petitioners and one the whites.

We suggested earlier that while the Type I pattern might seem more natural for an invitation council than a scheduled council, Mr. Thomas said that it would be perfectly acceptable for visitors to propose that the location of the scheduled council be the fire of the respondents. (Again, this was what took place in Washington in 1954 [note 9].) Under what circumstances might petitioners make such a proposal in historic times? The circumstances would be those in which the petitioners felt pressed by time and events. In the colonial era the journey over the forest path between designated fires was, as the elaborate welcome speeches still say, a long and arduous one, involving dangers of many kinds. Matters of business could not always wait for the orderly process of extending a formal invitation (stages 1–3 in the Thomas version) which added an entire round trip to the sequence. The speaker for the warriors at the 1747

Philadelphia council opened with a statement about the conflation of protocol, saying that the white officials might well be surprised by the warriors' "unexpected Visit" which was occasioned by "critical and dangerous" recent events.[20] The method of upstreaming thus awakens us to a significant detail: when petitioners are in the position of visitors we should expect to find some indication of "surprise" on the part of the host-respondents. This would apply equally to an invitation or a scheduled council: in both cases the petitioners have not arrived by express invitation.

Case 3: Philadelphia, 1736

This council is somewhat exceptional in the colonial records in that the preliminaries to the scheduled phase are well documented, both in the sense that the details of the 1732 Philadelphia council, whose proposals the chiefs had come to answer in 1736, are known (Wallace 1945: 47–49; Boyd 1938: xxiii–xxv) and in the sense that Weiser kept close track of activities at Shamokin where the earlier invitation to return to Philadelphia was renewed. We also have a detailed description of the Rubbing Down of Bodies rite at the wood's edge (Stenton) in the official minutes (Boyd 1938: 4). (The principal articles in the greeting, each marked by a string of wampum, are even set apart by the roman numerals I, II and III.) From our previous analysis we can see that the situation of visitors arriving at one's council fire is always ambiguous until the visitors' intentions are known: they could be coming either to present proposals of their own (as at Philadelphia in 1747) or to answer proposals, i.e., either as petitioners or respondents. It will be recalled that in 1736 it was President Logan who spoke first during the business phase of the council which took place after the Indians had been escorted to the Great Meeting House in town. While his speech was extremely brief compared with the long speech by the chiefs that followed, it clearly established Pennsylvania as the petitioner (the chiefs, he said, "were now come to return their Answer" to proposals made in 1732). In this case, then, the petitioning party was in the position of the host rather than, as in the two previous cases, the visitor. This council cannot be considered a Type I council.

Case 4: Easton, November, 1756

This council, we pointed out, involves another kind of ambiguity, that centering on location and the allocation of the roles of host/ visitor. Teedyuscung played on this ambiguity to establish himself as host, thereby subtly enhancing his claim to Easton as Delaware territory. He also led off during the business phase of the council, presenting proposals which an inexperienced Governor Denny responded to. Although the allocation of roles on this occasion was the reverse of that in the 1736 Philadelphia council (the Indians rather than the whites being in the position of host-petitioners), we can see that both councils were built on the same underlying plan in which the petitioner was host. This is, of course, the identical plan of the scheduled council in Mr. Thomas's version which exactly replicates the Easton council by having the Indians as host-petitioners. We will call councils of this type "Type II" councils.

As we have seen with the previous set of councils (Type I), one council in the modern version provides a prototype for two historic councils. Such is the heuristic value of the method of upstreaming. One final point emerges from the analysis. We have shown that although it was an invitation council in the modern version that provided the prototype for Type I councils, this type is not confined to invitation councils. Of the seventeen councils in the larger Pennsylvania sample which have been closely analyzed, nine fall into the Type I category, and of these only three have as their principal business the extending of an invitation. The remainder have other types of main business. Can Type II councils be invitation councils? There are eight such councils in the larger Pennsylvania sample and none of these is an invitation council. There is a simple logical reason for this state of affairs: while petitioners may journey to a foreign council fire for some purpose other than giving an invitation, they *must* travel to a foreign council fire in making an invitation just to make their intentions known; one cannot give an invitation by sitting at home.

CONCLUSIONS

We can sum up our findings on speaker precedence in the form of two basic rules of council protocol (rules (1) and (2)) and their corollaries (rules (1') and (2')). We can predict the order between the Indian and white sides of the fire at all the Pennsylvania councils on the basis of these rules, and this suggests far wider applicability. These rules might at least serve a useful purpose heuristically as we upstream to a larger sample of the historic records in future work.

Rule (1): Hosts deliver the ceremonial welcome and extend hospitality to visitors.

Rule (1'): Visitors answer the ceremonial welcome and may expect hospitality.

Rule (2): Petitioners set the council's agenda and state the first substantive proposals. (They "kindle the fire.")

Rule (2'): Respondents answer all proposals made by the petitioners
before introducing business of their own.

The overall event sequence of a council, at least through its first
"cycle," can be encapsulated in a brief formula, the shift between
the first pair of numbered rules and the second pair marking the
shift between major phases:

$$(1) \rightarrow (1') \rightarrow (2) \rightarrow (2')$$

It is then only necessary to determine the allocation of roles among
the participants on a given occasion to predict their order in council.
It is suggested that the four Pennsylvania councils discussed in this
paper may represent the full range of possible council types in the
colonial period:

Type I
- Case 1: Indians (1) → Whites (1') → Whites (2) → Indians (2')
- Case 2: Whites (1) → Indians (1') → Indians (2) → Whites (2')

Type II
- Case 3: Whites (1) → Indians (1') → Whites (2) → Indians (2')
- Case 4: Indians (1) → Whites (1') → Indians (2) → Whites (2')

This schema may prove useful in various ways. If, for example,
details are lacking on the preliminaries of a scheduled council, as is
so often the case in the colonial records, we would still have a
reasonable basis for explaining the order of speakers on a particular
occasion if there is some mention, even passing mention, of who
invited whom, or who presented or received an invitation wampum,
or who was returning an invitation wampum now. From this and
the council's location, which can nearly always be determined, we
should be able to predict the *ideal* order of speakers, and this could
be compared with the actual order followed on a given occasion.
This brings us to a second possible application. As we suggested
earlier, only rarely does the matter of speaker precedence appear to
have been disputed. The rules of council protocol, whether they in
fact had the form we have given them in the participants' minds or
some other form, were widely, if for the most part tacitly understood
and followed. The rare occasions when someone's right to the floor
was challenged are particularly valuable for the kind of approach
we have been taking, since in defending his or someone else's
privilege, the speaker might find it necessary to resort to "basic
principles" which would otherwise remain inexplicit. These principles
sometimes sound surprisingly like our rules of protocol.[21]

NOTES

1. Italicized native words are given in Cayuga, except as noted in footnote
3. The reason for the choice of this language over the other Five Nations

languages will emerge in due course. A longer version of the present paper can be made available on request (Foster 1979). A monograph dealing not only with the question of speaker precedence but with the general structure of council protocol is under preparation. This monograph, or a companion piece to it, will contain extensive annotated native texts of council speeches.

2. Fenton is one of the few white men who have been privileged to witness the Condolence Ceremony (Fenton 1946a). He has written extensively about its program and symbolism. In addition to the sources cited, see Fenton (1950), Hewitt and Fenton (1944; 1945). A number of features, some of which we shall be describing at a later point, were borrowed more or less intact from the Condolence Ceremony into council protocol: the practice of greeting visitors outside the village with strings of wampum to wipe away their tears, clear their eyes and open their throats; the leading of visitors by the arm to the council house; the abbreviated "Condolement" inserted during the opening ceremonies for leaders that had died since the last meeting; and so on. The use of what was essentially a death rite as the template for forest diplomacy, far from revealing a preoccupation with the macabre on the part of the Iroquois, was actually highly appropriate since many of the councils were concerned with redressing the excesses of frontier violence.

3. Morgan described the council system under the term *Ho-de-os'-seh* (1901, I: 103) which Chafe (1967: 51, item 510) renders phonemically as *hoťíashě̇ʔ*, a close cognate of the Cayuga term now in use.

4. In the Condolence, the Confederacy still divides into an "Elder Brotherhood" (sometimes also called the "Three Brothers' Side") consisting of the Mohawk, Onondaga and Seneca, and a "Younger Brotherhood" (or the "Four Brothers' Side") consisting of the Oneida, Cayuga and adopted Tuscarora and Tutelo. When a chief dies, the brotherhood sustaining the loss—the side to which the chief's tribe belongs—automatically becomes, until the completion of the ceremony, the Mourning Side, while the opposite brotherhood becomes the Clearminded Side. The ceremonial rights and duties of individual participants depend entirely on which side they, as members of particular tribes, belong.

5. The Iroquois distinguish "interpreter" from "translator" (*te-Hawě̇natě̇:nyǒhs* 'he changes the words'). Unlike today's simultaneous translators at international conferences who are trained, with the help of electronic gear, to provide a running literal translation of speeches, the interpreters at Indian-white councils had considerably more latitude to summarize the gist of the speaker's remarks. The usual practice was to wait until the speaker had finished a speech, if it was short, or a section of a longer speech; if there were several groups present each was accorded the honor of receiving a translation in his language even if he understood the language of the speaker perfectly well. The interpreter, who was bridging not only linguistic but cultural worlds, was thus an integral part of the communicative process at a council.

6. The reason for this, as we shall see, is that the modern speeches, while subject to certain changes since the colonial period, are actually far more complete than the historic accounts, particularly on finer procedural points,

although the latter, which are far more numerous, comprise a voluminous literature.

7. The selection of the Pennsylvania-Iroquois councils for the present discussion is arbitrary though not unmotivated. The first half of the eighteenth century in many ways represents the high-water mark of the Confederacy's political power in the Northeast (for a general review, see Wallace 1969), and the apex of forest diplomacy as well. As the historic accounts go, the Pennsylvania councils are also among the most richly described in the colonial records.

8. Such active knowledge stems, I believe, from two beliefs held by many supporters of the Confederacy today: first, a deeply rooted conviction that the League has never ceased to function from aboriginal times to the present as a fully independent legally constituted government (see note 11); and second, a practical hunch that the white man needs to be reminded of the old agreements from time to time. A third possible factor, less easily defined, has to do with the Iroquoian view of the alliance as an organic entity that needs constant tending: the polishing of the Chain of Friendship which is forever accumulating dust and rust; the clearing of the forest path which is forever becoming overgrown with "obstructions"; the building up of the council fire which is ever in want of "fuel."

9. The single occasion I refer to was a council held between Six Nations chiefs and the Commissioner of Indian Affairs in Washington in 1954. A photograph taken on this occasion shows the Commissioner and a number of the chiefs sitting around a long table where the belts described in the next paragraph and the "King George" silver pipe are shown. A similar reading occurred in London before a Parliamentary committee in 1930, an event mentioned by Edmund Wilson in his *Apologies to the Iroquois* (Wilson 1960: 258); and trips made to Geneva in the days of the League of Nations and to San Francisco during the formation of the United Nations are favorite stories on the Six Nations Reserve. It is not known whether the belts were actually read on these occasions, but the writer is now attempting to carry the council tradition back in time with hopes of linking it up ultimately with the last great councils of the post-Revolutionary era.

10. Cayuga, Onondaga and Mohawk. Mr. Thomas was installed in a Condolence Ceremony held in 1974 at which he received the title Dawenhethon (phonemically *teyohŏwé:thŏ:?*), the eighth in the Cayuga roster (No. 40 in the roster overall (Fenton 1950: 66)). This title belongs to the Snipe Clan. The previous holder, Augustus Williams, died in 1972. Mr. Thomas also teaches in the Native Studies program at Trent University.

11. I have summarized this project elsewhere in a brief report which contains drawings of the two belts (Foster 1978). A rapid oral translation of the speeches was obtained using a second tape recorder, playing the speeches back on the first line at a time. This rough translation has been transcribed and annotated. More recently the essential but far more arduous process of transcribing and segmenting the native texts has been begun: this will take several years to complete. Already a good deal of new light has been shed on the elaborate metaphorical language of council oratory. Mr. Thomas has

himself prepared excellent English summaries of the texts accompanying the two belts (1975; 1975a).

The speeches accompanying the belts take the form of a dialogue between a generalized white man and a generalized Iroquois, a format which follows the basic council pattern of two sides of the fire addressing each other alternately. The first belt to be read, the Friendship Belt (*teHonané:tshō:t* 'they [masculine] have joined hands/arms'), describes the formation of the alliance between the Six Nations and the Dutch. The second belt, properly the Two Paths Belt (*tekhní: teyohá:te?* 'the two paths') but sometimes called in English the Two Row Belt (for the two rows of purple beads running parallel the length of the belt), traces the evolution of the alliance through the French, British and finally American "periods," i.e., to the present day. Each successive white government had agreed to the proposition that the laws and customs of the Indians and the white men should remain in separate canoes: the paths of these canoes should neither drastically converge nor diverge but remain parallel through time. As we shall see presently, the purpose of a renewal council is to see if the party to whom the belts are read still "respects" this arrangement; in the sense that this was the proposition placed before the participants in each historic stage described, the readings draw to a suspenseful climax in the staged event itself or in any renewal council which might be scheduled today.

12. The Washington council of 1954 (see note 9) is an instance of the latter type; on that occasion the Six Nations assumed responsibility for the reading of the belts at a foreign council fire.

13. In the Condolence Ceremony the Clearminded faction, whose speaker has been chanting the Roll Call of the fifty chiefs, stops by the entrance lane to the Mourners' longhouse and receives the wood's edge welcome there before being escorted to the longhouse (see Fenton 1946a: 112 ff. for a description).

14. The recurrent metaphors of council oratory revolve around the same concern for the clearing of channels between designated fires: the maintenance of the Path, the polishing of the Chain, etc.; and these channels are also the principal motifs of wampum belts (Foster 1977).

15. This is a departure from the historic councils where visitors usually returned thanks for the greetings immediately afterwards, this phase of the council being the sole business of the first day which was followed by a period of rest and private consultation before proceeding to the main place of council.

16. Here, speech and gesture unite in a single purposive act: the terms for "invitation," "invitation wampum," and "agreement" all revolve around the notion of extending arms (or hands) across the fire. These are verbal constructions incorporating the noun root *-nĕtsh(a)-* 'arm' (sometimes 'hand' in the context of the formal speeches). We see this root in the messenger's announcement *aetshiné:tsha:?* 'they take you by the arm'; in the term for the invitation wampum, *enĕtshatiyōtáhkwa?* 'that which stretches a person's arm'; in the term for escorting visitors to the place of council, *ĕyetshinĕtshí:neht* 'they will lead you by the arm'; in the general terms for the invitation itself, e.g., *ethínĕtsha:?* 'we've got them by the arm', *ōkhínĕtsha:?* 'they've got us

by the arm', etc.; in the name of the Friendship Belt, *teHonanȇ:tshõ:t* 'they have joined/linked arms'; and in a great many other expressions in the speeches.

17. The privilege of having one's body "rubbed down" is thus accorded to anyone who has made a journey over the forest path, and not just a foreign emissary. This further bears out the notion that some attention must be paid to the channel of communication, here the agent carrying the message, before dealing with substantive matters.

18. Fenton has applied the method of upstreaming in tracing the history of the Condolence itself (see sources cited in note 2), as well as in treating Iroquois suicide patterns (1941a), settlement patterns (1951) and the Eagle Dance (1953). It would be easy to exaggerate the factor of change while trying to pay it just due. Suppose we wanted to make a statement about the grammar of English at an earlier stage and all we had were some fragments of written texts from this stage: we would be overlooking an invaluable resource if we excluded what we know about the grammar of contemporary English in attempting to reconstruct the earlier stage. This would not mean that we would have to be blind to the ways the language has changed during the intervening time.

19. This trip occurred in 1743. Weiser described the opening in these terms: "A String of Wampum was given by Tocanontie in behalf of the Onondagoes to wipe off the Sweat from their (the Deputies & Messenger's [i.e., Weiser's party's]) Bodies. . . . All this was done by way of a Song the Speaker walking up & down in the House. After this the Deputies & Messengers held a Conference by themselves and appointed Aquoyiota to return thanks for their kind reception with another String of Wampum Aquoyiota repeated all that was said in a Singing way walking up and down in the House. . . . the Council was now Opened . . ." (Wallace 1945: 163).

20. Protocol allowed for such an abridgment of the ideal sequence. Just as interesting, it allowed for the opposite tendency, the stretching out of the sequence over considerable periods of time. The latter tendency might arise as a diplomatic way of saving face. When the governor of Virginia proposed, via Weiser, at the Onondaga council of 1737 that the Iroquois come to Williamsburg to treat with the Southern Indians, with whom the Iroquois claimed on another occasion to be engaged in a war which would "last to the End of the World" (Wallace 1945: 167), the normal expectation was that such a council would take place within a year, at the most. The Iroquois did not want to offend Pennsylvania which was acting on Virginia's behalf and so did not want to make an outright refusal of the invitation, but they succeeded in having the matter put on ice by suggesting Albany as an alternate location, a location that they knew their enemies would be reluctant to agree to. The council did eventually materialize—in 1751, *fourteen years later*—and then only because of further goading by Pennsylvania at councils held at Onondaga in 1743 and 1750 (Wallace 1945: 160 ff., 304 ff.) and a special ceremony to readmit Virginia to the Chain of Friendship at the Lancaster treaty of 1744 (Boyd 1938: 41 ff.; Wallace 1945: 184 ff.).

21. One such instance occurred at the Lancaster treaty of 1744, a Type II council with the whites as host-petitioners. It was generally agreed that

the white side of the fire should lead off during the business phase of the council, but the situation was complicated by the fact that this side comprised three groups who all had proposals to make to the Six Nations. It was agreed that Pennsylvania's role on this occasion would mainly be to "introduce" the colonies of Maryland and Virginia who had allowed the chain to accumulate a great deal of rust and who would therefore need to be readmitted to the alliance. The problem was determining which of the new members should speak first, a problem which was compounded by the existence of a squabble between Virginia and Maryland over their common border and a bold attempt during the rest period by Colonel Thomas Lee of Virginia to bribe the chiefs privately to have the floor before Maryland. The Iroquois had been given to understand that the invitation had emanated from Maryland, and they were not the least swayed by Lee's maneuverings. As soon as the governor of Pennsylvania had delivered the welcome address, which he did by virtue of the council's being held in his territory and his being the spokesman for the white side of the fire (Rule (1)), Canasatego, the great Onondaga orator-chief, rose to answer for the Six Nations (Rule (1')), at the same time setting the council firmly on the rails:

> We thank you [the governor of Pennsylvania] for giving us Time to rest; we are come to you, and shall leave it intirely to you to appoint the Time when we shall meet you again. We likewise leave it to the Governor of *Maryland*, by whose Invitation we came here, to appoint a Time when he will please to mention the Reason of his inviting us. As to our Brother *Assaragoa* [Virginia], we have at this present Time nothing to say to him, not but we [do not] have a great deal to say to *Assaragoa*, which must be said at one Time or another; but not being satisfied whether he or we should begin first, we shall leave it wholly to our Brother *Onas* [Pennsylvania] to adjust this between us, and to say which shall begin first. (Boyd 1938: 44)

In the ensuing days, Pennsylvania led off by formally introducing Maryland and Virginia, saving its own business until later, and Maryland stated the first substantive proposals. Canasatego's statement is one of the most explicit formulations of Rule (2) in the Pennsylvania literature.

CHAPTER TWELVE

Translation Glosses
and Semantic Description

HANNI WOODBURY

INTRODUCTION

One of William Fenton's characteristics as an anthropologist is his excellence as a field worker. Indeed, this attribute is an important source of the high quality of his work. Much of what is known and understood of Iroquoian culture is attributable to Fenton's remarkable eye for fine detail and his seemingly tireless efforts as a field worker and theoretician to learn Iroquoian culture well enough to become a creditable participant. Good data collection yields productive theory, as it has in Fenton's case.

In this paper I want, in a small way, to carry on in his tradition, by reexamining the complementary roles of field worker and those whom the field worker consults as experts in their language and culture. It has occurred to me that we Iroquoianists have neglected to explore, and fully use, the knowledge our consultants bring to their task; that is to say, we have ignored or taken for granted the fact that they are bicultural. Not only are they experts in Iroquoian language and culture, but they share *our* expertise in Euro-American language and culture. This raises the issue I address in this paper: how can we incorporate this knowledge of two cultures into our methodologies and theoretical constructs? In this paper I explore the problem through language, taking Onondaga as my example. But linguists and ethnographers share a number of problems and I intend this paper as an example which can suggest ethnographic method as well. Thus, to begin with, I would like to point out what I think is the connection.

One way of thinking of the anthropological task is as one of translation, which is to say that it is not exempt from the Whorfian problem. As members of *a culture*, with all that this implies, anthropologists must face the issue of how to keep that from interfering with the process of understanding *a different culture*. Inevitably we must translate in order to try to understand. We must ask how the activities we are observing differ from similar activities in our own culture; we must ask how a linguistic form we encounter can be rendered (that is, how it can be matched) by one in our own language; and so on. The problem is familiar from the large literature on ethnographic semantics. The question this literature raises is: how can we develop culture-free descriptive categories, and if that is not possible, what other techniques can we devise to help prevent distortions?

This is where, as American Indianists, we have a precious resource in the fact that many native Americans are bicultural. As participants in two cultural systems they are especially sensitive to the degree of overlap that exists between similar categories of the two cultures. We have already reaped the benefit of such extensive knowledge through the work of J. N. B. Hewitt, who was not only bicultural and bilingual, but who was also a linguist. His skill as a translator documents my point. In fact, my acquaintance with his work, together with my field experiences with skilled bilinguals, stimulated the ideas I develop in this paper.

Translation is an activity in which an expression in one language is encoded into another in such a way as to retain its original meaning. I urge the point in this paper that when one has the good fortune of being assisted in one's research by individuals who are experts in two languages (or cultures), one would do well to extend the task of one's informants. Not only should they be sources of cultural information, but they should also take part in the task of translation. In working with language it soon becomes clear that translation is a process that requires a number of steps. This is why linguists distinguish between translation glosses and true translations. Glosses are rough approximations (in the language that is shared by linguist and informant, i.e., the contact language) of the meanings that are signaled by the forms in the language under study (i.e., the target language). Glosses to some extent ignore the lack of fit between categories in the two languages. The step of acquiring glosses is, however, absolutely essential for the development of true translations. I show in this paper how true translations can be derived from series of related glosses. It is in the acquisition of related sets of glosses that bilingual informants are particularly helpful. In addition, their glosses generally are excellent approximations of the meanings in the target language.

The method I describe can be adapted to ethnography. Glosses are the linguistic equivalent of comparisons the *bicultural informant* makes between the two cultures of which he is a member. Again, the equivalences he notices will tend to be significant ones. It will be the task of the ethnographer to derive "true cultural translations" from these comparisons by specifying the differing systems underlying the cultural expressions being compared. This can be done by making cross-comparisons in the manner I outline below.

CHARACTERISTICS OF TRANSLATION GLOSSES

> We would like to assume that the metalinguistic operation of defining is a cultural universal. That is to say, all languages furnish a way of asking "What's an X? " and in all cultures at least children make use of this device . . . We therefore believe that it is possible to obtain tentative definitions from naive speakers of any language.
> But we would like to make a much stronger assumption still: the definitions elicitable from informants by asking them, in their language, "What's an X? " . . . are not completely random; on the contrary, they will show a certain recurrent pattern for any X, and it is this pattern which constitutes the culturally shared structure of the meaning of X. (Weinreich 1967:42)

Let us extend Weinreich's insight to the bilingual situation. Then his "defining" becomes glossing, for a gloss is a kind of definition, one that is rendered in a bilingual's other available language. I will suggest that bilinguals' choices of translation glosses in a contact language (here English) are significant, and that treating these choices as nonrandom occurrences helps to provide systematic insights into the semantic structure of the target language (here Onondaga).[1]

That translation glosses are slippery customers is common knowledge. Warnings to this effect are dutifully delivered and accepted, but since, it seems, we cannot accomplish grammatical analysis without access to meaning, it is hard to know what to do about the warnings. A second characteristic of translation glosses has, with one important exception (Dixon 1971), been virtually ignored in the literature. It is their nonrandomness, or put differently, the fact that translation glosses bear a realtionship to the linguistic forms they gloss. For bilinguals, the posssible results of glossing activities are rather narrowly limited, at least if these activities are confined to the strictly *referential* functions of language use. There are, broadly, two possible situations: that in which a word of the target language apparently matches a form in the contact language rather well, and that in which there is only a partial semantic overlap between the two languages' forms. Except for the possibility of error, three and only three mutually exclusive outcomes of glossing activities are possible: (1) an informant will provide a gloss without further ado; (2) he will become aware that he either does not know or has temporarily forgotten the equivalent item in the contact language, in which case he will provide synonyms or near synonyms; or (3) he will provide a gloss which is the nearest equivalent in the target language, knowing that no *real* equivalent exists. The last of these outcomes often results in a linguistic form together with an explanation. The one thing a properly bilingual informant (*properly bilingual* to be defined below) would almost never do would be to provide a gloss that has *no* relationship to the requested item. The three alternatives are extremely interesting because they seem to indicate that speakers have *slots*, as it were, for linguistic forms and their related referential meanings. When they have forgotten a surface form they know it, and they do not randomly substitute a different one. Similarly, bilinguals are often aware of poor lexical matches in the two languages they control, and they are often quite adept at pinpointing the areas of mismatch.

One way of characterizing the method of the bilingual informant is to say that apparently he finds the gloss which overlaps in terms of at least some of its criterial elements with the form in question and that he then proceeds to point to ways in which the two words are alike and unlike one another. Presumably he holds the contexts of the two utterances constant during this process. Seemingly bilinguals have knowledge of the semantic structures of the two languages they control. They compare these, and then make use of the comparisons when they are asked to produce glosses. The product of this activity is a set of two matched folk definitions. Our job as linguists is to treat these as data to be examined in terms of theoretical constructs that are suitable to their analysis. An important point is— and this is like Weinreich's contention—that an investigator can go to any number of bilinguals and find a large amount of patterning in their choices of translation glosses.

The task of this paper is to suggest ways in which a bilingual's knowledge of *two* languages can be used systematically to discover the semantic structure of the target language. The meanings of single lexical items as well as their morpho-syntactic characteristics can and should be investigated in order for the comparison between languages to be revealing (Conklin 1967:121). The approach is not new so far as semantic analysis is concerned. It invokes a combination of paradigmatic and definitional methods as was suggested by Dixon (1971).[2] What is new, as far as I know, is the suggestion that translation glosses are devices that can be systematically used to supplement the results of the two more basic methods. The reasons why we would wish to use them are rather obvious: first, the semantic structure of English is better known at this point than that of many other languages. Used with care this knowledge can be made available for the discovery of the semantic structure of other languages. Secondly, and much more importantly, these suggestions overtly recognize, as well as examine, a procedure which has remained largely implicit in our analyses of unfamiliar semantic systems. The use of translation glosses is unavoidable in treating large areas of the lexicon. Kinship terminologies, pronominal sets, and a few other special vocabularies are exceptional in this respect. This is so because they may be treated as finite sets, because often they are structured on the basis of a minimal set of semantic features, and because it is at least conceivable that informants could define their elements ostensively. But the analysis of verbal meanings, for example, would be largely impossible were we to disallow the use of translation glosses. In doing semantic analyses we are confronted with a procedural problem, namely, that meanings of single lexical items, let alone grammatical meanings, cannot be fully known until the whole system is examined. The procedural problem becomes a *logical* one when we attempt to analyze open-ended sets of elements. We deal with finite sets by treating our solutions as provisional until the entire set has been analyzed, after which the provisional solutions are adjusted. But it makes no sense to think in terms of provisional solutions when analyzing open-ended sets. In such cases completeness is a statistical concept and it becomes necessary to use a number of approaches which, taken together, do not depend so heavily on completeness for the validity of their findings. I suggest in what follows, that the implicit use of translation glosses be replaced by a set of standards and procedures for their acknowledged use.

It is appropriate at this point to develop criteria of bilingualism which will protect this approach against errors that are due to insufficient mastery of one of the two languages. *Bilingualism* is usually treated as rather a broad category. For example, "the practice of alternately using two languages will be called *bilingualism* and the persons involved, *bilingual*" (Weinreich 1974:1). In the context of the discussion to follow, it is useful to narrow the scope of the concept *bilingual* to refer to an individual who has *grown up* in a setting which required the practice of alternating between two languages. This requirement leaves out all those individuals who have acquired the second language *as* a second language at some later stage in their life. *Bilingual* in this sense, then, refers to an individual who can be presumed to have internalized the semantic structures of two languages in a rather complete way, despite the fact that he may feel more comfortable with one or the other language in specifiable situations or linguistic contexts.

Among speakers of the Iroquoian languages, it is exceptional to encounter a monolingual speaker. The fact that a language has few or no monolingual speakers, means that the process of contact between two languages is complete, if we take the speaker as the focal point of language contact. Such a language does not exist, as it were, outside of the contact situation. This condition offers us a unique opportunity to take seriously and to study systematically the products of our informants' translation skills, and to develop methods that will check the accuracy of their folk definitions. Variability among speakers due to variations in their skill between the two languages, and hence *variation* in terms of the interference of one semantic system with the other, are reduced to a minimum in this situation. It is of great interest in this connection to compare glossing behavior as it is manifested in dictionaries of closely related languages. For example, comparisons among dictionaries of the northern Iroquoian languages show remarkable agreement in terms of the English translation glosses that are provided for cognate forms. This cannot be due to mere chance or to the incredible analytic skill of the linguists who prepared these dictionaries. We still have too much to learn about semantic systems to believe that. It seems clear that the agreement finds its source among the speakers of these languages even though the *reasons* for their unanimity may be complex. As linguists we have a tendency, despite warnings to the contrary, to take our informants' word that X in their language means roughly Y in ours. I believe that it is possible, by studying their matched productions in two languages, to become more precise in our own analytic and translation efforts.

Identifying the Semantics of Direction

All languages encode spatial concepts in one way or another. Among these are those referring to direction. Usually they are expressed on more than a single linguistic level. Thus *up* and *down* are overtly directional, but *come* and *go* express direction as an intrinsic property of these particular verbs, so that their meanings can be analyzed into more basic elements, at least one of which will signify direction. Sometimes direction is encoded morphologically. For example, the prefixes of *import* and *export* bear this semantic function. On the level of meaning, too, direction need not be a unitary phenomenon. For example, direction may pertain to the end result of an activity, or it may describe the activity itself. Again, direction may or may not be relative to a reference point which in turn may or may not be related to pragmatic dimensions describing elements of the speech situation, e.g., person and space. The distinctions are subtle ones, but a thorough analysis requires their discovery and elucidation. To illustrate questions that were raised at the beginning of this section, we will focus on semantic elements of direction in Onondaga, attempting to establish their presence or absence, their content, and their manner of interacting with other semantic elements.

Onondaga belongs to the Six Nations group of the Northern Iroquoian languages. It is spoken on reservations in northern New York and Canada. The grammatical details that are pertinent to the discussion are largely in the realm of derivational morphology, that area of word formation processes in which meanings are affected. The crucially important derivational morphemes are listed in Table 12.1, together with each morpheme's syntactic and semantic functions.

We will consider three sets of examples. The sets consist of a number of constructions all of which share a verb root in common. The verb roots are, first, -e- which bilinguals gloss 'come, go, walk' depending on the presence or absence of various derivational affixes; second is -v- which is glossed 'pull, push, fall, alight, happen'; third is -hninu- which is glossed both 'buy' and 'sell'. These verbs were chosen, in part, because their counterparts in English have been much analyzed (e.g., Bendix 1966; Bierwisch 1969; Fillmore 1971, 1977; Gruber 1967; Katz 1967), and this spares us from having to make a parallel analysis of English meanings. I have in mind, too, that ethnographers, social anthropologists, and psychologists have shown interest in orientation systems. An investigation into their linguistic manifestations may be of interest to them.

The method of analyzing the meanings of the target language's forms consists, as a first step, of listing all the constructions based on a given Onondaga verbal root which produce variations in the English lexical items that are used to gloss the constructions. The choice and range of English glosses is treated as significant. As a second step, we note the presence of the chosen glosses as well as the absence of possible related ones in comparing the English items in search of common semantic elements. For the third step, we assign the common semantic elements of the glosses as part of the meaning of the Onondaga root which is the only element that is shared by all of the constructions. As a final step, we compare the Onondaga constructions with one another, noting formal similarities and differences among them, and we again perform cross-comparisons with those semantic elements of the translation glosses co-occurring with them. Any residues must be compared to formally similar elements that occur in construction with other verb roots. The method is confined, it should be observed, to constructions which have not

Table 12.1. Table of Grammatical and Semantic Functions

Derivational Morpheme[a]	Grammatical Functions	Semantic Functions[b]
Semi-reflexive -at-, -atv-	Intransitivizes: 1 Marks loss of direct objects of transitives 2 Marks loss of indirect objects of indirect transitives unless subject & direct object are coreferent, in which case direct object is lost	Middle voice: marks action with respect to agent or his (inalienable) possession 2 Renders stative verbs active 3 Reassigns case role of lost noun phrase to surface subject
Causative -ht-	1 Transitivizes intransitives 2 Marks presence of new subject adjunct	1 Former actor of active intransitive or patient of stative intransitive becomes patient of new transitive 2 New subject becomes agent
Dative -ʔs-	Transitivizes: marks the addition of indirect object to intransitives, transitives, and indirect transitives.	1 New case roles associated with dative: source, goal/beneficiary, replacive. 2 Restricted to verbs taking inanimate direct objects and animate indirect objects.
Inchoative -ʔ-		Marks inception of a new event or state
Cislocative[c] (-)t-	Adverbial; marks overt allative-like adverbial adjunct	1 Direction of action or event toward reference point 2 Place or result of action or event near reference point
Trans-locative[c] h-	Adverbial: marks overt ablative-like adverbial adjunct	1 Direction of action or event away from reference point 2 Place or result of action or event away from reference point.

[a] Only those variants of each derivational morpheme which occur in the examples are listed.

[b] The semantic functions of each morpheme do not all occur simultaneously; rather they are selected by each root in terms of its membership in various grammatical and semantic classes.

[c] Only the semantic functions having to do with direction are listed for these morphemes.

been petrified into idiomatic expressions, since the problem of how to analyze idioms is still far from being solved. What follows is intended as an example of a method. It should be emphasized that the greater the number of semantically related forms that are examined in this way, the greater will be the accuracy of the final analysis.

The verb root -e- 'come, go, walk'

Consider the following examples:

1 *a* v́the? 'he'll come'
  v-t-h-e-? TENSE-CISLOC-he-verb root-ASP

 b hv́he? 'he'll go'
  h-v-h-e-? TRANSLOC-TENSE-he-verb root-ASP

 c tshá? hakwá nheyakáwè:nu ' where she went'
  tsha? hakwa n-he-yakaw-e-nu ADV # direction # PART-Transloc-she-verb root-ASP

 d tshá? hakwà nityakáwè:nu 'where she came from'
  tsha? hakwa ni-t-yakaw-e-nu ADV # direction # PART-CISLOC-she-verb root-ASP

 e íhe? 'he's walking'
  i-h-e-? EMPTY MORPH-he-verb root-ASP

 f nutáwe? "thence it would come" (Hewitt 1903: 198, line 4).
  n-u-t-a-w-e-? PART-EMPTY MORPH-CISLOC-TENSE-it-verb root-ASP

From the translation glosses in 1 it is simple to see that the Onondaga verb root -*e*- which occurs in each of the six examples only partially matches the meanings of English *come, go,* and *walk*. An approximate analysis of the English verbs is:[3]

 come: MOVE PROGRESSIVELY TO ANY REFERENCE POINT, INCLUDING ONE ASSOCIATED WITH EITHER SPEAKER OR ADDRESSEE

 go: MOVE PROGRESSIVELY TO ANY REFERENCE POINT, INCLUDING ONE ASSOCIATED WITH THE ADDRESSEE, BUT NOT INCLUDING ONE ASSOCIATED WITH THE SPEAKER

 walk: SELF-PROPELLED PROGRESSIVE MOVEMENT ON FOOT (RESTRICTED TO ACTORS OF THE CLASS OF ANIMATES POSSESSING FEET)

The semantic element shared by the three English words is MOVE PROGRESSIVELY, and our assumption is that since the six constructions in 1 are built upon a single Onondaga verb root, that the meaning of this root will (at least) contain that element which all the glosses share.[4] It may of course contain others, which do not go to make up definitions of the English words. These must be uncovered by contrasting various complex forms containing the Onondaga root, and by contrasting this particular root with others having related meanings. In this paper the first two steps, i.e., the comparison between English and Onondaga constructions and comparisons among different Onondaga constructions that are based on a single root will be emphasized. Only fleeting consideration is given to contrasts among elements with related meanings.

Examples 1*a* - *d* show that the glosses 'come' and 'go' are associated with the cislocative and the translocative morphemes, respectively. Hence we should assign directional meanings to these morphemes. This decision is supported by example *e* which lacks locative prefixes and whose gloss 'to walk' also lacks directionality. Examples *c*, *d*, and *f* provide a clue concerning the nature of the directionality that is marked by the locative prefixes. When the partitive is in construction with the verb root -*e*- it refers to a particular place or reference point with respect to which the action that is signified by the verb root takes place. Notice that the partitive marks a goal expression in *c* (i.e., 'where (the place) she went') and a source expression in *d* and *f* (i.e., 'where (the place) she came from'). Examples *c* and *d* form a minimal pair with contrasting locative prefixes, so that the difference in the interpretation of the partitive must be due to them. One way of interpreting this division of labor in signifying different nuances of meaning among the verb root, the locatives, and the partitive is as follows: the verb root describes progressive movement but is neutral with respect to direction; the partitive signals the fact that the movement takes place in relation to a reference point; the locatives, finally, encode the direction of the movement that is described by the verb. The glosses of *c* and *d* show what reference points the partitive signals. Rather than describing it as now a goal and now a source, we can say that it is much like the proximate place adverbial *here*, i.e., it refers to the vicinity of the speaker or some other object or person acting as reference point. This is so, because the gloss 'where she came from' presupposes a known goal (i.e., near X) but calls for a specification of the place of origin (i.e. somewhere not near X), whereas the gloss 'where she went' presupposes a known place of origin (i.e., near X) but calls for a specification of the goal (i.e., somewhere not near X). In each case the location near X is known and used as reference point.

We conclude that English *come* and *go* differ from Onondaga -*e*- insofar as the fomer are inherently directional whereas the Onondaga verb root lacks a directinal semantic component. But further, the constructions as whole entities differ from their English glosses. Gruber has argued convincingly that both *come* and *go* must be defined in terms of their possible goal expressions. That is, *come* and *go* differ in that the former may incorporate the meaning of either the proximal or the distal place adverbs (i.e., here, there) as a semantic element describing a goal expression (e.g., *will you come to my party?* and *I'll come to your party*) whereas *go* contains only the distal deictic as goal (e.g., *I will go to your party* but not **will you go to my party?*). The directional meanings that are added to -*e*- when the locatives are in construction with it differ from the *come* and *go* directions in that they use only the proximate meaning as reference point, and in the presence of the partitive, this element functions either as goal or as source. Hence the glosses of *a* and *b* must be taken as mere approximations of the actual meanings expressed by these Onondaga constructions, which are more nearly rendered by 'he'll come (to here)' and 'he'll go (from here)'.

A second difference in meaning between Onondaga -*e*- and the three English verbs occurring in the glosses is associated with the kinds of subjects that these intransitive verbs can take. Example *1f* shows that -*e*- does not require animate subjects, just like English *come* and *go*. This is not so for English *walk*. That is to say, that *walk* leaves something to be desired as a gloss for the construction in *1e*, because its selectional restrictions do not match those of the Onondaga root.

We conclude that a possible definition of Onondaga -*e*- is TO MOVE PROGRESSIVELY IN A WAY THAT IS CHARACTERISTIC OF THE REFERENT DESCRIBED BY THE SUBJECT. With this definition in hand we can see that the overlap between Onondaga -*e*- and any *one* of the translation glosses is imperfect. But we did find that what overlap there is is significant. An important finding for the thesis of the paper is that the translation glosses were an indispensable part of the analysis of the constructions' actual meaning.

The verb root -v- 'fall, pull down, push down, alight, happen'

Compared to 1 the examples in 2 display a much more diverse set of translation glosses:

2 *a* taheyá?tv̀hta? 'I pulled him down'
   t-a-he-ya?t-v-ht-a?   CISLOC-TENSE-I/him-body-verb root-
                         CAUS-ASP

 b takuta?sv́hta? "thence they let themselves down" (Hewitt 1903: 182, line 9). (also "they alighted")

c hwaʔheyáʔtv̀hta? 'I pushed him down'
　 h-waʔ-he-yaʔt-v-ht-aʔ　TRANSLOC-TENSE-I/him-body-verb
　　　　　　　　　　　　 root-CAUS-ASP
d waʔtknóʔtsyv̀ʔnha? 'my teeth fell out'
　 waʔ-t-k-noʔtsi-v-ʔ-nha?　TENSE-DUALIC-I-tooth-verb root-
　　　　　　　　　　　　　 INCH-ASP
e niyá:wv̀ʔi 'it has happened / came to pass (in this way)'
　 ni-yaw-v-ʔ-i　PART-it-verb root-INCH-ASP

Approximate definitions of the English verbs that are used in the glosses of example 2 are:

> *pull:* X CAUSES Y TO MOVE TOWARD X
> *alight:* X CAUSES SELF TO MOVE DOWN ONTO Y
> *push:* X CAUSES Y TO MOVE AWAY FROM X
> *fall:* (IT) HAPPPENS, X MOVES DOWN
> *happen:* (IT) COMES ABOUT (BY CHANCE)

Leaving aside *happen* for the time being, we find that the common property of these definitons is the element MOVE. The glosses of *a - c* contain the locative adverb 'down'. Since the gloss of *d* includes 'fall' which has DOWN as one of its sense components, we can identify DOWN as a second shared element. Hence we provisionally define -*v*- as MOVE DOWN. Examples *a - c* each contain the causative transitivizer -*ht*-. Its presence marks the verb root as intransitive, since, in Onondaga, the causative affix is restricted to intransitive roots. Semantically, the causative identifies the subject as causer and the object as patient of the action this verb describes. These three constructions contrast with *d* derivationally. In *d* the causative of *a - c* is replaced by the inchoative morpheme. While the causative in these constructions is associated with the idea that the action is intentionally initiated by the causer, the inchoative suggests the inception of an action or a state that is unintentional, that is, it simply happens. This is just the difference we find between English *pull down, alight,* and *push down,* on the one hand, and *fall* on the other. A difference between *fall* and the Onondaga construction in *d* is marked by the occurrence of the dualic. Independent evidence (comparisons among Onondaga forms with and without the dualic) indicates that the dualic in *d* marks a change of state (supplementing the notion of the inception of a new state which is marked by the inchoative) so that 'fall out' is not simply an unintentional process in Onondaga, as it is in English. Rather, this example describes the unintentional inception of a transition from one state to another.

　　Examples *a* and *b* contrast with *c* in terms of direction. In *a* and *b* direction is marked by the cislocative and in *c* by the translocative.

In English *push down* and *pull down* differentiate between direction away from or towards the agent, respectively. But the array of examples *a - c* provides evidence that the directionality we associate with *push* and *pull* is not like that which is encoded by the Onondaga locative morphemes. Observe that it makes sense to say that the direction of the action in *a* and *c* is toward or away from the causer, but it is nonsense to say that the glosses 'alight' and 'let oneself down' can refer to direction toward the causer. In *b* it is not the direction of the activity that is signaled by the cislocative, but rather the location of its end result in relation to the causer of the action. That is, if the end result is in the vicinity of the causer, then the cislocative is used.[5] This meaning also is reasonable for examples *a* and *c*. That is important, for one of our goals must be to find a *constant* semantic function that holds between a given root and a particular derivational morpheme.[6] Examples *a* and *c* can now be interpreted to mean X CAUSED Y TO MOVE DOWN TO HERE and X CAUSED Y TO MOVE DOWN TO NOT HERE. So that the contrast between the cislocative and the translocative, when these are in construction with -*v*-, resembles that of the English elements *here* and *there* more nearly than it does the contrast we associate with *pull* and *push* where the directional elements modify the action itself rather than the result of the action.

We have found similarities and differences in the functions of the cislocative and translocative morphemes depending on whether they occur in collocations with -*e*- (sec. 2.1.) or -*v*-. In both cases we find that the reference point of the locatives is a location in the proximity of the subject's referent. The difference is that when the locatives are in construction with -*e*- their directional meaning modifies the action signified by the verb directly, so that the progressive movement of -*e*- takes place in a certain direction, but when the locatives are in construction with -*v*-, their directionality pertains to the end result of the verb's action. So the locatives plus -*v*- encode the place where the downward movement which that root describes ends. In constructions with -*e*- the partitive had the function of marking the presence of source or goal expressions. This is precluded for the verb root -*v*-, for the partitive has a different function (to be discussed below) when it occurs with that root. The function of marking the presence of a goal expression with -*v*- is taken over by the locatives when they are in construction with that root. The verb root -*v*- is semantically more complex than -*e*-, for apart from the components of movement which are a part of the sense of each of these roots, -*v*- also has a directional component over and above those that are marked by locatives. It is the direction DOWN and we may assume that MOVE is directly modified by DOWN. Hence examples such as *2a - c* in which the locatives occur, are quite complex in the way they encode direction.

In construction with *-v-* the partitive has a specialized idiomatic effect on the meaning of the verb root. It abstracts the action that the verb describes, as it were, so that the gloss 'to fall' of *2d* (*-v-* plus inchoative) becomes 'to happen' (*-v-* plus partitive and inchoative) in *2e*. This metaphoric extension of the literal meaning of MOVE DOWN is familiar to us from the English set *fall* vs. *befall* as well as *fall* in the sense 'occur'.[7]

The verb root -hninu- 'buy, sell'

Analysis of this verb root involves yet greater complexities. The following set of examples is pertinent:

3 *a* waʔhahninúʔ kaʔsé:htaʔ   'He bought a car'
   waʔ-ha-hninu-ʔ ka-ʔseht-aʔ   TENSE-he/it-verb root-ASP # it-vehicle-NOUN SUFFIX

  b waʔshakohninúʔ kaʔsé:htaʔ   'He bought a car from someone'
   waʔ-shako-hninu-ʔ   ka-ʔseht-aʔ   TENSE-he/someone-verb root-ASP # it-vehicle-NOUN SUFFIX

  c waʔshakohninúʔs kaʔsé:ht-aʔ   'He bought a car for someone'
   waʔ-shako-hninu-ʔs-∅ ka-ʔseht-aʔ   TENSE-he/someone-verb root-DAT-ASP # it-vehicle-NOUN SUFFIX

  d waʔhatvhninúʔ kaʔsé:htaʔ   'He sold a car'
   waʔ-ha-atv-hninu-ʔ ka-ʔsehta-aʔ   TENSE-he/it-SR-verb root-ASP # it-vehicle-NOUN SUFFIX

  e waʔshakotvhninúʔs kaʔsé:htaʔ   'He sold a car to someone'
   waʔ-shako-atv-hninu-ʔs-∅ ka-ʔseht-aʔ   TENSE-he/someone-SR-verb root-DAT-ASP # it-vehicle-NOUN SUFFIX

  f waʔshakotvhninúʔs koʔsé:htaʔ   'He sold a car for someone'
   waʔ-shako-atv-hninu-ʔs-∅ ko-ʔseht-aʔ   TENSE-he/someone-SR-verb root-DAT-ASP # someone's-vehicle-NOUN SUFFIX

English *buy* and *sell* refer to an event in which the ownership of goods is transferred from seller to buyer in consideration of equivalent value in legal tender, which flows from buyer to seller. Approximate English definitions for the two terms are:

buy: X TRANSFERS Y FROM Z FOR MONEY
sell: X TRANSFERS Y TO Z FOR MONEY

Now English *buy* and *sell*, as Fillmore (1977) has pointed out, "focus" on the buyer, the seller, and on the goods which pass between the two, leaving the money "out of perspective" as he terms it. In order to bring the money into perspective, speakers of English usually use verbs like *spend*, *cost*, or *pay*. There is morphological evidence that the Onondaga verb root also focuses on the buyer, seller, and the goods, for when reference to money is involved in a sentence, then the instrumental morpheme is affixed to the basic verb root, i.e. -*hninu*- becomes -*hninu-ʔt*- in sentences such as *neʔ hothwistahsvnuni waʔhaʔse:htahnínùʔtaʔ* 'he bought a car with his savings' (literally: the he-has-money-saved he-it-car-buy-used).

A second well-known characteristic of the English verbs *buy* and *sell* is that they are not mirror images of one another, for while *Harry bought the car from Mary* and *Mary sold the car to Harry* can truthfully refer to the same event, yet the initiative lies with the buyer when the event is described with the verb *buy* and with the seller when *sell* is used. In the first instance the agent is also the goal or beneficiary of the goods and in the second the agent is also their source. Because the role of money is suppressed for these lexical items, and in order to express their case role correctly, we posit a derived semantic level where these two words are described as follows (on the basic level MONEY is needed to distinguish *buy* and *sell* from *take* and *give*, respectively):

buy: X TRANSFERS Y FROM Z TO X
sell: Z TRANSFERS Y FROM Z TO X

The directional element (which describes the flow of goods) of English *buy* and *sell*, then, is invariant, but its reference points vary between source and goal.

Turning now to the examples in 3 we find that -*hninu*- is an indirect transitive, because it can occur in sentences with three noun phrase adjuncts without the need for derivational morphemes (see 3*b*). Secondly, in comparing the two subsets of 3 we find the gloss 'buy' associated with *a - c* and 'sell' with *d - f*. We note that the gloss 'sell' occurs always and only in connection with constructions containing the semi-reflexive morpheme. Further comparison of the Onondaga constructions shows that the two subsets of 3 are formally asymmetric. However, the two subsets of glosses show apparent symmetry. Observe that while both *b* and *e* refer to three noun phrases (buyer, seller, and car), only the verb in *e* contains a dative morpheme. Table 1 shows that one of the grammatical functions of the dative morpheme is to derive indirect transitives from transitives. What has happened in *e* is that a basically *indirect* transitive root, i.e., one taking three noun phrase adjuncts, has been intransitivized by the semi-reflexive (see Table 1 for this morpheme's functions) with the result that the stem has lost its ability to take an indirect object. The dative in *e* is needed to retransitivize the stem so that it can once more take three noun phrases as adjuncts. Hence the semi-reflexive which changes the meaning from 'buy' to 'sell' represents a cost on the grammatical level due to its status as an intransitivizer. Examples *c* and *f* are also formally asymmetrical, and for the same reason. The semi-reflexive occurs in *f* but not in *c*. In addition, the noun phrases accompanying the verb phrases contrast: the root glossed 'car' is prefixed with the neuter third person pronominal prefix in *c* and with the feminine/indefinite third person possessive in *f*. Remembering that -*hninu*- is an indirect transitive, we conclude that the dative in *c* may mark the presence of a *fourth* noun phrase in that construction. Now the gloss of *c* begins to make sense. It may be an elliptical way of saying 'he bought a car (from someone) for someone'. Because of the presence of the semi-reflexive in *f*, the verb phrase can only take three noun phrase adjuncts (the three basic ones, minus the indirect object whose absence is marked by the semi-reflexive, plus a new indirect object whose presence is signaled by the dative). This is where the possessive construction is handy, since it collapses two noun phrases into one. The gloss of *f*, 'he sold a car for someone' is thus only an approximate rendering of the more literal 'he sold it to someone, someone's car'. This discussion shows that the asymmetry of the two subsets of 3 is due to the occurrence of the semi-reflexive, and that the apparent symmetry of the two sets of glosses is misleading.

Since 'buy' becomes 'sell' when the semi-reflexive occurs we need to investigate how that morpheme can appropriately signal the seeming change of direction of the verb's action. We once more assume that speakers' choices of the glosses 'buy' and 'sell' are informative. Since the single root -*hninu*- is glossed 'buy' as well as 'sell' we are justified in assuming that these encode a unitary set of sense components. Our definitions for the English items suggest the common element TRANSFER as a possible candidate. But -*hninu*- is an indirect transitive and the absence of locatives in 3 leads us to suspect that a directional element must occur as an element encoded by the root. The choice of either TO or FROM would solve both of these problems at once. Inspection of the data shows that with this root the dative marks the addition of a beneficiary or goal, a relation that is expressed by *to* in English. Hence we must choose FROM as the element we are looking for. Observe that this element suggests a direction, i.e., from a source. With the definition TRANSFER FROM in hand, it is easy to see why the semi-reflexive is admirably suited to encode the switch from 'buy' to 'sell', for *buy* has someone other than the agent as source, and *sell* has the agent *himself* as source and one of the important functions of reflexives is to signal *action with respect to the self*. Substituting TRANSFER FROM (a source) for each of the occurrences of 'buy' or 'sell' in 3, we find that the sense of the glosses is perfectly maintained: the gloss of *a* is elliptical; we can say that the literal meaning is HE TRANSFERRED A CAR FROM (SOMEONE AS SOURCE) that is to say, 'he bought a car'. Example *b* is HE TRANSFERRED A CAR FROM SOMEONE (AS SOURCE), 'he bought a car from someone'. The morphological evidence that the sentence in *c* involves four underlying noun phrases has been presented above. The construction means HE TRANSFERRED A CAR FROM (SOMEONE AS SOURCE) TO SOMEONE, 'he bought a car for someone'. The glosses of *d - f* have 'sell'. In terms of our new definition *d* means HE TRANSFERRED A CAR FROM HIMSELF (AS SOURCE), 'he sold a car'; *e* means HE TRANSFERRED A CAR FROM HIMSELF (AS SOURCE) TO SOMEONE, 'he sold someone a car'; and *f* is HE TRANSFERRED SOMEONE'S CAR FROM HIMSELF (AS SOURCE) TO SOMEONE, 'he sold someone's car to someone'. We conclude, then, that the semi-reflexive is functioning in an entirely regular way. It does not change the nature of the directional element; rather, it intransitivizes the root, and assigns the vacated case role, in this case the source, to the agent of the action that the verb describes. It is the regularity of the semi-reflexive's behavior that makes this analysis particularly convincing.

In this third set of examples, we have found additional sources of directionality. Although direction is a basic part of the meaning of *-hninu-* it is not one of its semantic components in the same sense as is DOWN for the verb root *-v-*. The directionality of *-hninu-* is related to its transitivity, that is, to a grammatical characteristic of this root. In addition we found that the dative morpheme is an element capable of encoding direction by means of its function as transitivizer. Further, because of the semi-reflexive's ability to reassign case roles to alternative noun phrases, we have seen that this element is able to affect processes relating to direction. The difference between English *buy* and *sell* and *-hninu-* lies in the case roles that are used as reference points for the direction of the flow of goods that is described by the transaction. *Buy* and *sell* have goal and source, respectively, as reference points. In contrast, *-hninu-* confines itself to the source as reference point, leaving the rest of the operations to the many-layered derivational morphology.

SUMMARY AND CONCLUSIONS

In this paper I have attempted to make explicit an approach that has been implicit in many linguistic analyses of unfamiliar languages. Working with such languages, linguists are actually forced to assume a correlation between constructions in a target language and their glosses in a more familiar one. The object of admitting this in public is to try to develop approaches that reduce *assumed* correlations to a minimum. Nonidiomatic derivational sets in the target language and sets of corresponding glosses that are produced by bilinguals yield, as we have seen, voluminous data for analysis. By focusing on a single set of meanings, those of direction, we have been able to infer distinctions of some subtlety. This would not have been possible had we not investigated the sets of translation glosses with as much care as we did the constructions they glossed.

NOTES

1. Notational conventions: (1) for the body of the text and for English examples: capitals mark semantic elements. Glosses are enclosed in single quotes, except that the translation of examples from J. N. B. Hewitt's text (1903 ARBAE 21) are enclosed in double quotes to show that they are direct quotes. Italics mark words, parts of words, or sentences that are mentioned rather than used. They are also used for emphasis. (2) for Onondaga examples: grammatical morphemes are identified by capitals; # marks word boundaries; - marks morpheme boundaries; ´ marks high pitch; ` marks heavy stress; in forms having only ´ high pitch and heavy stress fall together; ADV = adverbial particle; ASP = aspect; CAUS = causative; CISLOC = cislocative; DAT = dative; INCH = inchoative; PART = partitive; SR = semi-reflexive; TRANSLOC = translocative.

Apart from the examples I have taken from J. N. B. Hewitt, the Onondaga data are from my own field work at the Onondaga reservation in Nedrew, N.Y., which began in 1972 and has continued off and on until the present. My principal informant is Harry Webster, whom I thank heartily for all his help. I am indebted to Anthony Woodbury for his helpful comments on an earlier version of this paper. Another version of the paper was read at the 1977 Annual Meeting of the American Anthropological Association at Houston, where Ives Goddard, Eric Hamp, and Michael Silverstein were most helpful in their comments on the definitions of English lexical items that are proposed in the body of this paper.

2. Examples of these two approaches are Bendix 1966; Bierwisch 1969; Binnick 1968; Conklin 1955; Dixon 1971; Goodenough 1956; Gruber 1967; Lounsbury 1956, 1964a; McCawley 1972; Weinreich 1967.

3. The English analysis of *come* and *go* in this section and of *buy* and *sell* later owes much to Gruber 1967.

4. The fact that the translation glosses share at least one semantic element is partial evidence that our informants are familiar with the semantic structure of this particular lexical set.

5. *2b* also contrasts with *2a* and *c* in terms of reflexive action. The semi-reflexive in *2b* intransitivizes the verb which has been transitivized by the causative. The semi-reflexive then functions to assign the case role of patient, which has been vacated by the intransitivizing process, to the noun phrase which occupies the causer/actor case role. Hence a single noun phrase, the subject, is causer, actor, as well as patient and X MOVES DOWN Y becomes X MOVES DOWN (SELF) (Woodbury 1976).

6. The prepronominal prefixes, among which the partitive and the locatives are numbered, each have rather diverse sets of semantic functions. For a detailed account of these, see Lounsbury 1953. Specific semantic functions of each of the derivational morphemes are selected by a root's membership in various grammatical and semantic classes.

7. The collocation of -*v*- plus partitive and inchoative contrasts with others in which the incorporated noun roots denoting 'thought/mind' and 'abstract matter' have the function of abstracting the meaning of the root in different ways (Woodbury 1975:136). They are not considered here because they lack concrete directional elements.

CHAPTER THIRTEEN

Agreskwe, A Northern Iroquoian Deity

IVES GODDARD

The Northern Iroquoian deity Agreskwe, frequently mentioned in the seventeenth-century sources in connection with warfare, has sometimes been identified with the sun (e.g., Thwaites, note in JR 5:286), apparently following the discussion by Lafitau (1974–1977, 1:106). An examination of the sources, however, shows that Agreskwe had the function of a god of war, among other attributes, and was wholly distinct from the sun, though the latter might also be prayed to in time of war. The present brief note is intended to draw attention to the basic facts about Agreskwe, and to point out some of the problems that remain in interpreting what we know about him.[1]

In the seventeenth century, Agreskwe is referred to in the *Jesuit Relations* as Agreskoüé, among the Mohawks, and as Agriskoüé (Agriskoué, Agriskoue) among the Mohawks, Oneidas, and Onondagas (JR 53:224, 228, 234, 238 [Mohawk]; 53:264, 266, 280, 294 [Onondaga]; 57:96 [Mohawk]; 57:122 [Oneida]; 57:146, 156 [Onondaga]; 58:204 [Oneida]). In passages dealing with the Hurons he is called Aireskouy (Aireskoi, Aireskui), a form also used by Isaac Jogues in describing the Mohawks (JR 33:224 [Huron]; 39:12 [copied from the passage in 33:224]; 39:208, 214, 220 [Mohawk]).[2] Lafitau (1724, 1:126, 127, 132, 206; 2:189) explicitly identifies these as linguistic variants of the same name, which he gives as Iroquois Agriskoué and Huron A$_{\mathrm{l}}$reskoui (the former sometimes without the accent, and the latter sometimes with a misplaced or omitted iota subscript). Cuoq (1882:225) gives the Mohawk name in the missionary orthography as Akreskwe, glossed in French as 'Akreskoué'. The form used by Megapolensis (Jameson 1909:177) in his 1644 account of the Mohawks is Aireskuoni, which will be discussed below in connection with Jogues's form. The spelling Agreskwe adopted in this paper reflects an anglicization of the presumed Mohawk pronunciation.

The most general statements about Agreskwe describe him as the "Master of life" (JR 53:225), as representing "a secret idea of the Divinity and of a first Principle, the author of all things" (JR 33:225), as "le grand Demon & le grand genie du Païs" (not named, but the reference is clear; JR 42:150), and as "a spirit to whom they are in the habit of addressing themselves, as to a divinity, for all sorts of Things" (JR 57:97). Charlevoix (1866, 3:157) reports a resolution by Christian Mohawks in 1670 "not to permit any public invocation of Agreskoué, or even recognize him as Author of Life," and from the "notebooks of the early missionaries" Cuoq (1882:225) quotes: "Iah Niio te haiatoten n'Akreskwe, katiken rawenniio tsi tionnhe?" 'Agreskwe is not God; is he the master of our life?' and "Oriwakon hetsewenniiostha n'Akreskwe, iahte hawenniio tsi sonnhe" 'It is useless for you to take Agreskwe as master; he is not the master of your life'.

More specific attributes appear in a number of passages. Father Isaac Jogues gave much information on the subject in a letter written from Rensselaerswyck in 1643 while a captive of the Mohawks (JR 39:175–225):

> They have recourse in their necessities to a demon whom they call Aireskoi, to whom they offer, as it were, the first-fruits of everything. When, for instance, a Stag [i.e. deer] has been taken, they call the eldest of the hut or of the Village, to the end that he may bless it or sacrifice it. This man, standing opposite the one who holds some of the flesh, says with a loud voice: "Oh, Demon Aireskui, we offer thee this flesh, and prepare for thee a feast with it, that thou mayst eat of it, and show us where are the stags, and send them into our snares,—or, at least, that we may see them again in the winter," etc.; or, in sickness, "to the end that we may recover health." They do the same in fishing, war, etc. (JR 39:207–9)

In connection with the torture of a woman Jogues wrote:

> And, as often as they applied the fire to that unhappy one with torches and burning brands, an Old man cried in a loud voice: "Aireskoi, we sacrifice to thee this victim, that thou mayst satisfy thyself with her flesh, and give us victory over our enemies." The pieces of this corpse were sent to the other Villages, there to be eaten. During the winter, at a solemn feast which they had made of two Bears, which they had offered to their demon, they had used this form of words:

"Aireskoi, thou dost right to punish us, and to give us no more captives" (they were speaking of the Algonquins, of whom that year they had not taken one; these are, moreover, their chief enemies), "because we have sinned by not eating the bodies of those whom thou last gavest us; but we promise thee to eat the first ones whom thou shalt give us, as we now do with these two Bears,"—and so they did. (JR 39:219–21)

A somewhat more complex account of the corresponding Huron deity was given by Father Paul Ragueneau in 1648:

There remained in their hearts a secret idea of the Divinity and of a first Principle, the author of all things, whom they invoked without knowing him. In the forests and during the chase, on the waters, and when in danger of shipwreck, they name him *Aireskouy Soutanditenr*, and call him to their aid. In war, and in the midst of their battles, they give him the name of *Ondoutaeté* and believe that he alone awards the victory. Very frequently, they address themselves to the Sky, paying it homage; and they call upon the Sun to be witness of their courage, of their misery, or of their innocence. But, above all, in the treaties of peace and alliance with foreign Nations they invoke, as witnesses of their sincerity, the Sun and the Sky, which see into the depths of their hearts, and will wreak vengeance on the treachery of those who betray their trust and do not keep their word. (JR 33:225)

Here Ragueneau is misleading about the expression *Aireskouy Soutanditenr;* the second word is not part of the name (as taken by Tooker 1964:82) but a verb form meaning 'have mercy on us' ('miserere nobis'—Bressani in JR 39:13).

The clear distinction between Agreskwe and the Sun in Ragueneau's account is noteworthy and should be borne in mind in connection with Jogues's description of the behavior of his Iroquois captors:

Thanks being then rendered to the Sun, which they believe to preside in wars, and their muskets being fired as a token of rejoicing, they made us disembark, in order to receive us with heavy blows of sticks. (JR 39:185)

It is clearly unwarranted to describe this incident as the firing of a volley in honor of Agreskwe (Charlevoix 1866, 2:143). The distinction made by the Huron between the Sun and the God of War is clear in the account of the torturing of an Iroquois prisoner in September 1636:

Before he was brought in, the Captain Aenons encouraged all
to do their duty, representing to them the importance of this
act, which was viewed, he said, by the Sun and by the God
of war. (JR 13:61; whence Charlevoix 1866, 2:109, with
incorrect date and conflation of the two deities under the
name "Areskouy")

Not completely resolved is the meaning of Ragueneau's statement
that in war the Hurons gave Aireskouy the name Ondoutaeté. Ondoutaeté (Ondoutaehte, JR 23:153–55) is elsewhere described as specifically the god of war, who appears in various guises including
that of a dwarf (JR 10:183; see Tooker 1964:89; Trigger 1969:91).

The references reviewed above give the necessary background for
interpreting and evaluating the statements about Agreskwe made by
Lafitau, whose ethnological theories sometimes becloud the ethnographic facts he reports. His most explicit statement is as follows:[3]

The *Aireskoui* of the Hurons, and the *Agriskoué* of the
Iroquois, is so much the God of Warriors that they use hardly
any other name at all in their invocations when they have
taken up the tomahawk, and it is principally on those
occasions that they invoke him by that name. (Lafitau 1724,
1:206)

Elsewhere he provides more detail:

The war song is sung in a council-lodge in which everyone
gathers, . . . and it is the war chief who gives the feast. . . .
the dogs that are put into the kettle are the main component
of the sacrificial offering in it—an offering marked by the
addresses they make to Aireskoui (the God of War), to the
Great Spirit, and to the Sky, or to the Sun, whom they
entreat to light their way, to give them victory over their
enemies, and to bring them back safe and sound to their own
country. (Lafitau 1724, 2:189)

Another passage implies a conflation of the four deities mentioned:

The Great Spirit, the Sky, and the Sun, who are jointly their
deity *(leur Divinité commune)*, are also their God of War. It is
he whom they invoke on all their military expeditions and to
whom they entrust all the success of their undertakings.
(Lafitau 1724, 1:205–6; followed by the passage quoted above)

However, this conflation must be understood in the context of Lafitau's general thesis of universal heliolatry:

The sun was so much the hieroglyphic symbol of divinity among all nations that all the names given to the gods of paganism referred to the sun. . . . The sun is the divinity of the American peoples, with none of those known to us excepted. . . . The Huron *Aireskoui* and the Iroquois *Agriskoué* are also the sun, which is their divinity as it is that of all the Americans. (Lafitau 1974–1977, 1:104, 106)

Lafitau goes on to claim that Tharonhiawagon (the name of the Good Twin in the Iroquois cosmological origin myth) is another name for Agreskwe, though he recognizes that its meaning ('sky-grasper') is inappropriate to the sun and suitable only for a supreme being.[4] It seems clear, then, that the conflations of Iroquoian deities that appear in his writings are expressions of his general ethnological theories rather than of Iroquoian ethnographic realities. In fact, his recognition of a narrower function for Agreskwe is shown by his (totally fanciful) etymology of Huron *Aireskoui*, which derives from it both Greek *Ares* and Latin *Mars*, the names of the ancient Gods of War (Lafitau 1974–1977, 1:103, 148).

A late reference to a White Dog Sacrifice to Tharonhiawagon at Grand River in 1798 in response to a vision (Tooker 1970:115) cannot be taken as a significant indication that Tharonhiawagon was treated like a war god in the earlier period. The events of 1798 must be evaluated as part of a nativistic revival that may have involved recombinations of older elements. Finally, it should be noted that Hewitt also explicitly rejected the equation of Tharonhiawagon with the Sun or with Agreskwe (Hodge 1907–1910, 2:719; Hewitt 1928:468).

What has been presented here so far about Agreskwe derives from a reading of historical sources and direct ethnographic statements. Other information, which must be reckoned with even if its import is not completely clear, comes from a linguistic analysis of the forms of his name itself; it may be taken as an illustration of the importance of philological control of the data in ethnohistorical research. In the Iroquois villages in 1669 and the following years the French recorded the forms Agreskoüé and Agriskoüé. The correspondence between *e* and *i* suggests the pattern of vowel epenthesis found in original Proto-Iroquoian *$*nk$ clusters, whereby this shows up as Mohawk *nek* and Oneida *nik* (Lounsbury 1978); however, there are no citable parallels for a putative Proto-Iroquoian *$*krsk$ cluster, and the treatment of *$*nk$ can only show that a correspondence *kresk/krisk* (between two unidentified languages) is not unreasonable. The form Agreskoüé was recorded among the Mohawk (JR 53:224ff.), and Cuoq (1882:225) cites this as a Mohawk form in the missionary spelling Akreskwe. This could not be a word in modern Mohawk, because *kr* is not a possible cluster in that language—all original *kr sequences are broken up by an epenthetic e and are reflected in Mohawk ker. It is likely, however, that in the seventeenth century this epenthesis of e had not yet taken place (Michelson 1981). Also quite unclear is the status of Hewitt's Mohawk form $\bar{A}regw\breve{e}^{n}s'gw\breve{a}'$ 'the Master or God of War' or $Aregw\breve{e}^{n}s'kw\breve{a}'$ 'The reason or cause for absence' (Hodge 1907–1910, 1:923; 2:719). Lafitau's Huron form, here normalized as Aireskoui (with the first i written for the iota subscript of the missionaries' Huron orthography), shows the expected Huron sound change of Proto-Iroquoian *k (except in certain clusters, such as *sk) to whatever the iota subscript represents—perhaps a voiced velar fricative ($[\gamma]$) or, as in Wyandot, a [y]. The final i may be compared to the perfective ending -i, as in Huron oki 'spirit' (phonemically /ohki/, from Proto-Iroquoian *$otki$, beside Mohawk $\acute{o}tk\bar{o}$ 'spirit' and related forms which show replacement of -i by the more common perfective ending -$\bar{o}$), and the final e of $Akreskwe$ calls to mind the common noun ending -$e^{?}$ which has a tendency to replace other endings. Since the morphological analysis of the variants of this name is unclear, however, the significance of the different final vowels is necessarily uncertain.

It remains to account for the fact that Jogues and Megapolensis use what appear to be forms of the Huron name when describing the Agreskwe of the Mohawks. Jogues's use of Aireskoi (in Latin) is most easily accounted for by the reasonable assumption that this is simply in fact the same Huron name as that recorded by Lafitau. Either Jogues learned of Aireskoi among the Huron before being captured by the Iroquois, or he learned the name from his Huron fellow-captives at the time of the incidents he describes. In either case his use of the name would seem to indicate a close similarity between the Huron Aireskoui and the Iroquois Agreskoué, specifically in the context of warfare, in agreement with Lafitau's discussion but in contrast to what is implied by Ragneneau's statement that in war Aireskoui was called Ondoutaeté. In any event Jogues's use of the Huron form Aireskoi provides a straightforward explanation for the Aireskuoni of Megapolensis. Megapolensis was the Dutch pastor in Fort Orange at the time of Jogues's escape from the Mohawk in 1643, and he in fact aided Jogues and visited him several times in hiding (Jameson 1909:248, 252). Megapolensis's generalized account of the Mohawk bear sacrifice to "Aireskuoni," written in 1644 (Jameson 1909:177), is so similar to Jogues's account of a sacrifice that he witnessed of two bears to "Aireskoi" (JR 39:221; quoted above) that Jogues must have been Megapolensis's source. It is not surprising then that Megapolensis used an altered form of the name used by Jogues.

The records examined make it clear that the Northern Iroquoian deity Agreskwe was an important member of the aboriginal pantheon. What is not clear is whether he is better considered a War God with certain nonmartial functions, or a spirit of generalized functions that included special powers in connection with warfare and other dangerous activities. A true War God seems out of place in northeastern North America; the Fox *maneseno·ha* 'Spirit of War' (animate form of *maneseno·wi, maneseno·hi* 'war') (Michelson 1930:160–61) and Unami Delaware *i·la·anət·u* 'War Spirit; comet' seem hardly to have the same prominence or to approach the range of contexts in which Agreskwe is mentioned. On the other hand the strong emphasis in the sources on the war functions of Agreskwe cannot lightly be dismissed. It can only be hoped that further study will shed more light on the matter.

NOTES

1. I became interested in Agreskwe while editing Fenton's chapter on "Northern Iroquoian Culture Patterns" for the *Handbook of North American Indians* (Fenton 1978). The present article is offered in appreciation for his scholarship and friendship, with apologies for exercising my editorial prerogative to make an anonymous addition on this subject to his chapter, and as an expansion and explanation of my conclusions about Agreskwe there reported.

2. Thwaites's index also has a reference to JR 13:221, a page which has nothing about Agreskwe. Perhaps this is an error for 13:61, quoted above.

3. In translations from Lafitau (which are mine from the 1724 edition and Elizabeth L. Moore's from the 1974 edition), I normalize his spellings as Aireskoui and Agriskoué. The present paper was written before Vol. 2 of Lafitau (1974–1977) appeared, which is why both Lafitau (1724) and the modern edition are cited in different places.

4. In an Onondaga version of the myth, Tharonhiawagon is given his name by his grandmother when he divines that he and his brother came from the sky and declares "I myself then will continue to grasp with both hands the place whence I came" (Hewitt 1928:486, 641; also in Hodge 1907–1910, 2:719); elsewhere Hewitt glosses the name 'he grasps the sky (by memory)' (Hewitt 1903:137). This name is complementary to that of his grandfather, the chief of the sky people, *haōhwętsyawá?ki* 'he holds the earth' or *tehaōhwętsyawá?khō?* 'he holds the earth dually (by his two hands)' (Hewitt 1903:137, 150; 1928:553, 610 n.53 [phonemicized except for accent]; the names are confused in the heading in Hewitt 1928:470).

III

Iroquoian Origins: Problems in Reconstruction

INTRODUCTION

This last group of papers exemplifies the recent stepped-up interest among Iroquoianists to coordinate the results from historical linguistics and archeology to resolve outstanding problems of Iroquoian prehistory: the location of the Iroquoian homeland, the origin of tribal and linguistic divisions, prehistoric migrations and, in general, the development of Iroquoian culture before contact with Europeans.

The problem of the rather anomalous or "intrusive" cultural position of the Iroquois remains as compelling today as it was forty years ago when Fenton summed it up in a classic review article (Fenton 1940). How could one explain the presence of politically centralized, matrilineally organized horticulturalists in the Northeast, surrounded by a "sea" of less centralized, patrilineal, often nonhorticultural Algonkians, speaking a completely unrelated set of languages? At the time that Fenton was writing, it was generally believed that the Iroquoians had migrated to their historic seats only a few centuries before contact. This migration was variously posited as originating in the St. Lawrence Valley, the Southeast, or the far West. By the 1950s the migration hypothesis had begun to crumble as archeologists failed to discover any plausible sites outside New York State which could be claimed either for the Iroquoian homeland or as the paths of migration, and instead began to amass a considerable body of evidence for an in-place occupation stretching well back before the appearance of certain telltale signs of horticulture in the archeological record. The *in situ* hypothesis holds sway today. Significant features such as horticulture and the Confederacy are now

237

explained primarily as the products of diffusion and/or internal development, rather than as having been brought by Iroquoian speakers into the Northeast from elsewhere. The complex interplay of common inheritance, migration, and diffusion provides a focus of study for those interested in reconstructing the past.

In the first paper, Dean Snow traces the development of Iroquoian economic, social, technological, and religious subsystems through time on the basis of archeological remains interpreted in the light of insights from ethnohistory, ethnology, and historical linguistics. He reconstructs long-distance trade relations from the distribution of trade goods. From house plans he infers the existence of extended family residential units. The presence of mortars and pestles from A.D. 900 implies the use of maize by that time. Evidence for the emergence of clans and elaborate rituals comes from mortuary remains. The culture prehistory which emerges is especially rich because of the material drawn from various subdisciplines.

Marianne Mithun reconstructs some aspects of the Proto-Iroquoian environment and culture from a comparison of vocabularies of the modern Iroquoian languages. A Proto-Iroquoian lexicon is reconstructed by the comparative method; then inferences are made from the meanings of the reconstructed words about the existence of objects and concepts in the proto-culture. Words for varieties of flora and fauna, aspects of fishing and hunting technologies, types of food and cooking equipment, articles of clothing and household utensils, as well as ritual practices are reconstructed first for the Proto-Iroquoians of four millennia ago, then for the Proto-Northern-Iroquoians of two millennia ago, and finally for the more recent Proto-Five Nations community. The ecological and cultural elements of the proto-cultures reconstructed by this method agree significantly with those posited by archeologists on the basis of different sets of data.

James Wright investigates the origins of Iroquoian-speaking peoples using archeological evidence. He proposes that Iroquoians have been present in the Northeast for at least 6000 years. This occupancy is hypothesized on the basis of a basic continuity through time in technology, religion (mortuary practices), and settlement and subsistence patterns of the Ontario Iroquois, ancestors of the historic Huron, Petun, Neutral, and Erie. To demonstrate the continuity, he traces the cultural development of the Iroquoian co-tradition from its Archaic base, through a major period of cultural change between 1500 B.C. and 100 B.C. related to climatic and technological changes, up into the period of corn cultivation between A.D. 500 and 800.

Wallace Chafe uses linguistic evidence to reconstruct population divergences and recontacts among Northern Iroquoian peoples. He posits an early Proto-Northern-Iroquoian speech community which was ruptured by the departure of the Tuscarora and the Cayuga. The remaining Northern community then split again when, first, the Huron left, then the Seneca, then the Onondaga. Sometime later, the Cayuga returned to the area, developing particularly close ties with the Seneca. Finally, the Oneida and Mohawk separated. To illustrate the method of reconstruction, Chafe traces the development of the verb 'they drank' in each of the languages from a presumed Proto-Northern-Iroquoian word.

Nancy Bonvillain investigates post-Contact divisions in the Mohawk community and their outside contacts by examining dialectal divergences. She details phonological differences among the Caughnawaga, Oka, and Akwesasne dialects, then compares some of the words each has borrowed from other languages. Caughnawaga and Oka Mohawk are found to be more similar to each other than either is to Akwesasne Mohawk. This fact is attributed to the geographic distances separating the communities. The Caughnawaga and Oka dialects, situated closer to Montreal, are shown to have undergone heavy French influence, while the Akwesasne dialect exhibits stronger influence from other Indian languages.

William Engelbrecht compares ceramic rim sherds from eight sites in the Niagara Frontier to chart the locations and migrations of the Erie during the sixteenth and seventeenth centuries. The sites were occupied by two contemporaneous Erie communities, both moving progressively southward. On the basis of "coefficients of agreement" of ceramic attributes, he orders the sites chronologically. The order is the same as that proposed by Marian White on other grounds. Engelbrecht next calculates "coefficients of homogeneity" of attributes for each site which indicate that while Seneca and Cayuga pottery was becoming progressively more homogeneous through time, Erie pottery was becoming more heterogeneous, due to an influx of Seneca and Cayuga pottery. He then considers alternative historical explanations for the presence of these types among the Erie.

The picture of the prehistoric Iroquois which emerges from work in any of the subdisciplines is tantalizing and necessarily spotty. Archeologists can recover only those aspects of culture which have left material traces, and linguists, only those linguistic aspects which remain part of the modern languages. Neither provides a full picture alone, but their combination, interpreted according to insights from ethnohistory and ethnology concerning cultural systems as wholes, yield relatively detailed insights into Iroquois life before contact.

CHAPTER FOURTEEN

Iroquois Prehistory

DEAN R. SNOW

The development of anthropology in North America over the past dozen decades has explicitly involved the integration of ethnology, archaeology, linguistics, and bioanthropology. Most large departments reflect this historical development in their present structures, and most anthropologists see the discipline as a rational composite of these subdisciplines (notwithstanding those that prefer to redivide it in imaginative ways). Yet despite our past history and present good intentions, there is a persistent tendency for our subdisciplines to talk past or even ignore one another in their customary progress. The annual meetings of the American Anthropological Association have become a congeries of disparate sessions rather than an integrative enterprise, and more and more anthropologists avoid them in favor of national meetings of their respective subdisciplines. Regional meetings seem to preserve the internal disparity of national A.A.A. meetings while only rarely providing a sense of regional integration. The annual reunion of Iroquoianists, for which William Fenton is and has been primarily responsible, is one of a small number of topically defined regular meetings at which anthropologists from all subdisciplines still come together for productive discussion. Rather than being a vestige of old-time anthropology, I suspect that gatherings like that of the Iroquoianists, which have drawn upon scholars internationally without becoming cumbersome undertakings, will become even more important in the future. I offer this article with that in mind.

What follows is not the exposition of an esoteric archaeological problem, or a summary of regional prehistory, but rather a summary of the prehistory of the Iroquois as we now understand it. I doubt that such a focus would be possible without the stimulating perspectives offered by linguists, ethnologists, and bioanthropologists, which have more often than not found expression in the crisp autumn air of Rensselaerville, the usual site of the Iroquoianist meetings. I have attempted to pull ideas together in a way that will satisfy the Iroquoianist even though this has entailed a subversion of some hoary subdisciplinary traditions. Among other things, and perhaps most importantly, I have attempted to avoid the jargon and style that have become standard in archaeology but too often preclude the integration of lines of evidence from other subdisciplines. I trust that my readers will not conclude that this abandonment of familiar comforts on my part will require a suspension of belief on theirs.

To obtain a complete archaeological culture prehistory for the Iroquois we must make regional comparisons based on more than one or two artifact classes. To do that we must define each phase using several criteria that can be used consistently from case to case and that together get us closer to a definition of whole cultures. My own approach has been to define fourteen categories under Clarke's (1968:101–28) four general headings of economic, social, technological, and religious subsystems (Table 14.1). All fourteen can be observed directly or inferred from archaeological *or* ethnohistorical data, making cultural systems so defined truly comparable. However, categories such as "inferred seasonal movements" require reference to more than one site, forcing me to make a priori decisions about whether or not certain archaeological sites or historical references are attributable to a single cultural system, a requirement that could end with my assuming what I should be trying to discover. My solution for this problem has been to divide the Northeast into river drainage "containers" within each of which I assume that there was only one cultural system at any given time level (Snow 1973). This approach is only beginning to yield results, some of which are discussed below, but may end with our having a much better understanding of the prehistory of Northeastern cultures rather than just the prehistory of a few artifact types.

Economic Subsystem
   1. Site types and distribution within the area
   2. House types and distribution within settlements
   3. Food resources and seasonality
   4. Seasonal movements

Social Subsystem
   5. Household unit
   6. Settlement unit
   7. Other inferred institutions
   8. Inferred community activities

Technological Subsystem
   9. Artifact types

10. Trade goods
11. Raw materials
12. Specific activities

Ideological Subsystem
13. Mortuary site types
14. Burial programs

Table 14.1. The cultural system as defined by four subsystems and 14 lines of evidence that can be inferred from either archaeological or ethnohistorical data.

NORTHERN IROQUOIAN ORIGINS

For almost thirty years, the issue of the origins of the Five Nations and other Northern Iroquoians has been couched in terms of a presumed choice between an *in situ* evolution out of some earlier entity and a relatively late prehistoric immigration. As archaeological evidence has accumulated, it has become clear to most investigators that such a forced choice has created a simplistic and therefore false dichotomy. "The *law of the excluded middle* may demand instant obedience in formal logic, but in history it is as intricate in its applications as the internal revenue code" (Fischer 1970:10). In fact, the *in situ* hypothesis is no longer a topic of lively discussion (MacNeish 1952; 1976). Nearly all archaeologists now accept the sequences of phases shown in Figure 14.1. The Owasco tradition, which embraces a series of phases in the Mohawk and central New York drainages, was once thought by Parker, Ritchie and others to have been attributable to "Algonkians" (Ritchie 1969:300). Mac-Neish's assertion that the Owasco ceramic tradition was carried by Iroquoians and led directly into the later Iroquois tradition in New York, though controversial at first, is now generally accepted, and the discussion over Iroquois origins has largely dissipated.

The new problem as I see it is not that the old hypothesis has disappeared with the acceptance of the *in situ* hypothesis, it has merely been pushed back to an earlier level. Certainly the Iroquois were not always in place, having risen from a frozen torpor under glacial ice. Moreover, their historical position as a wedge between Algonquian-speaking communities and their clear links with the Cherokee and others to the south all suggest a northward intrusion at some point in the past. This northward movement may not have originated any farther south than modern Pennsylvania, but even movement of that magnitude is significant. It can be argued that the A.D. 1600 distribution of languages in the Northeast might be explained as the consequence of Proto-Eastern Algonquian moving to

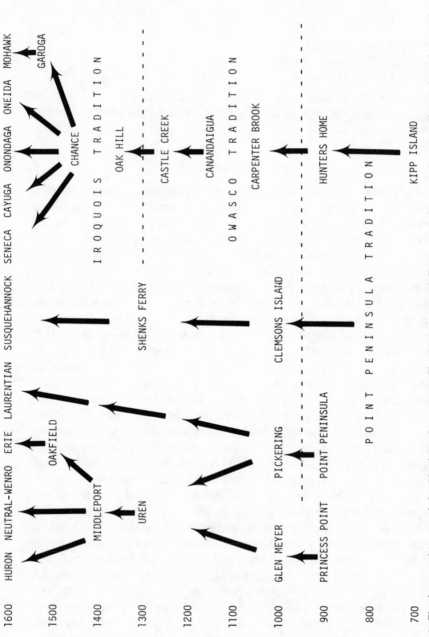

Fig. 14.1. The later prehistory of the Northern Iroquoians. The Nottoway and Tuscarora, who were linguistically northern but residentially southern, are excluded. All dates are approximate. Derived from Ritchie (1969), Ritchie and Funk (1973), Tuck (1978) and Wright (1972).

the coast and expanding southward as it broke up into roughly eighteen descendant languages. Goddard, who favors this view (pers. comm.), has estimated that the Eastern Algonquian languages have been separated from the other Algonquian languages for about 2000 years (1978:70). As I have argued elsewhere, however, there are no archaeological data to support this hypothesis and many to contradict it.

There are two moderately well-defined phases for the period 1250–300 B.C. in New York, the Meadowood Phase of western and central New York, and the Orient phase of the Hudson Valley and Long Island (see Figure 14.2). The Orient phase may have ended by 700 B.C., but the Meadowood phase appears to have persisted until 300 B.C. Ritchie and Funk (1973:96) now see Meadowood as being both earlier and culturally separate from the Point Peninsula tradition, but it is significant that Ritchie (1969:206) saw strong formal similarities between the two before their temporal separation was noticed. Most archaeologists now see a strong continuity through the Point Peninsula, Owasco, and Iroquois ceramic traditions, a continuity that takes us along an essentially unbroken line of development from the first century A.D. down to the historic Iroquois. In this case, examination of the larger cultural systems through the use of the criteria listed in Table 14.1 indicates that continuity characterized the entire cultural system, not just ceramics. Ritchie has generally held the view that there are two more phases that should be included under central New York in Figure 14.2, Middlesex and Squawkie Hill. He sees each as presenting a discontinuity in the sequence. I have argued, however, that each of these phases is based on evidence from cemeteries alone, and that they indicate participation of Meadowood and Canoe Point in Adena and Hopewell mortuary cults respectively. Thus I see Middlesex as evidence of the ideological subsystem of the Meadowood system, and Squawkie Hill as related in the same way to Canoe Point (Snow 1978:88). There is no clear discontinuity in the central New York sequence.

Many archaeologists also accept the hypothesis that Point Peninsula phases developed out of the Meadowood phase. Acceptance of this idea pushes our unbroken cultural continuum back to 1200 B.C. This is well within the 3500–4000 year depth that Lounsbury (1961:11; 1978:334) has suggested for the split between Cherokee and Northern Iroquoian. In other words, Northern Iroquoian could not have split off from Cherokee much after 3800 years ago, and we have archaeological evidence of cultural continuity for almost that long in central New York. Moreover, the eastern New York sequence is different and separate from that of central New York for that same long time span. The distribution of Meadowood components is very

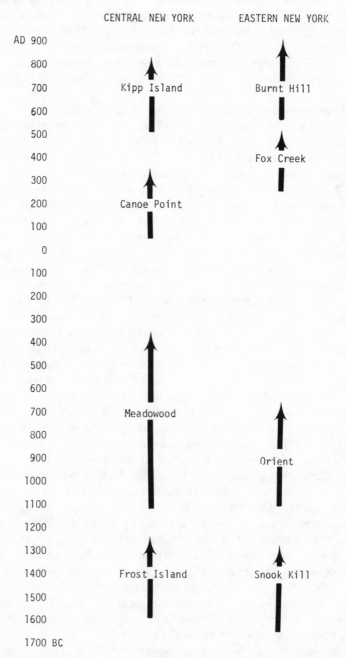

Fig. 14.2. Phase sequences for central New York and eastern New York, the latter area defined as Long Island and the Hudson drainage apart from the Mohawk tributary drainage

similar to that of the historic Iroquois, they being most numerous in central New York and the Mohawk drainage. It appears to have been present as well along the St. Lawrence River in New York and the parts of Québec and Ontario closest to New York (J. Wright 1972:42). There is some evidence for a Meadowood presence in the upper Delaware drainage, and data emerging from Robert Funk's long-term investigations in the upper Susquehanna drainage indicate that it is there as well (Funk 1976:278).

Another implication of Lounsbury's time range for the Cherokee-Northern Iroquoian split is that it must have taken place late in or after the Late Archaic period (4000–1700 B.C.). That period saw the coexistence of three separate adaptations in the Northeast, the Lake Forest, Maritime, and Mast Forest adaptations. Some archaeologists prefer to call the last "Narrow Point" and refer to all three as traditions (Tuck 1978). Some also contend that they must necessarily have been temporally distinct within this long period. I see all three, however, as separate adaptations as much as separate cultural traditions and conclude from several lines of evidence that all three persisted in different parts of the Northeast for the entire twenty-three-century period. Most importantly for present purposes, I have seen no convincing evidence of major population movements into or even within the Northeast during the Late Archaic period. Thus on the basis of present archaeological evidence, the Northern Iroquoians were either here prior to 4000 B.C. or arrived after 1700 B.C. An implication of the first possibility is that the Cherokee would have split off and moved southward out of the Northeast 3500–4000 years ago (1500–2000 B.C.), a movement that no one has seriously suggested and for which I have seen no archaeological evidence.

Despite the logical difficulties and the lack of supportive evidence, several links between Late Archaic archaeological evidence and Iroquoian speech communities have been proposed by other archaeologists. Douglas Byers (1961:49) once suggested that Iroquoian speech was carried into the Northeast by bearers of the Lamoka complex, a variant of the Mast Forest adaptation. Ritchie (1969:105) properly dismissed this proposal as "dubious in the extreme," though he may have done so for the wrong reasons. Tuck has argued more recently that the distribution of broad side-notched points in the Eastern Woodlands argues for an origin of the Lake Forest Laurentian complex to the southwest of our region, and that the bearers of this variant of the Lake Forest Archaic were early Iroquoian speakers (Tuck 1977:39). James Wright (1972) sees continuity over time from the Lake Forest Archaic (or at least its Laurentian variant) to the Ontario Iroquois, and therefore shares Tuck's view. Sanger (1975:73) extends this identification to the Maritime Archaic by speculating that ". . .

the inhabitants of Maine around 4000 B.P. spoke a language more closely akin to Iroquois than Algonkian." Tuck's hypothesis is weak because it equates a major migration with the presumed movement of a single artifact class, broad side-notched points, which may not even have origins outside the Northeast. Sanger's hypothesis is basically an unsupported impression rather than an explicit argument, and does not deal with archaeological evidence showing how Iroquoians might have arrived in Maine much less how they departed before the end of prehistory. Thus I see no convincing evidence to indicate that Iroquoians were present anywhere north of Pennsylvania during the Late Archaic. The distributions of the three adaptations (or traditions) of the Late Archaic are such that the identification of any one of them with Iroquoians would require not only their migration into the Northeast, but their subsequent retreat to the homelands of historic Iroquoians, movements the data will not support.

Taken together, the evidence indicates an arrival of Iroquoians in New York after the end of the Late Archaic (1700 B.C.) but before the emergence of Meadowood (1200 B.C.). These brackets mark off five centuries within which we should conduct our search for the first arrival of Iroquoians north of Pennsylvania. This is consistent with Lounsbury's (1978:336) view that the evidence favors "a long occupation of the area of central New York State and north-central Pennsylvania, extending back in time for perhaps as much as four millennia, with expansions or migrations first to the south and then to the north and immediate west." Archaeologically, the only logical choice is the Frost Island phase, which appears in central New York around 1600 B.C. and from which the Meadowood phase appears to have derived. Steatite (soapstone) bowls are an important Frost Island artifact class. Frost Island bowls tend to be unsmoothed on their exterior surfaces, and in this and other respects they resemble the bowls of southeastern Pennsylvania rather than those of eastern New York and southern New England. Trade and travel connections of the Frost Island phase were with the region to the south, primarily along the Suquehanna River, and the projectile points and bowls diagnostic of Frost Island are found primarily along the banks of the Susquehanna, its major tributaries, and through the Finger Lakes district. The Frost Island cultural system contrasts with both the Mast Forest and Lake Forest systems that preceded it in central New York. The site distribution and inferred food resources are more strikingly riverine for Frost Island, and subsistence seems neither as diffuse as the preceding Mast Forest system nor as adapted to northern resources as the Lake Forest system. Technological links are also with the southern Susquehanna drainage, and Frost Island mortuary site types and burial programs were new to New York. Frost Island preferences for sites along major streams (Ritchie 1969: 157), and the presence of domesticated squash in the Eastern Woodlands by 2300 B.C. (Chomko and Crawford 1978) combine with other lines of evidence to suggest reasons for the northward expansion of people responsible for this phase. The argument is too lengthy to detail here, but it seems likely that these people were in possession of several semi-domesticates and perhaps even a domesticated plant or two by 1700 B.C. This plus the knowledge of appropriate storage techniques would have been sufficiently advantageous to explain their own expansion and the displacement of the previous inhabitants of central New York. Thus the hypothesis favoring the interpretation of Frost Island as an immigrant phase is supported by evidence for a place of origin, the sudden appearance of a whole new cultural system, and a clear explanatory mechanism. Rouse's (1958) stringent criteria for the demonstration of a prehistoric migration are all met.

MEADOWOOD CULTURAL SYSTEM

Both habitation and burial sites are known for the Meadowood phase. Diagnostic remains include Vinette 1 pottery, the thin side-notched Meadowood point type, cigar-shaped pottery pipes, thin ovate cache blades, birdstones, trapezoidal and rectanguloid gorgets, copper beads and adzes, and shell disk beads. There is no unequivocal evidence for the presence of maize horticulture, but Meadowood remains are rarely found in back-country sites away from the main streams, a settlement pattern that suggests a shift away from the older system involving seasonal hunting and collecting in remote parts of drainage areas, to one involving more intense food extraction (or even production) around more permanent settlements. Maize could have been grown at these sites, and there was certainly heavy use of near-cultigens such as *Chenopodium* (goosefoot) (Ritchie 1969:189). Grayson's (1974) observations regarding the heavy and efficient use of faunal resources at the Riverhaven No. 2 site combine with this and Ritchie's observation of storage pits at several sites to suggest that the carriers of the Meadowood phase may well have mastered efficient food preservation and storage techniques that would have facilitated the new settlement pattern even if cultigens were not yet available to them.

Perhaps the most interesting aspect of the Meadowood phase is the elaborate burial ceremonialism that goes with it. The dead appear to have been kept above ground and the bones cremated and buried at periodic intervals, often accompanied by red ocher and food offerings. The diagnostic items listed in the previous paragraph were also included, the cache blades sometimes numbering in the hundreds per grave lot (Ritchie 1969:196–200). Also found in New York at a slightly later time level are other burial sites which parallel the Meadowood burial sites in many ways but which contain artifactual remains that can be directly traced to the contemporaneous Adena culture of Ohio. Ritchie (1969:201) defines this as the separate Middlesex phase even though all the components discovered thus far have been burial sites. This is in line with his interpretation of the appearance of Adena remains in the Northeast as being the consequence of the migration of small groups out of Ohio (Ritchie and Dragoo 1960). Grayson (1970) has convincingly challenged this interpretation, and it seems clear to me that Ritchie's migration hypothesis is inconsistent with both the archaeological evidence and our understanding of how human communities behave. Ritchie (1969:202) observes that in nineteen Middlesex components he has examined, slightly over half the traits present can be attributed directly to Ohio Adena, whereas slightly less than half "can be accommodated within the Point Peninsula culture," which as we have seen once also accommodated the Meadowood phase. Thus it seems more likely to me that what we really have is a mortuary system that begins as a Meadowood analogue of the Adena system. By the time the Meadowood phase evolved into the beginning of the Point Peninsula tradition it became a direct participant in the Adena system. I do not see Middlesex as a separate phase. Cemeteries that can be clearly related to Meadowood habitation sites have produced four dates that average about 750 B.C. Adena-like mounds that Ritchie classes as Middlesex cannot be dated directly, but similar sites in New Jersey and Delaware have produced two dates that average around 450 B.C. It seems likely that what we are seeing is a gradual intensification of Meadowood participation in trade and burial practices centering in the Adena homeland of southern Ohio over a period of three centuries.

The importance of the above discussion is that it brings the issue of long-distance trade in North America into sharp focus. During the florescence of Adena and later Hopewell culture in Ohio, exotic raw materials and luxury items made from them were transported hundreds and sometimes thousands of kilometers from their points of origin. Conch shells from the Gulf of Mexico are found in sites all the way to Ontario. Native copper from the margins of Lake Superior is found all over the East. So is silver from Ontario, galena from the Mississippi Valley, mica from the southern Appalachians, grizzly bear canines from the Rocky Mountains, and so on. One could conclude that this complex redistribution was the end result of a protracted pattern of small individual trade exchanges between the members of adjacent communities were it not for the fact that an elaborate and relatively consistent pattern of mortuary behavior was conveyed as well. The extent and complexity of the pattern suggests formal gift exchange between corporate groups, and concerted long-distance travel to effect it. The example of obsidian serves to make this point. Gary Wright (1972) has noted that all the obsidian in Ohio appears to have come from Yellowstone Park (4,000 km away) and was deposited in graves between A.D. 100 and 200, a very short time span. Moreover, more than half the total known to date was found in a single grave, probably that of the person who went after it in the first place. Wright infers a widespread formal trading network in the Eastern Woodlands in which demand was maintained by consignment of the traded luxury goods to grave lots. The roots of the system probably go back at least to the Late Archaic, when exotic Ramah chert from Labrador regularly made its way into Northeastern sites.

Elisabeth Tooker (1971) has come to some of the same conclusions by way of an almost exclusively ethnological approach. She observes generally that although North American clans recruited members by means of some principle of kinship, they did not function as kin groups. Rather, clans tended to function as corporate groups charged with the maintenance of particular rituals, and there are strong cross-cultural similarities in their structure as religious groups. She presents a strong argument favoring the prehistoric existence of a widespread trade network as the most reasonable explanation for these cross-cultural similarities. I have not seen a more reasonable alternative hypothesis. Unfortunately, I think that Tooker weakens her argument by using the term "empire" in place of "network" and suggesting not just a Mexican inspiration for it but Mexican control of the system. Although there may have been some Mexican participation and inspiration, I see no reason why the North American network could not have arisen and operated independently from Mexico.

Tooker and Wright come to very similar conclusions independently and on the basis of both different data sets and different analyses. I think that we must conclude that the Middlesex complex is evidence of the participation of prehistoric New York Indians in a widespread trade network. I suspect that Wright is correct that the materials traded were passed in the context of formal gift exchange between trading partners, although I would specify that the individuals were acting as leaders of corporate groups rather than as independent entrepreneurs. Indeed, this was the form preferred by nearly all Native American groups at first contact with European traders. The corporate groups in the Meadowood system were probably clans as defined by Tooker, exogamous groups for which recruitment was usually unilineal. There was probably a totem, but descent from either the totem or from some human founder would not necessarily have been claimed. Tooker (1971:364) argues that clans "did not develop as a device to maintain knowledge of genealogical connections between lineages, but rather were a device to establish and maintain relationships with non-kin through the fiction of kinship." Thus we do not need migrations to explain the appearance of Adena traits in the Northeast, and we have a mechanism to explain both the emergence of clans and the adoption and maintenance of the elaborate ritual implied by Meadowood mortuary remains. I see no reason to infer the existence of a priesthood as some have, for in Mexico at least, this is an institution that by definition operates well above the clan level as a permanent full-time maintainer of public ritual. The Meadowood case is probably much closer to the historical Northwest coast institution of clan-based maintenance of ritual and trade through powerful and highly respected clan leaders. Adena style sites elsewhere in the Northeast are rare, and their presence can be best explained by reference to the same mechanism. They are not strongly associated with the Orient phase of the Hudson Valley and Long Island.

The pottery types of the Point Peninsula ceramic tradition develop smoothly out of Meadowood beginnings. However, Point Peninsula ceramics were adopted by many communities in the Northeast and it is simply not possible to talk in terms of a Point Peninsula culture except perhaps for the specific southern Ontario phase bearing that name. J.V. Wright (1972:45) has noted that types of this ceramic tradition appear to have been adopted by the resident Archaic communities of southern Ontario and simply added to their existing inventories. My own research has suggested a similar pattern in Maine. Thus, while the Meadowood phase is tightly contained within the areal distribution of historical Northern Iroquois, and may well turn out to be a distinct cultural system in the terms I outlined earlier, the Point Peninsula tradition will almost certainly turn out to be a single dimension that cuts across several cultural systems. Nonetheless, the three Point Peninsula phases of central New York, Canoe Point, Kipp Island, and Hunters Home, appear to represent at least a major part of Northern Iroquois culture history when they are redefined as cultural systems.

CANOE POINT CULTURAL SYSTEM

Although the settlement system of Meadowood culture may have started out as central-based wandering, it almost certainly evolved to semi-permanent sedentary with the emergence of Canoe Point

(A.D. 200). There were probably relatively large villages that were occupied year round and relocated every few years. No such sites have been found in New York, but Ritchie and Funk (1973:349–52) regard the contemporaneous Donaldson site in Ontario as analogous. That site produced two house plans about 7×5m and 5×3m, respectively, each with a single hearth. We can infer an extended family residential unit. It seems likely to me that in central New York the emergence of clans, which has been hypothesized on both ethnological and archaeological grounds, began in Meadowood culture around 1000 B.C. and was completed by the time its carriers were fully involved in the Adena trade network. The institution would have persisted into Canoe Point culture. There is still no direct evidence for maize, but they continued to make efficient use of mammals, fish, nuts, plants such as goosefoot and perhaps squash. The presence of nutting stones but the absence of the mortars and pestles one might expect to attend maize cultivation suggest that we may never find maize for this time level.

Perhaps the most interesting aspect of Canoe Point culture are the "Squawkie Hill phase" mounds that go with it much the same way Middlesex goes with Meadowood. Two radiocarbon dates from each indicate contemporaneity and their spatial distributions are about the same. There are no other burial sites known for Canoe Point, and Squawkie Hill is defined entirely on the basis of burial sites. I see no reason to separate them as distinctive entities, particularly since early Point Peninsula sherds were found in the fill of Lewiston mound. What I am calling the Canoe Point cultural system therefore includes both. It seems likely that the trade network and the clan institutions that served as nodes within it never lapsed after their emergence sometime after 1000 B.C. By this time (A.D. 200), however, the center of the network was Ohio Hopewell. The Canoe Point religious subsystem is represented by mounds containing both primary and secondary burials, the latter being either bundle burials or cremations. Most are accompanied by lavish offerings of Ohio platform pipes, copper ear ornaments, copper beads and axes, pearl beads, gorgets, mica sheets, points of Flint Ridge chert, and other well-known Hopewell paraphernalia. These trade items were used exclusively in burials and do not turn up in village refuse. Conversely, items of local manufacture do not turn up in burials. This exclusivity explains why Canoe Point and Squawkie Hill remains did not fall together obviously before the advent of radiocarbon dating, and perhaps why migration hypotheses were once so popular. For reasons we do not yet understand, the Hopewell trade network collapsed around A.D. 500 and the religious subsystems of cultures all over the Eastern Woodlands turned inward. As we shall see, this does not imply that any of them entered a dark age. Indeed, among these early Iroquoians other cultural subsystems continued to thrive.

Kipp Island Cultural Systems

Kipp Island culture grew out of Canoe Point, the settlement subsistence systems maintained as before. Even now (A.D. 700) some trade persisted, for we find banded slate pendants, shark teeth, and platform pipes of both local and nonlocal manufacture. However, there is no longer a clear distinction between those items included in village refuse and those that might be found with burials. The burial pattern continued as before, the apparent confusion of primary, secondary, flexed, bundle, and cremation burial probably being simply the result of saving the dead for periodic burial rites. Those that died some distance from home were apparently cremated to facilitate transportation, for there is no evidence of on-site cremation. The recently deceased were buried flexed while those that had been dead for some time had their disarticulated bones bundled for burial. Cemeteries were situated some distance from habitation sites, but mounds were no longer constructed.

Hunters Home Cultural System

Hunters Home culture emerges as the last to carry pottery of the Point Peninsula tradition around A.D. 900. House forms and settlement patterns remain as previously, but mortars and pestles are now present and we presume that maize has been added to the list of subsistence resources. There is the same low level of long-distance trade, and although burial programs appear to have remained as before, fewer and fewer artifacts were making their way into graves. Grave goods consist usually of elbow pipes and iron pyrites buried with adult men. It seems clear that lavish grave offerings were simply no longer regarded as being as important as they once were. It must also be clear, however, that this too in no way indicates a cultural decline, for the prehistoric Iroquoians were about to use their new broader subsistence base as a springboard into the new cultural forms of the Late Woodland period.

Owasco Cultural System

Owasco culture and the beginning of the Late Woodland period date to about A.D. 1000. The analogous Glen Meyer and Pickering cultures emerge at about the same time in southern Ontario. All were clearly carried by Iroquoian speakers. This is not to say that all the pottery assigned to the Owasco ceramic tradition were made by Iroquoian speakers, for the potters of Algonquian communities in the Hudson and Delaware drainages as well as elsewhere in the Northeast adopted many central New York Owasco styles. It is clear, however, that Owasco communities of the Mohawk and upper Susquehanna drainages were Iroquoian speaking: It was during the time span of Owasco that maize, beans, and squash became central to the subsistence subsystem. Nucleation caused villages to become less numerous but larger, a process that did not necessarily entail an increase in the population growth rate. The vestiges of long-distance trade withered away as warfare increased. Warfare was also accompanied by the emergence of a new settlement pattern that favored relatively secure elevated sites away from major streams, as well as a shift to safer overland travel in place of travel on major streams. By A.D. 1150 large villages were palisaded, their walls sometimes supplemented by exterior ditches and interior earthworks. Small seasonal sites indicate a continued reliance upon hunting, fishing, and gathering. However, deer now predominate in bone refuse, and there is some evidence that fishing might have declined by the Owasco-Iroquois transition around A.D. 1300. A sharp increase in serious tooth decay in Owasco burials points to increased reliance on carbohydrate foods, and is therefore further indication of the increasing importance of agricultural food production.

A new burial pattern emerged in which the dead were almost always buried soon after death in primary flexed burials, indicating an abandonment in New York of the old practice of saving bodies for periodic burial. The old pattern appears to have been retained by some communities in Ontario into historical times. At the same time, emphasis upon grave goods changed such that Owasco burials are accompanied only by an occasional pot for a child or a pipe for an adult male.

Our information on Owasco suggests that as these communities coalesced into larger but fewer settlements, they also became more self-sufficient and isolated from one another. The clans that had grown up in the context of Early and Middle Woodland period trade networks now began to find themselves sometimes residing together in fortified villages, their old trading functions gone and their ritual responsibilities changed. I believe that it is no coincidence that Wallace Chafe's (1972 Iroquois Conference) estimate of 1000 B.P. for the breakup of Proto-Five-Nations Iroquois closely approximates the emergence of Owasco in central New York. It seems to me that many of the social mechanisms such as trade and travel that would have preserved a single-speech community disappeared around A.D. 1000.

The Iroquois longhouse began to emerge as an architectural form at about the same time. The Maxon-Derby site contained the remains of both an old style 6×7m house and a presumably later 18×8m longhouse, as well as an intermediate 10×7m house. Ritchie and Funk (1973:213–25) report only small round houses at the Sackett site (A.D. 1130), but plans of the site indicate long lines of post molds that probably point to partially excavated longhouses. By A.D. 1300, the longhouse was certainly the standard dwelling and the social institutions that accompanied that settlement pattern in historical times must have been in place or emerging. Trends toward elaborate decoration of pottery vessels and pipes, and evidence of increasing violent death and even cannibalism, combine to indicate some of the ways in which nonsubsistence activities adapted and changed with the larger evolving cultural system (Ritchie 1969:275–300; Ritchie and Funk 1973:359–61).

The emergence of the Five Nations from an earlier common cultural system has been studied ceramically by Whallon (1968) and Engel-brecht (1972). Cultural divergence can also be seen in larger site features; storage pits occur in sites in the Mohawk and Susquehanna drainages, but were not much used in central and western New York. Throughout Iroquoia, the trends begun before A.D. 1300 continued after that date as well. Longhouses attained lengths of over 30m. With advancing time we see first a 65m longhouse at Furnace Brook, then a 103m house at Howlett Hill, then a 123m house at the Schoff site as the prehistoric Onondaga built successive villages near Syracuse (Tuck 1971; 1978a). From 1300 to 1600, the trend toward the protective location of villages intensified such that as houses attained record lengths they also came to be located on high defensible hills. Moreover, village size increased from an Owasco average of a hectare (2+ acres) up to 3 or 4 hectares.

IROQUOIS CULTURAL SYSTEM

It is possible at this point to generate a brief description of historic Iroquois culture using the same four subsystems that I used to outline its prehistoric antecedents. In the economic subsystem, subsistence depended heavily upon maize-beans-squash horticulture, supple-mented by hunting, fishing, and gathering along lines practiced since 1000 B.C. Hunting appears to have declined in terms of per capita energy expenditure on it, with species other than white-tailed deer now relatively unimportant. The corresponding settlement pattern now involved perennial palisaded villages in protected locations away from major streams and linked to hunting and fishing sites by overland trails. The pattern has been defined as semi-permanent sedentary (Beardsley et al. 1956). The longhouse was now the standard house type. Implications for the social subsystem are lineage household units and village units comprised of two or more clans (Fenton and Tooker 1978:467).

Inferred social institutions center upon widespread warfare. The League appears to have been essentially a phenomenon of the historic period, and participation in long-distance trade had dwindled to almost none at all by A.D. 1000. Archaeological evidence for both warfare and cannibalism increases sharply after that date.

The artifact types of the historic Iroquois include several diagnostic ceramic and lithic types that were also widely used by non-Iroquoians in the Northeast. Raw materials tended to be of local origin. The complex evolution of Iroquois clay pipes has proven to be a useful line of combined archaeological and ethnological investigation. Indeed, pots and pipes provided an important outlet for artistic impulses among late prehistoric, early historic Iroquois.

In the religious subsystem, mortuary sites were primarily cemeteries containing flexed primary burials. The old pattern of retaining the remains of the dead above ground for periodic burial (probably just before a village was moved) was apparently abandoned by A.D. 1000 in central New York, although something like it appears to have been retained by Huron communities. Grave goods were limited to a few personal belongings.

This discussion has shown that it is possible to discuss cultural systems in terms of either ethnohistorical or archaeological data, or both of them in combination. It is no longer necessary, or even excusable, to discuss prehistoric cultures in the narrow terms of ceramic or lithic traditions. Moreover, it is no longer excusable to invoke wholesale migrations, military conquests, despotic priesthoods, or other imaginary institutions for which there are no vestiges of ethnological evidence to explain archaeological evidence from the prehistoric Iroquoian continuum. In time we will be more sure of the time-space distribution of that continuum outside of central New York such that future summaries will not have to be as restricted in scope as this one. Similarly, further research will almost certainly clarify the initial appearance of Iroquoians in the Northeast prior to 1000 B.C.

CHAPTER FIFTEEN

The Proto-Iroquoians: Cultural Reconstruction from Lexical Materials

MARIANNE MITHUN

The chance to catch a glimpse of the past is tempting to almost everyone.[1] Tastes of what life must have been like before modern memory can be gleaned from a number of different kinds of sources: lore passed down from parents to children, old documents, archaeological discoveries, language. Each of these resources provides unique contributions. Documentation can furnish very specific facts. Archaeology can uncover information no one thought to pass down in legend form. Often traces of traditions which disappeared too long ago to be remembered by storytellers and historians or which left no material mark are passed down from one generation to the next in vocabulary. Ethnohistorical, archaeological, and linguistic tools can each uncover pieces of daily life in Proto-Iroquoia. Each has its own limitations, but together, they reveal a much richer picture of Iroquoian life in early times than any one alone. In the sections which follow, the method of cultural reconstruction from linguistic materials will be outlined, then some conclusions will be drawn concerning the life of the Proto-Iroquoians, the common ancestors of all modern Iroquoian peoples.

THE METHOD OF LINGUISTIC RECONSTRUCTION

Traces of earlier cultural elements still present in language are detected in the following manner. Sets of words are sought in related languages that are similar in both form and meaning from one language to the next. Such similarities can be due to several causes: common inheritance, borrowing, onomatopoeia, parallel creation, or chance. Words similar because of common inheritance, cognates, are

259

assumed to have evolved from a word in the common parent language. If a word was present in the parent language, in this case Proto-Iroquoian, there is a good chance that the referent of the word was part of the lives of the speakers of that language, the Proto-Iroquoians.

The Identification of Cognates

Compare the words for 'man' in the various Iroquoian languages: [2]

'man' M. ú:kweh   Oe. ú:kweh   Oo. õkweh   C. õ:kweh
S. õ:kweh H. onhoüoy W. o:meh T. v́:kweh Ch. ayuwi

The words are close but not identical in form. Examination of other cognate sets reveals that the differences in form from language to language are systematic. When Tuscarora and the Five Nations languages show *kw* in certain environments, Cherokee, Huron, and Wyandot show *w*. Next to nasalized vowels, Wyandot *w* becomes *m*.

'color' M. -ahsohkw- Oe. -ahsohkw- Oo. -ahsohkw- C. -ah-
sohkw- S. -ahsohkw- H. -ahsohw- W. -ahsohw- T. -ah-
θuhkw- Ch. -hsuhwi-

The sound correspondences are systematic because when the original Iroquoian *kw changed to *w* in Cherokee and Huron, the sound changed in every word containing *kw in those languages at that time. If the expected, systematic sound difference does *not* appear in a modern word, we know the word was not part of the language at the time of the sound shift.

<u>The accurate identification of cognates depends upon a thorough understanding of the sound shifts which have occurred in each language since the parent language first divided.</u> For a detailed discussion of the sound shifts and their conditioning environments, see Mithun (1979).[3]

Other causes of lexical resemblances across different languages can seriously interfere with the correct identification of cognates if undetected.

Borrowing. Words in different languages may be similar because one language borrowed the word from the other or because they both borrowed the same word from a third source. Compare the words below:

'cat' M. takò:s Oe. takò:s Oo. takus C. taku:s S. taku:tsi.
T. ta:ku:θ

The words are strikingly similar in form and have exactly the same meaning. In fact, they are *too* similar to be cognate. In Tuscarora, proto *t became (ʔ)*n* before vowels, as in the example below:

'two' PNI *tekni M. tékeni Oe. tékni Oo. tekníh Su. tiggeni C. tekhni: H. teni W. tendi T. né·kti:

This happened to all *t*'s in all words present in Tuscarora at the time of the shift. If the word for 'cat' had been part of Tuscarora then, the modern Tuscarora word would be

T. *na:ku:θ

The *t* in the actual form, T. *ta:ku:θ*, shows that the word was borrowed. In fact the word was probably borrowed from the Dutch into all of the Iroquoian languages about 300 years ago. Notice how different the words for 'cat' are in the Iroquoian languages that were not in contact with the Five Nations:

'cat' Su. tzidtze N. tose Ch. wehsa

Often systematic sound differences are the only basis from which to distinguish borrowed words from cognates, so if a word does not contain sounds which have shifted, borrowing may not be detectable.

Borrowed words tell us little about the life of the Proto-Iroquoians, but if not identified as loans, they can be seriously misleading. It would be a mistake, for example, to hypothesize the presence of domestic cats in Proto-Iroquoia on the basis of these borrowed words. Nevertheless, borrowings whose source is identified can provide information about contacts between groups—in this case the Dutch and the Iroquois.

Onomatopoeia. Notice how similar the words for 'crow' are in the modern Iroquoian languages:

'crow' Oe. kà:kaʔ Oo. káhkah C. káʔka:ʔ S. káʔka:ʔ W. yahkáʔa Ch. kho:ka

It is tempting to assume that these words all evolved from the same word in Proto-Iroquoian. This would be unjustified. The word could easily have been created independently by each modern group. Crows may simply have sounded alike to all of them.

Parallel Creation. Compare the words for 'church' in Mohawk and Oneida:

'church' M. onuhsatokv́hti Oe. onuhsatokv́hti

The words are identical in form and meaning, and are probably not borrowings. Yet they are not descended from a single term in Proto-

Mohawk-Oneida either. They became part of the languages after contact, long after the groups had separated from each other. Both were formed from existing cognates, *-nuhs- 'house' and *-tokvhti- 'holy'. Although the pieces were part of the Proto-language, the compound was not. Care should be taken in assigning the referents of analyzable terms to Proto-cultures.

Chance. Each of the Iroquoian languages has approximately fifteen distinctive sounds, most of them roughly the same from language to language. It would not be impossible for two languages to form words consisting of the same sounds in the same order. It is less likely, but still not impossible, that the words might have relatable meanings. Such chance similarities would be misleading if mistaken for cognates.

Several factors aid in the detection of chance resemblances. For one, the probability of identity by chance decreases drastically as the length of words increases. Newly created words in Iroquoian tend to be quite long. Second, the probability of similarity due to chance is greatly reduced if the word fits into a cognate semantic complex. If words for 'cornsilk' are similar to two languages, they are more likely to be cognate if words for 'corn', 'cornhusk', 'corncob', 'ear of corn', 'kernal', 'cornstalk', etc., are also similar.

The identification of cognates thus involves the discovery of words similar in form and meaning which show systematic sound correspondences and the elimination of similarities due to borrowing, onomatopoeia, parallel construction, or chance.

Inferences from Proto-Lexicon to Proto-Culture

The existence of a set of cognate words for an object provides good evidence for the existence of the object in the Proto-culture, but the fact that certain terms for an object are not cognate does not constitute evidence that the object was unknown to speakers of the Proto-language. Compare the words for 'knee' in the Iroquoian languages:

'knee' M. okwítsha? Oe. otsinikú.ta? Oo. okẽhì?na? C. áõtsha?
S. áõsha? T. awvtkwé:θeh Ch. ni:ke:ni

Although no word can be reconstructed for 'knee' in Proto-Iroquoian, we are not justified in concluding that the Proto-Iroquoians lacked knees. Words come and go in every language.

Just as sounds and vocabulary change over time, so do the meanings of words. Compare the terms below:

'corn tassel' M. otsì:tsya? Oe. otsi:tsya? Oo. otsí?tsya?
S. otsí?tso:t T. utsi?tsíhsteh Ch. utsi:tsati

The cognate set suggests that corn tassels could have been part of Proto-Iroquoian culture around 4000 years ago. In fact, this term, which does have the specialized meaning 'corn tassel' in Seneca and Cherokee, means 'hops' in Onondaga and is a general word for 'flower' or 'beer' in the other languages. The fact that other terms for corn culture are not cognate for this period indicates that corn was probably not a part of Proto-Iroquoian culture and that the original meaning of the root *-tsi?tsy- was 'flower'. Semantic shifts are often detectable from differences in meaning among cognates.

The Depth of Reconstruction

The age attributable to reconstructions depends upon the relationships among the languages in which cognates are found. If languages L_1, L_2, and L_3 are related as shown in Figure 15.1 below, and cognates are found in L_1 and L_3, the word must have been in these languages at time t_1, before they separated. If cognates are found only in L_2 and L_3, we can be sure only that the word was present at time t_2. An understanding of the historical relationships among the languages of the family is thus crucial to correct reconstruction.

THE IROQUOIAN FAMILY

Perhaps four thousand years ago, the ancestors of the modern Iroquoians separated into two groups. One group, which became the modern Cherokees, migrated toward what is now Tennessee and the Carolinas. Perhaps two thousand years later, a second group left. This group, the ancestors of the Tuscaroras, Nottoways, and Meherrins, eventually settled in eastern North Carolina and Virginia. After some time, the remaining Northern Iroquoians divided again. Some of these, later known as the Hurons and eventually part of

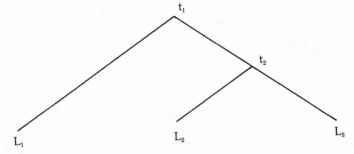

Fig. 15.1. Relationship of languages and time of development of cognates

the Wyandots, moved into Ontario. The others subsequently separated into a western group, (Seneca-Cayuga[4]), Onondaga, Susquehannock (=Andaste=Minqua=Conestoga), and an eastern group (Oneida-Mohawk). The existence of several other Northern Iroquoian communities is on record: Laurentian (Hochelagan, Stadaconan), Wenro, Neutral, Erie, and Tionontati (=Petun=Tobacco Nation). Because the languages of these last peoples disappeared with little or no documentation, their exact status within the family is uncertain, but they were clearly part of the Northern Iroquoian community which remained after the departure of the Tuscarora-Nottoway group.

The relationships among the Iroquois languages are shown schematically in Figure 15.2.

The crucial roles of Cherokee, Tuscarora, and Nottoway in the reconstruction of Iroquoian language and culture are apparent from the sketch of the family. To reconstruct a word for Proto-Iroquoian (PI), it is necessary to find cognates in Cherokee and *any* other language in the family. To reconstruct a Proto-Northern word (PNI), cognates must be found in either Tuscarora or Nottoway and any other Northern language.

RECONSTRUCTABLE SEMANTIC COMPLEXES

A number of terms for fauna, flora, and material culture can be reconstructed for Proto-Iroquoian, Proto-Northern Iroquoian, and the

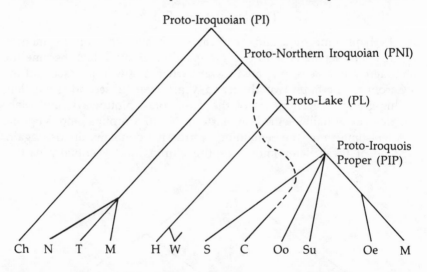

(Ch = Cherokee, N = Nottoway, T = Tuscarora, M = Meherrin, H = Huron, W = Wyandot, S = Seneca, C = Cayuga, Oo = Onondaga, Su = Susquehannock, Oe = Oneida, M = Mohawk)

Fig. 15.2. Relationships among Iroquois languages

Proto-Iroquois Proper community. If a term can be traced no further back than PIP, we do not know whether it was present in PI or not.

Fauna

To reconstruct a term for PI, it is necessary to find cognates in Cherokee and any Northern language. Since Cherokee is now spoken in quite different ecological areas (North Carolina and Oklahoma) than the other languages (Pennsylvania, New York State, Quebec, Ontario), this is not always possible. Terms for animals not found in both places can be reconstructed only if they have remained in the language but undergone semantic shift.

Mammals. The Proto-Iroquoians probably lived among wildcats, wolves, deer, chipmunks, and skunks:

'wildcat' M. kv̀:reks Oe. kv̀:leks Oo. kẽhes S. hẽ:es W. yĕric
T. kv́hreks Ch. kvhe

'wolf' M. okwáho Oe. okwáho Ch. wahya *PNI*

'deer' Su. haagw T. á:kweh N. aquia Ch. ahwi *PI*

'chipmunk' M. ohryò:kv? Oe. tsihlyò:kwv? C. *tsihnyókẽ:?* *PI*
S. tsihó?kwaes (L. caiognen) H. ohioen W. ju?eẽ
T. tsyuhrú?kv Ch. khiyu:ka

'skunk' M. atì:ru Oe. atì:lu H. tiron W. atí:ro^n T. né?rv?
Ch. ti:lv

The semantic shifts in the last cognate set are interesting. The modern Mohawk, Oneida, Huron, and Wyandot terms now mean 'raccoon'.

Several terms are reconstructable for at least PNI and may go back to PI. Words for 'elk' are similar, but the Cherokee term may rather be cognate to PNI 'deer'. A second term for 'elk' is shared by the western PNI languages:

'elk' Su. hrwha Oo. sganiungachrówa T. tsyuhwarhù:weh
Ch. ahwa u:thana

'elk' C. tekatsián?ẽtõ:t S. jonóẽ?ta? H. sondareinta
W. utsindára^{n}ta?

The presence of foxes and weasels can be traced back through vocabulary:

'fox' M. tsítsho? Oo. tsítsho?. Su. sisshw T. katsíhtshu
Ch. tsuhla

'weasel' M. onú:kwet   'weasel'   Oe. onú:kote?   'weasel'
S. hanõ:ko:t   'weasel'   T. θenv́:ku:t   'mink'   Ch. thane:kwa
'mole'

Note the different glosses in this last set. The Delaware word for
'mink' *winingus*, which sounds strikingly similar to the Iroquoian
words, is a descriptive term meaning 'dirty face', so the possibility
of borrowing should not be ruled out. Words for 'dog' appear to be
cognate at least to PNI and perhaps to PI:

'dog' Oo. tsí:hah   S. tsi:yæh   T. tsihr   N. cheer   Ch. kihli

The Proto-Northern Iroquoians knew not only wolves, deer, wildcats, chipmunks, skunks, elk, fox, weasels, and dogs, but also beavers
and others:

'beaver' C. tsó?taka? ('mink') H. toutayé ('castor') T. tsyu?ná:kv
'otter' M. tawí:ne   Oe. tawi:né   W. tawí^{n}de   H. tsabouinecq
T. tsa?kawì:nv?

The Five Nations (PIP) community knew porcupines and their
quills, raccoons, skunks, squirrels, and woodchucks:

'porcupine' M. onhè:ta? ('quill')   Oe. onhè:ta?   Oo. onhé?ta?
C. kanhé?ta?   S. kahé?ta?   T. uhé?ta? ('quill', borrowing)
'raccoon' M. atí:ru   Oe. ati:lú   H. tíron   W. ati:ro^n
'skunk' M. anì:ta?s   Oe. anì:ta?s   Oo. ēní?ta?s
W. (Potier) nditátsia   W. a^{n}di?tátsi?a
'squirrel' M. aró:sv   Oo. háese?   S. tha:wa:sǫ.t   H. arousen
W. arú:se^n
'woodchuck' Oe. ona:kút   Oo. oná:kot   W. (Potier) ondakent
W. u^{n}dáyä^n

Reptiles. Frogs and toads can be reconstructed for PI:

'bullfrog' S. kwanõno:h   Ch. khanu:nu
'frog' W. tside?esk?   T. né:kre:?   Ch. te:hka
'toad' M. otskwà:rhe?   Oe. kwale:lé?   Oo. skwá?æk   C. skwá?ahta?
('frog')   S. tsinõskwaes ('toad')   T. runv́θkwarv?   Ch. walu:si

Interestingly, Zeisberger gives the Delaware word for 'toad' as *tsqual-
lac*.

General terms for snakes and lizards can be reconstructed for PI.
The final vowels in the Mohawk and Onondaga words for 'snake'
are verb roots 'be in water':

'snake' M. oná:to ('blacksnake') Oe. ona:tú Oo. oná:toh ('water snake') C. haná:tõh ('blacksnake' or 'water snake') S. hanõ:toh ('water snake') N. antatum Ch. inata

'lizard' M. tsyahré:na Oe. tsyahle:nás ('yellow spotted lizard') S. tsá:enǫs 'chameleon' T. rurakwnyv́hre? ('red spotted lizard') Ch. thayo:ha:li:/tiyoha?li ('fence lizard')

The Northern Iroquoians also knew turtles:

'turtle' H. angyahouiche W. gá?wic T. rá?kwihs

In addition to frogs, toads, lizards, and turtles, the Five Nations community (PIP) distinguished two other kinds of turtles and salamanders:

'turtle' M. a?nó:wara? Oe. a?no:wál Oo. ha?nó:wa: C. k?anó:wa: S. ha?no:wa?

'snapping turtle' M. ronyáhte? ('turtle clan') Oe. lanyáhtv ('turtle clan') Oo. kanyahtẽh C. kanyáhtẽ: S. kanyáhtẽ:

'salamander' M. tó:tis Oe. to:tis Oo. to:tis C. tó:tihs S. to:ti:s

Insects. The Proto-Iroquoians had lice:

'lice' M. otsì:nu? Oe. otsì:nu C. tsí?nõ: S. tsi?nõ:h Ch. thi:na

It appears that they were bothered by mosquitoes:

'mosquito' H. tachiey/teschei W. téce Ch. dosa

Northern and southern words for 'katydid' look similar, but this could be due to onomatopoeia:

'katydid' S. tsiskæ:kae T. tsiské:ke: Ch. tsiki:ki:

Terms for 'bee' are formed alike in all of the Northern languages, from the term for 'hive', *-?nahkõht-, which could itself come from a root for 'barrel' or 'drum', *-?nahkw-:

'bee' M. otsi?nahkuhtahkwà:ne   Oo. nahkõtahkwàhne
C. k?anáhkõtha? S. o?nõhkõ:t W. o?ndáhko^{n}t T. ru?tahkv
N. ronuquam

The Five Nations languages and Huron and Wyandot (PL) share terms for 'ant', for 'butterfly', and for 'tick':

'ant' M. tsiki?nhotstókh(w)i   Oe. tsyonhotstókwi
Oo. tsi?nhóhstòhkwi? C. tsi?nhṍhkwehẽh S. tsihṍstohkwẽ?
H. stinonchoquey W. tsithõsyúkhe?

'butterfly' M. tsi$^{?}$ksinà:nawv　Oe. kanà:wv　Oo. hanáhwẽh
C. tsi$^{?}$taná:we:　S. otsí$^{?}$tanõ:wẽ:$^{?}$　W. thame^{n}dúme^{n}　(Ch. ka-
mama)
'tick' M. oséhto　Oe. oséhtu　Oo. oséhtõh　C. oséhtõh
S. koséhtõh　W. osetõk

Birds. The reconstruction of bird names is generally risky because
of the high frequency of onomatopoeia. Some Iroquoian bird names
which appear to match are those for 'whippoorwill', 'quail', 'kingfisher', 'turkey', 'robin', 'chickadee', perhaps 'eagle', and of course
'crow':

'whippoorwill' M. kwa$^{?}$kóryv　Oe. kwa$^{?}$ko:lí　Oo. kwe$^{?}$kóhnyẽ$^{?}$
kwa$^{?}$kónyẽh　C. kwé$^{?}$kohnyẽ$^{?}$　S. kwé$^{?}$ko:nyẽ$^{?}$　H. vhoiroq
W. meyuríha　T. kwa$^{?}$kórhyeh　Ch. waku:li
'quail' M. kóhkwayv　Oe. kóhk*wai*　Oo. kóhkowih　C. kóhkowi:$^{?}$
S. kóhkawi$^{?}$　W. (Potier) okõaki　T. kúhkwih　Ch. ukhkwe:hi
'kingfisher' S. tha:sæ:h　Ch. tsa:lohi
'turkey' W. détõta$^{?}$　T. kv̀:nv$^{?}$　N. kunum　Ch. khv:na
'robin' M. tsiskó:ko　Oe. tsisko:kó　Oo. tsiská$^{?}$ka$^{?}$　C. tsiskoko$^{?}$
T. tsiskú:ku　Ch. tsi:skwo:kwo/tsiskó:ko　(Del. tscisgockus)
'chickadee' M. taktsiré:ri　　Oe. tsiktsile:lé　　C. tsiktsí:ye:$^{?}$
T. nektsiré:re　Ch. tsikilili
'eagle' M. à:kweks　Oo. há$^{?}$koks　C. shá$^{?}$kõks　H. sondaqua
W. sondakwe^{n}　T. stá:kwi　Ch. awohili/awoha$^{?}$li

All of these words, with the possible exceptions of 'turkey' and 'eagle'
could easily be onomatopoeic. The word for 'robin' matches nicely
among the Iroquoian languages, but it also matches those in Amerindian languages all over North America.

In addition to all of the birds mentioned above, the Proto-Northern
Iroquoians also knew passenger pigeons, blackbirds, and partridges:

'pigeon' M. orí:te$^{?}$　Oe. olí:te$^{?}$　H. orittey　T. urí:$^{?}$ne$^{?}$
'blackbird'[5] M. tsyò:kwaris　Oe. tsyókwalis　Oo. tsyó$^{?}$kìsta$^{?}$
C. ts$^{?}$okris　S. tsoko:ki:h　T. θu$^{?}$krihst
'partridge' M. ahkwé:sv　Oe. ohkwe:sv́　C. kwé:sẽ$^{?}$　H. acoissan
W. kwe$^{?e}$disẽ$^{?}$a$^{?}$　T. uhkwé:θv$^{?}$

Besides these, the Proto-Five Nations (PIP) community knew ducks,
bluejays, gulls, flickers, snipes, great horned owls, and perhaps geese:

'duck' M. só:ra　Oo. so:wæk　S. so:wæk
'bluejay' M. terì:teri$^{?}$　Oe. tlì:tli　Oo. tíhtih　C. tí:ti:$^{?}$　S. tí$^{?}$ti:$^{?}$

'gull' M. tsyohwàtstaka?we? Oe. tsohwv́tstaka?we
Oo. tsyohwě́hstaka? C. ts*ohwě́?staka? S. tso:wě́?staka?
(T. tsyuhv́?θtaka?, borrowing)

'flicker' M. kwitò:kwito Oo. kwitótutu C. kwitú?kwitu:?
S. kwitó?kwito?

'snipe, plover, woodcock' M. tawístawis Oe. tawístawi
Oo. tahwístahwis tawístawis C. towístowi:? S. towístowi?
(T. tawístawis 'snipe clan', borrowing)

'goose' M. káhuk Oe. káhuk Oo. káhõk C. hő:ka:k S. hõ:ka:k
H. ahonque W. yáhõk

The term for 'goose' is probably onomatopoeic but may go back to
PL, since Wyandot shows it with the sound change of *k to *y*.

Hunting

Although terms for game animals can be reconstructed for PI, little
pertaining to hunting can be established for that period. This of
course does not prove the absence of hunting in Proto-Iroquoian
culture.

Words for hunting equipment can be traced back to PNI. Two
roots for 'bow' can be reconstructed, although one may have originally
meant 'stick'. In addition, terms for 'bowstring', 'arrow', 'arrowfeathers', and 'arrowhead' are cognate. Words for 'quiver' are later, independent constructions:

'bow' ('stick'?) C. atóta:? S. káeo?ta? ('gun') (L. cacta) H. a?ta?
N. ata T. á?neh ('bow' or 'gun')

'bow' M. a?v́:na? Oe. a?v:ná? Oo. a?ě́:na? 'pole' C. a?ě́:na? 'pole'
S. wa?ě̃:nõ? (L. ahena) W. a?ě̃:nda

'bowstring' M. orv́hsa? Oe. olv́:sa? Oo. kaěsó:tà:? C. kaěsota:?
S. kanóhsota:a? W. yarésha T. urv́:θeh

'arrow' C. k?anõh S. ka?nõ? H. anda W. ú?ⁿda? T. ú?teh (Ch.
ga?ni 'bullet')

'arrowfeathers' Oe. kahlà:tu? Oo. ohæ?ta? C. ohá?ta? S. óæ?ta?
W. yará?to? T. yera?nv́hstha?

'arrowhead' C. *kah*ná?ya? W. onda?ye/yauⁿgya?

The verb 'hunt' can be reconstructed for PIP. The *t* in Tuscarora
shows that it was a borrowing:

'he hunts' M. rató:rats Oe. lató:lats Oo. ható:wæts C. ható:wa:s
S. hato:wæs T. ratú:ra:ts

Flora

The reconstruction of significant flora referents is rendered difficult
by the collection techniques of philologists. The domain is enormous
to begin with and translations of plant names are seldom specific
enough to yield the results crucial to homeland hypotheses.
Several tree names can be traced back to Proto-Iroquoian:

'red oak' M. karíhtu   Oe. kalíhtu   OoZ. garihti   C. ko:weh
S. okowæˀ   H. ontuiere ('acorn')   T. kù:reh   N. coree   Ch. ku:le
('acorn')

'hickory' T. waht   Ch. waneˀi

'soft maple' C. kóhso:ˀ   S. kóhso:ˀ   T. hakv́hsu:ˀθ   Ch. khu:si
('beech')

'plum' M. onáˀuhsteˀ (L. honnesta)   H. tonestes   W. daˀᵃtu:nẽsti
Ch. kwanunsdiˀi

A word for a potato-like tubor, perhaps Jerusalem artichokes or
ground nuts, can be reconstructed for PI:

'potato' M. ohnvnà:taˀ   Oe. ohnvnà:taˀ   Oo. oné:nòhkwˀ
C. ohónˀataˀ   S. onónòˀtaˀ   N. anton   T. ù:nv́:θeh   Ch. nu:na

In addition to these, the Proto-Northern Iroquoians must have
lived among elm, slippery elm, basswood, and pine:

'elm' M. oká:ratsi   Oe. kalánikwala   Oo. kahó:kàhtaˀ   C. kháõka:ˀ
S. kaõkæˀ   W. (Potier) karakõat   T. karátkwar

'slippery elm' M. ohò:ksera   Oe. ohò:kseli   Oo. ohóksæ:ˀ
C. ohóhskraˀ   S. oska:aˀ   W. hucuyà:ra   T. kúˀks

'basswood' M. ohósera   Oe. ohósela   Oo. ohóhsæ:ˀ   C. ohó:traˀ
S. o:osæˀ   W. (Potier) ohochra   T. uhústraˀ

'pine' M. ohnéhtaˀ   ('gum')   Oe. ohnéhtaˀ   Oo. ohnéhtaˀ
H. xahⁿdéhtaˀ   W. (Potier) andeta   T. uhtéhneh

The Proto-Five Nations community (PIP) knew these plus white
ash, birch, hemlock, sugar maple, willow, balsam fir, and perhaps
tamarack:

'white ash' M. káneru   Oe. ká:nlo   Oo. ká:ne   S. kanyõh

'birch' M. oná:ke (birch bark)   Oe. ona:ké   Oo. ná:ket   T. ùná:kyeh
(borrowing)   (Ch. u:ne:ka 'white')

'hemlock' M. onvˀtaˀú:weh   Oe. onv:taˀ   Oo. oné:taˀ   C. kanéˀtẽˀs
('evergreen')   S. onéˀtaˀ   (L. Lanneda)   W. (Pot) onnenta (evergreen)   T. ù:nv́:ˀteh (borrowing)

'sugar maple' M. wáhta   Oe. wáhta   Oo. ohwáhta   C. ohwáhta?
S. wahta?   H. ouhatta   W. wahta
'willow' M. ó:se   Oo. oséhta?   C. oséhta?   S. oséhta?
'balsam fir' M. otshohkó:tu   Oe. otshohko:tú   Oo. tshohkó:tõ
C. otsho?kó:tõ?   S. sohko:tõh
'tamarack' M. kanv̀:tv?s   Oe. kanv?tv̀:sa?   Oo. kané?tẽ?s
C. kané?tẽ?s   S. kané?tẽ?s   W. (Potier) kannentens   T. kanv́?tvs
(borrowing)

The term for 'balsam fir' is a verb meaning 'it's lumpy', presumably referring to the bark, and the term for 'tamarack' is analyzable as 'falling evergreen' (it does loose its needles), so both could have been developed independently by each group or easily borrowed.

Agriculture

No agricultural terms have been reconstructed for Proto-Iroquoian. A number can be found for Proto-Northern Iroquoian, however. The Proto-Northern Iroquoians distinguished wild animals from domesticated ones:

'wild animal' M. káryo?   Oe. kályo?   Oo. ka:yó?   C. kanyo:?
S. kanyo:?   H. ayot   T. ká:ryu:?
'domestic animal' M. -nahskw-   Oe. -naskw-   Oo. -naskw-   C.
-nahskw-   S. -nõskw-   T. -tahskw-

A second cognate set for tame animals appears to have developed from PNI. It cannot be proven that the term is cognate in Tuscarora rather than borrowed, since it does not contain any of the sound sequences which shifted in that language. The root *-nahskw- is always incorporated, while the root *-tshenẽ? is not, probably because it is basically a verb root:

'domestic animal' M. katshé:nv?   Oe. katshe:nv́?   Oo. katshé:nẽ?
C. katshé:nẽ?   S. kashe:nẽ?   T. katshè:nv?

Terms for tapping maples match among the Five Nations languages, but because of their length and analyzability, it is likely that the word spread by diffusion. They are built on the root *-hkar- 'wood chip', because maples were tapped by the insertion of hollowed wooden pegs:

'he tapped it' M. wahahkaró:tv   Oe. wahahkalo:tv́   C. ahahká:otẽ?
S. wá:keotẽ?

The verb 'plant' appears cognate in PNI, but again, it is impossible to determine whether the Tuscarora term is inherited or borrowed:

'he plants' M. rayv́thos Oe. layv́thos Oo. hayéthwas
C. hayé:thwas S. hayĕ:thwas H. achienqua (you would plant)
T. rayv́thuθ

The root for 'field', *-heht-, is cognate in all of the Northern languages, but it also means 'meadow', so provides no special evidence of early agriculture.

The corn complex is an interesting puzzle. At contact, of course, the Iroquois cultivated corn extensively. Corn seems to have arrived relatively recently in the Northeast, however, certainly after the initial breakup of the Iroquoian family. Lexical reconstruction bears this out. Two stems for 'corn' appear in the Northern Iroquoian languages:[6]

PNI *-nēh- M. onv́ha? 'seed', 'pit' onvhakv̀:ra 'white corn'
Oe. kanv́he? 'seed' Oe. onvhakv̀:lat 'Indian corn' Oo. onéha?
'corn' C. onéhē? 'corn' S. onéõ? 'corn' H. onneha 'bled'
W. dunĕha 'corn' T. unv́heh 'corn'

PNI *-nēhst- M. ó:nvhste? 'corn' Oe. o:nv́ste? 'corn' OoS. oninchta
pepin Su. onaeste 'corn' H. onesta 'semences de citroüilles'
W. tsunĕstat 'seed' T. u:v́nhsneh 'seed'

There is a good chance that both of these words originally referred to seeds in general. The words for 'cornhusk' match among the languages and the Tuscarora word is clearly a cognate rather than a borrowing:

'cornhusk' M. onó:ra? Oe. -nol-otshu 'to husk' Oo. onó:ya?
C. onó:nya? S. -nowi- T. utù:reh Ch. nu:laki 'to shuck corn'

This could have originated as a general term for husk, however, and only later become specialized for corn. Words for 'corn tassel' do not match, except where the word for 'flower' (*-tsi?tsy-) is used.

An interesting cognate is the verb 'pound corn', which goes back to PI. It is found in Northern words for 'pestle' as well as a basic verb and in the Cherokee word for 'flour':

'pound (corn)' M. ahsísa 'pestle' iehsisà:tha? 'cornmill' Oe. ahsísaht
'pestle' Oo. ahsísàhtha? 'pestle' C. kasísahtha? 'pestle' H. achisa
'pillions à battre' W. ahsí:sa 'pestle' Ch. isa 'flour'

It is not at all clear, however, that the substance originally pounded was corn. It could have been any kind of grain or nut until the term became specialized for corn.

Additional words pertaining to corn and its preparation can be reconstructed for the Proto-Five Nations community. In most cases, because they do not contain the crucial phonological sequences, it is impossible to determine whether the Tuscarora counterparts are cognates, which would make the terms reconstructable for PNI, or borrowings, which would take them back only to P5N:

'cornsilk' M. ókera   S. okyo:t   T. ukrú?reh

'corncob' M. skanuhkwv́:?v   Oo. onóhkwà:yẽ?   C. onóhkw?ẽ:?
S. onõhkwẽ?ẽh

'cooked, ground corn' Oe. ono?khwísv 'cooked, ground corn'
Oo. onó?òhkwa? 'ground corn'   S. onó?khwishæ? 'boiled, sweet-
ened corn'

'mush' M. otsískwa? 'falseface mush'   Oo. otsíkwa?   C. otsískwa?
S. otsískwa?   T. utsískweh

'mortar' M. ka?ní:ka   Oe. ka?nikáhta?   Oo. ká?nikàhta?
C. k?aníka*h*tha?   S. ka?níkahta?   H. andiata   W. ya?díyata?
T. u?tikáhneh

'husk products' Oo. katsíhsa?   C. katsíhsa?   S. katsíhsa?   W. (Potier)
katiatsísta   T. utsíhseh

The word for 'bread' clearly goes back to at least PNI and perhaps PI:

'bread' M. kanà:taro   Oe. kanà:talok   Su. canadra   C. oná?ta:?
H. o^{n}da?tara   T. utá?nareh   N. gotatera   Ch. gadu

The Five Nations languages (PIP) share cognates for 'grain', 'dough', and 'winnow'. The verb 'winnow' could have originated simple as 'shake', however. This and 'grain' can be traced to PL because of the Huron and Wyandot cognates:

'grain' M. onv́tsya? 'wheat' onvtsyakv̀:ra 'rice' ('white grain')
Oo. oná:tsya? 'wheat'   C. oná:tsa? 'grain'   S. onõ:tsa? 'wheat'
onõ:tso:t 'oats' ('standing grain')   W. (Potier) ondatsa   H. andotsa
'espèce de bled'

'dough' M. oshè:rha?   Oe. oshè:lha?   Oo. oshé?æ?   C. oshéa?
S. oshé?æ?

'winnow' *-?shew-   M. sà:shew 'winnow' ie?shewà:tha? 'winnowing
basket' ('one uses it to winnow')   H. easeuëouha 'I winnow'
W. o^n?shewata? 'winnow'

A word for flour matches back to PNI, but it is not a provable cognate. It is based on a verb root *-the?t- 'pound' and could have been developed independently in each language:

'flour, cracked wheat, powder' M. othè:sera   Oe. othè:tsla?
Oo. othé?tshæ?   C. othé?thra?   S. othé?shæ?   H. ottecha
W. uteaca   T. uthé?tsreh

Words for 'beans' and 'tobacco' appear to go back to PNI, but again, the Tuscarora terms are not provable cognates. The Huron and Wyandot do not match.

'bean' M. osahè:ta? Oe. osahè:ta? Oo. óhsahè?ta? C. osáhe?ta? S. osáe?ta? (L. sahe) T. θáhe? (H. ogaressa W. uya:resa?)
'tobacco' M. oyv̀:kwa? Oe. oyv̀:kwa? Su. ojeengqua Oo. oyé?kwa? C. oyé?kwa? S. oyé?kwa? T. ù:yv́?kweh 'smoke' (H. houan houan)

The Proto-Northern Iroquoians must have gathered many berries and fruits:

'fruit', berry' M. káhi Oe. káhik Oo. óhya? C. ohya? S. o:ya? T. úhyeh

Aquatic Subsistence

One semantic complex appears to be quite old. The set of words relating to water suggests that the Proto-Iroquoians lived near a large river or lake:

'water' M. awv̀:ke 'in a lake or river' Oe. awv̀:ke 'in a lake or river' Oo. awé?ke 'in a body of water' (L. ame 'water') H. aoüen 'water' W. mé?ye 'in water' T. à:wv? 'water' N. auwa/owan 'water' Ch. ama 'water'
'be in water' M. -o- Oe. -o- Oo. -o- C. -o- S. -o- H. -o- W. -u- T. -u- Ch. -u-
'lake or large river' M. kanyá:tara? Oe. kanya:tále? Oo. kanyá:tae? C. kanyátae? S. kanyotae? H. gontara W. kayo^{n}tare? T. unyá:tareh (borrowing) Ch. vdali
'bathe' M. -atawv- Oe. -atawv- Oo. -atawẽ- C. -atawẽ- S. -atawẽ- H. attahoüan T. -a?nawv Ch. atawo?a
'row a boat' M. -kawe- Oe. -kawe- Oo. -kawe- C. -kawe- S. -kawe- T. -kawe- Ch. -kawe-
'fish' M. kv́tsyu? Oe. kv́tsyu? Oo. otsyó?ta? C. otsó?ta? S. kẽtsõh (L. quejon) H. titsiay- T. kv́tsyv- N. kaintu Ch. atsat?i
'fishhook' C. atáhstẽthra? S. kastõ?shæ? W. distsúhkwa T. uttsúhneh Ch. suhdi

Besides these, a number of terms can be reconstructed for Proto-Northern Iroquoian:

'boat' M. kahuwé:ya? Oe. kahu:wá? Oo. kahó:wa? Ch. kháõwa? S. ka:õwõ? T. uhv̀:weh

'current' M. -hnaw- ohná:wa? Oe. -hnaw- -ahnawvht 'downstream' (current falls) Oo. -hnaw- ohnáwahnhò:ta? 'trout' C. -
hnaw- ohná:wa? S. -hnõw- o:nõwõta:se:h 'whirlpool'
W. ua^{n}duwa T. -htaw- uhta:weh

'fishscales' M. yótstare? Oe. ótstale? Oo. ósta? C. osta?
S. osta? T. ú:θneh

'fish roe', 'milt' H. oocayé T. uθrà:yeh

'fish roe', 'milt' M. onè:tara C. oné?ta:? S. oné?ta:e? H. andé
W. yaderi

'fishhook and line' M. à:rya C. -ahny- T. úhryeh

'foam' M. ohwá:tsta? Oe. ohwv̀:tsta? Oo. ohwé?sta?
C. ohwé?sta? S. o:wé?sta? W. uhméstu T. uhwásneh

'eel' Oo. okṍtèhna? C. kṍ:te S. ké?ta? T. kv́?neh N. kunte
H. oskeendi L. esgueny M. tyawerú:ko Oe. tyawelu:kó
H. tyauoirongo W. tameronko

'sturgeon' H. hixrahon W. (Potier) karaon W. yehrowha
T. kárha

'crab', 'crayfish' M. otsi?eróhta? Oe. yotsi?elóle Oo. otsí?è:ya
('clawed') C. tsí?o: S. otsí?ehta? H. tsiea W. tsi?e:ra?

'oyster', 'mussel' Oo. ohnóhsa? C. kahnóhsa? S. o:nṍstake:?
('oyster stew') W. yahdósya? T. uhtúhseh

'sand' M. o?nehsarúhtehwa? Oe. o?néhsa? Oo. o?néhsa?
C. o?néhsa? S. o?néhsa? H. adecque W. ya?désya?
T. u?téheh N. oter

'island' ('land in water') M. kawè:note? Oe. nikahwe:nóte?
Oo. kahwéhno? C. ohwéhno:t S. o:wé:no? H. ahoindo
W. kawé:du?, yawenda T. yuhwè:nu (borrowing)
Ch. uhnaluolv?i

'river' M. kahyúha? Oe. kawyhúha Oo. kẽhyṍhwa? C. kihú:?u
S. kẽhõ̀:te? H. eindauh*aein* T. kahyvháhreh Ch. huni:hiv

Material Culture

The rapid change in the way of life of most Iroquoians within the
past three hundred years has resulted in heavy replacement of terms
for tools and utensils.

In the area of clothing, a term for 'leggings' is clearly reconstructable
for PNI and perhaps for PI:

'leggings' M. ká:ris Oe. ká:lis Su. khaalis Oo. ká:is káisæ:?
C. kaisra? S. káishæ? H. ariche W. uri:sa N. orisrag Ch. aliyo

A term for 'shoe' or 'moccasin' goes back to PNI:

'shoe' M. áhta 'shoe' ahtahkwahú:we 'moccasin' (original 'shoe')
Oe. áhta 'shoe' ahtakwahú:we 'moccasin'   Su. atackqua
Oo. ahtáhkwaʔ   C. ahtáhkwaʔ   S. ahtáhkwaʔ   (L. atta/atha)
H. atakwa   N. otagwag   T. uhnahkwahv̀:weh 'moccasin'

Another cognate set for shoe, Huron *arassiou*, Wyandot *aracu*, and
Cherokee *alasulo* is probably analyzable as something like 'on the
foot'.

The verb 'sew' goes back to PNI:

'sew' M. -ʔnikhu-   Oe. -ʔnikhu-   Oo. -ʔnikhõ-   C. -ʔnikhõ-   S.
-ʔnikhõ-   H. dandiche 'je recouds'   T. -ʔtikw-

Terms for 'hemp' and 'thread' go back at least to PIP, as does a
term for a type of gown or petticoat. The Tuscarora term for 'hemp'
appears to be a borrowing because of the simplification of the *ts*
cluster:

'hemp' M. kv́tskara 'mat' ('hemp in it')   Oo. oséka:ʔ   C. kẽtska:ʔ
('mat', 'blanket', 'towel', etc.)   S. óskæ:ʔ   H. ononhasquara
T. úhskareh   N. nikarara 'linen'

'thread', 'string' M. ahserí:ye   Oe. ahsli:yéʔ   Oo. ohsí:yæʔ
C. ohsí:yaʔ   S. ohsi:yæʔ   H. taetchiron (donne moi de la corde)
W. yatsea

'petticoat', 'skirt' M. kà:khareʔ 'slip'   kaʔkhá:res 'long shirt'
Oe. kà:kaleʔ 'dress, gown'   kakaláksv 'bad skirt'   Oo. kaʔkhwáes
'long skirt'   C. kakha:ʔ   S. kaʔkha:aʔ   W. yaʔkharetsiʔ

A number of household utensils can be reconstructed. Pipes and
jugs can be traced back to PI:

'pipe' M. kanv́:nawv   Oe. kanu:náwvʔ   Su. chanoona
Oo. kanónawẽ̀ʔta   H. noo oüen   W. yanadúme   T. uʔnv̀:weh
Ch. ganvnowa

'jug' M. kátsheʔ   Oe. kátsheʔ   Su. kaatzie   Oo. katsheʔtaʔ
C. katshéʔtaʔ   S. kashéʔtaʔ   H. asseta   W. yatceʔtaʔ   T. utsheh
Ch. -atsi-

Baskets, wooden troughs, kettles, dishes, bowls, cradleboards, and
perhaps harnesses go back to PNI:

'basket' Oe. waʔahsli:yó (good basekt)   Oo. kaʔáhsæʔ   C. kʔáhtraʔ
S. kaʔáshæʔ   H. atonsha   W. tatòhcraye   T. uʔáhθreh

'trough or wooden bowl' M. kaʔú:waʔ   Oe. kaʔú:waʔ
Oo. kaʔõ̃:waʔ   C. kʔá:õwa?   S. kaʔõ̃:wõʔ   T. uʔv̀:weh

'pot' or 'kettle' M. ú:ta   Oe. u:ták   Su. owntack   L. undaco
T. nʔnawehv̀:weh

'dish' M. katsyv̀:tha? 'dipper' Oe. kátsyv 'cup' Oo. ká:tsyẽ:?
C. katsẽ? S. katsẽ? H. adsen W. hatci^n T. katsyv tha? 'dipper'

'cradleboard' M. kárhu? Oe. kálhu? Oo. ka:hõhsæ:?
C. ká:hõhfra? S. kẽ:õshæ? W. (Potier) harhónchra T. uhrhátsteh
'harness', 'burden strap' M. okéhta? Oe. okéhta? Oo. okéhta?
C. kakéhta? ('scarf', 'necktie') S. kakéhta? 'sash traditionally worn
over shoulder' T. ukéhneh 'burden strap'

The word for 'harness' is related to a verb to 'carry something over
the shoulders', so its use in 'harness' could be a later independent
innovation.

In addition to the bows and arrows mentioned earlier, axes and
knives can be reconstructed for PNI:

'axe' M. ató:kv? Oe. ato:kv́? Su. adwgen, hadoogen C. ató:kẽ?
S. ato:kẽ? (L. addoque) H. atouhoin W. atu:yẽ? T. (a?)nú:kv?
'knife' M. à:share? Oe. à:shale? Oo. á?sha:? S. kakanya?shæ?
H. assara W. a?sha:? T. θharé?ku 'get that knife'

Besides these, pails, spoons, and barrels can be reconstructed for
PIP:

'pail' M. kanà:tsya? Oe. kanà:tsi? Oo. kaná?tsya? C. kaná?tsa?
S. kanṍ?tsa? H. andatson W. (Pot) kandatsa T. kaná?tsya?
(borrowing)

'spoon', 'ladle' M. atókwa Oe. atókwat Oo. ató:kwat
S. atókwa?shæ? H. estoqua

'barrel', 'drum' M. ka?náhkwa? Oe. ka?náhkwa?
Oo. ka?náhkwa? C. k?anáhkwa? S. ka?nṍhkwa? H. anderoqua
W. aha$^{n?}$dahku:ri T. u?náhkweh (borrowing)

On a larger scale, the Cherokee word for 'room' is cognate with
Northern 'house'. It is not unlikely that the two were essentially the
same thing. A term for any arching, protruding structure, such as
porch, bridge, or shed, can be traced by PNI.

'bridge', 'porch' M. áhskwa? Oe. áskwa? Oo. -askw- waskóhwi
'bridge' C. ahskwa? S. waskóõh T. úskweh H. aqua

Rafters can be traced back to P5N:

'rafter' M. kanáhsta? Oo. kanásta? ('post') C. kanáhsta?
S. onõ:sta? H. andaste W. kandasta (Pot)

Social Traditions

An interesting cognate involves the word 'clay'. The word is used in both the Southern and Northern Iroquoian languages for 'chimney' and for 'clan' as well. It could be that the languages independently extended the term for 'chimney' to 'clan':

'clay', 'chimney', 'clan' M. oʔtá:raʔ Oe. oʔta:láʔ Oo. oʔtá:ẽʔ 'mud?
S. kaʔta:aʔ T. uʔnyehreh N. odeshag W. yaʔtara Ch.
-hstahlv:ʔi

None of the names for clans can be traced back, however, except where the animal name can be reconstructed:
Words for 'family', 'marriage', and 'spouse' go back to PNI:

'family' M. -hwatsir- Oe. hwatsil- Oo. -hwatsiy- C. -hwatsiy-
S. -hwatsiyæ-

'marry' M. -nyak- Oe. -nyak- Oo. -nyak- C. -nyak- S. -nyak-
H. sangyoue 'tu es marié' T. -tyak- N. gotyag 'marriage'

'spouse' M. -nahkw- Oe. -nahkw- C. -nahkw- ('marriage') S.
-nõhkw- H. eatenonha 'ma femme' T. -tahkw- N. gotyakum

The Proto-Iroquoians practiced medicine:

'medicine' M. onúhkwaʔ Oe. onúhkwaʔt Oo. onõhkwáʔtshæ
C. onőhkwʔathraʔ S. onőhkwaʔshæʔ H. énonquat
W. nóhkwaʔ T. unvhkwáʔtsreh Ch. nvwoti

'witch' M. ótku Oe. átku Oo. ótkõʔ C. kotkõʔ S. otkõʔ
H. oki W. uki T. útkv Ch. asgina

'bewitch' M. -aʔvn- Oo. -aʔen- C. -aʔẽn- S. -atõ:nõ- Ch. atu:n

The Proto-Northern Iroquoians had the concept of luck. (The Tuscarora is a likely but not provable cognate.):

'luck' M. -ateraʔshw- roteraʔshwi:yo 'he is lucky' Oe. -atlaʔsw-
lotlaʔswi:yo Oo. -atæ:ʔsw- hotæ:ʔswíyoh C. -atraʔsw- ho-
traʔswí:yo: S. -atæʔsw- hotæʔswi:yo: T. -atraʔsw- rutraʔswí:yu:

Dancing can be traced back at least to PNI:

'I danced' Oe. wa:tkátkweʔ Oo. waʔtkátkwaʔ C. atka:t
S. oʔtka:t T. wátkatkw

Singing and rattles go back at least to PIP:

'I sang' M. waʔkatervnó:teʔ Oe. waʔkatlvnó:tvʔ ('I played an instrument') Oo. waʔka:tẽ:nòtẽʔ C. akatrẽnó:tẽʔ S. oʔkatẽno:tẽʔ
H. otoronte 'il chante' W. yareunda 'song'

'rattle' M. ostawv̀:sera   Oo. kastá:wẽˀsæ:ˀ   C. ostáwˀẽtraˀ
S. kastŏ́wẽˀsæˀ W. ostameⁿsra   T. ustawv́ˀtsreh (borrowing)

CONCLUSION

The picture that emerges of the Proto-Iroquoians through their vocabulary is one of a people living near water and relying heavily on fishing. They must have known wolves, wildcats, deer, possibly elk, foxes, weasels, chipmunks, dogs, and skunks, as well as frogs, toads, snakes, and lizards. They were probably bothered by lice and mosquitoes. They may have listened to katydids, whippoorwills, quails, kingfishers, robins, chickadees, and crows, and watched eagles and turkeys. They lived among oak, hickory, beech, and plum trees, and ate tubers, some kind of meal which they may have made into bread, and fish. They smoked pipes and practiced medicine.

The Proto-Northern Iroquoians lived the same kind of life, and also knew otters, beavers, turtles, bees, pigeons, blackbirds, and partridges. They hunted with bows and arrows in forests of elm, slippery elm, basswood, and pine. They had domestic animals, wore leggings and moccasins, and sewed. They put their children on cradleboards and carried loads with burden straps. They used axes and knives, made baskets, wooden troughs, and dishes. They married, had families, and believed in luck.

The Proto-Five Nations community knew these things and others. They lived among porcupines, raccoons, squirrels, and woodchucks, three kinds of turtles, salamanders, mudpuppies, ducks, bluejays, gulls, flickers, snipes, great horned owls, and possibly geese. They hunted in forests of white ash, birch, hemlock, sugar maple, willow, balsam fir, possibly tamarack. They may have tapped sugar maples for syrup. They had hemp and wore skirts and petticoats. They grew corn and beans. They pounded the corn with mortars and pestles into meal, from which they made cornbread and mush. From the husks, they made mats. They used pails, barrels, and spoons. They sang, danced, and used rattles.

The picture is colorful, but gaps remain where no cognates are to be found. Total absence of cognates for an entire semantic field, such as corn cultivation in Proto-Iroquoia, indicates the possible absence of that cultural complex, but does not prove it beyond doubt. The lack of a specific cognate in isolation proves nothing. Interpreted in conjunction with hypotheses arrived at from archaeological and ethnohistorical resources, however, the linguistic data contribute a rich source of information about the past.

NOTES

1. I would like to thank Reginald Henry, Dean Snow, and Jack Campisi for their comments on an earlier draft of this paper.

2. I am grateful to Annette Jacobs and Dorothy Lazore of Caughnawaga, Quebec, and to Mary McDonald, of Ahkwesahsne, New York for the Mohawk examples cited here, abbreviated M. The symbols u and v used in the Mohawk and Oneida data stand for nasalized vowels [ũ] and [ʌ̃]. The Oneida (Oe.) is from Floyd Lounsbury (personal communication), Clifford Abbott, "Oneida Dictionary" (manuscript), and my own notes from Winnie Jacobs, of Syracuse, New York. The Onondaga (Oo.) is from my notes from Reginald Henry, from Hanni Woodbury (personal communication) or (Oo.Z) from David Zeisberger, *Indian Dictionary* (Cambridge: John Wilson and Son, 1887). The Cayuga (C.) is from my own notes from Reginald Henry and James Skye of Six Nations, Ontario. The Seneca (S.) is from Wallace Chafe, *Seneca Morphology and Dictionary* (Washington: Smithsonian Press, 1967), and from my notes from Myrtle Peterson of Steamburg, New York. In the Onondaga, Cayuga, and Seneca examples, the symbols ẽ and õ are used for the nasalized vowels in these languages. The Andaste or Susquehannock (Su.) material is cited in the original transcription of Johan Campanius, *Lutheri Catechismus, Oftwesatt pa American-Virginiske Spraket* (Stockholm: 1696), pp. 157–60. The Laurentian (L.) is cited in the form found in H. P. Biggar, *The Voyages of Jacques Cartier* (Ottawa: Public Archives of Canada Publication 11, 1924). The Huron (H.) is taken from Gabriel Sagard-Theodat, *Dictionnaire de la langue Hvronne* (Paris: 1632). The Wyandot (W.) is from C. Marius Barbeau, "Huron-Wyandot Traditional Narratives," *Translations and Native Texts* (Ottawa: National Museum of Canada Bulletin 165, 1960), unless specified as W. (Potier), in which case it comes from Pierre Potier, Radices huronicae [1751], *15th Report of the Bureau of Archives for the Province of Ontario for the Years 1918–1919*, Alexander Fraser, ed., Toronto: Clarkson W. James, 1920, pp. 159–455. The Tuscarora (T.) is from my own field notes from Mr. Elton Green of Lewiston, New York and Mr. Robert Mt. Pleasant, of Six Nations, Ontario. The Nottoway (N.) is given as transcribed by John Wood in his "Vocabulary of the Language of the Nottoway Tribe of Indians" (Manuscript, American Philosophical Society, Freeman and Smith No. 2478, Philadelphia, 1820). The Cherokee (Ch.) is from Duane King, "A Grammar and Dictionary of the Cherokee Language" (Ph.D. dissertation, University of Georgia, Athens, 1975). (In the Tuscarora examples, the symbol v represents a nasalized schwa [ə̃], the symbol e represents [æ], and a represents [a].) The v in Cherokee represents [ʌ̃].

3. Marianne Mithun, "Iroquoian," in *Native Languages of North America: An Historical and Comparative Assessment*, ed. by Lyle Campbell and Marianne Mithun (Austin: University of Texas Press, 1979), pp. 133–212.

4. It appears that the Cayuga actually separated from the rest of the Northern Iroquoians earlier, sometime after the departure of the Tuscaroras but before that of the Hurons. They later rejoined the Seneca, never quite losing their identity, until relatively recently, when they separated definitively.

For a detailed discussion of this hypothesis consult Wallace Chafe and Michael Foster (1981).

5. Mohawk, Cayuga, and Seneca all share a dialect split, whereby for some speakers, the affricate is palatalized:

*tsy > [džy]

while for others, it is not:

*tsy > [dz].

All words containing this sequence thus have two alternants:

M. tsyò:kwaris/tsò:kwaris
C. tsy?okris/ts?okris
S. tsyoko:ki:h/tsoko:ki:h.

6. Dean Snow informs me that there is no clear evidence for corn in New York until A.D. 1000, although some presume it to be present as early as A.D. 500.

CHAPTER SIXTEEN

The Cultural Continuity of the Northern Iroquoian-Speaking Peoples

JAMES V. WRIGHT

Starting with Father Jérôme Lalemant in A.D. 1641 (Thwaites 1896–1901: 193–95), considerable attention has been directed toward the origins of the Iroquoian-speaking peoples of northeastern North America. Most of the early origin hypotheses involved a late Iroquoian migration out of the south that resulted in a displacement of indigenous Algonkian-speaking peoples. The proposals of James B. Griffin (1944) and Bertram Kraus (1944) followed by the work of Richard S. MacNeish (1952) led to a replacement of the migration hypotheses with an archaeologically based *in situ* theory. For a critical assessment of the earlier origin hypotheses as well as the *in situ* theory, see B. G. Trigger (1970).[1]

In essence, the *in situ* theory states that the historic Iroquoian-speaking peoples of northeastern North America are not recent intruders from the south but rather that they are the product of a long, prehistoric development that took place in the general area of their historic homeland. MacNeish proposed that four regional subdivisions diverged from a relatively common Point Peninsula culture base (400 B.C.-A.D. 600) to result in 1. the Huron/Neutral/Erie, 2. Seneca/Cayuga, 3. Onondaga/Oneida, and 4. Mohawk. Subsequent research has modified and refined many aspects of the *in situ* theory (Emerson 1961; Lenig 1965; Noble 1969, 1975; Pendergast 1966; Pratt 1976; Ramsden 1977; Ritchie 1952, 1965; Ritchie and Funk 1973; Stothers 1977; Tooker 1967; Tuck 1971; White 1961; Wright 1966; Wright and Anderson 1969; and others), but all have reinforced the *in situ* aspect of the theory. One obvious question arising from the *in situ* theory is, "How long were the Iroquoian peoples resident in the northeast?" At a hypothetical level it has been recently suggested that the Iroquoian peoples of the historic period represent the end product of a cultural development that began in the Laurentian Archaic some 6000 years ago (Wright 1972; Tuck 1977). It is to this question that the present paper will address itself with reference to that portion of the Northeastern Iroquoian Co-tradition that gave rise to the Huron, Petun, Neutral, and Erie. A co-tradition "is the over-all unit of culture history of an area within which the component cultures have been interrelated over a period of time" (Bennett 1948: 1), and as used in this paper refers to the relationships between the various archaeological traditions that terminate in the historic Iroquoian peoples of northeastern North America. In terms of political entities the historic end products of the co-tradition are 1. Huron/Petun/Neutral/Erie; 2. Onondaga/Oneida/Mohawk; 3. St. Lawrence Iroquois; and ??? Seneca? Cayuga? Susquehannock? As indicated by the question marks, evidence regarding the relationships of the last three tribes is limited and equivocal.

At a hypothetical level, I would propose that the Ontario Iroquois tradition (Huron/Petun/Neutral/Erie) and the other segments of the co-tradition will eventually be traced back to the Laurentian Archaic and that the cultural continuity implied in such a proposal will be analytically demonstrable. An addition of at least 4500 years would have to be added onto the slightly more than 1000 years currently accepted for segments of the co-tradition under consideration. While such a proposal is fraught with interpretational and theoretical pitfalls it is, in my opinion, a valid and necessary construct.

Underlying the specific proposal is a theoretical premise; and by theory I mean an assumption based upon principles independent of the phenomena under consideration. The assumption is that if all facets of a prehistoric culture or cultures, such as technology, religion (mortuary practices), settlement and subsistence patterns, maintain an essential continuity through time and terminate in a historic cultural and linguistic grouping, there is a rational basis for the proposal that the cultural tradition(s) traced by archaeology represent the ancestral generations of the historic grouping regardless of the time dimension involved. Basic to this assumption is the proposition that, given the levels of society under consideration, a cultural/linguistic population cannot be replaced by a different cultural/linguistic population during prehistoric times without creating a discontinuity of such magnitude that it can be readily distinguished in the archaeological record.

Cultural replacements have been recorded in the prehistory of Canada; the most dramatic being the expansion out of northern Alaska around A.D. 900 of the Thule ancestors of the present-day Inuit (McGhee 1978) and the expansion of a portion of the Athabascan peoples into the barren grounds and adjacent forests around 600 B.C. (Gordon 1975; 1976). These two major movements of prehistoric people, the Inuit and the Athabascans, however, represent exceptions to the rule in the prehistory of northern North America where most native groups appear to have occupied their historic homelands for a considerable time period. This not only appears to be true for the Iroquoian peoples of the lower Great Lakes-St. Lawrence but also for the Algonkian-speakers of the Canadian Shield (Wright, 1981), the majority of the tribes of the West Coast (Mitchell 1971; MacDonald and Inglis 1976), and others. Contractions and expansions of con-temporaneous prehistoric populations are common but are generally limited in extent and associated with phenomena such as climatic change that favors one cultural adaptation over another.

At this point a basic question must be asked: What is the basis for assuming that language and culture neatly correlate with any particular prehistoric assemblage through time and space? Dr. B. G. Trigger has been the most articulate scholar in terms of the critical evaluation of the various hypotheses that have been applied to Iroquoian culture history (Trigger 1970; 1976). I am in essential accord with many of his assessments and the differences are more ones of degree and emphasis than kind. The dendritic model of Iroquoian culture development, for example, can only be viewed as a simplistic device of temporary utility; to look upon it as anything more concrete abuses both data and reason. It is a tool, a framework if you will, within which certain forms of data can be manipulated for specific purposes. Also, the role of diffusion and particularly stimulus diffusion in Iroquoian culture history has been underemphasized by archae-ologists just as have the interaction through time of the various changing elements of the co-tradition and the relationship of these elements to adjacent non-Iroquoian cultures. But Iroquoian archae-ologists must continue to put their local, chronological sequences into better order before the roles of diffusion and interaction at either general or specific levels can be effectively evaluated within the given limitations of the discipline. This, of course, does not mean that any archaeologist can afford to ignore the impact upon his sequences of major diffused elements such as horticulture, but rather that a major emphasis of his research should focus upon analytically demonstrable trends and developments that, in turn, constitute the essential in-gredients for more sophisticated analyses and realistic syntheses.

Trigger's comments regarding the hazards of correlating language with archaeological data in the absence of historical records, however, are only partially valid (Trigger 1976: 6). The probability of language diffusion into the prehistoric societies under consideration without an equivalent diffusion of other elements recognizable in the archaeological record seems slight. Although the association of a language with any prehistoric culture can never be proven, the assumption of a language association with an unbroken archaeological sequence that terminates with a historic language group would appear to be a more valid option than the possible alternatives. Neither culture nor language "mutates" out of thin air—both are the products of long, complex developments. Observations regarding Latin-speaking Celts of the Roman Empire or present day English or French-speaking Iroquoians pertain to a level of phenomenon not pertinent to the present discussion.

However, I do agree with the statement "It appears to me that nothing but needless difficulties can be gained by confusing political entities with 'ethnic divisions' and by this muddled process further confusing them with archaeological cultures" (Trigger 1970: 40). The political entity called "the Huron" is not the same level of phenomenon as the ethnic groups that historically represented the component parts of the Huron. Gross ethnic groupings or constellations, however, can be recognized in the archaeological record along with their contractions, expansions, amalgamations, or disappearances. When their developments can be traced through time it is, in my opinion, a valid assumption that the historically documented language groups can be related back to their prehistoric ancestry. This certainly does not mean that a particular prehistoric site or complex can be called Huron but rather should be recognized as one of the contributing elements to what historically became known as the Huron. Recent evidence suggests that the Iroquoian political units of the historic period were likely very late, even proto-historic, developments (Tuck 1971; Ramsden 1977; Finlayson, Dawkin and Tripp 1977). While prehistoric cultures cannot be equated with historic political units per se, they can be recognized as the contributing cultural ancestry of political groups of the historic period. Some historically distinct groups such as the Huron and Petun, on the one hand, and the Mohawk and Oneida, on the other, shared very similar archaeological cultures for at least a portion of their respective developments.

Pertinent to the ethnic/linguistic association with prehistoric cultures is the suggestion that adjacent Algonkian-speaking peoples shared in the same archaeological cultures that gave rise to Iroquoian-speakers (Trigger 1970: 43). Such a situation has been proposed for the Algonkian-speaking Munsee division of the Delaware (Ritchie 1949a; 1965: 299–300). The evidence from Ontario and Quebec, however, indicates that there is no particular difficulty in distinguishing the archaeological cultures of Algonkian-speaking peoples from Iroquoian even when the former have shared the same ceramic tradition for over 800 years (Ridley 1954; Wright 1965; 1969). When the *total* archaeological cultures of Iroquoians and adjacent Algonkians are examined in detail it is apparent that there are significant differences particularly in the areas of lithic technology, settlement and subsistence patterns. For too long, rudimentary and selective analyses that focus on a single facet of the material culture—pottery—have created a false impression of cultural homogeneity when actually considerable heterogeneity exists. The archaeological data base is sufficiently biased without compounding the situation with simplistic analytical techniques and incomplete analyses.

THE TIME DEPTH OF THE ONTARIO IROQUOIS TRADITION

The cultural developments involved in the Ontario Iroquois tradition have been traced by the direct historic approach to approximately A.D. 800. One segment of this tradition, the Princess Point/ Glen Meyer development has been pushed back to nearly A.D. 500 (Noble 1975; Stothers 1977). Ongoing and future research will undoubtedly continue the process of extending the time depth of the Ontario Iroquois tradition as well as the other segments of the Northeastern Iroquoian Co-tradition in a fashion that will generally be acceptable to most scholars. Difficulties are encountered, however, when we attempt to extend the tradition beyond A.D. 500. Undoubtedly the complex events revolving around the adoption of a horticultural subsistence base between A.D. 500 and A.D. 1000 have blurred the proposed ancestral connections with the preceding Initial Woodland hunting bands.

Prior to A.D. 1300 two discrete cultural developments are involved in the early portion of the Ontario Iroquois tradition—the Pickering branch in the east and the Glen Meyer branch in the west (including the preceding Princess Point complex). After this period an apparent conquest and absorption of the Glen Meyer people by the Pickering branch created the broad cultural horizon from which the historic Huron, Petun, Neutral, and Erie developed (Wright and Anderson 1969). The approximate boundary between the separate Pickering and Glen Meyer sequences is a line running north from Toronto to Georgian Bay. This same boundary was noted earlier as the separation point between eastern and western variants of Laurentian Archaic based upon a distributional study of selected classes of artifacts (Wright 1962). I would agree that the use of the term Laurentian to include the western variant overextends the taxonomic utility of the concept and that the designation in Ontario should now be restricted to the eastern variant which is related to developments in southern Quebec, the northern New England states and northern New York (Ritchie 1969: 79–83). The western variant would then fall into the potpourri of an unnamed entity related to assemblages that extend northward from the Appalachian uplands into Canada and of which Laurentian is only one regional expression (Tuck 1977).

With the introduction of pottery and other traits during the Initial Woodland period this same boundary line in the Toronto area maintains itself with the Saugeen culture occupying southwestern Southern Ontario (Wright and Anderson 1963; Finlayson 1977a) and the Point Peninsula culture occupying southeastern Southern Ontario (Wright 1967; Johnston 1968). Thus from Archaic times up to approximately A.D. 1300 there appear to be distinct regional developments in the eastern and western portions of Southern Ontario. Further cultural variants within each of these geographical regions should also be anticipated but the groups within each major region share more with each other than with their counterparts in the other region.

The Western Region

This region extends west from Toronto to include the area bounded by Lake Erie, Lake Huron and the western end of Lake Ontario with the exception of the southwestern extremity in the Windsor area. The prehistory in the latter area appears to relate more closely to developments taking place in adjacent Michigan and Ohio.

In terms of the late Archaic in the Western Region, only the local sequence along Lake Huron in Bruce County is at all well known. Called originally the Inverhuron Archaic (Kenyon 1959), the sequence has been traced from approximately 1700 B.C. to later than 900 B.C. (Wright 1972b; Ramsden 1976) and can be demonstrated to have been ancestral to the subsequent Saugeen culture of the Woodland period (Wright 1972b: 56–57; Finlayson 1977: 596–602). It has been proposed that Saugeen culture history can be traced from 700 B.C. to A.D. 800 (Finlayson 1977). If the terminal date is correct then we have a cultural tradition in Bruce County that overlaps the Archaic and Woodland periods and spans 2500 years. Presumably similar, regional cultural developments were taking place with regard to related peoples that shared in the Saugeen cultural pattern.

Despite some very minor evidence of Michigan-derived Terminal Woodland material along the coast of Bruce County there appears to be a cultural hiatus between the late Saugeen culture and a mid-fourteenth-century limited reoccupation from the east by an element of the Ontario Iroquois tradition (Wright 1974). The fate of the Saugeen culture in Bruce County is unknown. Finlayson, however, on the basis of ceramic attribute data, has speculatively suggested that to the south, a region more suited to initial horticulture, the Saugeen culture may have evolved into the Princess Point culture and, thence, to Glen Meyer (Finlayson 1977: 611–12). However, at an equally speculative level it may be suggested that Princess Point culture moved into Ontario probably from Michigan. If my hypothesis of a conquest and absorption of the Glen Meyer people by the Pickering branch at A.D. 1300 is correct (Wright 1966; Wright and Anderson 1969), then this lengthy cultural development is truncated. If, on the other hand, a less draconian explanation for the apparent cultural discontinuity involving Glen Meyer and Pickering can be demonstrated, then we have a sequence that extends to the historic period. From the late Archaic period to the historic period the only major disruptions in the cultural development of the Western Region occur between Saugeen and Princess Point and Glen Meyer and Pickering. My views regarding the latter are known; only future research will resolve the former.

The Eastern Region

The situation in the Eastern Region is quite different. A local Laurentian Archaic sequence in the middle Ottawa Valley has been revealed in the excavation of two adjacent but temporally distinct components. The Allumette Island site (Kennedy, n.d.) produced a date of 3290 B.C. ± 80 (S–509) while the Morrison Island site (Kennedy 1967) was dated at 2750 B.C. ± 150 (GSC–162). Not only do the stone, bone, and copper technologies and the burial patterns at the two sites indicate a clear cultural continuity but biologically the two populations appear to be inseparable (Pfeiffer 1977). Unfortunately there are, as yet, no terminal or very late Laurentian Archaic sites that have been analyzed from the region. At the East Sugar Island site on Rice Lake, late Laurentian Archaic materials were found with Point Peninsula pottery but the nature of the deposits precluded any statement regarding contemporanity as opposed to accidental association (Ritchie 1949). Ongoing work at the McIntyre site, also on Rice Lake, by Dr. Richard B. Johnston should help fill the gap. On the basis of surface collections (Johnston 1968a), the McIntyre site appears to be essentially a late expression of the Laurentian Archaic with a number of lithic traits, particularly the projectile points, exhibiting close parallels with the subsequent Point Peninsula culture of the Woodland period.

With few exceptions the investigation of Point Peninsula culture in Ontario has focused on either the middle Ottawa valley (Emerson 1955; Watson 1972) or the Rice Lake area (Johnston 1968; Spence and Harper 1968; Ritchie 1949). Sites in the former area have been radiocarbon-dated between 500 B.C. and A.D. 200 while in the latter region the dates range from approximately 100 B.C. to A.D. 300. Due to the limited material and frequently mixed deposits of the Ottawa valley sites it is very difficult to establish a chronology although a rough sequence is possible. In the Rice Lake region, on the other hand, excavation has concentrated on the burial mounds and the limited examination of habitation sites has produced too little material for effective seriation. Unfortunately, the extensive excavation of a major Point Peninsula occupation area, the Ault Park site on the St. Lawrence River, has never been adequately reported upon.

From Point Peninsula culture we move to the early Pickering branch of the Ontario Iroquois tradition beginning sometime prior to A.D. 800 and extending in a relatively well-documented sequence to the populations that composed the Huron and Petun of the historic period (Wright 1966; Wright and Anderson 1969; Kenyon 1968; Ridley 1958; Reid 1975). An examination of the earliest described Pickering component, the Miller site (Kenyon 1968)[2] reveals certain connections with the preceding Point Peninsula culture despite the rapid changes resulting from populations of hunters becoming reliant upon corn agriculture. Most of the stone tool classes such as hammer and anvil stones, abraders, polished adzes, scrapers, projectile points, biface blades, and drills are found on Point Peninsula sites. Also, the high frequencies of scrapers characteristic of Point Peninsula sites is also typical of early Pickering sites. Other artifact traits that span the Point Peninsula–Pickering transition are unilaterally barbed harpoons with line hole, bilaterally barbed and conical bone points, steatite elbow pipes and ground slate pendants, columella and copper beads, notched pottery markers, sinew-stones, copper and bone awls, and utilized or modified linear flakes. The retention of side-notched and stemmed projectile varieties on early Pickering sites also supports the proposed transition out of Point Peninsula as do the ceramic attributes. Early Pickering vessels are characteristically decorated by dentate stamping (Kenyon 1968) which also includes pseudo scallop shell and dragged stamp (personal examination) as well as other techniques and motifs typical of Point Peninsula pottery. Paradoxically, the bossing attributes of early Pickering vessels are more typical of late Laurel ceramics than Point Peninsula. The evidence for the transition of Pickering out of Point Peninsula is mirrored in New York state where the ancestry of Owasco culture has been attributed to the preceding Point Peninsula culture (Ritchie 1965: 253–57).

In the Eastern Region the major breaks in the proposed continuity from Laurentian Archaic to the historic Iroquoian populations occurs between the very late Archaic period and the beginnings of the Woodland period. The cultural continuum of Point Peninsula culture from circa 700 B.C. to the transition into Pickering culture needs considerable refinement. From A.D. 800 up to the historic populations, the development is on a relatively firm basis.

It can be appreciated that the quantity and quality of data necessary to analytically demonstrate cultural continuity, especially during periods of rapid change related to diffused concepts from outside, is considerable. Archaeological excavation in Southern Ontario has been heavily slanted towards the large Iroquoian village sites dating between A.D. 800 and the historic period. As a result the earlier Archaic and Initial Woodland segment of the development has been, to a considerable extent, neglected. There is a pragmatic reason for this neglect—the large Iroquoian sites guarantee a high return in data relative to money and manpower expended whereas the small Archaic and Initial Woodland camp sites with their frequently mixed and thin deposits, present the reverse situation. In the one instance in Southern Ontario where considerable research has been directed towards Archaic and subsequent Initial Woodland sites, however, a cultural continuity has been demonstrated as witnessed by the Inverhuron tradition of the Western Region (Wright 1972b; Finlayson 1977). Stratified sites or, less preferably, sites with superpositional deposits, should be sought, and excavation techniques must guard against the dangers of component mixture that would naturally result in a false image of cultural continuity. Analytical techniques will have to be refined in order to fully exploit the relatively meager forms of data available from the early sites. It is anticipated that for a considerable period the comparative exercise will have to rely upon widely dispersed sites. In the long run tight control of local sequences will serve prehistory better and will very likely reveal that the cultural heterogeneity now being recognized within the various late Iroquoian groups (Ramsden 1977) also applies, albeit probably to a lesser extent, to the preceding Archaic and Initial Woodland populations.

Three major facets of the Northeastern Iroquoian Co-tradition cultural development are considered: the generalized Archaic base from which it is speculated to have evolved; the major period of cultural change between 1500 B.C. and 1000 B.C. related to climatic and possible technological changes; and the final period of rapid change related to the adoption of corn agriculture between A.D. 500 and A.D. 800.

I. Formative Laurentian: The term Formative Laurentian was first used by William A. Ritchie (1955: 8), to describe an early population that entered the northeast "through the deciduous forest belt bordering the Great Lakes in Altithermal times." The same author, however, has clearly stated that the Laurentian Archaic developed *in situ* in the northeast from the hypothetical "formative" culture base (1965: 83). More recently, James A. Tuck has made an examination of Laurentian and has come to the conclusion that there ". . . are two 'Laurentians'—that defined strictly for the upper St. Lawrence region and that which is even less well defined 'typologically' or geographically and presently appears older than that in the upper St. Lawrence" (Tuck 1977: 33). On the basis of distribution studies of projectile point varieties and information from widely scattered sites, it has been tentatively suggested that the formative base of which Laurentian is only one regional expression extends "from the Appalachian uplands to suggest a continuous distribution northwards from western North Carolina–eastern Tennessee to New York and Canada" (ibid.). These materials pertain to elements of the Early (8,000–6,000 B.C.) and Middle (6,000–4,000 B.C.) Archaic periods (Wright 1978).

What has made Laurentian Archaic distinctive from this formative assemblage of broad, side-notched points, simple and hafted scrapers, biface blades and drills, has largely been diffused traits from other regions. Diagnostic Laurentian Archaic traits such as ground slate lances and points, gouges, and ulus, are early elements in the Maritime Archaic and very likely diffused from the coast to be adopted by the interior Laurentian populations (Tuck 1977: 34–35). It might also be pointed out that another Laurentian diagnostic, the bannerstone (atlatl weight), must have originated in the southeastern United States.

A number of years ago Frank Speck, in considering the relationship of the Cherokee and the northern Iroquoians, stated "The roots of migration followed in the course of Iroquoian dispersion still defy explanation. Archaeology holds the answer" (Speck 1945: 22). Archaeology still does not have the answer. However, should future research validate the proposal of an early, generalized Archaic lithic technology extending from North Carolina to Canada from which Laurentian evolved as one regional development, then the archaeological gap between the northern and southern Iroquoian-speaking peoples may have at least been partially bridged.

It is becoming increasingly clear that the role of diffusion in the formation of archaeological cultures is of paramount importance. Years ago, William N. Fenton stressed the possible role of ongoing diffusion as a means by which Iroquoian traits of southeastern North American origins were transmitted to the Iroquoian-speaking peoples of the Northeast (Fenton 1940). Paradoxically, the majority of the archaeological traits that appear to distinguish the Laurentian Archaic from related complexes have their origins on the northeast coast of North America (Tuck 1977: 34). Archaeology has a long way to go in its efforts to elucidate the factors that gave rise to the Laurentian Archaic, and certainly a number of the forces involved are probably beyond the capabilities of the discipline to detect. Despite the magnitude of the task and the equivocal nature of much of the data the potential exists for archaeology to provide testable hypotheses concerning Iroquoian origins, hypotheses that can be subjected to the critical scrutiny of other concerned scholars. Unless the problem is viewed from a broad perspective, however, and supported by rigorous analytical processing of data, it is unlikely that hypotheses capable of attracting the attention of other disciplines will be generated.

II. The Period of Rapid Change between 1500 and 1000 B.C.: The major disruption in the proposed development took place 3500 to 3000 years ago. If the continuity hypothesis is wrong and a cultural replacement took place, then it would most likely have occurred during this period. On the other hand, this was a time of population shifts that appear to be related, in a complex fashion, to both technological and climatic changes. In opposition to the replacement hypothesis it is proposed that diffusion resulting in technological change exerted forces on the culture of the indigenous Laurentian Archaic peoples with sufficient intensity and brevity to blur but not eradicate the cultural continuity with later populations.

New traits that appear are birdstones, pipes of both stone and pottery, gorgets, and pottery; all are items with southern origins. Quantitative changes take place in the tool kit such as the marked increase in the manufacture of end scrapers and biface blades. A new projectile point variety appears, the Meadowood point (Ritchie 1971: 35–36), associated with finely made cache blades and end scrapers manufactured from bifacially formed blades.

Late Archaic traits that carry through into Woodland cultures such as Point Peninsula and Saugeen are as follows: point styles including the typical cavalier manufacturing pattern; ground celts; hafted scrapers; asymmetric hafted knives; wedges, drills; strike-a-lights; most rough stone categories and other minor items. Settlement and subsistence patterns appear to be essentially unchanged as are the trading patterns for native copper, marine shells, and certain silicious materials. The burial practices of Meadowood culture (Woodland period) have their roots in the preceding Glacial Kame and related burial complexes of the Archaic period (Ritchie 1965: 131–34, 179–200). Finally, the possibility of biological continuity from Laurentian Archaic to historic Iroquois has been suggested, albeit in a tentative manner (Anderson 1968: 60). Another study of Archaic population affinities, however, found a Laurentian population in New York state to compare more closely with a Maritime Archaic population from Newfoundland than it did to another Laurentian population in the Ottawa valley (Pfeiffer 1977). It appears that the physical anthropological complexities are similar in magnitude to the archaeological ones.

In the past, based upon the linguistic relationship of the northern Iroquoians to the Cherokee, it has been assumed that the former broke off from their southern kinsmen at some undetermined date and penetrated to the north to become an enclave surrounded by Algonkian-speakers. Early archaeological constructs regarded Iroquoian material as being late and assumed that earlier material in the same region had been left by the original Algonkian-speaking occupants who were forced out by Iroquoian peoples (Parker 1916a). This position was reflected in the titles of a number of early archaeological works (Ritchie 1944; Wintemberg 1931).

The first specific replacement hypothesis stated that ". . . it seems possible that Lamoka was the means by which the Iroquoian language was introduced into a region otherwise occupied by speakers of Algonkian languages" (Byers 1959: 256). Recently, the essential element of this replacement hypothesis has been revived. Using an archaeolinguistic model correlated with drainage systems, Dean Snow (1977) has suggested that the Laurentian Archaic were Algonkian-speakers and that the earliest penetration of the Iroquoians out of the south can be seen with the appearance of the Frost Island phase of the Susquehanna tradition (Ritchie 1965: 155–63). The Frost Island phase falls within William A. Ritchie's Transitional Stage dated between 1300 and 1000 B.C. and, therefore, fits within the period of rapid change under discussion. The only dated component of the phase comes from the O'Neil site in central New York (Ritchie 1965: 156), with a reading of 1250 B.C. and is in close agreement with the glotto-chronological estimate for the separation of the Iroquoian and Cherokee languages between 3500 and 3800 years ago (Lounsbury 1961). There is little resemblance, however, between the Frost Island assemblage and the subsequent Woodland assemblages that develop into the various historic Iroquoian populations. I would agree with William A. Ritchie's statement that "The Frost Island phase seems to have expired without clear survivals" (Ritchie 1965: 163).

In place of Douglas Byer's and Dean Snow's replacement models, I would suggest that two related factors resulted in such rapid changes in the indigenous Laurentian Archaic culture that the discontinuity between the Archaic and Woodland periods is more apparent than real. These factors were climatic and technological.

About 1500 B.C. a major climatic deterioration affecting the northern latitudes resulted in major shifts in prehistoric populations adapted to different ecosystems. In the northwest this climatic event (Nichols 1967, 1967a, 1967b), resulted in the abandonment of the eastern barren grounds of Keewatin District by the Shield Archaic people with a subsequent reoccupation from the northwest by Palaeo-Es-kimos (Wright 1972a; Gordon 1975; 1976). The ripple effects of this prolonged and geographically erratic event in the north may be reflected in certain archaeological data far to the south. In the Lake Nipissing region, for example, Laurentian Archaic sites that should date as early as 4000 B.C. have been located (unpublished infor-mation). By 1000 B.C. and probably earlier, the region is occupied by late Shield Archaic hunters (Ridley 1954). If, for the region involved, the assumption is correct that the specific archaeological cultures were adapted to specific environments, then it would follow that the marginal replacements of one culture by another could represent a more sensitive indicator of climatic change affecting flora and, thereby, fauna then pollen analysis in lieu of plant macrofossils and heavy pollen.

Similarly, in the northern latitudes of the northeast the same climatic deterioration (Nichols 1974; Jordan 1975), was having a dramatic impact upon maritime-adapted cultures. It appears that around 1800 B.C. Palaeo-Eskimos began expanding down the Labrador coast and their descendants and/or followers would eventually oc-cupy the entire coastal regions of Newfoundland and overlap onto the northshore of the Gulf of St. Lawrence into Quebec (Tuck 1976; Fitzhugh 1976). The Palaeo-Eskimo expansion was made at the expense of the previous Maritime Archaic Indians (Tuck 1975; McGhee and Tuck 1975; Fitzhugh 1972). The pertinence of this event to the Laurentian Archaic will become apparent shortly. It should also be noted that the contact zone between the Laurentian Archaic and the Maritime Archaic occurred in the middle St. Lawrence valley in the area of Trois-Rivières (Marois and Ribes 1975).

The third major population shift involving adjacent contemporaries of the Laurentian Archaic was the advance out of the mid-Atlantic states by the Susquehanna tradition around 1300 B.C. or earlier (Ritchie 1965, 1969; Dincauze 1975). The areas involved in this event are the Potomac, Susquehanna and Hudson-Mohawk drainages (Witthoft 1953: 16), Long Island and the Finger Lakes–Seneca River region of central New York (Ritchie 1965: 155), and southern New Brunswick (Sanger 1975).

Why the Susquehanna tradition advanced into central New York and what happened to the migrants after 1000 B.C. are still unresolved problems although, as has already been mentioned, Dean Snow (1977) would argue that the migrants developed eventually into the historic Iroquoian-speaking peoples. My view of this hypothesis has already been expressed.

An important element in the events of 1500 B.C. to 1000 B.C. has been the shifting geographic locations of both the Laurentian Archaic and their neighbors. New traits and concepts that appear during this period are likely the result of increased physical contact situations with concomitant diffusion. Although the effects of the northern climatic deterioration around 1500 B.C. may have had only a marginal impact upon the biome of the Laurentian Archaic, the cultural implications of this event were possibly profound.

In addition to the geographic shifting of Archaic populations in the second millennium before Christ there is a basis for suspecting that a new technological element was introduced into the area around 1000 B.C.—the bow and arrow. It has been suggested that some time prior to 1500 B.C., the Palaeo-Eskimos, who were moving down the coast of Labrador, introduced a bow technology to the indigenous Maritime Archaic peoples and received, in return, the toggling harpoon head (Tuck 1976a: 87). As has been mentioned earlier, the Laurentian Archaic received the majority of their diagnostic traits via diffusion from the Maritime Archaic (gouge, ground slate lance, point and ulu, and plummet), and the distributions of these two Archaic populations overlapped in the Trois-Rivières area. It thus appears that there was a diffusion pattern from the Maritime Archaic up the St. Lawrence River into Laurentian Archaic territory. By approximately 1000 B.C., a distinctive point variety associated with finely flaked triangular blades and end scrapers manufactured from the former, was grafted onto the late Laurentian assemblage. The appearance of these new traits correlates with the introduction of ceramics and, thus, the beginning of the Woodland period. The Meadowood projectile point (Ritchie 1971: 35–36) has long been recognized as one of the major diagnostics of the Meadowood culture that occupied essentially the same area as the preceding Laurentian Archaic. What has not been explicitly commented upon are the apparent attribute differences between the Meadowood point and late Laurentian Archaic points with which it has been recovered in direct association (Levesque, Osborne, and Wright 1964). First, the Meadowood points are characterized by a symmetry of form that is atypical of the associated late Laurentian points. Second, the Meadowood point is significantly thinner than the other point varieties with which they are found. At the Batiscan site, Adena and Brewerton side-notched point varieties were recovered in association with Meadowood points. According to Ritchie (1971), Adena points and Brewerton side-notched points range in thickness from 6mm to 11mm and from 6mm to 13mm respectively, whereas the Meadowood points rarely exceed 4mm in thickness.[3] It might also be noted that there are no good Laurentian prototypes in terms of both form attributes and knapping technique for the Meadowood point.

It is proposed that the bow and arrow was adopted by Maritime Archaic hunters from the Palaeo-Eskimos and was then transmitted to the Laurentian Archaic via an established diffusion system up the St. Lawrence River. An alternative to this hypothesis would be that late Shield Archaic hunters (circa 1500 B.C.) adopted the bow from Palaeo-Eskimos in southern Keewatin District and environs and/or Labrador. This proposal has the advantge of offering a possible explanation for the quantitative increase of end scrapers and bifaces in Laurentian Archaic. Perhaps both of these Archaic populations, Maritime and Shield, who were in potential contact situations with Palaeo-Eskimos, recognized the utility of the bow. The situation at the Batiscan site and other sites of equivalent and later temporal placement suggest that the bow did not immediately replace the javelin but was added to the extant weaponary and only through time gained a preeminent position. A rigorous attribute and metrical analysis should detect significant differences between projectile points intended for propulsion by a bow as opposed to a throwing board.

The contribution that the bow made to a more efficient exploitation of the environment is unknown. We can only assume that its utility was sufficient to result in its adoption and, it eventually replaced the earlier javelin.

The preceding has suggested that rather than reflecting a cultural replacement, the cultural changes between 1500 and 1000 B.C. were the product of diffused concepts and traits coming from both the northeast and the south. The changes that took place in a relatively short span of time, however, have only blurred the continuity from late Laurentian Archaic into the Woodland period. Settlement pattern, subsistence, and mortuary practices maintain a continuity through this period as do essential elements of the technology despite the proposed addition of the bow and perhaps associated quantitative changes such as the marked increase in the frequencies of end scrapers and biface blades.

III. The Cultural Transition of A.D. 500 to A.D. 800: The nature of this period of change is quite different from that previously discussed. It was during this time, at least in Southern Ontario, that the transition from hunters to farmers took place. By approximately A.D. 500, corn was introduced into Southern Ontario (Stothers 1977) and by A.D. 700 ". . . the settlement pattern data definitely indicates a semipermanent mode of village life" (Noble and Kenyon 1972). The process of hunters being transformed into farmers and the concomitant social changes involved must represent one of the most interesting challenges facing Iroquoian archaeologists today. There is already evidence to suggest that certain of the changes involved in women becoming the main food producers as opposed to men can be detected by archaeological means. However, this particular research problem is only pertinent to the central theme of this paper inasmuch as it has only been recently that archaeologists have recognized the cultural continuity between the preagricultural hunters and their agricultural descendants who historically became the Iroquoian-speaking peoples of northeastern North America. While significant changes took place during this period they were not sufficient to mask the basic cultural continuity that eventually led to the historic period.

SUMMARY

It has been proposed that the historic Iroquoian-speaking peoples of northeastern North America are the descendants of a long cultural development that begins with the Laurentian Archaic. Such a proposal entails the consideration of more than six thousand years as the valid domain of Iroquoian archaeologists. Many aspects of the proposal are speculative, based as they are on limited and often equivocal evidence. Given the present level of data, however, the proposal is, in my judgment, based on a more solid foundation than the only major alternative—cultural replacement. It might be suggested that such speculative constructs serve no purpose or, at the worst, constitute a disservice to the discipline. Archaeology or, for that matter, science in general cannot function without hypotheses. The continuity hypothesis of Iroquoian origins outlined in this paper is intended to present a broad perspective of the events leading to the historic Iroquoian-speaking peoples of northeastern North America. If in so doing it reduces the all too often restricted time-space and particularistic view of archaeology and, at the same time, stimulates the critical assessment of other disciplines such as linguistics, then it will have been a potentially useful exercise. The hypothesis of six thousand years of cultural continuity for the Iroquoian peoples has yet to stand critical assessment. It is hoped that by putting such a hypothesis forward, testing can begin and through confirmation, negation and/ or modification contribute to the resolution of a problem that has attracted the attention of scholars for more than three hundred years.

NOTES

1. I wish to acknowledge with gratitude the critical assessments of an enlarged version of the paper by the following National Museum of Man colleagues: Drs. Gordon Day, Robert McGhee, and the late Roscoe Wilmeth. [This paper was completed in 1979 and represents the writer's thinking at that time—Eds.]

2. The single radiocarbon date of A.D. 1115 ± 70 (S–108) from the Miller site is rejected; on the basis of other Pickering culture dates and seriation, an estimated age for the village is A.D. 800.

3. W.A. Ritchie's fractions have been converted into millimetres.

CHAPTER SEVENTEEN

How to Say They Drank in Iroquois

WALLACE L. CHAFE

Suppose a speaker of one of the extant Northern Iroquoian languages (Mohawk, Oneida, Onondaga, Seneca, Cayuga, or Tuscarora) wanted to report an event in which several women took a drink of something. If a speaker of English had the same sort of thing in mind, he or she might say, "They drank." Corresponding expressions in these other languages are:

Mohawk:	waʔkūtihnekîˑraʔ
Oneida:	waʔkūtihnekíhLA
Onondaga:	waʔkūtihneˑkíhæ?
Seneca:	oʔwatiˑnékeæ?
Cayuga:	akaehnékEaʔ
Tuscarora:	waʔkàˑyáˑihr

It can be seen that the form of these words differs considerably from language to language, with the "western" languages (Seneca, Cayuga, and Tuscarora) showing marked differences not only among each other, but also with respect to the "eastern" languages (Mohawk, Oneida, and Onondaga). With the latter languages the words are more resemblant, though they still differ in some respects.

These words differ also in the ranges of their meanings. The reader can note that the English sentence, "They drank," covers a broad range of possible drinkers. It does not in itself specify whether they were humans or animals (they might, for example, have been several deer), whether they were male or female, or how many of them there were. The Iroquois words, on the other hand, do make some distinctions of these kinds, though not all of them make the same distinctions. A speaker of the relevant language who heard one of the first four words listed above would understand that the drinkers were not male but either women or animals, and that there were at

least three of them—there could not have been just two. The Cayuga
word, on the other hand, would be understood to mean that the
drinkers were women—they could not have been men or animals.
But like the English word "they," the Cayuga word fails to specify
whether there were two or more than two. The Tuscarora word is
different still. It specifies that the drinkers were human, not animals,
but nothing about their sex. It is like the first four words in indicating
that there were more than two. Thus, while all of these words could
be said when the drinkers were a group of three or more women,
they vary with respect to the other possibilities to which they can
be extended.

I am going to try to trace the development of both the forms and
meanings of these six words from a hypothesized Proto-Northern-
Iroquoian stage which probably existed in the neighborhood of two
thousand years ago, at which time the ancestors of the speakers of
these languages are thought to have constituted a single speech
community. My plan is not only to show some of the kinds of things
that led to the differences which now exist among the Northern
Iroquoian languages, but also to reconstruct from linguistic evidence
some of the population divergences and recontacts which seem to
have been characteristic of this family. All of my suggestions will
of course be hypothetical; we have no direct access to this kind of
prehistory. I can only say that I believe them to represent the most
plausible reconstructions that can be made on the basis of evidence
currently available (which is considerably more extensive than will
appear from the examples cited here). More detailed reconstructions
and more data are available in Chafe (1977) and Chafe and Foster
(1981).[1] The somewhat complex discussion which follows may be
easier to understand if the reader will refer at each stage to Fig.
17.1, proceeding from the bottom up.

We are concerned with the various ways in which the Northern
Iroquoian languages now and in the past have expressed what I will
call our target meaning: "they drank," where "they" is feminine and
plural, involving three or more individuals. I use this target meaning
because it serves to illuminate especially well several important facets
of Iroquoian linguistic prehistory. At the Proto-Northern-Iroquoian
stage it is likely that this meaning was expressed by a word *waʔá·ihrʔ.
The asterisk shows that this is a reconstruction, not an actually
attested word. The word contained four distinguishable elements, or
morphemes. First was a prefix waʔ- which indicated that the speaker
was reporting a factual event, not one that he or she believed would
or might happen. Second was another prefix whose underlying form
was -ya-, carrying the meaning that the event was performed by one
or more humans, but not by a single male. The more common form

of this prefix was -ye-, but the variant -ya- was used before a few verb roots beginning with i, including at least those meaning "drink" and "die." Following that prefix came the verb root -ihr-, meaning "drink." Finally there was a suffix -ʔ (a glottal stop), showing that what the speaker had in mind was a particular single event. The underlying form of the word, then, was *waʔ-ya-ihr-ʔ. By a phonological change which had already occurred at that time, the y was dropped after the glottal stop. An accent was automatically placed on the next to last syllable, which was also lengthened. Hence the actual form *waʔá·ihrʔ.

It may help the reader keep track of the ranges of meanings involved in this word and the words to follow if they are thought of in terms of a matrix, as shown in Figure 17.2, where differences in gender are shown in rows and differences in number in columns (Matrix 1). In general, with the exception of anthropomorphized pets and the like, the masculine-feminine distinction applies in these languages only to humans. Sometimes masculine and feminine are included together in a single "human" category: the first two rows of Figure 1 in opposition to the third. Similarly, the second and third rows together are sometimes set off against the first: a distinction between masculine and "nonmasculine." In the columns, indicating number distinctions, there is sometimes a coalescence of dual and plural into a "nonsingular" category (two or more, whereas plural means three or more). With this kind of diagram the range of possible genders and numbers of drinkers conveyed by the reconstructed word *waʔá·ihrʔ can be shown as in Matrix 2. That is, with one exception, the drinkers might have been one or more humans, regardless of gender or number. The one exception was the masculine singular category; the prefix used for a single male was different from that used for any other combination of one or more humans. Thus at this Proto-Northern-Iroquoian stage the world of drinkers, or of agents in any action, was divided into three parts: single male humans, humans otherwise, and nonhumans. Our word *waʔa·ihrʔ expressed the "humans otherwise" possibility, and thus included our target meaning in which three or more women were involved.

Sooner or later there arose a split within the Proto-Northern-Iroquoian community by which a segment of the population migrated away from the parent or "mainstream" group, as shown by the line moving up and to the left in Fig. 17.1. This splinter population may have been ancestral to both the modern Tuscarora and the Cayuga. I will thus refer to the language that developed within this group as Proto-Tuscarora-Cayuga. Among these people, but not in the mainstream community, a change took place whereby an element -ka- was added in front of the -ye- prefix to convey the idea that

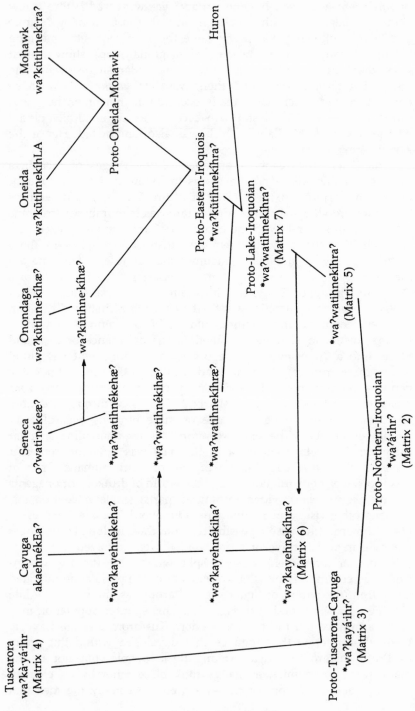

Fig. 17.1. Reconstruction of ways of saying "they drank"

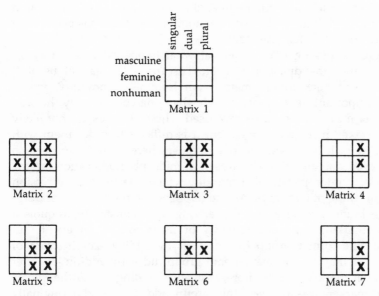

Fig. 17.2. Matrices of gender and number in meanings of "they drank"

more than a single human was involved in an action. The word we are interested in thus changed to *wa²kayá·ihr²*. The meaning of this word was the somewhat more restricted one shown in Matrix 3. Through the addition of -ka- it excluded the singular feminine category, which of course was still expressed by the original word without the -ka-.

This group did not remain together long, but itself split in two. It is plausible to suppose that, if the hypothesis of a temporary Tuscarora-Cayuga unity is valid, the ancestors of the Tuscarora moved on toward their eventual home in the North Carolina area, while the ancestors of the Cayuga remained in the Northeast. In the Tuscarora segment there now arose a way of distinguishing dual from plural participants in an action. Although the same distinction came to exist in most of the other languages also, the Tuscarora way of marking it is totally different and must have developed independently. It involved the prefixing of the so-called duplicative or dualic prefix *te-* (in Tuscarora eventually *ne-*) to the singular form of the verb. While the same prefix is found in the other Northern Iroquoian languages and in fact in Cherokee as well, it has this dual marking function only in Tuscarora. As a consequence, our word *wa²kayá:ihr²* came to be narrowed to only a plural (three or more) meaning, since the dual meaning had come to be marked in this other way. The new range can be shown as in Matrix 4. The present-day Tuscarora word, as shown in the upper left-hand corner of the chart, is *wa²kà·yá·ihr*, where the final glottal stop has been lost through phonological change, and the antepenultimate syllable has been given a fallen pitch and lengthened.

Instead of looking immediately at what happened in the Cayuga segment after the division of Proto-Tuscarora-Cayuga, let us shift our attention back to the mainstream Iroquois community, where several important developments were changing considerably the way our target meaning would be expressed. These changes are not likely to have taken place all at once, but it is difficult to order them with respect to each other and for our purposes here there is no need to do so. For one thing, there was a significant modification in the system of gender and number marking which affected the expression of our meaning in two ways. As had happened in the Proto-Tuscarora-Cayuga branch, there arose also among the mainstream Iroquois a way of marking the nonsingularity of the actors in an event. But whereas the former group had done it by adding -*ka*- in front of the gender marker, the mainstream group did it by adding -*ti*- after the gender marker. Furthermore, instead of adding -*ti*- to the *human* gender marker -*ya*- or -*ye*-, this group added it to the originally *nonhuman* marker -*wa*-, thus creating in the nonsingular a distinction between masculine and nonmasculine rather than between human and nonhuman as in Proto-Tuscarora-Cayuga. The range of meaning embraced by the new prefix combination -*wati*- was that shown in Matrix 5.

Another change involved the introduction of an "incorporated noun root" into the verb meaning 'drink'. The root in question had the form -*hnek*- and its meaning was 'drink (noun)' (or usually 'water'), as opposed to 'drink (verb)'. Thus, whereas the original word included only the verb root -*ihr*- 'drink', as is still the case in Tuscarora, the mainstream Iroquois expression came to be -*hnek-ihr*-, literally 'drink a drink'.

Finally, instead of dropping the final glottal stop as the Tuscarora did, the mainstream Iroquois inserted the vowel *a* between the glottal stop and the preceding consonant. Thus the word which came to express our target meaning was now **wa²watihnekíhra²*. This word is shown on the chart above and to the right of Proto-Northern-Iroquoian.

The ancestors of the Cayuga must meanwhile have returned to contact with the mainstream Iroquois. In fact, the evidence suggests that they moved in and out of such contact several times. Each time, they influenced or were influenced by the language of the mainstream group. For our present example it is necessary at this point to note that sooner or later the Cayuga language assimilated from the other Iroquois both the incorporated -*hnek*- and the vowel *a* before the final glottal stop, but that it stubbornly refused to give up the "human nonsingular" prefix combination containing -ka-. In this case, where the prefix now occurred before -hnek-, the form was -kaye-. Thus through these contacts with the other Iroquois the Cayuga word came to be *wa?kayehnekíhra?. In the chart this word is shown as a development out of Proto-Tuscarora-Cayuga, but with an arrow showing the direction of influence from the mainstream Iroquois group.

Although Cayuga did not assimilate the Iroquois nonsingular marker -ti- in this case, it did assimilate it in other prefix combinations, though still in its own ways and not by a wholesale adoption of the mainstream system. What is important to us here is the fact that through the adoption of -ti- to mark a masculine nonsingular category, Cayuga came to distinguish masculine from feminine in the nonsingular. Thus -kaye- came to be restricted to feminine referents in Cayuga, as it did not in Tuscarora. The eventual range of meaning of the Cayuga word cited at the end of the last paragraph thus came to be that shown in Matrix 6.

Sometime after it had loaned its nonsingular marker -ti- to some Cayuga contexts (but not completely enough to displace -kaye-), the mainstream Iroquois language acquired a third person *dual* marker with the form -ni-. This marker was extended by analogy from the first and second person prefixes, where it already existed. It would seem that the Cayuga, having partially assimilated in their own way the -ti- marker of nonsingularity, now distanced themselves again from the mainstream community; at least they did not now participate in the adoption of this dual marker. To this day Cayuga has never acquired a dual-plural distinction in the third person. But in the mainstream language a result of this new development was a restriction of the meaning of *wa?watihnekíhra?* to a range which excluded dual, as shown in Matrix 7. In Fig. 17.1 this stage is identified as Proto-Lake-Iroquoian, the reconstructed language hypothesized as ancestral to Huron, Mohawk, Oneida, Onondaga, and Seneca.

Through the developments described we have now arrived at the meaning ranges which characterize the languages today. In Tuscarora we find the range shown in Matrix 4, in Cayuga that shown in Matrix 6, and in the other Northern Iroquoian languages that shown in Matrix 7. The Cayuga word arrived at so far was *wa?kayehnekíhra?*, the Proto-Lake-Iroquoian word *wa?watihnekíhra?*. The changes yet to be described will not modify the range of meanings expressed by these words, but for the most part only their phonological shapes. In one case we will see a new morphemic element added.

The Lake Iroquoians, a unified community up to this point, now began to divide successively into the various distinct groups we know today. First to leave, apparently, were the ancestors of the Huron, whose language was spoken until recently but is now extinct. Because of some uncertainty as to the form our word eventually acquired in Huron, I will leave that language out of further consideration. The next split in the mainstream community may have divided it into an Eastern Iroquois group, the ancestor community of the Mohawk, Oneida, and Onondaga, and a western group ancestral to the Seneca alone.

A relevant change in the language of the Eastern Iroquois was the addition of an element -ka- to precede the already established prefix combination -wati-. Probably this was not the nonsingular marker -ka- which we saw earlier added to -ye- in Proto-Tuscarora-Cayuga, but rather a nonhuman marker -ka- which had long existed as an alternate of -wa-. In other words, the new combination *-kawati- contained a kind of reduplication of the nonhuman marker, perhaps because the force of -wa- was no longer clear. This sequence was subject to a longstanding phonological process whereby *awa was simplified to ŭ. Hence the resulting form was *waʔkŭtihnekíhraʔ. In Mohawk this is virtually the form found today, except that the next to last syllable has acquired a long, falling-pitched vowel; the modern Mohawk word is waʔkŭtihnekî·raʔ. In Oneida, a close relative of Mohawk, there is little difference except that at the end of a phrase or sentence the final syllable is whispered, so that the pronunciation is waʔkŭtihnekíhLA. The capital letters at the end indicate voicelessness.[2]

The events which led to the modern Cayuga, Seneca, and Onondaga words were more complex, and involved several interactions among those languages. To begin with, we can suppose that among the ancestors of the Seneca, and at first only in their language, the pronunciation of the vowel a became fronted to æ when this vowel was preceded by r. Thus our word came to be pronounced in Seneca *waʔwatihnekíhræʔ. Meanwhile among the Cayuga, who apparently had remained aloof from the Lake Iroquoians while the latter were separating into Huron, Eastern Iroquois, and Seneca, several phonological changes of considerable importance had taken place. One was the loss of r under certain conditions which included those found in our example word. Another was a change in the accent pattern whereby under certain conditions an accent which was originally on an odd-numbered syllable (counting from the left) was shifted to an even-numbered one. Again our example fits the necessary conditions. As a result of these two developments the word changed in Cayuga from *waʔkayehnekíhraʔ to *waʔkayehnékihaʔ, losing its r and shifting its accent back one syllable. It would seem that subsequently the Cayuga and Seneca came into particularly close contact, to the extent that various phonological changes were either copied from one language into the other, or took place in both simultaneously. For one thing, it appears that both of the Cayuga changes just mentioned were assimilated by the speakers of Seneca, as shown on the chart by the arrow leading from the Cayuga to the Seneca branch. In fact, these changes were overassimilated, in the following sense. Whereas both the loss of *r* and the shift of the accent to even-numbered syllables were restricted in Cayuga to certain limited conditions, in Seneca these same changes were adopted without limitations: *r* was lost everywhere, and a new accent pattern developed in which only even-numbered syllables were accented. For our present example, however, the result was parallel to that seen in the Cayuga word; the Seneca word was now **waʔwatihnékihæʔ*. In addition, whatever the mechanism may have been, both languages now underwent a change in common whereby, through a restricted kind of "vowel harmony," the vowel in the next to last syllable of these words was changed to coincide with the preceding, accented vowel. The Cayuga form became then **waʔkayehnékehaʔ*, the Seneca **waʔwatihnékehæʔ*.

After this last case of interinfluence, the Cayuga and Seneca must have parted company for good, with subsequent phonological changes taking place independently in the two languages to yield the words we find today. Before we consider these final changes, however, we must take note of another important development. It seems that during this recent period the Seneca and Onondaga were in close enough contact that two of the changes which had already occurred in Seneca were assimilated by the Onondaga. One was the fronting of *a* to *æ* after *r*. In Onondaga, however, this change was generalized to all the back vowels: not only did *a* become *æ* but *o* became *e* and *õ* became *ẽ* wherever there was a preceding *r*. But concomitantly, it would seem, the *r* itself was dropped, just as it had been earlier in Seneca and earlier still in Cayuga. The Cayuga loss of *r* always remained restricted to certain contexts, but in both Seneca and Onondaga the loss was complete. The spread of these changes to Onondaga must have taken place quite recently, subsequent to the contact that David Zeisberger had with the Onondaga in the mid-eighteenth century (Horsford 1887), but before Abraham Le Fort collected the Onondaga vocabulary which was published in Schoolcraft (1852:482–93). One can speculate that the Onondaga borrowed these habits of pronunciation from the Seneca during the post-Revolutionary period, or perhaps even as a consequence of the spread of the Handsome Lake religion. The final form of our word in Onondaga was *waʔkũtihne·kíhæʔ*.[3]

We can note finally that both the Cayuga and Seneca words changed their forms considerably as a result of changes peculiar to each of those languages. From *waʔkayehnékehaʔ Cayuga arrived at the present pronunciation akaehnékEaʔ. Both the change of the initial syllable waʔ to a and the change of the penultimate syllable eh to E (a voiceless vowel) were manifestations of a uniquely Cayuga process which weakened the pronunciation of odd-numbered syllables originally ending in ʔ or h. In addition we see the loss of the y from the earlier kaye sequence, now kae. Seneca went on to change *waʔwatihnékehæʔ to oʔwati·nékeæʔ. The initial waʔ was changed to oʔ, the h between the i and n was replaced by a lengthening of the vowel, and the h between two vowels was dropped. There has been a great deal of relatively recent phonological change in Seneca, of which these are a few typical examples.

I have tried to illustrate how changes in certain prefixes have changed the range of meanings of Iroquoian words, how the addition of elements such as the incorporated noun root meaning 'drink' have further changed the composition of such words, and how phonological change has further remolded the words into shapes quite different from what was there originally. But my main purpose has been to show how changes of these various kinds give evidence for divergences and recontacts among the prehistoric Iroquoian peoples. In particular we have seen evidence for a short-lived Tuscarora-Cayuga unity, succeeded by a long period during which the ancestors of the Cayuga entered, left, and reentered the influence of the mainstream Iroquois, above all the Seneca. We have seen evidence that the Cayuga were at some time prestigious enough that the Seneca copied features of their speech. And lastly we have seen that the Onondaga were quite recently influenced by the Seneca in a similar way. It is an intriguing task to try to unravel the prehistory of these languages, and it is rewarding that we can at the same time, to some extent, unravel the prehistory of their speakers as well.

NOTES

1. I want to acknowledge a considerable debt of gratitude to several Iroquoian linguists who contributed data and advice which has been incorporated here: to Michael Foster for information on Cayuga and for allowing me to extract this discussion from our longer joint treatment of these matters (Chafe and Foster 1981); and to Marianne Mithun and Hanni Woodbury for information on Tuscarora and Onondaga, respectively, as well as for other advice on specific points.

2. Oneida and some Mohawk dialects have *l* where the other languages have *r*.

3. The lengthening of the antepenultimate vowel follows a familiar pattern in Onondaga, whose origins, however, are still not well understood.

CHAPTER EIGHTEEN

Mohawk Dialects:
Akwesasne, Caughnawaga, Oka

NANCY BONVILLAIN

1.0. INTRODUCTION

The three dialects of Mohawk, a Northern Iroquoian language currently spoken by Mohawk Indians in Ontario, Québec and New York State, provide a basis for contemporary and historical comparison. Contemporary or synchronic analysis of phonological patterning demonstrates the differences and similarities among the dialects today and allows us to understand how they have diverged. The differences among the dialects can be accounted for in view of the historical relationships and locations of the populations. Historical or diachronic analysis of specific phonological and lexical changes leads to an understanding of the processes and influences which have affected the language and its speakers.

The data for this study were collected from the dialects of Akwesasne (St. Regis) and from Caughnawaga and Oka. Data for Akwesasne and Caughnawaga were obtained through my own field work; data for Oka were obtained from J. A. Cuoq's *Lexique de la langue iroquoise* (1882).

A brief note on transcription: Akwesasne and Caughnawaga words are written in phonemic notation. Data from Oka are given by Cuoq in the Jesuit writing system devised for Iroquoian languages in the seventeenth century. It is quite adequate phonemically except for Cuoq's omission of glottal stop, ?, but since this sound does not differ in the three dialects in its occurrence of patterning, its omission in Cuoq's work does not affect this study.

2.0. HISTORICAL BACKGROUND

The Mohawk reserves in Québec were originally established as mission villages. In the 1650s, French Jesuits based in Québec City began expeditions into Iroquois territory along the Mohawk River in present-day New York State. These expeditions had very little initial success. However, throughout the rest of the seventeenth century, the missionaries made a number of devout converts who were attracted to the new mission of St. Francis Xavier des Prés established in 1667 north of Montréal at La Prairie (JR 55:33–35). Ten years later, the mission shifted near to its present site just outside Montréal bordering on the St. Louis rapids (JR 60:275–77). The Mohawks called the site Caughnawaga (kahnawâ:ke) 'on the rapids'. By 1683, the Mohawk population at the mission had greatly increased and numbered over two hundred (JR 62:237). Around 1720, another mission was founded at Oka or Lake of Two Mountains at the Ottawa River near Montréal. This was the final mission site of a group of Mohawk converts who had been settled by Sulpician missionaries on the Island of Montréal in the 1670s (Fenton and Tooker 1978:472).

Although people from various other Iroquois and even some from Algonkian groups came to live at these missions, they maintained their Mohawk character and language through intermarriage and incorporation of outsiders into the Mohawk social structure. The French influence on the two missions was similar throughout the historical period and their Canadian experience has been the same too.

The mission of St. Francis Regis (Akwesasne), located about eighty miles southwest of Montréal along the St. Lawrence River, was established in the mid-eighteenth century (Hough 1853:107; Fenton and Tooker 1978:473). Its population consisted of migrants from Caughnawaga and Oka and of converts from Mohawk and Oneida villages in New York. Later, there were also converts from Algonkian groups, notably the Abenaki. Again, these groups were all integrated into the linguistically and culturally dominant Mohawks. After its divergence from the older missions, Akwesasne became more independent of the dominant French influence of the growing city of Montréal. Also, after the American Revolution and throughout the nineteenth and twentieth centuries, Akwesasne came under increasing Anglo influence, both from Canadian and American farmers and from their respective governments.

In the context of these historical events, we can now turn to the dialects themselves.

3.0. PHONOLOGICAL PATTERNING AND CHANGE

The major differences among the Mohawk dialects are those of phonological patterning. However, we can briefly review the sound inventories of these dialects.

3.1. Phonological Inventories

The consonant inventories of the three Mohawk dialects contain ten phonemes, all but one of which are identical. The nine identical consonants are the following: three stops, *t, k, ʔ*; an affricate, *j*; two spirants, *s, h*; a nasal, *n*; and two semi-vowels, *y, w*. Each dialect also contains a resonant; in Akwesasne it is *l* but in Caughnawaga and Oka it is *r*. Lounsbury has reconstructed **r* for Proto-Iroquoian, but both *r* and *l* occur in various modern Iroquoian languages (1978:341). Since Akwesasne has had a large number of Oneida settlers, it is possible that the *l* at Akwesasne has come, in part, from Oneida influence.

The vowel inventories of the three dialects are identical, containing four oral vowels, *i, e, a, o*, and two nasalized vowels, *v, u*.

3.2. Phonological Patterning

As stated above, differences in phonological patterning are crucial in the sound differentiation of the three Mohawk dialects.

The difference in patterning occurs in the reflexes of the sequences of stops and spirants with a following *y*.

3.2.1. /stop + y/

The underlying sequences of *t + y* and of *k + y* have one reflex of manifestation in Caughnawaga and one in Akwesasne, but the reflex is different in the two dialects. In Caughnawaga, **ty* and **ky* sequences are replaced by the palatal affricate *j*. In Akwesasne, **ty* sequences merge with *ky*, so that contemporary *ky* sequences may be derived from underlying **ty* or **ky*.

The examples given below from the data illustrate these occurrences. Note that the data from Caughnawaga and Akwesasne are written phonemically whereas the historical data from Oka are written in Jesuit script which differs from phonemic notation in the representation of nasal vowels and palatal consonants. That is, phonemic vowels *v* and *u* are written "en" and "on" in Jesuit script, respectively; the palatal consonants *y* and *j* are written "i" and "tsi", respectively.

The reflexes of /stop + y/ sequences can be shown in the following data:

Oka (1882)	Caughnawaga	Akwesasne	Gloss
ano*k*ien	anó:*j*v	anó:*ky*v	muskrat
*t*iaweronko	*j*awerú:ko	*ky*awelú:ko	eel
en*t*ie	v*j*e	v*ky*e	noontime
*t*io*t*ierenton	*j*ojervhtu	*ky*o*ky*elvhtu	first

There are two additional examples in the corpus which illustrate the historical change involved when *y* follows an obstruent:

Oka (1882)	Caughnawaga	Akwesasne	Gloss
*tei*ohiotsis	*j*ohyò:tsis	*ky*ohyò:jis	salt
*tei*onnhonskwaron	*j*onhúhskwaru/	*ky*ohnúhskwalu/	cow
	*j*ohúhskwaru	*ky*onhúhskwalu	

In these examples, the words from the 1882 manuscript begin with the segment teio- (phonemically *teyo-*). It is composed of two prefixes: *t(e)-* which is the duplicative verbal prefix, and *-yo-*, which is a personal pronominal prefix marking 3rd person singular feminine/ neuter. At some point, the epenthetic vowel *-e-* was lost, resulting in the sequence *tyo-, inadmissable in both the Caughnawaga and Akwesasne dialects. In Caughnawaga, as we have seen, *ty — j, while in Akwesasne *ty — ky, resulting in the surface *j*ohyò:tsis and *ky*ohyò:jis, respectively.

3.2.2. ts + y

The underlying sequence of *ts + y is manifested differently in the Caughnawaga and Akwesasne dialects. In Caughnawaga, the *y* is lost, resulting in surface *ts*. This sequence occurs voiceless as [ts] or voiced as [dz] following rules of allophony (see Beatty 1974). In Akwesasne, *ts + y merges and is palatalized to become the palatal afficate *j*. These correspondences can be demonstrated:

Oka	Caughnawaga	Akwesasne	Gloss
*tsi*atak	*ts*á:ta	*j*á:ta	seven
kate*tsi*ens	yuté*ts*vts	yuté*j*vts	she doctors
kahon*tsi*	kahú:*tsi*	kahú:*jo*	it's black
kana*tsi*o	kaná:*tso*	kaná:*jo*	Ottawa (there's a bucket)
khon*tsi*	kó*tsu*	kv*ju*	fish

It can be noted that the sequence *ts* in Caughnawaga may be derived either from underlying *ts or from *tsy. The origin of any given word with a *ts* sequence becomes obvious, however, when the Caughnawaga form is compared to an Oka form where *tsy* occurs or when compared with Akwesasne where underlying *ts remains unchanged but underlying *tsy is replaced by *j*.

Words with Underlying *ts:

Caughnawaga	Oka	Akwesasne	Gloss
onv*ts*a	onen*ts*a	onv*ts*a	arm
o*ts*o?kó:tu	o*ts*ohkoton	o*ts*o?kó:tu	balsam fir

Words with Underlying *tsy:*

onátsa	onatsia	onája	wheat
kaná:tso	kanatsio	kaná:jo	ottawa

Finally, in Akwesasne Mohawk the pattern of *ts* + *y* → *j* is consistent with the more general rule of *s* + *y* → *j*. For example, the verb form /téja?k/ 'break it (one break)!' is derived from the underlying *te-s-ya?k*. In this word, *-s-* is the marker for 2nd person singular subject. When combined with the verb stem *-ya?k*, the rule of phonological change applies. That is, the combination of *s* + *y* here results in the surface *j* in *téja?k*.

3.3. Resonant Metathesis or Loss

A third difference among the Mohawk dialects involves change in the order of sounds (metathesis) or loss of resonants in certain positions. Words with sequences of *rh* (*lh* in Akwesasne) and *nh* have varied reflexes. In Caughnawaga, the underlying sequence of *resonant + h* is either maintained or the resonant is lost and *h* alone remains.

In Akwesasne, underlying *resonant + h* is maintained or metathesis occurs, resulting in *h + resonant* sequences. Variation occurs both in the community as a whole and in the speech of a single speaker; such variation is common in speech communities especially for phonological variables in the process of change. As a general but not total rule, older speakers use the resonant + *h* sequences while younger speakers use *h* + resonant. Although both variants coexist in Akwesasne speech, the sequence of *h* + resonant has a higher frequency among younger speakers and may become the typical pattern in the future. Younger speakers have a certain difficulty producing resonant + *h* sequences, especially when the resonant is *n*.[1]

The following examples illustrate underlying *resonant + h* sequences. Variations are noted as they occur.

Oka	Caughnawaga	Akwesasne	Gloss
kannhoha	kanhóha	kanhóha/ kahnóha	door
teionnhonskwaron	jonhúhskwaru/ johúhskwaru	kyonhúhskwalu/ kyohnúhskwalu	cow
tsionnhowane	tsuhó:wane?	juhnó:wane?	whale
orhotsera	ohótseri	olhótseli/ ohlótseli	stringbean, waxbean, greenbean
otskwarhe	otskwà:rhe?	otskwà:lh?/ otskwà:hlo?	frog

3.4. *Loss of Word-Final Consonants*

A fourth change of historical importance demonstrated in the data is the loss of consonants in final-position in some words. For example, Cuoq gives the form *enskat* 'one' in 1882. The modern word in both Caughnawaga and Akwesasne, *vhska* lacks the final *-t*. The word for 'wild goose' shows an interesting variation. In Akwesasne today variation exists between *káhuk* and *káhu*. Cuoq gives only *kahu* (written "kahon"). The significant change, i.e., loss of final *-k*, must have predated the 1882 work of Cuoq. As mentioned, variation exists at Akwesasne between the two forms although *káhu* is heard more frequently. Most speakers are not quite sure which form is more "correct," but all do recognize both as possibilities.

The process of final-consonant loss has affected words borrowed from French into Mohawk. Cuoq gives the word for 'oats, grain, porridge' as *rawenn*, borrowed from the French 'l'avoine'. In Caughnawaga, the final *-n* is retained in *arowén*. However, in Akwesasne there is variation of *olawén, olawé* and *olawv*. In all examples, the borrowed words do retain their "foreign" character in stress placement, keeping French stress on the final syllable in contrast to strong stress rules in Mohawk where stress is usually on the penultimate syllable and almost never occurs finally. The three variants occurring at Akwesasne show different treatment of the word-final *-n*. The variant *olawén* is closest to its French source and retains the final consonant. The form *olawé* has lost the final *-n*. Since *n* occurs very rarely in word-final position except in imperatives where the verb stem ends in *n*, its loss in the noun *olawé* fits this foreign word into Mohawk sound patterns. The final variant *olawv* illustrates the process of vowel nasalization. Here, an underlying sequence of oral vowel and nasal consonant undergoes loss of the consonant with a resulting nasalization of the adjacent vowel. Again, speakers do understand all three variations whether or not they themselves use all of them.[2]

4.0. Lexical Change

An important stimulus for lexical change in Mohawk has been the influence of foreign words (i.e. from French and English) borrowed into Mohawk. Naturally, other kinds of lexical change have occurred but comparison will be made here between words in the three dialects which have come from foreign sources.

The following list does not contain all of the borrowed words in Mohawk (see Bonvillain 1978); rather, it contains a sampling of lexical changes since the late nineteenth century.

Oka (1882)	Caughnawaga	Akwesasne	Gloss
atewirarha	rapahpót	lapahpót	barbote
oserha	rasós	ohsè:hla	gravy
		lasós	gravy
otsikwa	otsíhkwa	ojíhkwa	tuber
	rakarót	ojíhkwa	carrot
sotar	rasotár	sotál	soldier
(akenistenha)	akwatvt	istv:ha?	my aunt

The consonant inventory of Mohawk (as well as of the other Iroquoian languages) lacks labials. However, labial or labio-dental consonants (specifically *p, b, m, f, v*) occur in the European languages with which Mohawk has been in contact. Since the seventeenth century when Mohawk-French contact began, the Mohawk language has employed two strategies in dealing with the sounds of foreign words. The first method, as is typical of early interlinguistic contact, was to substitute Mohawk consonants for the French labials.[3] In addition, certain consonant clusters which were inadmissable in Mohawk were broken up by epenthetic vowels.[4]

The second, and historically later, method has been the incorporation of the labial consonants with the borrowed words. Presumably this has been the result of speakers' becoming more accustomed to the foreign sounds through greater contact and bilingualism. An example of this process is *rapahpót*, derived from the French 'la barbote'. Note that the French voiced stop *b* is phonemicized as *p* according to rules of stop allophony in Mohawk[5] (see Bonvillain 1973). The labial *m* is incorporated invariably as *m*, for example in the word *májis* 'matches.' The foreign labials *p-b* and *m* have been incorporated into the phonemic system of the Akwesasne and Caughnawaga dialects. They presently occur in words of French and English origin. Although these sounds are extremely limited in their occurrence, they behave as Mohawk phonemes since the rules of allophony applying to indigenous stop consonants apply to them as well; i.e., *p-b* occur in accordance with rules which apply to the occurrence of indigenous *t-d* and *k-g*.

This process of incorporation of labial consonants into Mohawk is in contrast to what has occurred in some of the other Iroquoian languages where foreign labials are still replaced by indigenous phonemes. Perhaps the explanation for the greater acceptance of foreign sounds in these dialects of Mohawk lies in their close proximity to centers of foreign influence and their long history since the seventeenth century of intensive intercultural and interlinguistic contact.

The first examples to be discussed are the words for 'barbote'. Cuoq gives the Oka word as *atewirarha*. At Caughnawaga and Akwesasne today the word is *rapahpót* and *lapahpót*, respectively, derived from the French 'la barbote'. The French definite article 'la' is incorporated into the noun itself in Mohawk. The word also retains French stress on the final syllable in contrast to the dominant Mohawk pattern of penultimate stress. The older word *atewirarha* is currently unknown at both Caughnawaga and Akwesasne; it has been completely replaced.

A second example consists of the words for 'gravy'. Cuoq gives the Oka word (1882) as *oserha*. In Akwesasne two words are in use: *ohsè:hal* and *lasós*. The first corresponds to the older Oka word and the second is a borrowing from the French 'la sauce'. In Caughnawaga, only the borrowed *rasós* occurs. At Akwesasne there has been some specialization in the meanings of the two words. Generally, *ohsè:hla* is used for 'thick gravies, mush, dough' while *lasós* is used for 'gravy'.[6]

The increased acceptance of French words at Caughnawaga over the past two centuries can be understood in view of the great influence of French language and culture there due to the proximity of the city of Montréal. After the establishment of the St. Regis mission, French influence on the Akwesasne dialect began to wane at the same time that it was increasing at Caughnawaga.

Other examples of the greater French influence in Caughnawaga are the words for 'tuber' and 'carrot'. The general word for 'tuber' is the same in all dialects: *otsikwa* (Oka); *otsíhkwa* (Caughnawaga); and *ojíhkwa* (Akwesasne). At Akwesasne, *ojíhkwa* is used for all tubers, i.e., beets, carrots, turnips, etc. There are no individual words for each variety although differences can be expressed with descriptive phrases, for example, *ojí:nekwal nikajihkò:tv* 'carrot' (literally: yellow or orange tuber). In Caughnawaga, however, a separate word for 'carrot' is used: *rakarót*, derived from the French 'la carrotte'. Again, the definite article 'la' (here *ra*) is incorporated into the Mohawk word, also keeping final-syllable stress. Caughnawaga informants reported that *otsíhkwa* would not be used for 'carrot' although in context it would be understood.

The word for 'wheelbarrow' also shows difference between the Caughnawaga and Akwesasne dialects. In the former, the word is *raparoét*, derived from the French 'la brouette', while in the latter, the word is *paroét*. The contrast has to do with the inclusion in Caughnawaga of the French definite article 'la' (here, *ra*) and its omission in Akwesasne.

The pattern of article inclusion at Caughnawaga and its omission at Akwesasne occurs in the words for 'soldier'. For Oka, the word reported for 'soldier' is *sotar*, derived from French 'soldat'; at Akwesasne the word is similar, *sotál;* but at Caughnawaga it is *rasotár.* There are two possible interpretations for the segment *ra-* in this last form. One is that *ra-* is derived from the French article by analogy with such words as *rasós* 'la sauce' and *rakaröt* 'la carrotte.' In this case, the segment *ra-* can be seen to have the generalized meaning of the French definite article or even of marking a word of French origin. In the case of *rasotár,* the actual article heard with the masculine noun 'soldat' is 'le' rather than the feminine 'la'. If the Caughnawaga dialect were simply imitating French, the word in Mohawk would be **resotár.* Therefore, the incorporation of *ra-* has resulted from some other process. Purely by chance, all of the other words borrowed into Mohawk with French articles happen to be feminine. The change of "le" to *ra-* is a step in the regularization of borrowed words.

Another interpretation of the segment *ra-* in *rasotár* is possible although not as likely. That is, it may be an example of the use of the marker for singular masculine subjects which is *ra-* (*la-* in Akwesasne). In this way, the word *rasotár* would perhaps better be translated as 'he is a soldier' or even 'he soldiers'. The major problem with this hypothesis is that although the word may fit one of the canonical requirements of verbs, it lacks any of the complex verbal affixes which also occur on well-formed verbs. For this reason, the first interpretation presenting *ra-* as a regularization of the French 'definite article' is preferred. Also, there are no examples in the dialects of the use of foreign words as verb stems.

A final, and most interesting, example of French borrowing at Caughnawaga is the word for 'my aunt' *akwatvt,* derived from 'tante'. In the Mohawk word, the prefix *akwa-* is the required possessive prefix for 1st person singular possessor. In Akwesasne, the word used for 'my aunt' is *istv:ha?* which also means 'my mother'. At Caughnawaga, the meaning of *istó:ha?* (traditionally 'my mother, my mother's sister') has been restricted; it is used now only for 'my mother'. At Akwesasne its meaning has in fact expanded so that to the older meanings of 'mother' and 'mother's sister' has been added 'father's sister' as well. The Caughnawaga dialect uses the loan *akwatvt* for both maternal and paternal 'aunt'.

The word *akwatvt* is structurally unusual too. All other Mohawk kin terms are structurally verbs and contain pronominal prefix markers, most belonging to a series of transitive prefixes which indicate the relationship between speaker and referent. For example, the term for 'my father' *rake?níha?* (*lake?níha?* at Akwesasne) contains the prefix *rak(e)-,* expressing the agent-patient relationship of 'he to me'. This kin term parallels in structure the transitive verb form *rak-hró:ris* 'he's telling me'. However, *akwatvt* contains instead a possessive prefix used with possessed nouns. It is formed, not on the pattern of kinship terms such as *rake?níha?*, but on the pattern of possessed nouns such as *akwáhta?* 'my shoe'. Obviously, the construction *akwa-tvt* is used not for semantic but for structural reasons. Since the segment *-tvt* is not recognized as a native verb stem and therefore cannot be incorporated into obligatory verbal structures, the only alternative is to treat it as a simple noun, capable of being possessed.

5.0. SUMMARY AND CONCLUSIONS

The major dialect split in Mohawk based on phonological characteristics among the mission populations is between the Mohawk spoken at Akwesasne and that of Caughnawaga/Oka. After the establishment of the mission of St. Regis in 1760, the two populations were geographically and socially separated. Changes in phonological patterning took place in both groups. But the differences in the shifts and mergers have resulted in sound patterns which distinguish Akwesasne from Caughnawaga.

French influence in Caughnawaga has meant a greater amount of borrowing than in Akwesasne, easily explainable in view of the historical divergence of the two groups. Later, English contact at Akwesasne became more widespread and has since resulted in a number of English loan words.

NOTES

1. Lounsbury suggests Proto-Oneida-Mohawk underlying sequences of *-hnh-* and *-hlh-*. Some elderly speakers at Akwesasne retain this pattern and will attempt to produce it in full when asked for careful speech; e.g., 'cow' *kyonhúhskwalu* or *kyohnúnskwalu* is given as *kyohnhúhskwalu*. The latter is said with some hesitation.

2. The loss of word-final *-t* has occurred in two proper names borrowed from French into Akwesasne: 'Marguerite' has become *kuwákeli* and 'Charlotte' has become *walisá:lo*, both without the French final *-t*. The consonant *-t*, however, does appear when the word is followed by a locative suffix, i.e., in *kuwakelíthne* and *walisalóthne*, 'at Marguerite's house,' and 'at Charlotte's house,' respectively.

3. Many instances of this process occur in French proper names, for example *waník* for 'Monique'. See Bonvillain 1978 for others.

4. For example, *katelí* for 'Catherine' (phonemically: *katrín*).

5. The rule for stop allophony produces voiceless stops word-finally and preceding consonants while voiced stops occur preceding vowels and semivowels.

6. It may be that the retention of the article "la" at Akwesasne in the already cited *lasós* from "la sauce" occurs for reasons other than regularization. Since monosyllabic words are extremely rare in Mohawk, the inclusion of *la-* here may be done simply to provide an additional syllable.

CHAPTER NINETEEN

The Kleis Site Ceramics:
An Interpretive Approach

WILLIAM E. ENGELBRECHT

The focus of this paper is the Kleis archaeological site located south of Buffalo, New York.[1] The site is of general interest since it is probably the last major village occupation in the area in the seventeenth century. Also, some of the Kleis site ceramics are more reminiscent of the Seneca area than the Niagara Frontier. This paper discusses the dating of the site, the nature of the ceramics found at the site, and the relationship of this site to others in western New York. In addition, an attempt will be made to interpret the results of the ceramic analysis in terms of human behavior and to place this behavior in its historic context. Given the inadequacies of the historical and archaeological records for the sixteenth and early seventeenth century in western New York, a series of suggested interpretations are offered.

The Kleis site is one of a number of large village sites south of Buffalo. The material found on these sites falls into the general archaeological classification, Iroquoian. In addition, some of the sites, like Kleis, contain articles of European manufacture. Marian White examined much of the historic evidence pertaining to the seventeenth-century occupation of the Niagara Frontier and concluded that the group in question was probably an eastern branch of the Erie (1971). No detailed historic description of the Erie exists. In the mid-1650s the Upper Iroquois (Seneca, Cayuga, Onondaga, and Oneida) are said to have attacked and dispersed the main body of the Erie which was probably to the south and west of the Niagara Frontier (Fenton 1940).

It is commonly assumed that sixteenth and seventeenth century horticultural villages shifted their location every eight to twenty years in order to find new arable land and sources of firewood. This assumption is supported by statements of early observers among the

Huron. Thus, village sites in an area might represent successive locations of the same community. Marian White hypothesized that the village sites south of Buffalo represented the successive southward movement of two contemporaneous communities which were located seven to ten miles apart. Marian White considered geographical position, change in ceramic styles, and the amount and kind of trade material present on these sites in order to infer chronological ordering (1961). She identified the last sites in the sequence as the Kleis and Bead Hill sites (1976:129). These sites probably date to the 1640s. The area south of Buffalo appears to have been largely uninhabited during the rest of the century.

The fate of the inhabitants of the Kleis and Bead Hill sites is unclear. They could have been absorbed by other groups. It is also possible that they moved south, perhaps occupying a site in the Cattaraugus Valley such as the Silverheels site, or a site even further to the south such as the Ripley site near Ripley, New York or the 28th Street Site in Erie, Pennsylvania. Pottery from these sites should be examined with this problem in mind. If in fact the population that we are dealing with represents an Eastern branch of the Erie, then its disappearance might be related to a statement of Gendron to the effect that the Erie were obliged to move away in order to escape their enemies to the west (Gendron 1868:8). These enemies were probably the Neutral who were north and west and who were expanding into the Niagara Frontier at this time (White 1976). There is evidence of some Neutral villages east of the Niagara River in the 1640s and there may have been disputes between the Neutral and Erie over hunting territory (especially for beaver). The relocation of the Erie occurred about a decade before the main body of the Erie were defeated and dispersed by the New York Iroquois. This fits the abandonment of the area south of Buffalo in the 1640s.

Brainerd-Robinson coefficients of agreement were calculated using ceramic attributes between eight of the village sites south of Buffalo, including the Kleis site (Brainerd 1951; Robinson 1951). These coefficients provide an indication of the relative similarity of the ceramics from two sites. The higher the coefficient, the more similar the ceramics from the two sites. For example, the Brainerd-Robinson coefficient between the Kleis and Ellis sites is 183, whereas the coefficient between the Kleis and Buffum sites is 159. This means that the Kleis site ceramics are more similar to those of the Ellis site than to those of the Buffum site.

Ceramically similar sites in an area are assumed to be closer in time than sites in the same area which are less similar. Thus, we assume that the Kleis and Ellis sites are closer in time than the Kleis and Buffum sites, since the Brainerd-Robinson coefficient is higher between the Kleis and Ellis sites than between the Kleis and Buffum sites. In order to infer chronological ordering among a group of sites, a matrix containing coefficients is ordered so that the highest coefficients are nearest the diagonal, with the value of these coefficients decreasing as one moves away from the diagonal. By doing this, highly similar sites should be located near one another in the matrix. From their arrangement within the matrix, the relative chronological relationship between sites may be inferred. After a process of trial and error, the ordering shown in Table 19.1 was achieved for the eight sites south of Buffalo. The Kleis site appears at one end of the matrix while the Buffum site appears at the other end. Since no trade goods have been found on the Buffum site while numerous trade goods have been found on the Kleis site, the ordering of sites from early to late would appear to be as follows: Buffum, Goodyear, Eaton, Newton-Hopper, Green Lake, Simmons, Ellis, and Kleis. This ordering agrees closely with the ordering achieved by Marian White using different methods and in some cases slightly different ceramic samples. Thus, both the present study and past studies place the Kleis site as the last of the sites studied.

Table 19.1. Coefficients of Agreement among Niagara Frontier Erie sites

	Buffum	Goodyear	Eaton	Newton-Hopper	Green Lake	Simmons	Ellis	Kleis
Buffum		181	181	181	182	179	164	159
Goodyear			182	184	186	181	167	161
Eaton				187	183	184	170	160
Newton-Hopper					184	186	170	160
Green Lake						184	174	169
Simmons							177	171
Ellis								183
Kleis								

Table 19.2. Coefficients of Agreement among sites representing the western villages of the Niagara Frontier Erie

	Buffum	Eaton	Green Lake	Ellis	Kleis
Buffum		181	182	164	159
Eaton			183	170	163
Green Lake				174	169
Ellis					183
Kleis					

On the basis of geographical evidence, these sites are believed to represent two contemporaneous groups of people. Therefore some of the sites listed in Table 19.1 were no doubt occupied simultaneously. Five of these sites: Buffum, Eaton, Green Lake, Ellis, and Kleis are believed to represent successive occupations by the western community, while Goodyear, Newton-Hopper, and Simmons represent occupations by the eastern community. In Table 19.2, coefficients from the five sites representing the western community have been arranged so as to infer chronological ordering. The probable movement of the eastern and western communities is illustrated in Figure 19.1.

Since the Kleis site is the most recent of the sites under consideration, one may ask if the ceramics at this site differ from those of earlier sites. In order to answer this question, the present study makes use of a coefficient of homogeneity in order to discover possible change in ceramic patterning over time (Whallon 1968). This coefficient gives a measure of the relative homogeneity of the ceramics at a single site as opposed to the coefficient of agreement which gives a measure of similarity between two sites. The higher the coefficient, the more homogeneous the ceramics from a site. Thus, the coefficient provides a method for comparing ceramic diversity between sites.

Coefficients of homogeneity were calculated for each of the Niagara Frontier sites under consideration. The results are as follows:

Buffum	.74
Goodyear	.80
Eaton	.80
Newton-Hopper	.79
Green Lake	.78
Simmons	.75
Ellis	.66
Kleis	.67

The sites are listed in the relative chronological order determined from Table 19.1. While there is an increase in ceramic homogeneity between Buffum and Goodyear, from then on there is a general trend toward ceramic heterogeneity through time. The Ellis and Kleis sites, the most recent sites examined, are by far the most heterogeneous ceramically.

In a similar earlier study (Engelbrecht 1971) the author examined ceramics from nine Seneca sites and a Cayuga site (Genoa Fort). To the author, some of the ceramics found on the Ellis and Kleis sites seemed similar to pottery found on Seneca and Cayuga sites. In order to test this impression, coefficients of agreement were generated

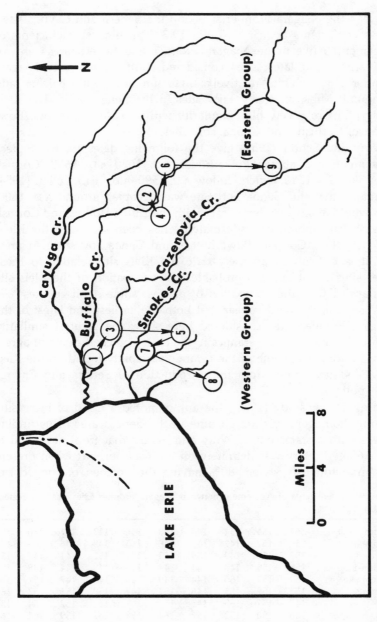

Fig. 19.1. Niagara Frontier sites: 1. Buffum; 2. Goodyear, 3. Eaton, 4. Newton-Hopper, 5. Green Lake, 6. Simmons, 7. Ellis, 8. Kleis, 9. Bead Hill

between the Niagara Frontier sites and the Seneca and Cayuga sites. These coefficients appear in Table 19.3. The highest coefficients of agreement between the Niagara Frontier and Seneca areas are for the earliest and latest sites considered. Buffum, an early Niagara Frontier site, exhibits relatively high similarity with Belcher and Richmond Mills, relatively early sites in the Seneca area. The Kleis site exhibits relatively high similarity with the Dutch Hollow, Powerhouse, Cornish, and Genoa Fort sites.

Wray and Schoff (1953) give the following dates for the Seneca sites mentioned above: Powerhouse A.D. 1630–A.D. 1650, Cornish A.D. 1590–A.D. 1616, Dutch Hollow A.D. 1590–A.D. 1615. Follett (1954) estimated that the Genoa Fort Site was occupied around A.D. 1600. This would make it contemporary with the Dutch Hollow and Cornish sites. A fair amount of trade material has been found on the Kleis, Dutch Hollow, Cornish, Powerhouse, and Genoa Fort sites. At present, it is difficult to precisely date the Kleis site relative to these other sites but it appears probable that occupation of the Kleis site overlapped with the occupation of at least some of these sites.

In general, it would appear that both the earliest and latest of the Niagara Frontier sites considered here show the greatest similarity with contemporaneous ceramics to the east. The coefficients of agreement indicate that some of the ceramic variability found on the Kleis and Ellis sites comes from the introduction of Seneca and Cayuga style pottery.

In an earlier study (1971), the author noted a trend of increasing ceramic homogeneity through time in the Seneca area. This finding agrees with a statement of Wray and Schoff that from A.D. 1630 to A.D. 1650, "Pottery was definitely on the way out, but when present was monotonously styled, 80% having the notched or fringed rim

Table 19.3. Coefficients of Agreement between Niagara Frontier Erie sites and Seneca and Cayuga sites.

	Belcher	Richmond Mills	Adams	Cameron	Dutch Hollow	Factory Hollow	Cornish	Warren	Powerhouse	Genoa Fort
Buffum	162	164	154	144	148	146	143	147	150	156
Goodyear	156	157	147	141	146	145	149	146	148	154
Eaton	153	154	143	139	143	141	142	141	147	152
Newton-Hopper	155	155	148	141	144	140	143	144	148	154
Green Lake	153	157	150	144	149	145	148	147	152	157
Simmons	153	157	155	146	151	147	150	151	153	160
Ellis	142	151	155	145	152	147	151	152	154	158
Kleis	136	150	152	157	164	158	162	159	164	163

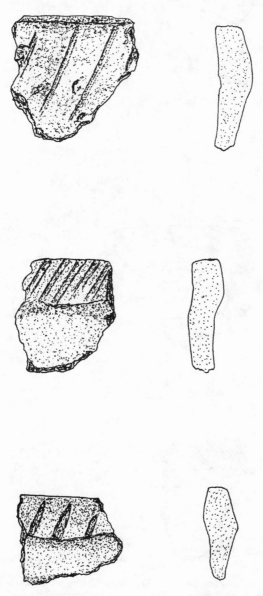

Fig. 19.2. Rim shards from the Eaton Site. These shards were randomly selected from rim shards in the Buffalo State College collection. Eaton rim shards were among the most homogeneous examined.

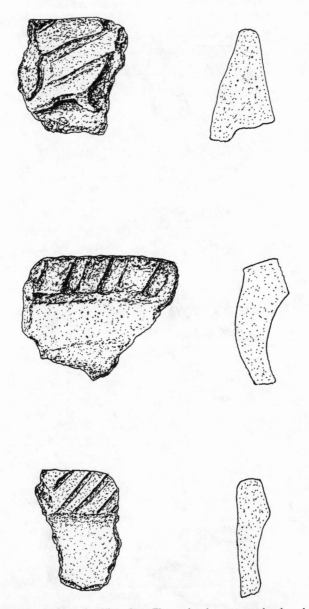

Fig. 19.3. Rim shards from the Kleis Site. These shards were randomly selected from a box of shards in the possession of Richard Buchauer. Kleis Site rim shards were among the most heterogeneous examined. Note the variation in rim profile.

decoration" (1953:57). Thus, while sites in the Niagara Frontier show increased heterogeneity, sites in the Seneca area exhibit the reverse trend. This suggests that the direction of ceramic innovation was from the Seneca area to the Niagara Frontier, with Seneca style pottery being found in the Niagara Frontier, but little Niagara Frontier style pottery appearing on Seneca sites.

INTERPRETATION

In this section an attempt will be made to interpret the results of the preceding analysis in terms of past human behavior. Specifically, the concern will be with explaining the presence of Seneca and Cayuga style pottery on the Kleis site. Interpreting the results of such an analysis is difficult since alternative interpretations are possible. Furthermore, the archaeological record only imperfectly reflects most areas of human behavior. Five possible explanations will be presented. None of these may be the real explanation, or the real explanation may involve a number of factors.

An attempt will be made to evaluate the likelihood of each explanation in terms of certain assumptions. Four of these assumptions follow:

1. Women were the potters among the Iroquois. Sagard observed women making pottery among the Huron and it seems reasonable to assume that this was true for the groups under consideration as well.

2. Trade was becoming increasingly important, both in the Seneca area and in the Niagara Frontier. This trade involved the exchange of animal pelts, especially beaver, for items of European manufacture such as metal tools, kettles, and cloth. The Kleis site contains many items of European manufacture.

3. The Niagara Frontier Erie did not have direct access to either English, French, or Dutch trade goods. Most of their trade goods probably came from the Seneca. The Seneca traded with the Dutch (Stewart 1970:17–18) but there is no record that the Erie did so, nor did the Erie trade with the French. Their nearest neighbors to the northwest were the Neutral, who were forced to trade with the Huron for French goods. Since the Neutral did not have direct access to European goods, they seem an unlikely source of supply for the population in the Niagara Frontier.

4. At the time that the Kleis site was occupied, population in the Seneca area appears to have been larger than that in the Niagara Frontier. The Seneca had four contemporaneous villages (two large and two small) while there were two large villages in the Niagara Frontier. This assumption needs to be tested by careful measuring

of the occupation areas involved, as well as systematic surveying for possible additional contemporaneous sites in both areas.

Explanation 1 (Trade Pots): Seneca and Cayuga pots were traded to the Niagara Frontier

This explanation has been used by a number of investigators including MacNeish (1952) to account for ceramic variability on Iroquois sites. While this explanation does take into account the increasing importance of trade, it does not fit with what we assume to be the nature of that trade (pelts for European items). Also, ceramic vessels are both heavy and breakable and seem unlikely items to be traded. Furthermore, adequate sources of clay appear to be widespread in New York. One method of moving heavy, bulky objects like pottery would be by canoe, but there is no direct water route between the Ellis and Kleis sites and the Seneca and Cayuga sites. A recent study by Underwood (1977) was concerned with tracing the minerals found in New York Iroquois potsherds to specific clay deposits. While the results of this study were inconclusive, technical studies of this nature have the potential for shedding light on the question of whether or not a pot is of local manufacture. At present, while Explanation 1 could account for the observed ceramic variation, it does not appear probable.

Explanation 2 (Stimulus Diffusion): Niagara Frontier potters borrowed Seneca and Cayuga pottery styles

This explanation would require Niagara Frontier potters to visit the Seneca area and then to return to the Niagara Frontier with new ideas of pottery manufacture which they then put into practice. This explanation would gain some support if a motive for such visits could be established. One possible stimulus for such visits would be the desire to acquire European trade goods. As mentioned earlier, it is assumed that the Seneca were trading with the Dutch but the Niagara Frontier population was not. Thus, the Seneca may have been playing the role of middleman between the Niagara Frontier population and the Dutch. Marian White (1971) suggested on ecological grounds that much of the Niagara Frontier would have been a good habitat for beaver. Therefore pelts from the Niagara Frontier may have been traded to the Seneca in exchange for trade goods.

An argument against this explanation, however, deals with the traditional role of women in Iroquois society. As mentioned earlier, it is assumed that women were the potters. Traditionally, however, intertribal trade is seen as a male activity and women are not viewed as playing an important role in it. While it is possible that some women accompanied men on these trading expeditions, this kind of activity would seem to conflict with traditional female domestic duties. For this reason, such visits on the part of females to other tribal areas were probably infrequent and Explanation 2 seems somewhat unlikely. If Niagara Frontier women did make such visits, the likelihood of their borrowing Seneca pottery styles is unknown.

Explanation 3 (Capture): Seneca and Cayuga women were captured and taken back to the Niagara Frontier. While there, they made pottery after the fashion of their former home

This is a fairly common interpretation of ceramic similarity between geographically distant Iroquois sites. Marriage by capture was one of the forms of marriage stressed by an earlier generation of anthropologists including J. F. McLennan (1865). Also, the Iroquois practice of adopting captives has been well documented by Snyderman (1948) and others for the historic period. Thus, the capture explanation has the weight of anthropological tradition behind it. The Erie were not members of the famous League of the Iroquois so Seneca and Cayuga women might have been fair game for Erie raiders, whether or not the League was functioning at this time.

One would expect, however, that the Seneca would also have been capturing Niagara Frontier Erie women and one would further expect that this should be reflected in the ceramics found on Seneca sites. As mentioned earlier, it is assumed that the Seneca had a larger population at this time, one that would be capable of retaliating and capturing women from the Niagara Frontier. However, the ceramic analysis does not bear this expectation out. As stated earlier, Seneca ceramics are increasingly homogeneous, showing little Niagara Frontier influence. Thus, while Explanation 3 possibly accounts for the observed ceramic patterning, it does not seem to be a very likely explanation.

Explanation 4 (Lineage Fission): Seneca and Cayuga lineages moved to the Niagara Frontier

This explanation involves the movement of both men and women from the Seneca area to the Niagara Frontier. There is historic evidence that among the Huron, lineages occasionally left a community at the time that the village moved to a new location. Such a move might have been occasioned by population pressure or by factional disputes between members of different lineages. It is conceivable that some Seneca lineages moved to the Niagara Frontier because of population pressure, possibly finding reception among similar clans. This explanation fits with the assumption that the

Seneca population was larger than the Niagara Frontier population. The two large Seneca villages may have reached the maximum size consistent with the Iroquois economic system of the period and the existing social mechanisms for integrating members of a community. Heidenreich (1971:129–30) has argued that large Huron villages were potentially unstable and tended to break down into smaller components.

The reason that a Seneca or Cayuga lineage should choose the Niagara Frontier to live remains unclear. Two lines of inquiry, however, could be followed in order to further test this explanation:

1. If Seneca or Cayuga lineages settled at the Kleis Site, one would assume that the women would be living together and making Seneca or Cayuga style pottery. Systematic excavation of the Ellis or Kleis sites might then reveal intrasite clustering of ceramic styles. If Seneca or Cayuga style pottery were found in discrete areal clusters on these sites it would lend support to this explanation.

2. Projectile points and other lithic artifacts presumed to have been manufactured by males should be analyzed from all relevant sites. If Seneca and Cayuga men were moving to the Niagara Frontier, this should be reflected in stylistic diversity within these artifact classes.

Explanation 5 (Marriage): Individual Seneca and Cayuga women married Niagara Frontier men and went to live in the Niagara Frontier

This explanation is similar to Explanation 3 in that it involves the movement of females to the Niagara Frontier. (Explanation 4 involves the movement of both men and women.) Matrilocal residence is assumed to have been the most common residence pattern among both the Erie and the Five Nation Iroquois. However, there were probably exceptions to this rule. Cara Richards (1967) notes a number of cases of nonmatrilocal residence among the Huron of the early seventeenth century. If Seneca and Cayuga women married Niagara Frontier men and moved back to the Niagara Frontier, it would explain the observed ceramic patterning. The argument for this explanation rests on the importance of trade during this period. As mentioned in Explanation 2 (stimulus diffusion), the Seneca may have been playing the role of middleman between the Erie and the Dutch. This interpretation is strengthened if the Niagara Frontier was in fact a good supply of beaver. Hunt (1940) notes that by the 1640s the Iroquois were running out of beaver within their own territories. The establishment of kin ties between the Seneca and Cayuga on the one hand and the Niagara Frontier on the other might be viewed as a mechanism for acquiring beaver pelts or facilitating their flow to the Seneca and Cayuga.

Unlike Explanation 2, this explanation does not require Niagara Frontier women to leave their villages. Rather, Niagara Frontier men would have traveled to the Seneca area to trade pelts for European objects. On these expeditions they could have met and married Seneca or Cayuga women. Seneca men would not have had as much reason to travel to Niagara Frontier villages and would therefore have had less chance to meet and marry women from the Niagara Frontier. Therefore, Niagara Frontier women would have had less occasion to move to the Seneca area. This model of past behavior fits the observed ceramic patterning.

While none of the above explanations have been conclusively demonstrated, three of the five explanations involve the presence of Seneca or Cayuga women at the Kleis site. On the whole, their presence seems the most likely explanation for the Seneca and Cayuga style pottery found there. The explanations involving trade pots or stimulus diffusion seem less convincing.

It is conceivable that the presence of Cayuga and Seneca women at the Kleis site influenced intertribal relations. In the introduction it was noted that the Neutral may have been the group which forced the Erie population south of Buffalo out of the Niagara Frontier in the 1640s. If it was the Neutral and not the Upper Iroquois who forced this population to leave, then this could be related to the presence among the Erie of Seneca and Cayuga women. Later, however, in the 1650s, the Iroquois did attack and destroy the main body of the Erie, probably living to the southwest.

In an earlier study (1974) the author noted a general trend of increasing ceramic similarity between tribal areas through time (A.D. 1550–A.D. 1650). The author had not then examined material from the Kleis site, but the Kleis ceramics agree with this earlier finding. These data suggest increasing movement and communication throughout New York in the early seventeenth century. It is during this time that the incidence of European trade material increases dramatically on Iroquoian sites. It seems probable that the two trends are related. It also seems likely that such movement and communication were accompanied by the strengthening of various integrative mechanisms which crosscut individual tribal groups. The League of the Iroquois was probably one such integrative mechanism. Had the Niagara Frontier not been abandoned, this population too might have been incorporated into the League.

CONCLUSION

This study is concerned with the ceramics from the Kleis site. The ceramic assemblage is of interest because it contained some Seneca and Cayuga style pottery. The site itself is of interest because it is probably the last major village occupation just south of Buffalo in the seventeenth century.

The ceramics from this site were compared with those from seven other village sites south of Buffalo. Brainerd-Robinson coefficients of agreement were calculated between sites using computer-coded ceramic attributes. From these coefficients, the Kleis site was inferred to be the most recent. Coefficients of ceramic homogeneity were then calculated for each of the sites. It was found that the latest sites (Ellis and Kleis) were the most heterogeneous ceramically. At least some of the ceramic variability present on these sites seems due to the presence of Seneca and Cayuga style pottery. This impression is strengthened by an examination of coefficients of agreement which were calculated between the Niagara Frontier sites and some Seneca and Cayuga sites.

At least five different interpretations of this ceramic pattern are possible. The two most likely explanations are that Seneca (and perhaps Cayuga) lineages moved in toto to the Niagara Frontier or that Seneca and Cayuga women individually married Niagara Frontier men and moved to the Niagara Frontier. Other ceramic studies by the author have revealed a similar phenomenon, namely increased ceramic similarity between different areas. This suggests that the first half of the seventeenth century was a time of increasing movement and contact between populations in the Northeast.

NOTE

1. I should like to thank the following individuals and institutions who allowed me access to their collections from the Niagara Frontier: Richard Buchauer, Eden, N.Y.; The Buffalo and Erie County Historical Society; The Buffalo Museum of Science; Carlton Conklin, Collins, N.Y.; The Houghton Chapter of the New York State Archaeological Association; Howard Lindell, Amherst, N.Y.; Herbert Merlau, Cowlesville, N.Y.; The Museum of Anthropology, University of Michigan; The Rochester Museum and Science Center; Gordon Schmahl, Williamsville, N.Y.; The Department of Anthropology, State University of New York at Buffalo; Mike Taylor, West Seneca, N.Y.; Malcolm Willard, Tonawanda, N.Y. I should also like to thank Neal Trubowitz, Hope Isaacs, Lynn Ceci, Kathy Allen, and Jim Bradley for commenting on an earlier version of this paper. I am grateful to the students on my 1975 and 1977 summer field schools at the State University College at Buffalo

whose work enlarged the ceramic sample from the Eaton site. Finally, thanks go to the staff of the computer center at the State University College at Buffalo, and to the editors of this volume, who made many helpful suggestions.

IV

The Fenton Tradition and Fenton as Applied Anthropologist

INTRODUCTION

The papers in this volume reflect the considerable diversity of Iroquoian studies today. It should be apparent, however, that despite tendencies toward specialization along the lines of the separate sub-disciplines, there is a strong undercurrent of conviction shared among the writers that anything ultimately worth saying about the Iroquois can and should be said within the broader context of the culture history of a whole people. This is the hallmark of the Fenton tradition.

In the first of the two papers in this section, Fred Voget traces the development of Iroquoian studies from Morgan's time to 1970 against a background of theoretical developments within North American anthropology. His point is that although the field we know today has roots in the nineteenth century, it did not really come together as an "organization of diversity"—to use Wallace's phrase—until the 1940s when Fenton took over "the reins of Iroquois research from Parker and Hewitt and . . . set a more definite course linked to the writing of Iroquois culture history." The Fenton tradition has continued at Conferences on Iroquoian Research, to some extent drawing from theoretical developments within North American anthropology, but maintaining a certain distance and a special distinctiveness too.

The second paper, by Laurence Hauptman, is also concerned with evaluating Fenton's career, but from an entirely different point of view which might be characterized as Fenton's contribution as an applied anthropologist. For two years during the bleak period of the Great Depression, Fenton served as a community worker among the

Tonawanda Seneca. In that role he was in the unenviable position at the outset of his career of having to explain government policy, and particularly the controversial Indian Reorganization Act, to skeptical Iroquois, while at the same time not compromising his personal friendships or endangering his future research prospects. Commissioner Collier's notion of creating an Applied Anthropology Staff at the Bureau of Indian Affairs was an enlightened one typical of the Roosevelt era, but at the local level the anthropologist-as-federal-employee was confronted with an extraordinarily challenging and complex task of diplomacy. Hauptman's paper is especially welcome in the present collection, both because it sheds light on a little-known early period of Fenton's career and because it provides some rounding out of discussions by other writers in the volume who have confined their remarks regarding Fenton's contributions largely to his scholarship. Hauptman, like Wallace, helps us to know Fenton the man better.

Chapter Twenty

Anthropological Theory and Iroquois Ethnography: 1850 to 1970

Fred W. Voget

Introduction

The long acculturative history of the Iroquois and their role in the struggle for empire between France and England produced a wealth of documentation which has proven very useful in later ethnographic investigation. Indeed, because of its historical depth, this documentation has played an important part in shaping problems and research about the Iroquois.

It is interesting, and also a matter of theoretical importance, to see how the ethnographic literature of any culture region reflects theoretical emphases in the general development of anthropology. Theoretical developments in anthropology can be divided into three stages (Voget 1975), and these, with some modification, will be used to focus this review of Iroquois literature. These stages are as follows: (1) Evolutionism (ca. 1850 to 1880); (2) Culture-Historicism: (a) The Salvage Ethnography Phase (ca. 1880 to 1940) and (b) The Historical Upstreaming Phase (ca. 1940 to 1970); and (3) Differentiation and Specialization (ca. 1940 to 1970). Developments in Iroquoian archeology are not reviewed, except in a peripheral way.

Evolutionism

Evolutionist thinking, which dominated anthropological theory in the nineteenth century, emphasized human progress guided by natural laws. Human advancement was divided into three stages: Savagery, Barbarism, and Civilization. The evolutionist objective lay in charting the "mental" and "moral" advancement of mankind by arranging ideas, values, inventions, arts, and social institutions on a line of development from the simple to the complex. In this line of development one could read the gradual triumph of reason over passion and the emergence of law in societies.

Lewis Henry Morgan (1851), the first ethnographer of the Iroquois, not only described the Iroquois and their culture sympathetically but also sought to establish their culture as an evolutionary type. In Morgan's (1871; 1877; 1881) view, the Iroquois exemplified a stage called the Lower Status of Barbarism, and he used them especially to illustrate the "archaic" type of matrilineal descent. At that stage the "paternity of children was not ascertainable" and maternity alone provided the "savage mind" with its first glimmerings of descent (Morgan 1881:6).

Morgan's comparison of the Iroquois longhouse with other house types, including prehistoric remains, led him to conclude that the clan-based "communistic" society of the Iroquois was typical for early societies. He ended his classic work, *Ancient Society* (1877), with the prophecy that the ancient communal and fraternal values found in Iroquois society would be restored in the future development of mankind. The evidence for a primeval communism and the prophecy caught Marx's eye, and Morgan's evolutionary scheme was incorporated into the communistic theory of human progress (Engels 1942). As a type the Iroquois thus achieved a special international and political-evolutionary place in Western thought not held by other preindustrial societies.

CULTURE-HISTORICISM: THE SALVAGE ETHNOGRAPHY PHASE (CA. 1880 TO 1940)

Morgan had hardly set forth the place of the Iroquois in the evolutionary development of mankind than American ethnology began to move toward an historical orientation which rejected evolutionary theory and method. The beginning of this historical interest was marked in Iroquoian studies by ethnographic documentation of Iroquois technology, mythology, cosmology, political organization, social organization, and religious ceremonialism. Emphasis was on salvaging the details of traditional life by consulting living Iroquois, and especially written documents composed by Iroquois, in the hope that these sources and memories of former times would bring out a more complete and true picture of Iroquois culture, history, and thought. The architects of this approach were Horatio Hale, William M. Beauchamp, Arthur C. Parker, and J. N. B. Hewitt; and, to a lesser extent, F. W. Waugh, Alexander Goldenweiser, Erminnie A. Smith, and Harriet Maxwell Converse.

Hale set the tone for this salvage operation with publication of *The Iroquois Book of Rites* (1883). This work described and analyzed the Condolence Ceremony recited to alleviate the grief of those who had lost a chief and who came before the council to elevate a successor. Hale introduced brief descriptions of Iroquois history and government to bring out the meaning of the ceremony. His primary sources were Mohawk and Onondaga versions of rules governing the Iroquois League. He dated the versions around the middle of the eighteenth century. Much of his effort, therefore, lay in the translation of native texts. Hale's concern for ethnographic facts restrained evolutionary speculation and aided transition to a more historical orientation and methodology.

During the first three decades of the twentieth century, Hewitt and Parker carried much of the burden of Iroquois salvage ethnography. Parker's major contributions lay in describing general technology and methods of maize cultivation (1910), the new religion of Handsome Lake (1913), and the traditional organization of the Confederacy (1916). He also wrote about Iroquois prehistory (1922), history (1926), and folklore, especially of the Seneca (1926). Hewitt's interests centered on mythology and cosmology (1903–1928), religion (1895; 1902), and political organization (1920). The research of these two native Iroquoianists thus filled out complementary domains.

Hewitt's religiosity (Swanton 1938) may have directed him to Iroquois religion where he hoped to capture "primitive" thinking about the world and man's place in it. His study of Iroquoian cosmology was intended to preserve in as original a way as possible the "aboriginal thought" of Iroquois "philosophers" (Hewitt 1903:137). While Hewitt's concern with primitive thought did not encourage him toward historical inquiry, he did use historical data to advantage in the introduction to his study of cosmology (Hewitt 1928:453–63; see also 1933). His field work led to the production of ethnographic documents, a primary objective of those with the historical orientation.

Parker's archeological and museological interests focused attention on historical problems and prompted him to recover Iroquois artifacts, customs, beliefs, and art objects in the field. As curator of the New York State Museum at Albany, he was commissioned in 1904 to "secure all possible information concerning the history, customs, ceremonies . . . [and] traditions . . . of the . . . Iroquois Confederacy" (cited by Fenton 1968:11). While Hewitt (1920) used linguistic analysis to verify ethnographic facts, Parker turned to historic sources, in conjunction with ethnographic study, to establish historical-cultural facts about the Iroquois. Parker's historical interests stand out in *The Code of Handsome Lake, the Seneca Prophet* (1913), as well as in *The History of the Seneca Indians* (1926). His *Iroquois Uses of Maize and*

Other Food Plants (1910; cf. Waugh 1916) is a landmark, in that historical, ethnographic, and methodological interests converge in a first-rate salvage effort of Iroquois technology and economy.

The pattern of drawing upon historic source materials, archeological remains, and ethnographic and linguistic findings for general interpretation had been set earlier by William Beauchamp (1897; 1902; 1903; 1907) in studies of Iroquois technology, customs, folklore, and archeology. Beauchamp (1905) also turned out a lengthy history of the Iroquois in New York State. Parker admired Beauchamp (Fenton 1968:18–19), and—with regard to objectives and procedures—he undoubtedly drew upon Beauchamp's work.

Tracing the historical diffusion of culture elements was never an important objective of Iroquois studies during the salvage phase. Marius Barbeau (1917; 1917a) did use the distribution of culture elements to trace the "probable" relations and sources for Iroquois social organization as a counter to Morgan's and Goldenweiser's (1918) theories. Nathaniel Knowles (1940) followed a similar distribution procedure to determine the types of torture complexes and their probable origins among the Iroquois and other Indians east of the Mississippi. Inspired by Parker's monograph on maize, the German diffusionist, John Loewenthal (1921) compared subsistence tools and containers, and concluded that several culture streams had brought influences to the Iroquois from Mexico, the Antilles, and Northeast Asia.

As the salvage phase of Iroquois research drew to a close during the thirties, those who had participated in the work of recovery could be proud of their achievements. Moreover, new perspectives regarding Iroquois life and culture were beginning to emerge, as in the deeper appreciation of the importance of local organization based on the matrilineage and household (Goldenweiser 1913). Various accounts of the "Constitution" of the Iroquois League (Scott 1912; Parker 1916, 1918; Goldenweiser 1916; Hewitt 1917) pointed up the variability of Iroquois social organization. Such variability at times appeared to be a result of cultural diversity at the tribal level, or of vital changes accompanying European contact, or of the need to accommodate the Confederacy to changing conditions on the reserves. The sharp debate between Parker and Hewitt over the authenticity and interpretation of their respective accounts of the Iroquois Constitution underlined difficulties facing those who hoped to produce documents which would describe Iroquois culture as it existed before contact.

Salvage ethnography did not encourage an interest in theory and its application in the solving of problems. At the same time broad problems which would continue to be of interest and focus research objectives were laid out, e.g., the origins of the Iroquois, the status of women, the nature of the Confederacy, and the question of linguistic diversity. A basic methodology had grown up around these objectives, combining archeological, historical, ethnographic, and linguistic approaches to produce limited generalizations about Iroquois culture and culture processes.

Culture Historicism: The Historical Upstreaming Phase (ca. 1940 to 1970)

Around 1935 William Fenton began to take over the reins of Iroquois research from Parker and Hewitt and to set a more definite course linked to the writing of Iroquois culture history. During the next twenty years, Fenton advanced Iroquois research in six ways. First, in a series of "position papers" he kept scholars abreast of the state of Iroquois research and indicated problems which needed to be taken up next (Fenton 1940; 1948; 1951b; 1961). Second, he introduced "historical upstreaming" as the method most applicable to Iroquois problems, and, through the example of his own research, communicated this method and its objectives to others. Third, he worked to draw students of the Iroquois, both lay and professional, into a company which met together with some frequency, exchanged ideas, and agreed on research objectives (the early meetings at Red House, New York). Fourth, he organized scholarly effort around special problems, such as local diversity in Iroquois culture (Fenton 1951a) and the connections between northern and southern Iroquoian-speaking peoples (Fenton and Gulick 1961). Fifth, he drew attention to the wealth of historic and ethnographic materials available on the Iroquois, stressing the unique opportunities for studying change processes in the development of a culture area. Sixth, he worked assiduously to compile historical and ethnographic sources for easy reference and availability (Fenton 1949; 1957). Iroquois studies between 1935 and 1955 thus belong largely to William Fenton.

In "historical upstreaming" Fenton (1957:21) found the primary methodological contribution of ethnology to ethnohistorical studies. Three assumptions governed historical upstreaming: "1) that major patterns of culture remain stable over long period of time, producing repeated uniformities; 2) these patterns can best be seen by proceeding from the known ethnological present to the unknown past, using recent sources first and then earlier sources; 3) those sources which ring true at both ends of the time span merit confidence" (Fenton 1957:21–22). The method, Fenton (1957:22) admitted, contained a "built-in fallacy . . . the doctrine of uniformitarianism, which infers the past from present." Here, of course, the proof of inference of past from present must rest on structured continuities or pattern retention.

Fenton (1940) outlined the method of historical upstreaming in his first "position paper." Following precedent, he defined "Iroquois" in a linguistic sense and thus extended Iroquoian studies to include the Huron, Susquehannock, and Cherokee. The basic problems of Iroquois research revolved around their "intrusive linguistic and cultural position in the Northeast," and the meaning of this for a "final demonstration of their cultural origins" (Fenton 1940:165). Assuming that their intrusive position was a consequence of migration from another region, Fenton called for studies of cultural adaptations which followed Iroquois movement into their historic locations, as well as of adjustments resulting from contacts with Algonkians and Europeans. The broad objective of understanding Iroquoian culture origins required interdisciplinary cooperation in the following areas: (1) a "comparative study of Iroquoian languages"; (2) archeological studies [which] proceed from the known historic sites to the prehistoric period"; (3) the use of basic sources to rewrite Iroquois history "to show the changes in Iroquois culture that have occurred during 400 years of white contact"; (4) bibliographic work to permit a descriptive "historical ethnography"; and (5) determination of distinctive physical types and their probable correlations with linguistic boundaries (Fenton 1940:165–66). With the aid of "extensive genealogies," correlations with race mixture might be uncovered.

The 1940 position paper provided an outline of historic periods to correlate Iroquois history and cultural relations with other Indians and Europeans. In Fenton's perspective, the flow of exchanges between the Iroquois and their neighbors began with Algonkians, shifted to Hurons who had taken up an Algonkian-style hunting and trading economy, and then, during the eighteenth century, linked up with Siouan, Muskogean and Iroquoian groups in the southeast. By studying Algonkin-Huron trade relations and political alliances, Fenton (1940:188) developed new insights regarding the migration of the Iroquois into their historic homeland. Contact relations also pointed to cultural borrowings, such as the Feast of the Dead. "From the Nipissing, display of wealth spread to Huronia along with dog sacrifice, and from Huronia to Iroquois; and only after the contact period do mortuary goods appear in Seneca graves" (Fenton 1940:191). From the Algonkians the Iroquois also obtained important shamanistic elements, with Hurons again acting as transmitters, especially to the Seneca.

Though broadly historical in orientation, Fenton focused his attention on the authentication of facts about Iroquois culture and history. His method in effect was a kind of ethnographic historiography, which explains his unswerving determination to establish the true nature of recorded facts and events, and to keep theorizing about processes in check until full historical-ethnographic documentation was at hand. His early publications (1936; 1941a) reflect a contrapuntal movement between present and historically recorded facts about Iroquois culture. At the same time (Fenton 1937, 1940, 1941a, 1941b; Fenton and Deardorff 1943) he synthesized data on the Iroquois; and, through a combination of historic and ethnographic research, filled out poorly described complexes, and demonstrated their patterned continuities. The study of Iroquois suicide illustrates a model which he has used time and again in his research (1941, 1941a; 1941b; 1942). Finding that contemporary Iroquois used the poisonous water hemlock to commit suicide, Fenton applied his method of historical upstreaming and intertribal comparison to determine that the use of hemlock was unique to the Iroquois in the seventeenth century. Similarities between seventeenth century motives and practices and present-day ones underlined the continuity of pattern. Regarding cultural continuity, he concluded:

. . . once a fundamental pattern becomes established it tends to persist despite substitutions within its framework. The unconscious nature of pattern and the illogical character of cultures are shown by the fact that social systems may offer the individual patterns as guides for his conduct that lead to the fulfillment of mutually opposite values. (Fenton 1941a:135)

The emphasis on continuity of pattern, unconscious processes, contradictory values available to the individual in culture patterns, and the absence of logical and functional connections between patterns and institutions reflected views of American culture theorists, especially those who followed Boas. Consistent with this view of culture, Fenton (1941a:124, note 4) avoided psychological explanations of the suicide pattern and did not generate psychological hypotheses for future testing.

Attention to particulars, so characteristic of the historical approach, found ready application in problems of variability within a broader pattern or system. On the one hand, variability could be seen as resulting from external historical contact; or it might arise from special accommodations made by local groups living in different environments. Frank Speck apparently strengthened Fenton's interest in cultural variation by pointing to ceremonial variability among the Southwestern Pueblos. Fenton (1941b) tested the nature of traditional pattern and historic-ceremonial diversity among the Iroquois by comparing Seneca ceremonial cycles recorded by Morgan and Parker with his own field observations at Tonawanda.

The problem of local diversity in Iroquois culture was explored in a symposium held in 1949. The local, tribal, and national levels of integration available for the Iroquois afforded a good test of the "validity of the area-study approach to a culture . . ." (Fenton 1951a:4). Local adjustments of the "kinship state" of the Iroquois would provide a test of variation in political organization. Ever on the lookout for forces operating with similar effects in the past and present, Fenton (1951a:10) pointed out how localized processes everywhere induced the formation of groups with local economic interests, loyalties, leadership, work groups, dialects, and factions. In this context, Goldenweiser's observation that the "maternal family is political . . . and politics are local business" took on special meaning (cited by Fenton 1951:45). The *sadinonhsaat* ("they of one house," composite household and/or matrilineage) was the basic economic, cooperative, social, and political entity of the Iroquois, and had remained a highly localized unit.

> . . . The clans had their separate councils, but there was also, and still is, an ad hoc village council of ranking clan chiefs, elders, and others whose wisdom was respected. The public, or the assembly, still includes the local residents who are the sounding board of local opinion. As local residents they engage in such joint enterprises as work parties—hunting, lumber, railroading, steel gangs—sports, drinking, and war parties. The mutual aid society is primarily a local affair; only secondarily do clan, rank, and moiety intrude, and principally to the extent that its membership boasts a clan chief, who is also the ranking chief of the community, and perhaps a federal chief in the League; and out of deference to his position he may be asked to speak, but he may not have charge of the enterprise. The mutual aid society apparently had its beginnings as a society of males who banded together to assist the women of a clan to whom they were married and their own sisters. They were coresidents in a composite household, or at least of the settlement. (Fenton 1951:50)

In examining the impact of locality on Iroquois culture Fenton found that processes which worked to produce separatism or unity were at work equally among present-day Iroquois. While changes in culture patterns outwardly appeared different, a closer examination of their change processes often revealed similarities. Time and again changes in culture patterns validated the principle that uniform processes invariably produce uniform results.

Sorting out the relationship between local variability or heterogeneity and integrative tendencies or homogeneity is a continuing problem for anthropological researchers. It turns up, for instance, in the question of Iroquois origins—whether Iroquois culture developed in place over a long time; or was brought in relatively intact by immigrants; or was stimulated periodically in its development by the historic spread of innovative inventions. Beginning in the 1950s, the findings of archeologists (MacNeish 1952; Ritchie 1965; Tuck 1971; Wright 1966) suggested that Iroquois culture, while distinctive in certain respects, arose out of a more general regional substratum shared with other groups. The older theory put forward by ethnologists, that the Iroquois were relatively late intruders, no longer appeared valid in the light of archeological facts.

The accumulated weight of evidence from archeological, ethnological, linguistic, and historic sources increasingly required that Iroquois origins and culture history be viewed against a background of developments in Eastern North America, the Midwest, Caribbean, Europe, and even Mexico. When tracing cultural contacts through a comparison of culture elements, the degree of similarity in form necessary to establish connections between cultures always involves critical judgment and methodological problems. Moreover, the study of cultural origins and change through historic contact is complicated, since contact processes may induce divergences or convergences, stimulate the perpetuation of traditional forms, or introduce new forms which carry both old and new functions. The symposium on Cherokee-Iroquois connections indicated that these issues must again be considered in any attempt to reconstruct Iroquois culture history.

In 1945 Speck and Schaeffer compared mutual aid organizations of the Cherokee and the Northern Iroquois to see if they shared a common "archaic" substratum. By eliminating "superficial accretions . . . from European sources," and taking note of "more fundamental modifications effected by varying streams of influence . . . subsequent to their separation and dispersion," they reduced the mutual aid societies of the Iroquois and Cherokee to a common proto-historic "community-wide" organization (Speck and Schaeffer 1945:178–79). This differed from Fenton's interpretation: he saw the mutual aid organization as an outgrowth of clan and household.

In their comparative study, Raymond D. Fogelson and Paul Kutsche (1961:114–16) concluded that the longhouse and the clan were more important in Iroquois subsistence and mutual aid organizations than among the Cherokee. The traditional clan-based Iroquois organization differed from the community-type structure of the Cherokee. However, similarities between the aid societies in the two areas were not the result of the persistence of an ancient tradition shared by the Iroquois and Cherokee, but were the product of convergences in historic change. Similar cultural changes following contact with Europeans had brought similarities in form and practice to Iroquois and Cherokee mutual aid associations. Separate reviews of the data had produced three distinct interpretations. In his remarks on Fogelson and Kutsche, Fenton (1961:264) put forward the view that a community-type mutual aid association was established early throughout the Eastern Woodlands and this accounted for similarities between the Iroquois (Seneca in particular) and the Cherokee.

A comparison of Iroquois and Cherokee musical traditions also suggested the interplay of different cultural substrata (Kurath 1961:188). The Iroquois showed more influence from a northern winter cycle than the Cherokee, perhaps because of stronger agricultural influences among the latter. William C. Sturtevant (1961:200) questioned a division of musical and dance elements "into a preagricultural stratum with survivals among northern Algonquians, versus a later agricultural stratum typified by the Muskogeans. . . ." Horticulture was too ancient in the Northeast for such an interpretation. Comparisons of linguistic change suggested that the Iroquois and Cherokee may have separated some 3800 years ago (Lounsbury 1961:11–12).

Reconstructions of proto-Iroquoian culture took historically minded anthropologists beyond the controls of documentary sources. The tracing of culture elements often suggested multiple sources and periods of contact, and the use of terms, such as cultural "stratums" and "substratums" recalled similar terminology by German culture-historicists. The modern Stirring Ashes Rite of the Midwinter Ceremony was seen as a survival of a "new fire" rite at the winter solstice, reminiscent of an old culture complex sketchily described for the Aztecs (Tooker 1970:83). Fenton (1961:263) wondered whether the splint basketry of the Northeast was introduced by Swedes in Delaware, or whether Speck's suggested derivation from northeastern South American cultivators were correct. He observed (1961:263):

> If there were no historical records, we might pursue this
> line of reasoning relentlessly and derive a great deal of
> Iroquois culture through the Southeast from the forest of the
> eastern Amazon via the Antilles. Faint echoes in the language
> are supposed to reverberate that way.

Sturtevant (1961:200–201) underlined complications in correctly identifying elements belonging to particular complexes and then tracing them to their respective sources and periods. While the Iroquois corn ceremony (thõwi:sas) undoubtedly derived from the Cherokee, perhaps through Seneca captives who escaped from the Cherokee, the box turtle rattle did not diffuse as part of this ceremonial complex. Box turtle rattles, common in the Southeast where the turtles thrive naturally, were present in Archaic archeological sites in New York and Ontario, and hence must be a very old trait among the Iroquois. Present culture complexes, as Fenton and Deardorff (1943) discovered when analyzing the passenger pigeon complex, might include elements derived from different historical times and sources. The success of reconstruction, as Fenton and Deardorff (1943) skillfully demonstrated, lay in drawing upon all available data—historical, ethnographic, archeological, and linguistic. This combination of evidence brought out the relation of pigeon hunting to seasonal cycle and diet, the pigeon in myth, song, and ritual, as well as the persistence of traditional techniques and thought. Similar limited objectives and controlled documentation characterized Fenton's papers on "Masked Medicine Societies of the Iroquois" (1941), "Contacts Between Iroquois Herbalism and Colonial Medicine" (1942), and "The Roll Call of the Iroquois Chiefs" (1950).

Others found the culture-historical model developed by Fenton a natural and useful instrument in their work. Conklin and Sturtevant (1953:289) combined historical, ethnographic, and linguistic data in a description of Seneca musical instruments and the contexts in which each was used. They pointed out that "Musical instruments alone have persisted as a well-integrated complex of largely aboriginal material traits." Wallace's survey (1957; cf. Snyderman 1951; Trigger 1960, 1969) of historical sources disclosed that land tenure and political territoriality were linked to ideas of use, trespass, right of conquest, abandonment, and succession. Wallace Chafe's (1961) study of Seneca Thanksgiving rituals focused on the development of contemporary oral tradition and provided a close grammatical analysis of Seneca texts. While variation—individual, community, historical, contextual—is alluded to, the dynamics of variation were not described. The closest Chafe (1961:13) came to this was a suggestion that the introduction of references to Handsome Lake and the Four Beings in the Thanksgiving Ritual probably originated with the Seneca and then diffused to other Longhouses. Michael Foster (1974) gave more consideration to variation in Iroquois oral tradition in a descriptive analysis of ritual recitations in the Longhouse. Elisabeth Tooker (1970) combined historical and ethnographic materials in a comparative analysis to determine the history of the Midwinter Ceremony and the variations which developed on the several reservations. Despite the analytic control sought through historic documents, Tooker still could not complete the history of the ceremony. For instance, it remained unclear as to whether the White Dog sacrifice was a substitute for human sacrifice as Hewitt suggested, or the product of historic diffusion from Indians to the west who practiced dog sacrifice (Tooker 1970:102; cf. Blau 1964). A comparison of forms and their geographic distributions suggested that the Eagle-Calumet and Victory dances had changed through the introduction of elements derived from the Southern Plains (Fenton and Kurath 1951), whereas the torture complex revealed features traceable to the Southeast and Mesoamerica (Trigger 1969). Functional shifts, as from war to curing complexes (Fenton and Kurath 1951) were documented, as well as recombinations of traditional elements within the traditional ceremonial pattern (Tooker 1970). The role of historic figures in effecting cultural change likewise became a topic of study, particularly the religious and social reformer, Handsome Lake (Tooker 1970; Wallace 1969).

The empirical emphasis which culture-historicism brought to Iroquois studies did not foster the development of grand theoretical designs. No synthesis of Iroquois culture history resulted, though individual summaries dealing with limited areas laid the groundwork for future syntheses (Heidenreich 1971; Tooker 1964; Trigger 1969, 1976). By and large the empirical model of culture-historicism was well suited to Iroquois research, resulting in a steady buildup of credible facts and explanations through a constant reexamination of old problems, assumptions, and facts in the light of historical and ethnographic documentation (see, for example, Richards 1957; Smith 1970). In the controlled studies of culture-historicists the continuity of pattern through time stood out as a paramount fact underlying culture change. This was true for the riveting work-gang of Caughnawaga steel workers, which in size, organization, purpose, and spirit followed the ancient model of the war-raid party (Freilich 1958).

DIFFERENTIATION AND SPECIALIZATION: CA. 1940 TO 1970

The pervasive cultural-historical orientation in Iroquois studies tended to insulate the field from theoretical influences associated with structural-functionalism which entered North American anthropology during the first half of the present century. The trend toward theoretical differentiation and specialization also seems to have come late to Iroquois studies. For example, Stites's (1905) early study of the impact of economy on Iroquois social organization, which had a structural-functional orientation, went largely unrecognized. Tendencies toward differentiation and specialization appear around 1940 when Hunt (1940) argued that the favorable geographic location of the Iroquois in relation to the fur trade accounted for their political-military ascendancy and historic role in the Northeast. The importance of geographic and economic factors in the destruction of Huronia is generally accepted by Iroquoian scholars while recognizing the weight of other factors. A complex of historic, sociopolitical, tactical, economic, demographic, and ecological conditions figure in recent analyses of Iroquois political and military success (Smith 1973; Snyderman 1948; Otterbein 1964; Tooker 1963; Trigger 1960, 1963a).

John Noon (1949) made use of a social-structural and functional analysis to explain modifications made by the Confederate Council when forced to accommodate to the new demands of reservation living. Malinowski, Noon (1949:27–28; cf. Trigger 1963) noted, had "demonstrated that social structure was the basis of all positive social control . . . [and consequently] the activities of individuals and groups are coordinated by functionally integrated societal patterns whose operation is enforced by a system of reciprocating benefits and obligations." From this viewpoint Noon was led to focus attention on the way in which the Iroquois reorganized their traditional social and political structure, including values, in order to cope with the rapidly changing times.

Noon's structural-functional perspective went beyond the theoretical views of culture-historicists regarding the functional integration of institutions and of cultures. Except for Buell Quain's study (1937) in Mead's survey of cooperation and competition, no descriptive analysis of integrative tendencies in Iroquois culture according to predominant values or institutions has appeared. However, the structural-functional orientation applied by Noon to the study of political change among the Grand River Iroquois was used by Frederick Gearing (1962) in his study of the rise of the Cherokee state in the eighteenth century. The present writer (Voget 1951; 1953) drew attention to the formation of sociocultural categories of acculturation and the possible correlation of socioeconomic changes with modifications in the family and in kinship terminology. Sally Weaver (1972) examined medical beliefs and practices in conjunction with political strategies employed by the "progressive" Iroquois to win acceptance of modern medical ideas and therapy at Six Nations. "Higher" and "lower" status categories were distinguished "to provide the necessary background for understanding participation in matters of health and illness at the community level" (Weaver 1972:98). While interested in culture contact processes, Annemarie Shimony (1961) produced an excellent descriptive ethnography of the culture of "conservatives" at Six Nations during the 1950s. She found that a number of "pervasive themes" held the culture together—notably the *"theme of being an Indian,"* of "collectiveness," of "reciprocity and helpfulness," and of "mind" as a special attribute of Iroquois men (Shimony 1961:290). An interlocking of "the medical complex, . . . the life cycle, the social system, and the traditional political system" provided a degree of functional coherence among institutions, with the political integrated least with the others (Shimony 1961:290). However, the persistence of conservative traditions was held to be more a matter of ideology than a functional interlocking of institutions.

Martha Randle (1951) used the Thematic Apperception Test to uncover differential stress and anxiety experienced by men and women because of changes in roles necessitated by life on reservations. She found (1951:180) that home and children were of primary importance to Six Nations women and concluded: "The acculturative process was less destructive of the woman's pattern, and consequently the woman of today is more secure in her feminine role and more successful in accomplishments along the lines set by white patterns, than her masculine counterpart." Randle (1952) also surveyed the Waugh collection of myths to see if psychological types could be found. The mother's brother emerged as a "ruthless, cannibalistic bogey-man who takes wives away from his nephew, but at the same time he is the savior of that nephew and of the whole group" (Randle 1952:20).

Anthony Wallace (1951:61; 1952) applied a psychoanalytic framework to correlate elements of Iroquois personality with tendencies to accept "congenial" and to reject "uncongenial" culture elements. This psychological approach paralleled earlier attempts by culture-historicists to explain the acceptance or rejection of alien traits by a principle of cultural compatibility. In "Dreams and the Wishes of the Soul: A Type of Psychoanalytic Theory Among the Seventeenth Century Iroquois," Wallace (1958a) brilliantly illustrated how psychoanalytic theory could add unsuspected dimensions to understanding of the dream complex among the Iroquois.

From a study of Handsome Lake, Wallace (1956) went on to develop a psychological theory of change processes, which he called "revitalization." The Deganawida legend, which recounted a reorganization of early Iroquois political organization, could, he (1958) argued, be fitted into the several stages of change projected in the revitalization model. In The Death and Rebirth of the Seneca, Wallace (1969) combined the results of his psychoanalytic and acculturative researches with ethnohistory to produce a sophisticated and plausible culture history.

CONCLUSIONS

A survey of Iroquois ethnographic literature from 1850 to the present suggests the following:

1. The evolutionary direction given to Iroquois studies by Morgan was soon superseded by a special concern for the use of facts verifiable through historic and ethnographic documents in order to better understand and describe the life and culture history of the Iroquois.

This theoretical and methodological trend corresponded to tendencies then emerging in cultural anthropology.

2. The thrust of Iroquois research from around 1880 to the present has remained cultural and historical in orientation. There are two reasons for this. First, the vast number of documents available on the Iroquois because of their historic role in the Northeast encouraged historical investigation and methodology. Ethnographic references frequently occurred in these historic documents, and, as Iroquois became literate in their own language, they proudly wrote about their political system and its ceremonialism in order to preserve in writing what memory was unable to hold as change eroded the old life. The second reason for the constancy of the culture-historical purpose rests largely with William Fenton. Fenton not only defined the ethnographic and historiographic objectives and methodology of Iroquois studies but also, through his own researches, persuaded and encouraged others to follow his example. Fenton's role in Iroquois studies is very much like that of Boas in the development of American cultural anthropology. He has guided it into the mainstream of culture-historicism while welcoming the interests of others which add something new to the facts and understandings of Iroquois life and culture down through time.

3. The continuity in the cultural-historical orientation has meant that special theoretical developments in anthropology have not influenced Iroquois research in any major way. This is true for structural-functional theory as well as the trend toward theoretical differentiation and specialization which began around 1940. In some ways, the persistence of cultural-historical objectives and methodology in Iroquois studies from 1880 to the present lends support to Fenton's (1941a:135) conclusions about patterns, namely, that "once a fundamental pattern becomes established it tends to persist despite substitutions within its framework."

CHAPTER TWENTY-ONE

Between a Rock and a Hard Place: William N. Fenton in the Indian Service, 1935-1937[1]

LAURENCE M. HAUPTMAN

In the past decade, historians have increasingly analyzed United States governmental Indian policies of the New Deal era. Most studies have focused on Commissioner of Indian Affairs John Collier (Philp 1977), the Indian Reorganization Act (Kelly 1975: 291–312), or on individual Indian nations (Parman 1976). Although Commissioner Collier's employment of anthropologists in the Indian Service is generally well known (Taylor 1975: 151–62), no historian has evaluated the specific work of a single field anthropologist involved in this experiment. By examining the career of Indian Service community worker William N. Fenton from 1935 through 1937, the Indian New Deal as it functioned at the agency level can be better understood.

In December 1934, Commissioner Collier in a speech at Pittsburgh stressed the need to work closer with anthropologists. For more than a year previously, Collier had sent out questionnaires, held informal discussions with prominent anthropologists, most notably William Duncan Strong of the Bureau of American Ethnology, and had made other overtures to win the profession's support for his program. The Commissioner had borrowed this idea from the British Empire's use of social scientists to facilitate colonial ventures (Collier 1963: 217, 345–51). Moreover, his plan was a conscious effort to employ them in places where missionary influence was strongest previously (Philp 1977: 161–62). Consequently, at its best, the experiment, based on these suppositions, was bound to be resented by many Indians.

In 1935, Collier appointed Strong to head the newly created Applied Anthropology Staff of the Bureau of Indian Affairs. An entire generation of aspiring anthropologists, many of whom were out of work or were unable to secure academic positions because of the Great

Depression, received much of their field work training under the auspices of Collier's program, including Clyde Kluckhohn, Oscar Lewis, Gordon MacGregor, Morris Opler, Laura Thompson, and Ruth Underhill. Through the efforts of Strong, Fenton was appointed as community worker in the Indian Service at Tonawanda, receiving a salary of $2000 per year, subsidized use of his own automobile, and a small per diem of $3.50 a day for traveling expenses (FISP 1934a; 1934b; 1935a; 1935c). With a fresh climate of experimentation, money in his pocket and new mentors at the hustings "down below" (the Longhouse district at Tonawanda), Fenton assumed his position in February 1935.

The young anthropologist was no stranger to Iroquoia. In the two years prior to his appointment, Fenton had conducted field work among the Senecas on Iroquois social structure, ceremonial organization, and medicine for the Institute of Human Relations at Yale University (Fenton p.c., June 21, 1978). In the process, he had learned much from older Indians at "doings," witnessed the extraordinary sense of cooperation by reservation folk during the difficult times of the Great Depression, and developed acquaintances who played a significant role in his research and scholarship for the next four decades (Fenton 1978b: 187–92). Fenton's return to Seneca country, as he was well aware, was going to be different this time. When he entered the Tonawanda Reservation in February, he was "wearing a new hat." He was now a "Fed," part of Commissioner Collier's experiment in applied anthropology at the Bureau of Indian Affairs. Fenton, who was cognizant of Iroquois distrust and even open hostility toward United States officials, reflected this concern when he wrote Collier: ". . . I think I will get on better when in an unofficial capacity. There is strong feeling amongst the Iroquois about government agents" (FISP 1935b).

In his two and a half years of service, Fenton walked the fine line of survival. He had to contend with a do-nothing Indian agent, federal governmental Indian policies that were often at odds with Iroquois wishes, factional tribal politics, and, most importantly, the severity of reservation poverty intensified by the Great Depression. At the same time, Fenton was completing his dissertation requirement for the "good men" of Yale. On occasion, his professional goals as an aspiring anthropologist ran counter to his official duties. In a society with an historic distrust of Washington and Washington-directed Indian policies, the more Fenton wore an official hat, the more his ability to gather information for his dissertation suffered. Yet, if he ignored the Bureau's directives altogether, he could easily foresee finding himself unemployed at a time of the nation's worst depression. Consequently, Fenton often felt as though he were "between a rock and a hard place" (Fenton p.c., June 21, 1978).

Iroquoia was an exciting if unsettled place in which to serve in the mid-1930s. Political ferment caused by the referendum on the Indian Reorganization Act (Hauptman 1980) and a cultural renaissance as a result of the Seneca Arts Project (Hauptman 1979a: 282–312) deeply affected reservation life. Prominent Iroquois activists such as Alice Lee Jemison were receiving nationwide attention in their frequent verbal assaults on the Bureau of Indian Affairs (Hauptman 1979: 15–22).

The problems facing the Iroquois in the period were immense. The grim realities of poverty abounded. Health conditions, in particular, were abysmal. Tuberculosis had reached epidemic proportions at the Cattaraugus Reservation (CPP 1934), while pneumonia struck periodically, seriously affecting life in the Longhouse district at Tonawanda (Fenton 1976: 6). In the year preceding Fenton's appointment, approximately 50 percent of all Indians received public assistance from the New York State Department of Social Welfare (Hirsch 1936: 1). The Great Depression had made an already poor situation even worse. At Tonawanda, virtually everyone was out of work except those who had part-time employment in the gypsum mines at Akron, New York (Fenton 1976). Moreover, racial discrimination was apparent everywhere, restricting job opportunities. Those Indians lucky enough to find work were often paid wages lower than those of whites (Rickard 1973: 120–25).

Besides these problems, Fenton, from the beginning, had to contend with overcoming Iroquois distrust and suspicion about outsiders. One month after he started work, one Seneca, later to become Fenton's friend, wrote Collier inquiring about the stranger who "hangs around in our Reservation every day. . . ." The Seneca, in broken English, added:

> And besides he has meetings here at nights in our Reserve—
> and being in wrong party—he got acquainted with
> Underground. Works that all we know. He don't even talks to
> the Chiefs. We have chiefs here but there isn't no one knows
> what hes doing! and what he is for! So I think it got to be
> done something about this man . . . we believe hes another
> crooked and thats the reason, I am writing to you and find
> out whether is all satisfaction (FISP 1935d)

Collier responded by defining Fenton's role as "community worker at the New York agency to assist the Indians of the Tonawanda Reservation and other communities in organizing enterprises which will meet their social needs." Collier added that Fenton's role was to "promote group meetings, clubs and classes, especially for adults" and to cooperate with the Indians in all efforts to develop "economic, social and health programs, with the objective of fostering the growth of definite civic and social responsibilities" (ibid.).

Anthropologists working in the Indian service under Commissioner Collier frequently complained about having to work with the old-line Bureau personnel. No clearer example of these complaints can be provided than Fenton's relationship with W. K. Harrison, the Indian agent in New York. For over thirty years, Harrison had survived in his Salamanca post primarily by not rocking the boat. Silent as President Coolidge, Harrison was accepted by Iroquois largely because he did not bother them. They preferred "a smooth old gentleman who only appears to pay their annuities, attend councils, and is a nice symbol of the government" (FISP 1935J).

The two men, who were separated in age by nearly half a century, were light-years apart in their approach to the Iroquois and their problems. From the first days on the job, the young anthropologist suspected that Harrison was not "convinced of the practicality of the program involved, or what he expects of a community worker" (FISP 1935b). Harrison questioned the necessity of Fenton's frequent travels to Rochester and Buffalo, especially without the agent's prior permission. Outraged, Fenton wrote to the central office in Washington asking for the privilege of exercising his own judgment on the need to travel (FISP 1935J). He added:

> The old gentleman is anxious that I do not play politics, a situation which he can control by keeping me in Akron. I don't happen to be interested in politics, but I am interested in these Indians. While here, I can devote much time to studying them, but I have to go to Buffalo to arrange outside help for them; to get lecturers, to see people, who really listen when you write afterwards. (Ibid.)

Despite the agent's objections, Fenton continued his travels. The distance between Harrison's Salamanca office and Fenton's work at Tonawanda allowed the community worker some latitude from outside interference.

The debate over the Indian Reorganization Act consumed most of Fenton's attention during the first six months in his new position. The act granted Indians the right to organize for purposes of local self-government and economic independence. It provided for the establishment of tribal elections, tribal constitutions, and tribal corporations; a revolving loan fund to assist organized tribes in community economic development; and the encouragement of Indian employment in the Indian Service by giving them preference in hiring by waiving civil service requirements. Title II of the act affirmed that its purpose was "to promote the study of Indian civilization, including Indian crafts, skills and traditions." Under this section of the act, vocational and college scholarships as well as educational loans were also included. Other provisions of the Indian Reorganization Act ended the land allotment provisions of the Dawes General Allotment Act of 1887 and encouraged tribal conservation efforts by the establishment of Indian forestry units and by herd reduction on arid land. As passed by Congress and signed by President Roosevelt on June 18, 1934, the act required a tribal plebiscite before its acceptance. According to section 18: "This Act shall not apply to any reservation wherein a majority of the adult Indians, voting at a special election called by the Secretary of the Interior, shall vote against its application" (*U.S. Statutes at Large* 1934, XLVIII: 984–88).

The Iroquois, as individual nations in New York and collectively as a Confederacy in council at Onondaga, took exception to the Indian Reorganization Act and overwhelmingly voted it down in June 1935. Since a majority of eligible voters in the referendum had to vote against the act to nullify its enforcement, many viewed it as another white man's trick to dupe the Indians. Others, valuing their freedom from governmental interference, interpreted the act's new rules and regulations as an encroachment on their lifestyles and questioned the government's motives for reorganization, fearing that the changes would result in citizenship, taxation, and eventual land loss. Still others saw the act as mass legislation that offered more for western tribes without landbases or existing political structures (Hauptman 1980).

Besides keeping Collier informed of the turmoil on the reservations caused by the Indian Reorganization Act, Fenton held public meetings to explain the act's features. Acutely aware of the strong opposition to the act, Fenton faced a major dilemma: how to keep the trust of Indian friends who were also informants when one was associated with promoting an unpopular cause. It is clear from his correspondence that he had doubts about the legislation. Even before his appointment to the Indian Service, he had insisted that "the best thing to do with the groups in question would be to leave their government intact but to give them financial advice in the form of an accounting system" (FISP 1934b). He later supported the act because he feared the educational and economic programs provided would be lost if the act was rejected (Fenton p.c., September 28, 1977).

Throughout the months preceding the referendum, he was well aware of Iroquois criticism as a result of his house-to-house distribution of copies of the act. He urged the Bureau to send a representative to the reservations to swing the vote for passage: "They certainly will not vote for a measure which the Office of Indian Affairs does not deem of sufficient importance to send a speaker to the reservations to explain" (FISP 1935e). Subsequently, Collier sent Henry Roe Cloud, the noted Indian educator and superintendent of Haskell Institute to explain the act and conduct the referendum (FISP 1935f). Unfortunately, Roe Cloud's talks only confused the Indians more with his references to western tribes (FISP 1935h). To make matters worse, Fenton had to face the worst fate a white man can endure among the modern Iroquois—the wrath of raging clan mothers who blocked the polls at St. Regis and forced the two "feds" to switch the site of the election while under federal marshal protection (PP 1935). Fenton later reflected on the experience:

> The Wheeler-Howard Bill flopped, and I am not sure it is the fault of the Indian Service personnel. We worked and in several instances risked our necks to conduct the elections. Roe Cloud, who has no axe to grind in the matter, can tell you. When I originally contemplated the Indian service, I questioned the possibility of breaking faith with groups of Indians who had been my friends. I have been their friend. Many of them have expressed their feelings frankly to me about the IRA (Indian Reorganization Act), which they wholeheartedly doubted and no amount of persuasion would dislodge them, and have told me I may live to regain the status I once enjoyed as participant in their rituals and recreation. My connection with the Government has cast an awful pall upon my presence. They hate to think that their friend, whom they admit they like, is connected with the government. (FISP 1935J)

After this crushing defeat, Fenton turned his attention to specific areas of need. The applied anthropologist had now become more aware of the bottomless gulf between official expectations and the realities of Indian life in the period. Consequently, during the remainder of his tenure as community worker, he served the Iroquois as a concerned social problem solver rather than involving himself in the maelstrom of Iroquois politics. In the process, he regained much of the support he had lost in the referendum debacle. Moreover, he was able to make use of his anthropological training to serve the Iroquois, especially at Tonawanda.

Perhaps his most significant accomplishments were in the area of education. Fenton organized study clubs at Tonawanda which brought in outside speakers and allowed the younger Indians to learn from their elders on the reservation. He handled the necessary paperwork to help promising students on several Iroquois reservations secure educational loans to go to college. He also encouraged several students, who might never have thought of higher education, to enter Cornell, Dartmouth, and St. Lawrence. Quite significantly, he helped organize the first community library at Tonawanda which immediately proved successful (Fenton 1935: 46–48).

Fenton was also a major contributor to the success of Arthur C. Parker's Seneca Arts Project (Parker 1936: 13). This Works Progress Administration's project, under the auspices of the Rochester Museum and Science Center and based at Tonawanda and briefly at Cattaraugus, employed about one hundred artists working at separate times. It produced approximately five thousand works of art and reproductions, including wooden false face masks, bowls, cradleboards, ladles and spoons; silver brooches and earrings; woven baskets and burden straps; embroidered beadwork, moose hair and porcupine quillwork used for assorted costume designs; and paintings of Iroquois life (Hauptman 1979b: 282–312). Fenton and Cephas Hill, the assistant project supervisor at Tonawanda, visited nearly all the museums, historical societies and galleries in New York that contained Iroquois ethnographical material. There they photographed the collections for the benefit of the project artists who learned by copying these older examples of traditional Iroquois arts and crafts.

Fenton's other contributions to the project are clearly revealed in a letter dated October 25, 1935:

> During the week of October 14 to 19th, I made an analysis of techniques involved in the manufacture of woolen sashes which were still made a generation ago by the Seneca Indians. The analysis was made from photographs sent out by the Rochester Municipal Museum. We were able to set up working models of string, and with the help of an old woman (Sarah Hill) who remembered her grandmother making sashes, we were able to re-construct the process. The Tonawanda "Indian Arts and Crafts" project will now reproduce sashes which are only to be found in Museums. (FISP, 1935 1)

Fenton was responsible for securing the services of Roy Mason, the noted landscape painter, who gave lessons in technique to Ernest Smith, an artist on the project who became the premier painter of modern Iroquoia (Hill and Fenton 1935: 13–15). It is clear from interviewing the project's personnel that the Seneca Arts Project, which lasted from 1935 to 1941, not only provided employment for indigent Indians during the Depression, but also fostered community cohesiveness and pride among the Senecas and created for the

Rochester Museum one of the richest ethnological collections of art in the United States (Hauptman 1979a: 284).

Fenton also worked to improve health care at Tonawanda. His activities included securing a wheelchair for a disabled old woman, driving Indians to the hospital for check-ups, handling business matters for those seriously ill, lecturing on ways to improve public health on the reservation, and cooperating with state physicians to stem the ravages of disease. He convinced the family of William Gordon, leaders of the Longhouse, to commit their son Theodore, suffering from a serious case of tuberculosis, to a sanitarium, rather than relying solely on native herbal medicines and medicine society rituals. Through his special knowledge of Seneca mores, he "persuaded them that the songs might relieve the individual of conflicts arising out of not fulfilling the requirements of belonging to a certain society, but that Theodore had T.B., a white-man's disease, which their most potent rituals would not cure" (FISP 1935k). Fenton's applied anthropology had saved a life. As he subsequently wrote:

> The ethnologists have amassed volumes of data pertaining to the history and operation of Indian customs. Can this knowledge be put to any practicable use? The title Community Worker implies a method; one should work with groups rather than cases. The method should be designed to fit the customs of the people. (Fenton 1936a:7)

Throughout his tenure as community worker, Fenton attempted to cut through established procedures and red tape. He acted as an intermediary to secure funds from the New York State Department of Welfare for casket lumber for Longhouse funerals. He then borrowed three Indian laborers, members of the Salt Creek Mutual Aid Society, from the local public works project to dig the graves, all to the chagrin of off-reservation non-Indian funeral directors. Amazed at the work and the spirit of cooperation in the form of Iroquois singing societies, he attempted to advise both Washington and Albany to incorporate an understanding of Seneca lifeways into any and all programs for these Indians:

> Perhaps the modest example of these singing companies suggests a method of meeting social problems. A group of individuals band themselves together for the purposes of joint pleasures and mutual assistance. They elect their native leaders and solve the problems which every society has to meet in some traditional manner. Where these societies exist, they should be encouraged. The recognition of native

leadership and the delegation of responsibility promotes self-respect and independence. (Fenton 1936a:7)

His advice was virtually ignored; however, in other areas, Fenton was more successful in getting results. He helped get needed improvements for the bridges and roads, shingle the longhouse, and bring electrification to Tonawanda.

Fenton's career-long commitment to promoting Indian-language programs was evident during his tenure in the Indian Service. The experiment in the Iroquoian language that later materialized among the Oneidas in Wisconsin in the late 1930s under Morris Swadesh's and still later Floyd Lounsbury's direction, was worked out in correspondence and face-to-face contact at Yale in the period. Edward Sapir suggested a rough plan as early as the spring of 1935 whereby Fenton, Swadesh, and Stanley Newman would conduct linguistic research among the Iroquois. Fenton, in June 1935, suggested to Collier's assistant that programs could be set up on all the Iroquois reservations and that his Indian friend, Jesse Cornplanter, and the local Presbyterian Indian pastor, Peter Doctor, could be employed because of their considerable knowledge (FISP 1935i). It was Fenton's opinion that Asher Wright's Seneca hymnal should be rewritten. He added: "I can imagine no more worthy scientific achievement than writing a Seneca grammar. Teaching the Indians to write it would be a means of preserving the language." (FISP 1935k). Although there were many innovative strides made in promoting Indian language during the New Deal, funding never materialized for a New York-based program. Almost forty years later in the mid-1970s, a Seneca program was finally established (Myrtle Peterson, p.c., April 7, 1978).

On August 14, 1937, Fenton applied for a leave of absence—later changed to resignation—from the Indian Service after accepting an instructorship in the Social Sciences at St. Lawrence University (FISP 1937a). Nevertheless, he remained committed to his former charges. Subsequent to his request for a leave, Fenton wrote to the Office of Indian Affairs to help secure funds for Ernest Benedict's schooling at St. Lawrence, after his transfer from Syracuse University. He added: ". . . I am to be a member of the St. Lawrence faculty this coming year, and it is quite right that I will be in a position to help Ernest if he gets himself in any great difficulty" (FISP 1937b).

Fenton's success as a community worker led to his nomination for both Director of the Tonawanda Indian Community Building and Indian agent in New York to replace Harrison (FISP 1937a). Fenton had always had a feeling that he was learning "more from the

Indians than they did from me" (FISP 1938). The Senecas recognized the importance of his role when he returned for a visit in 1938:

. . . We visited Tonawanda and Allegany Reservations recently, and the way the Indians greeted us made Mrs. Fenton and me realize that they considered us part of them. It gave me a deep sense of personal satisfaction when one of the leaders said, "We were talking about you at the Singers Society (one of the Native Mutual-aid societies at the Longhouse)—what good times we had when you were here. You made us realize that some things were worthwhile." (Ibid.)

His interest in helping the Iroquois in the mid-1930s had outweighed nearly everything in his life. They were not simply people to be studied for anthropological observation but were generous, cooperative people who opened their homes, their pantries and their ceremonies to him.

The New Deal experiment with anthropologists, although serving the purposes of the Indian Bureau and the anthropologist, was indeed significant well beyond immediate Bureau administrative needs and the subsidization of the field work for anthropologists. It often provided concrete and dramatic benefits for those who served. In addition, what we know about twentieth-century native Americans and even what native Americans know about themselves is partly a result of the work done in the 1930s by applied anthropologists. Although the Indian New Deal failed miserably in its attempts to implement a uniform nation-wide Indian policy under the Indian Reorganization Act, it often succeeded in less formal governmental involvement on an everyday community level. In New York, through Fenton, it was responsible for contributing to an artistic revival, improved health care delivery, the promotion of Indian educational opportunities, and many other things. It is clear that the abyss between Washington and reservation life in the period was only capable of being overcome when the personnel at the local level were working in the context of tribal cultures and understood the people. Undoubtedly, the successes and failures of anthropologists in the field varied depending upon their temperament or that of their Indian constituency. Although there were other arduous assignments, most notably among the Navajos, few matched Fenton's appointment in difficulty. And few could match his record of commitment and accomplishment.

NOTE

1. The research for this paper was made possible in part by grants from the Penrose Fund of the American Philosophical Society, the Research Foundation of the State University of New York and the National Endowment for the Humanities.

List of Contributors

Thomas S. Abler, University of Waterloo
James Axtell, College of William and Mary
Nancy Bonvillain, State University of New York at Stony Brook
Jack Campisi, Red Hook, New York
Wallace L. Chafe, University of California at Berkeley
Gordon M. Day, National Museum of Man, Ottawa
William E. Engelbrecht, State University College at Buffalo
Michael K. Foster, National Museum of Man, Ottawa
Ives Goddard, Smithsonian Institution
Laurence M. Hauptman, State University College of New York at New
    Paltz
Charles M. Johnston, McMaster University
Marianne Mithun, State University of New York at Albany
Annemarie A. Shimony, Wellesley College
Dean R. Snow, State University of New York at Albany
William C. Sturtevant, Smithsonian Institution
Elisabeth Tooker, Temple University
Bruce G. Trigger, McGill University
Fred W. Voget, Southern Illinois University at Edwardsville
Anthony F. C. Wallace, University of Pennsylvania
Sally M. Weaver, University of Waterloo
Hanni Woodbury, affiliated with Columbia University
James V. Wright, National Museum of Man, Ottawa

Bibliography of References Cited

ABC = The American Board of Commissioners for Foreign Missions Archive, Houghton Library, Harvard University, Cambridge, Mass.

Abler, Thomas and Elisabeth Tooker 1978 Seneca. Pp. 505–17 in Northeast. Bruce G. Trigger, vol. ed. Handbook of North American Indians, Vol. 15. William C. Sturtevant, gen. ed. Washington: Smithsonian Institution.

Adams, J. T. 1961 The Explorations of Pierre Esprit Radisson. Minneapolis: Ross and Haines, Inc.

Adamson, John W. 1930 English Education, 1789–1902. Cambridge, Eng.: The University Press.

Allen, Wilkes 1820 The History of Chelmsford, From Its Origin in 1653, to the Year 1820, Together With an Historical Sketch of the Church and Biographical Notices of the Four First Pastors. To Which is Added a Memoir of the Pawtucket Tribe of Indians, With a Large Appendix. Haverhill, Mass.: P. N. Green, Printer.

American State Papers 1832 Documents, Legislative and Executive, of the Congress of the United States, From the First Session of the First to the Third Session of the Thirteenth Congress Inclusive: Commencing March 2, 1789 and Ending March 3, 1815. Vol. 4. Washington: Gale and Seaton.

Anderson, James E. 1968 The Serpent Mounds Site, Physical Anthropology. Royal Ontario Museum, Art and Archaeology Occasional Papers. Toronto.

BPP = British Parliamentary Papers 1836 Report from the Select Committee on Aborigines (1968). Shannon, Ireland.

Bailey, Alfred G. 1937 The Conflict of Europeans and Eastern Algonkian Cultures, 1504–1700: A Study in Canadian Civilization. *Publications of the New Brunswick Museum, Monographic Series 2.* Saint John, N. B.

Barbeau, Marius 1917 Parallels Between the Northwest Coast and Iroquoian Clans and Phratries. *American Anthropologist* 19(1):403–05.

——— 1917a Iroquoian Clans and Phratries. *American Anthropologist* 19(1):392–402.

Bauman, Richard and Joel Sherzer 1975 The Ethnography of Speaking. *Annual Review of Anthropology* 4 (9554): 95–119.

Baxter, James P. 1893 Christopher Levett of York. The Pioneer Colonist of Casco Bay. Portland, Maine: The Gorges Society.

Beardsley, Richard K., et al. 1956 Function and Evolutionary Implications of Community Patterning. Seminars in Archaeology: 1955. *Society for American Archaeology Memoir* 11:129–55.

Beatty, John 1974 Mohawk Vocabulary. *Occasional Publications in Anthropology, Linguistic Series* 2. Greeley, Colorado.

Beauchamp, William M. 1897 The New Religion of the Iroquois. *Journal of American Folk-Lore* 10(38):169–80.

———— 1900 Iroquois Women. *Journal of American Folk-Lore* 13(49):81–91.

———— 1902 Horn and Bone Implements of the New York Iroquois. *New York State Museum Bulletin* 50. Albany.

———— 1903 Metallic Ornaments of the New York Indians. *New York State Museum Bulletin* 73. Albany.

———— 1905 A History of the New York Iroquois, Now Commonly Called the Six Nations. *New York State Museum Bulletin* 78. Albany.

———— 1907 Civil, Religious and Mourning Councils and Ceremonies of Adoption of the New York Indians. *New York State Museum Bulletin* 113:341–451. Albany.

Bell, Andrew 1807 An Analysis of the Experiment in Education Made at Egmore Near Madras. London: T. Bailey, for Cadell and Davies.

Bendix, Edward H. 1966 Componential Analysis of General Grammar. *International Journal of American Linguistics* 32(2), Part 2, Publication 41.

Bennett, Wendell C. 1948 The Peruvian Co-tradition. Pp. 1–7 in A Reappraisal of Peruvian Archaeology. W. C. Bennett, ed. *Society for American Archaeology Memoir* 4 (2). Menasha, Wisconsin.

Berkhofer, Robert F., Jr. 1971 The Political Context of a New Indian History. *Pacific Historical Review* 40(3):357–82.

———— 1978 The White Man's Indian. New York: Alfred A. Knopf.

Bierwisch, Manfred 1969 On Certain Problems of Semantic Representations. *Foundations of Language* 5(2):153–84.

Biggar, Henry P., ed. *see* Champlain, Samuel de

Binnick, Robert 1968 On the Nature of the "Lexical Item." Pp. 1–13 in Papers from the Fourth Regional Meeting of the Chicago Linguistic Society. B. J. Darden, ed. Chicago: Univ. of Chicago Press.

Binns, Christopher A. P. 1979 The Changing Face of Power: Revolution and Accommodation in the Development of the Soviet Ceremonial System: Part 1. *Man* 14(19):585–606. London.

Bishop, Morris 1948 Champlain: The Life of Fortitude. New York: Alfred A. Knopf.

Blau, Harold 1964 The Iroquois White Dog Sacrifice: Its Evolution and Symbolism. *Ethnohistory* 11(2):97–119.

———— 1969 Calendric Ceremonies of the New York Onondaga. (Unpublished Ph.D. Dissertation in Anthropology, New School for Social Research, New York.)

Blau, Harold, Jack Campisi, and Elisabeth Tooker 1978 Onondaga. Pp. 491–99 in Northeast. Bruce G. Trigger, vol. ed. Handbook of North American

Indians, Vol. 15. William C. Sturtevant, gen. ed. Washington: Smithsonian Institution.

Bock, K. E. 1956 The Acceptance of Histories: Toward a Perspective for the Social Sciences. Berkeley: University of California Press.

Bonvillain, Nancy 1973 A Grammar of Akwesasne Mohawk. *Canada. National Museum of Man, Ethnology Division, Mercury Series Paper* 8. Ottawa.

—— 1978 Linguistic Change in Akwesasne Mohawk: French and English Influences. *International Journal of American Linguistics* 44(1):31–39.

Bourque, Bruce J. 1975 Comments on the Late Archaic Populations of Central Maine: The View from the Turner Farm. *Arctic Anthropology* 12(2):35–45.

Bouton, Nathaniel 1856 The History of Concord, from its First Grant in 1725, to the Organization of the City Government in 1853, with a History of the Ancient Penacooks, . . . Concord, New Hampshire: B. W. Sanborn.

Boyd, Julian P., ed. 1938 Indian Treaties Printed by Benjamin Franklin, 1736–1762. Philadelphia: Historical Society of Pennsylvania.

Brainerd, George W. 1951 The Place of Chronological Ordering in Archaeological Analysis. *American Antiquity* 26(4):301–13.

Brasser, Ted J. C. 1971 The Coastal Algonkians: People of the First Frontiers. Pp. 64–91 in North American Indians in Historical Perspective. Eleanor B. Leacock and Nancy O. Lurie, eds. New York: Random House.

—— 1974 Riding on the Frontier's Crest: Indian Culture and Culture Change. *Canada. National Museum of Man, Ethnology Division, Mercury Series Paper* 13. Ottawa.

Brown, Judith K. 1970 Economic Organization and the Position of Women Among the Iroquois. *Ethnohistory* 17:151–67.

Byers, Douglas S. 1959 The Eastern Archaic: Some Problems and Hypotheses. *American Antiquity* 24(3):233–56.

—— 1961 Second Comment on William Ritchie's "Iroquois Archaeology and Settlement Patterns." Pp. 47–50 in Symposium on Cherokee and Iroquois Culture. William N. Fenton and John Gulick, eds. *Bureau of American Ethnology Bulletin* 180(6). Washington.

CMS = Church Missionary Society 1817–1824 Archives. London, Eng.

CPP = Collier Personal Papers 1933–1941 John Collier Collection, Yale University Library, New Haven, Conn.

Campeau, Lucien 1977 [Review of] The Children of Aataentsic, by Bruce G. Trigger. *Revue d'histoire de l'Amérique française* 31: 437–40.

Campisi, Jack 1974 Ethnic Identity and Boundary Maintenance in Three Oneida Communities. (Unpublished Ph.D. Dissertation in Anthropology, State University of New York, Albany.)

—— 1974a Consequences of the Kansas Claims to Oneida Tribal Identity. Pp. 35–47 in Proceedings of the First Congress, Canadian Ethnology Society. Jerome H. Barkow, ed. *Canada. National Museum of Man, Ethnology Division, Mercury Series Paper* 17. Ottawa.

—— 1978 Oneida. Pp. 481–90 in Northeast. Bruce G. Trigger, vol. ed. Handbook of North American Indians, Vol. 15. William C. Sturtevant, gen. ed. Washington: Smithsonian Institution.

Canada. 1891 Indian Treaties and Surrenders from 1680 to 1890. 2 vols. Ottawa: Queen's Printer. (Reprinted: Coles, Toronto, 1971.)

Canada. Laws, Statutes, etc. 1869 An Act for the Gradual Enfranchisement of Indians, the Better Managemant of Indian Affairs, and to Extend the Provisions of the Act. 31 Victoria, Chapter 42. Ottawa: M. Cameron.

—— 1884 An Act for Conferring Certain Privileges on the More Advanced Bands of the Indians of Canada, with the View of Training Them for the Exercise of Municipal Powers. (Short Title: The Indian Advancement Act.) 47 Victoria, Chapter 28. Ottawa: M. Cameron.

Canada. Parliament. House of Commons 1874 Report: The Select Committee Appointed to Inquire into the Conditions and Affairs of the Six Nations Indians in the Counties of Brant and Haldimand in the Province of Ontario (Sessional Papers 11). Ottawa: Queen's Printer.

Carr, Lucien 1884 On the Social and Political Position of Women Among the Huron. *Reports of the Peabody Museum* 3:207–32.

Chafe, Wallace L. 1961 Seneca Thanksgiving Rituals. *Bureau of American Ethnology Bulletin* 183. Washington.

—— 1964 Linguistic Evidence for the Relative Age of Iroquois Religious Practices. *Southwestern Journal of Anthropology* 20 (3): 278–285.

—— 1967 Seneca Morphology and Dictionary. *Smithsonian Contributions to Anthropology* 4. Washington.

—— 1977 The Evolution of Third Person Verb Agreement in the Iroquoian Languages. Pp. 493–524 in Mechanisms of Syntactic Change. Charles N. Li, ed. Austin: University of Texas Press.

Chafe, Wallace L., and Michael K. Foster 1981 Prehistoric Divergences and Recontacts Between Cayuga, Seneca, and the Other Northern Iroquoian Languages. *International Journal of American Linguistics* 47(2):121–42.

Champlain, Samuel de 1922–1936 The Works of Samuel de Champlain [1626]. Henry P. Biggar, ed. 6 vols. Toronto: The Champlain Society.

Charlevoix, Pierre F. X. de 1866–1872 History and General Description of New France [1744]. John G. Shea, ed. 6 vols. New York: John G. Shea. (Reprinted: Loyola University Press, Chicago, 1962.)

Chomko, Stephen, and Gary W. Crawford 1978 Plant Husbandry in Prehistoric Eastern North America: New Evidence for Its Development. *American Antiquity* 43(3):405–08.

Clark, S. D. 1948 Church and Sect in Canada. Toronto: University of Toronto Press.

Clarke, George F. 1968 Someone Before Us: Our Maritime Indians. Frederickton, N.B.: Brunswick Press.

Colden, Cadwallader 1747 The History of the Five Indian Nations of Canada, Which are Dependent on the Province of New-York in America, and Are the Barrier Between the English and French in That Part of the World . . . 2 vols. London: T. Osborne.

—— 1958 The History of the Five Indian Nations Depending on the Province of New-York in America [1727]. Ithaca, N.Y.: Cornell University Press.

—— 1902 The History of the Five Indian Nations of Canada. 2 vols. New York: New Amsterdam Book Company.

Collier, John 1963 From Every Zenith. Denver, Colorado: Sage Books.

Conklin, Harold C. 1955 Hanunóo Color Categories. *Southwestern Journal of Anthropology* 11(4):339–44.

—— 1967 Lexicographic Treatment of Folk Taxonomies. Pp. 119–41 in Problems in Lexicography, F. W. Householder and S. Saporta, eds. 2nd ed. The Hague: Mouton.

Conklin, Harold C. and William C. Sturtevant 1953 Seneca Indian Singing Tools at Coldspring Longhouse: Musical Instruments of the Modern Iroquois. *Proceedings of the American Philosophical Society* 97(3):262–90. Philadelphia.

Converse, Harriet (Maxwell) 1908 Myths and Legends of the New York State Iroquois. Arthur C. Parker, ed. *New York State Museum Bulletin* 125:5–195. Albany.

Cranston, J. H. 1949 Etienne Brûlé: Immortal Scoundrel. Toronto: The Ryerson Press.

Cuoq, Jean-André 1882 Lexique de la langue iroquoise avec notes et appendices. Montreal: J. Chapleau.

Day, Gordon M. 1962 Rogers' Raid in Indian Tradition. *Historical New Hampshire* 17 (June): 3–17.

—— 1972 Oral Tradition as Complement. *Ethnohistory* 19 (2): 99–108.

—— 1973 The Problem of the Openangos. *Studies in Linguistics* 23:31–37.

—— 1975 The Mots Loups of Father Mathevet. *Canada. National Museum of Man, Publications in Ethnology* 8. Ottawa.

—— 1975a Early Merimack Toponymy. Pp. 372–89 in Papers of the Sixth Algonquian Conference in 1974. William Cowan, ed. *Canada. National Museum of Man, Ethnology Division, Mercury Series Paper* 23. Ottawa.

Deardorff, Merle H. 1951 The Religion of Handsome Lake: Its Origin and Development. Pp. 77–107 in Symposium on Local Diversity in Iroquois Culture. William N. Fenton, ed. *Bureau of American Ethnology Bulletin* 149(5). Washington.

De Forest, John W. 1851 History of the Indians of Connecticut from the Earliest Known Period to 1850. Hartford, Conn.: W. J. Hamersley. (Reprinted: Shoestring Press, Hamden, Conn., 1964.)

Desrosiers, Léo-Paul 1947 Iroquoisie. *Études de l'Institut d'Histoire de L'Amérique française*. Montreal.

Dincauze, Dena F. 1975 The Late Archaic Period in Southern New England. *Arctic Anthropology* 12(2):23–34.

Dixon, R. M. W. 1971 A Method of Semantic Description. Pp. 436–71 in Semantics, An interdisciplinary Reader in Philosophy, Linguistics and Psychology. D. D. Steinberg and L. A. Jakobovits, eds. Cambridge, Eng.: Cambridge University Press.

Druillettes, Gabriel 1933 Rapport du R. P. Druillettes envoyé en députation à la Nouvelle-Angleterre pour y conclure un traité de neutralité entre les colonies anglaises et françaises (1) 1651. *Le Canada Français* (juin): 941–49. Québec.

Edmonds, Walter D. 1968 The Musket and the Cross: The Struggle of France and England for North America. Boston and Toronto: Little, Brown and Company.

Emerson, J. Norman 1955 The Kant Site: A Point Peninsula Manifestation in Renfrew County, Ontario. *Transactions of the Royal Canadian Institute* 31(64):24–66. Toronto.

—— 1961 Problems of Huron Origins. *Anthropologica* 3(2):181–201.

Engelbrecht, William E. 1971 A Stylistic Analysis of New York Iroquois Pottery. (Unpublished Ph.D. Dissertation in Anthropology, University of Michigan, Ann Arbor.)

—— 1972 The Reflection of Patterned Behavior in Iroquois Pottery Decoration. *Pennsylvania Archaeologist* 42(3):1–15.

—— 1974 The Iroquois: Archaeological Patterning on the Tribal Level. *World Archaeology* 6(1):52–65.

Engels, Friedrich 1942 The Origin of the Family, Private Property and the State in the Light of the Researches of Lewis H. Morgan. New York: International Publishers.

FISP = Fenton Indian Service Papers. (Manuscript Collection in William N. Fenton's Possession.)

Farnham, Mary F., comp. 1901 Farnham Papers, 1698–1871. *Documentary History of the State of Maine 7*. Portland.

Fenton, William N. 1935 The Tonawanda Indian Community Library. *Indians at Work* 3(5):46–48.

—— 1936 An Outline of Seneca Cermonies at Coldspring Longhouse. *Yale University Publications in Anthropology* 9. New Haven, Conn. (Reprinted: Human Relations Area Files Press, New Haven, Conn., 1970.)

—— 1936a Some Social Customs of the Modern Seneca. *Social Welfare Bulletin* 7(1/2):4–7.

—— 1937 The Seneca Society of Faces. *Scientific Monthly* 44 (March): 215–38.

—— 1940 Problems Arising from the Historic Northeastern Position of the Iroquois. Pp. 159–251 in Essays in Historical Anthropology of North America. *Smithsonian Miscellaneous Collections* 100. Washington.

—— 1941 Masked Medicine Societies of the Iroquois. Pp. 397–429 in *Annual Report of the Smithsonian Institution for 1940*. Washington.

—— 1941a Iroquois Suicide: A Study in the Stability of a Culture Pattern. *Bureau of American Ethnology Bulletin* 128(14):83–137. Washington.

—— 1941b Tonawanda Longhouse Ceremonies: Ninety Years After Lewis Henry Morgan. *Bureau of American Ethnology Bulletin* 128(15):140–65. Washington.

—— 1942 Contacts Between Iroquois Herbalism and Colonial Medicine. Pp. 503–26 in *Annual Report of the Smithsonian Institution for 1941*. Washington.

—— 1944 Simeon Gibson: Iroquois Informant, 1889–1943. *American Anthropologist*, n.s., 46(2):231–34.

—— 1946 [Obituary] Twí-yendagon' (Woodeater) Takes the Heavenly Path: On the Death of Henry Redeye (1864?–1946), Speaker of the Coldspring Seneca Longhouse. *The American Indian* 3(3):11–15.

—— 1946a An Iroquois Condolence Council for Installing Cayuga Chiefs in 1945. *Journal of the Washington Academy of Sciences* 36(4):110–27.

—— 1948 The Present status of Anthropology in Northeastern North America: A Review Article. *American Anthropologist* 50 (3): 494–515.

—— 1949 Collecting Materials for a Political History of the Six Nations. *Proceedings of the American Philosophical Society* 93(3):233–38. Philadelphia.

—— 1949a Seth Newhouse's Traditional History and Constitution of the Iroquois Confederacy. *Proceedings of the American Philosophical Society* 93(2):141–58. Philadelphia.

—— 1950 The Roll Call of the Iroquois Chiefs: A Study of a Mnemonic Cane from the Six Nations Reserve. *Smithsonian Miscellaneous Collections* 111(15):1–73. Washington.

—— 1951 Locality as a Basic Factor in the Development of Iroquois Social Structure. *Bureau of American Ethnology Bulletin* 149(3):39–54. Washington.

—— 1951a Introduction: The Concept of Locality and the Program of Iroquois Research. *Bureau of American Ethnology Bulletin* 149(1):3–12. Washington.

—— 1951b Iroquois Studies at the Mid-Century. *Proceedings of the American Philosophical Society* 95(3):296–310. Philadelphia.

—— 1953 The Iroquois Eagle Dance: An Offshoot of the Calumet Dance; with an Analysis of the Iroquois Eagle Dance and Songs, by Gertrude P. Kurath. *Bureau of American Ethnology Bullein* 156. Washington.

—— 1953a A Calendar of Manuscript Materials Relating to the History of the Six Nations or Iroquois Indians in Depositories Outside of Philadelphia, 1750–1850. *Proceedings of the American Philosophical Society* 97(5):578–95. Philadelphia.

—— 1955 Factionalism in American Indian Society. *Actes du IVe Congrès International des Sciences Anthropologiques et Ethnologiques* 2:330–40. Vienna.

—— 1957 American Indian and White Relations to 1830: Needs and Opportunities for Study. Chapel Hill: University of North Carolina Press.

—— 1960 [Review of] Mohawk Baronet: Sir William Johnson of New York, by James Thomas Flexner. *Ethnohistory* 7(3):311–17.

—— 1961 Iroquoian Culture History: A General Evaluation. *Bureau of American Ethnology Bulletin* 180(25):257–77. Washington.

—— 1962 Ethnohistory and Its Problems. *Ethnohistory* 9:(1)1–23.

——, ed. 1968 Parker on the Iroquois. Syracuse, N.Y.: University of Syracuse Press.

—— 1969 Anthropology and the University: An Inaugural Lecture. State University of New York, Albany.

—— 1971 The Iroquois in History. Pp. 129–68 in North American Indians in Historical Perspective. Eleanor B. Leacock and Nancy O. Lurie, eds. New York: Random House.

—— 1971a The New York State Wampum Collection: The Case for the Integrity of Cultural Treasures. *Proceedings of the American Philosophical Society* 115(6):437–61. Philadelphia.

—— 1972 [Obituary] Howard Sky, 1900–1971: Cayuga Faith-Keeper, Gentleman, and Interpreter of Iroquois Culture. *American Anthropologist* 74(3):758–62.

—— 1972a Foreword. Pp. xiii-xxi in Cartier's Hochelaga and the Dawson Site, by James F. Pendergast and Bruce G. Trigger. Montreal and London: McGill-Queen's University Press.

—— 1975 The Lore of the Longhouse: Myth, Ritual and Red Power. *Anthropological Quarterly* 48(3):131–47.

—— 1976 Tonawanda Reservation, 1935: The Way It Was. (Speech at the Opening of Images from the Longhouse: Paintings of Iroquois Life by Seneca Artist, Ernest Smith, 1907–1975.) Rochester Museum and Science Center, Rochester, N.Y.

—— 1978 Northern Iroquoian Culture Patterns. Pp. 296–321 in Northeast. Bruce G. Trigger, vol. ed. Handbook of North American Indians, Vol. 15. William C. Sturtevant, gen. ed. Washington: Smithsonian Institution.

—— 1978a "Aboriginally Yours," Jesse J. Cornplanter, Hah-Yonh-Wonh-Ish, The Snipe, Seneca, 1889–1957. Pp. 177–95 in American Indian Intellectuals. Margot Liberty, ed. 1976 Proceedings of the American Ethnological Society. Robert F. Spencer, gen. ed. St. Paul: West Publishing Co.

Fenton, William N. and Merle H. Deardorff 1943 The Last Passenger Pigeon Hunts of the Cornplanter Senecas. *Journal of the Washington Academy of Sciences* 33 (10): 289–315. Washington.

Fenton, William N. and John Gulick eds. 1961 Symposium on Cherokee and Iroquois Culture. *Bureau of American Ethnology Bulletin* 180. Washington.

Fenton, William N. and Gertrude P. Kurath 1951 The Feast of the Dead, or Ghost Dance, at Six Nations Reserve, Canada. *Bureau of American Ethnology Bulletin* 149(7):143–65. Washington.

Fenton, William N. and Elisabeth Tooker 1978 Mohawk. Pp. 466–80 in Northeast. Bruce G. Trigger, vol. ed. Handbook of North American Indians, Vol. 15. William C. Sturtevant, gen. ed. Washington: Smithsonian Institution.

Fey, Harold E. and D'Arcy McNickle 1970 Indians and Other Americans: Two Ways of Life Meet. Rev. ed. New York: Harper and Row.

Fillmore, Charles J. 1971 Types of Lexical Information. Pp. 370–92 in Semantics, An Interdisciplinary Reader in Philosophy, Linguistics and Psychology. D. D. Steinberg and L. A. Jakobovits, eds. Cambridge, Eng.: Cambridge University Press.

—— 1977 The Case for Case Reopened. Pp. 59–81 in Grammatical Relations, Vol. 8. P. Cole and J. M. Sadock, eds. New York: Academic Press.

Finlayson, William D. 1977 The Saugeen Culture: A Middle Woodland Manifestation in Southwestern Ontario. *Canada. National Museum of Man, Mercury Series. Archaeological Survey* 61. Ottawa.

Finlayson, William D., John Dawkin and Grant Tripp 1977 A Preliminary Report of Archaeological Investigations at the New Toronto International Airport 1976. *Canada. National Museum of Man, Archaeological Survey*. Ottawa.

Fischer, David H. 1970 Historians' Fallacies. New York: Harper and Row.

Fiske, John 1900 The Discovery of North America. 2 vols. Boston and New York: Houghton, Mifflin and Company.

Fitzhugh, William A. 1972 Environmental Archaeology and Cultural Systems in Hamilton Inlet, Labrador: A Survey of the Central Labrador Coast from 3000 B.C. to the Present. *Smithsonian Contributions to Anthropology* 16. Washington.

—— 1976 Paleoeskimo Occupations of the Labrador Coast. *Society for American Archaeology Memoir* 31:103–18. Washington.

Fogelson, Raymond D., and Paul Kutsche 1961 Cherokee Economic Cooperatives: The Gadugi. Pp. 84–121 in Symposium on Cherokee and Iroquois Culture. William N. Fenton and John Gulick, eds. *Bureau of American Ethnology Bulletin* 180. Washington.

Follett, Harrison C. 1954 An Archaeological History of Cayuga County. *The Archaeological Society of Central New York Bulletin* 9(3):40–42.

Foster, Michael K. 1974 From the Earth to Beyond the Sky: An Ethnographic Approach to Four Longhouse Speech Events. *Canada. National Museum of Man, Ethnology Division, Mercury Series Paper* 20. Ottawa.

—— 1977 The Path, the Fire and the Chain: The Function of Channel in Eighteenth-Century Iroquois-White Councils. (Paper read at the 1977 Annual Meeting of the American Anthropological Association, Houston, Texas. Manuscript in Foster's possession.)

—— 1978 The Recovery and Translation of Native Speeches Accompanying Ancient Iroquois-White Treaties. *Canada. National Museum of Man, Ethnology Division, Canadian Studies Report* 5e-f. Ottawa.

—— 1979 Kindling the Fire at Iroquois-White Councils: An Exercise in Upstreaming. (Manuscript in Foster's possession.)

Freilich, Morris 1958 Cultural Persistence Among the Modern Iroquois. *Anthropos* 53(3–4):473–83.

Friends, Society of 1840 The Case of the Seneca Indians in the State of New York, Illustrated by Facts. Philadelphia: Merrihew and Thompson.

Frisch, Jack A. 1970 Revitalization, Nativism, and Tribalism Among the St. Regis Mohawks. (Unpublished Ph.D. Dissertation in Anthropology, Indiana University, Bloomington.)

Funk, Robert E. 1976 Recent Contributions to Hudson Valley Prehistory. *New York State Museum and Science Service Memoir* 22. Albany.

Gamst, F. C. 1969 The Qemant. New York: Holt, Rinehart and Winston.

Gearing, Frederick O. 1962 Priests and Warriors: Social Structures for Cherokee Politics in the Eighteenth Century. *American Anthropological Association Memoir* 93.

Gendron, François 1868 Quelques particularitéz du pays des Hurons en la Nouvelle France, remarquées par le Sieur Gendron, Docteur en Médecine qui a demeuré dans ce pays-là fort longtemps [1660]. I. B. deRocoles, ed. Albany: J. Munsell.

Goddard, Ives 1978 Eastern Algonquian Languages. Pp. 70–77 in Northeast. Bruce G. Trigger, vol. ed. Handbook of North American Indians, Vol. 15. William C. Sturtevant, gen. ed. Washington: Smithsonian Institution.

Goldenweiser, Alexander A. 1913 The Clan and Maternal Family of the Iroquois League. *American Anthropologist* 15:696–97.

—— 1915 Functions of Women in Iroquois Society. *American Anthropologist* 17(2):376–77.

—— 1916 [Review of] The Constitution of the Five Nations, by Arthur C. Parker. *American Anthropologist* 18(3):431–36.

—— 1918 The Diffusion of Clans in North America. *American Anthropologist* 20:118–20.

Gollin, Gillian L. 1967 Moravians in Two Worlds: A Study of Changing Communities. New York: Columbia University Press.

Goodenough, Ward H. 1956 Componential Analysis and the Study of Meaning. *Language* 32(2):195–216.

Gookin, Daniel 1970 Historical Collections of the Indians in New England [1792]. Jeffrey H. Fiske, ed. [No place]: Towtaid.

Gordon, Bryan H. C. 1975 Of Men and Herds in Barrenland Prehistory. *Canada. National Museum of Man, Mercury Series. Archaeological Survey Paper 28.* Ottawa.

—— 1976 Migod—8,000 Years of Barrenland Prehistory. *Canada. National Museum of Man, Mercury Series. Archaeological Survey Paper 56.* Ottawa.

Graham, Elizabeth 1975 Medicine Man to Missionary: Missionaries as Agents of Change Among the Indians of Southern Ontario, 1784–1867. Toronto: P. Martin Assoc.

Grayson, Donald K. 1970 Statistical Inference and Northeastern Adena. *American Antiquity* 35(1):102–4.

—— 1974 The Riverhaven No. 2 Vertebrate Fauna: Comments on Methods in Faunal Analysis and on Aspects of the Subsistence Potential of Prehistoric New York. *Man in the Northeast,* no. 8:23–39.

Griffin, James B. 1944 The Iroquois in American Prehistory. *Papers of the Michigan Academy of Science, Arts and Letters* 29:357–74. Ann Arbor.

Gruber, Jeffrey S. 1967 Functions of the Lexicon in Formal Descriptive Grammars. Technical Memorandum TM 3770/000/00. Santa Monica: Systems Development Corp.

Hale, Horatio E. 1883 The Iroquois Book of Rites. (Brinton's Library of Aboriginal American Literature 2) Philadelphia: D. G. Brinton. (Reprinted: University of Toronto Press, Toronto, 1965.)

Halevy, Elie 1961 England in 1815. London: A History of the English People in the Nineteenth Century. Translated from the French by E. I. Watkin. 6 vols. New York: Barnes and Noble.

Harlow, Vincent T., and Frederick Madden 1953 British Colonial Development, 1774–1834: Select Documents. Oxford: Clarendon Press.

Hatzan, A. Leon 1927 The True Story of Hiawatha, and History of the Six Nations Indians. Toronto: McClelland and Stewart.

Hauptman, Laurence M. 1979 Alice Lee Jemison: Seneca Political Activist, 1901–1964. *The Indian Historian* 12:15–22.

—— 1979a The Iroquois School of Art: Arthur C. Parker and the Seneca Arts Project, 1935–1941. *New York History* 40:282–312.

—— 1980 Raw Deal: The Iroquois View the Indian Reorganization Act of 1934. Studies on Iroquoian Culture. Nancy Bonvillain, ed. *Occasional Papers in Northeastern Anthropology* 6. Rindge, New Hampshire.

Heidenreich, Conrad E. 1971 Huronia: A History and Geography of the Huron Indians, 1600–1650. Toronto: McClelland and Stewart.

────── 1977 Ethnohistory: The Way It Should Be Written. *Queen's Quarterly* 84:627–32.

Henning, Charles L. 1898 The Origin of the Confederacy of the Five Nations. *Proceedings of the American Association for the Advancement of Science* 47:477–80. Salem, Mass.

Herskovits, Melville J. 1948 Man and His Works. New York: Alfred A. Knopf.

Hertzberg, Hazel W. 1966 The Great Tree and the Longhouse: The Culture of the Iroquois. New York: Macmillan.

Hewitt, J. N. B. 1895 The Iroquoian Concept of the Soul. *Journal of American Folk-Lore* 8(29):107–16.

────── 1902 Orenda and a Definition of Religion. *American Anthropologist,* n.s., 4(1):33–46.

────── 1903–1928 Iroquoian Cosmology. Pp. 127–339 in Vol. 21 and pp. 449–819 in Vol. 43 of the *Annual Reports of the Bureau of American Ethnology for the Years 1899–1900* and *1925–1926*. Washington.

────── 1917 [Reviews of] The Constitution of the Five Nations, by Arthur C. Parker; Traditional History of the Confederacy of the Six Nations, by Duncan C. Scott; and Civil, Religious and Mourning Councils and Ceremonies of Adoption of the New York Indians, by William Beauchamp. *American Anthropologist* 19(3):429–38.

────── 1920 A Constitutional League of Peace in the Stone Age of America: The League of the Iroquois and Its Constitution. Pp. 527–45 in *Annual Report of the Smithsonian Institution for 1918*. Washington.

────── 1933 Status of Women in Iroquois Polity Before 1784. Pp. 475–88 in *Annual Report of the Board of Regents of the Smithsonian Institution for 1932*. Washington.

Hewitt, J. N. B., and William N. Fenton 1944 The Requickening Address of the Iroquois Condolence Council. *Journal of the Washington Academy of Sciences* 34(3):65–85.

────── 1945 Some Mnemonic Pictographs Relating to the Iroquois Condolence Council. *Journal of the Washington Academy of Sciences* 35(10):301–15.

Hickerson, Harold 1962 The Southwestern Chippewa: An Ethnohistorical Study. *Memoirs of the American Anthropological Association* 92. Menasha, Wis.

────── 1970 The Chippewa and Their Neighbors: A Study in Ethnohistory. New York: Holt, Rinehart and Winston.

Hill, Cephas D., and William N. Fenton 1935 Reviving Indian Arts Among the Seneca. *Indians at Work* 2(21):13–15.

Hirsch, Harry M. 1936 New York State Indians. *Social Welfare Bulletin* 7:1.

Hodge, Frederick W., ed. 1907–1910 Handbook of American Indians North of Mexico. 2 vols. *Bureau of American Ethnology Bulletin* 30. Washington. (Reprinted: Rowman and Littlefield, New York, 1971.)

Horsford, Eben N., ed. 1887 Zeisberger's Indian Territory. Cambridge, Mass.: John Wilson and Son.

Hough, Franklin B. 1853 A History of St. Lawrence and Franklin Counties, New York, from the Earliest Period to the Present Time. Albany: Little and Company.

Howison, John 1821 Sketches of Upper Canada . . . to Which are Added Practical Details for the Information of Emigrants of Every Class; and Some Recollections of the United States of America. Edinburgh: Oliver and Boyd.

Hubbard, William 1848 A General History of New England from the Discovery to MDCLXXX. *Massachusetts Historical Society Collections*, 2d ser., Vol. 5.

———— 1865 The History of the Indian Wars in New England from the First Settlement to the Termination of the War with King Philip, in 1677. Samuel G. Drake, ed. 2 vols, Roxbury, Mass.: W.E. Woodward. (Reprinted: Kraus, New York, 1969.)

Hunt, George T. 1940 The Wars of the Iroquois: A Study in Intertribal Trade Relations. Madison: University of Wisconsin Press.

Hunt, William 1873 A History of the English Church (half title). London.

Innis, Harold A. 1956 The Fur Trade in Canada: An Introduction to Canadian Economic History [1930]. 2d ed. Toronto: University of Toronto Press.

JP = Sir William Johnson 1921–1965 The Papers of Sir William Johnson. James Sullivan et al., eds. 15 vols. Albany: University of the State of New York.

JR = Thwaites, Reuben G., ed. 1896–1901 The Jesuit Relations and Allied Documents: Travel and Explorations of the Jesuit Missionaries in New France, 1610–1791; the Original French, Latin, and Italian Texts, with English Translations and Notes. 73 vols. Cleveland: Burrows Brothers. (Reprinted: Pageant, New York, 1959.)

Jameson, J. Franklin, ed. 1909 Narratives of New Netherland, 1609–1664. New York: Charles Scribner's Sons. (Reprinted: Barnes and Noble, New York, 1959.)

Jennings, Francis 1968 Glory, Death, and Transfiguration: The Susquehannock Indians in the Seventeenth Century. *Proceedings of the American Philosophical Society* 112(1):15–53. Philadelphia.

———— 1975 The Invasion of America: Indians, Colonialism, and the Cant of Conquest. Chapel Hill: University of North Carolina Press.

Johnston, Charles M., ed. 1964 The Valley of the Six Nations: A Collection of Documents on the Indian Lands of the Grand River. Toronto: University of Toronto Press.

Johnston, Richard B. 1968 The Archaeology of the Serpent Mounds Site. *Royal Ontario Museum, Art and Archaeology Division Occasional Paper* 10. Toronto.

———— 1968a Archaeology of Rice Lake, Ontario Ottawa. *National Museum of Canada Anthropology Paper* 19. Ottawa.

Jones, Arthur E. 1909 "8Endake Ehen" or Old Huronia. *5th Report of the Bureau of Archives for the Province of Ontario for 1908*. Toronto.

Jones, William H. S. 1951 The Story of St. Catherine's College, Cambridge. Cambridge: The University Press.

Jordan, Richard 1975 Pollen Diagrams from Hamilton Inlet, Central Labrador, and Their Environmental Implications for the Northern Maritime Archaic. *Arctic Anthropology* 7(2):92–116.

Katz, Jerrold J. 1967 Recent Issues in Semantic Theory. *Foundations of Language* 3(2):124–94.

Kellaway, William 1961 The New England Company 1649–1776: Missionary Society to the American Indians. New York: Barnes and Noble.

Kelly, David G. Jr. 1975 Indian Title: The Rights of American Natives in Lands They Have Occupied Since Time Immemorial. *Columbia Law Review* 75:654–86.

Kelly, Lawrence C. 1975 The Indian Reorganization Act: The Dream and the Reality. *Pacific Historical Review* 44(3):291–312.

Kennedy, Clyde C. 1967 Preliminary Report on the Morrison's Island–6 Site. *Canada. National Museum of Man Bulletin* 206: 100–125. Ottawa.

—— n.d. The Allumette Island–1(AL1) Site. *Canada. National Museum of Man, Archaeological Survey* (Archives). Ottawa.

Kent, Donald H. 1974 Iroquois Indians. New York: Garland.

Kenyon, Walter 1959 The Inverhuron Site. *Royal Ontario Museum, Art and Archaeology Division Occasional Paper* 10. Toronto.

—— 1968 The Miller Site. *Royal Ontario Museum, Art and Archaeology Division, Occasional Paper* 14. Toronto.

Kimball, James 1878 The Exploration of the Merrimack River, 1638, by Order of the General Court of Massachusetts, With a Plan of the Same. *Historical Collections of the Essex Institute* 14(3):153–71. Salem, Mass.

Knowles, Nathaniel 1940 The Torture of Captives by the Indians of Eastern North America. *Proceedings of the American Philosophical Society* 82(2):151–225. Philadelphia.

Kraus, B.S. 1944 Acculturation: A New Approach to the Iroquoian Problem. *American Antiquity* 9(3): 302–18.

Kurath, Gertrude (Prokosch) 1961 Effects of Environment on Cherokee-Iroquois Ceremonialism, Music and Dance. Pp. 173–95 in Symposium on Cherokee and Iroquois Culture. William N. Fenton and John Gulick, eds. *Bureau of American Ethnology Bulletin* 180. Washington.

Lafitau, Joseph-François 1724 Moeurs des sauvages amériquains, comparées aux moeurs des premiers temps. 2 vols. in 1. Paris: Saugrain l'aîné.

—— 1974–1977 Customs of the American Indians Compared with the Customs of Primitive Times. William N. Fenton and Elizabeth L. Moore, eds. and trans. 2 vols. Toronto: The Champlain Society.

Landon, Fred 1922 The Diary of Benjamin Lundy. Pp. 110–33 in *Papers and Records, Ontario Historical Society*. Toronto.

Landy, David 1978 Tuscarora Among the Iroquois. Pp. 518–24 in Northeast. Bruce G. Trigger, vol. ed. Handbook of North American Indians, Vol. 15. William C. Sturtevant, gen. ed. Washington: Smithsonian Institution.

Latourelle, René 1966 Jean de Brébeuf. Pp. 121–26 in Dictionary of Canadian Biography, Vol. 1. Toronto: University of Toronto Press.

Leacock, Eleanor B. 1954 The Montagnais "Hunting Territory" and the Fur Trade. *Memoirs of the American Anthropological Association* 78. Menasha, Wis.

Leacock, Eleanor B. and Nancy O. Lurie, eds. 1971 North American Indians in Historical Perspective. New York: Random House.

Le Clercq, Chrétien 1691 Premier établissment de la foy dans la Nouvelle-France. 2 vols. Paris: A. Auroy.

Leder, Lawrence H., *see* Livingston, Robert

Lenig, Donald 1965 The Oak Hill Horizon and Its Relation to the Development of Five Nations Iroquois Culture. *Researches and Transactions of the New York State Archaeological Association* 15(1):1–114.

Lescarbot, Marc 1907–1914 The History of New France [1618]. W. L. Grant, trans. 3 vols. Toronto: The Champlain Society.

Lévesque, René, F. Fitz Osborne, and James V. Wright 1964 Le gisement de Batiscan: Notes sur des vestiges laissés par une peuplade de culture sylvicole inférieure dans la vallée du Saint-Laurent. *Canada. Musée National Études Anthroplogiques* 6. Ottawa.

Linton, Ralph 1940 Acculturation in Seven American Indian Tribes. New York, London: D. Appleton-Century Co.

Livingston, Robert 1956 The Livingston Indian Records, 1666–1723. Lawrence H. Leder, ed. Gettysburgh: Pennsylvania Historical Association.

Loewenthal, John 1921 Irokesische Wirtschaftsaltertümer. Eine Untersuchung zur Geschichte der ersten Entdeckung Amerikas A.D. ± 1000. *Zeitschrift für Ethnologie* 52:171–233.

Lounsbury, Floyd G. 1953 Oneida Verb Morphology. *Yale University Publications in Anthropology* 48. New Haven, Conn.

—— 1956 A Semantic Analysis of the Pawnee Kinship Usage. *Language* 32(1):158–94.

—— 1961 Iroquois-Cherokee Linguistic Relations. *Bureau of American Ethnology Bulletin* 180(2):11–17. Washington.

—— 1964 The Structural Analysis of Kinship Semantics. Pp. 1073–93 in Proceedings of the 9th International Congress of Linguists. Horace G. Lunt, ed. Cambridge, Mass., 1962. The Hague: Mouton.

—— 1964a The Formal Analysis of Crow- and Omaha-Type Kinship Terminologies. Pp. 351–93 in Explorations in Cultural Anthropology: Essays in Honor of George P. Murdock. Ward H. Goodenough, ed. New York: McGraw-Hill.

—— 1978 Iroquoian Languages. Pp. 334–43 in Northeast. Bruce G. Trigger, vol. ed. Handbook of North American Indians, Vol. 15. William C. Sturtevant, gen. ed. Washington: Smithsonian Institution.

Lubbock, John 1870 The Origin of Civilization and the Primitive Condition of Man; Mental and Social Condition of Savages. London: Longmans, Green.

Lurie, Nancy O. 1959 Indian Cultural Adjustment to European Civilization. Pp. 33–60 in Seventeenth Century America: Essays in Colonial History. James M. Smith, ed. Chapel Hill: University of North Carolina Press. (Reprinted: W.W. Norton, New York, 1972.)

Lydekker, John W. 1938 The Faithful Mohawks. New York: Macmillan; Cambridge, Eng.: The University Press.

MBPP = Maris Bryant Pierce Papers. Buffalo and Erie County Historical Society. Buffalo, New York.

MHSC = Massachusetts Historical Society 1792–1915 Collections. 10 series. 70 vols. Cambridge and Boston: The Society.

McCall, Daniel F. 1964 Africa in Time-Perspective. Boston: Boston University Press.

McCallum, James D., ed. 1932 The Letters of Eleazar Wheelock's Indians. Hanover, N.H.: Dartmouth College Publications.

McCawley, James 1972 Syntactic and Logical Arguments for Semantic Structures. Bloomington: Indiana University Linguistic Club.

MacDonald, George F. and Robert I. Inglis 1976 The Dig. *Canada. National Museum of Man*. Ottawa.

McGhee, Robert 1978 Canadian Arctic Prehistory. *Canada. National Museum of Man*. Ottawa.

McGhee, Robert and James A. Tuck 1975 An Archaic Sequence from the Strait of Belle Isle, Labrador. *Canada. National Museum of Man, Mercury Series. Archaeological Survey Paper* 34. Ottawa.

McIlwraith, Thomas F. 1930 The Progress of Anthropology in Canada. *The Canadian Historical Review* 11:132–50.

McLennan, J.F. 1865 Primitive Marriage. Edinburgh: Adam and Charles Black.

MacNeish, Richard S. 1952 Iroquois Pottery Types: A Technique for the Study of Iroquois Prehistory. *Anthropological Series 31, National Museum of Canada Bulletin* 124. Ottawa.

—— 1976 The In Situ Iroquois Revisited and Rethought. Pp. 79–98 in Cultural Change and Continuity. New York: Academic Press.

Malone, Dumas 1970 Jefferson the President: First Term, 1801–1805. Jefferson and His Time, Vol. 4. Boston: Little, Brown and Company.

Manley, Henry S. 1947 Buying Buffalo from the Indians. Pp. 313–29 in *Proceedings of the New York State Historical Association 45. New York History* 28. Cooperstown.

Marois, Roger J.M. et René Ribes 1975 Indices de Manifestations Culturelles de l'Archaïque: la Région de Trois-Rivières. *Canada. National Museum of Man, Mercury Series. Archaeological Survey Paper* 41. Ottawa.

Massachusetts Archives 326 vols. Secretary of the Commonwealth's Office, Boston.

Mellor, G. R. 1951 British Imperial Trusteeship, 1783–1850. London: Faber and Faber.

Michelson, Karin 1981 A Philological Investigation into Seventeenth-Century Mohawk. *International Journal of American Linguistics* 47(2):91–102.

Michelson, Truman 1930 Contributions to Fox Ethnology—II. *Bureau of American Ethnology Bulletin* 95. Washington.

Mitchell, Donald H. 1971 Archaeology of the Gulf of Georgia Area: A Natural Region and its Culture Types. *Syesis* 4.

Moore, Jacob B. 1824 Annals of the Town of Concord, in the County of Merrimack, and the State of New-Hampshire, from its First Settlement, in the Year 1726, to the Year 1823. With Several Biographical Sketches. To Which is Added, A Memoir of the Penacook Indians. Concord.

Morgan, Edmund S., ed. 1964 The Founding of Massachusetts: Historians and the Sources. Indianapolis, Indiana: The Bobbs-Merrill Company.

Morgan, Lewis H. 1851 League of the Ho-dé-no-sau-nee or Iroquois. Rochester, N. Y.: Sage; New York: Newman. (Reprinted as League of the Iroquois, Corinth Books, New York, 1962.)

—— 1859 The Indian Method of Bestowing and Changing Names. *Proceedings of the American Association for the Advancement of Science* 13: 340–42.

—— 1871 Systems of Consanguinity and Affinity of the Human Family. *Smithsonian Contributions to Knowledge* 17. Washington.

—— 1877 Ancient Society or Researches in the Lines of Human Progress from Savagery Through Barbarism to Civilization. New York: Henry Holt. (Reprinted: World Publishing Company, Cleveland and New York, 1963; Gordon Press, New York, 1976.)

—— 1881 Houses and House-life of the American Aborigines. (Contributions to North American Ethnology 4.) Washington: U.S. Geological and Georgraphical Survey of the Rocky Mountain Region.

—— 1901 League of the Ho-dé-no-sau-nee or Iroquois [1851]. Herbert M. Lloyd, ed. 2 vols. New York: Dodd Mead. (Reprinted: Human Relations Area Files, New Haven, Conn. 1954.)

Morison, Samuel E. 1972 Samuel de Champlain: Father of New France. Boston: Little, Brown and Company.

Murdock, George P. 1934 Our Primitive Contemporaries. New York: Macmillan.

NEC = New England Company Records. Guildhall Library, London, Eng.

NYA = New York Agency 1829–1880 Letters Received by the Office of Indian Affairs. National Archives, Washington.

NYCD = O'Callaghan, Edmund B., ed. 1853–1887 Documents Relative to the Colonial History of the State of New York; Procured in Holland, England and France, by John R. Brodhead. 15 vols. Albany: Weed, Parsons.

NYSL = New York State Library, Albany, N.Y.

Naroll, Raoul 1969 The Causes of the Fourth Iroquois War. *Ethnohistory* 16:51–81.

Newhouse, Seth 1880 Constitution of the Five Nations Indian Confederation. (A 16-page manuscript.) Manuscript 1359 in Bureau of American Ethnology Archives, Smithsonian Institution, Washington.

—— [1885] [Cosmogony of De-ka-na-wi-das' Government of the Iroquois Confederacy: The Original Literal Historical Narratives of the Iroquois Confederacy.] (Manuscript in Public Archives of Canada. Folder MG19F.26. Ottawa.)

Nichols, Harvey 1967 Central Canadian Palynology and Its Relevance to Northwestern Europe in the Late Quaternary Period. *Paleobotany and Palynology* 2:231–43. Amsterdam.

—— 1967a The Post Glacial History of Vegetation and Climate at Ennadai Lake, Keewaten and Lynn Lake, Manitoba, Canada. *Eiszeitalter und Gegenwart* 18:176–97. Ohringen.

—— 1967b Pollen Diagrams from Sub-arctic Central Canada. *Science* 155: 1665–68.

—— 1974 Arctic North American Paleoecology: The Recent History of Vegetation and Climate Deduced from Polen Analysis. Pp. 637–67 in Arctic and Alpine Environments. Jack D. Ives and Roger G. Barry, eds. London: Methuen.

Noble, William C. 1969 Some Social Implications of the Iroquois 'In Situ' Theory. *Ontario Archaeology* 13:16–28.

—— 1975 Van Besien (AfHd-2): A Study in Glen Meyer Development. *Ontario Archaeology* 24. Toronto.

Noble, William C. and Ian T. Kenyon 1972 Porteous (AgHb-1): A Probable Early Glen Meyer Village in Brant County, Ontario. *Ontario Archaeology* 17. Toronto.

Noon, John A. 1949 Law and Government of the Grand River Iroquois. *Viking Fund Publications in Anthropology* 12. New York.

Norton, John 1970 The Journal of Major John Norton, 1816. Carl F. Klinck and James J. Talman, eds. Toronto: The Champlain Society.

O'Callaghan, Edmund B., ed. 1849–1851 Documentary History of the State of New York. 4 vols. Albany: Weed, Parsons. *See also* NYCD.

O'Toole Francis J., and Thomas N. Tureen 1971 State Power and the Passamaquoddy Tribe: "A Gross National Hypocrisy." *Maine Law Review* 23(1):1–39.

Otterbein, Keith F. 1964 Why the Iroquois Won: An Analysis of Iroquois Military Tactics. *Ethnohistory* 11:56–63.

PAC = Public Archives of Canada. Haldimand Papers. Colonial Office Series, Ottawa, Canada.

PAO = Public Records and Archives of Ontario 1823–1834 Strachan Papers. Toronto, Canada.

PP = Parker Papers 1926–1941 Arthur C. Parker Collection. Rush Rhees Library, University of Rochester, Rochester, N.Y.

PRO = Public Records Office. Colonial Office Series. Barbados, United Kingdom.

Parker, Arthur C. 1910 Iroquois Uses of Maize and Other Food Plants. *New York State Museum Bulletin* 144(482):5–113. Albany.

—— 1913 The Code of Handsome Lake, the Seneca Prophet. *New York State Museum Bulletin* 163. Albany.

—— 1916 The Constitution of the Five Nations. *New York State Museum Bulletin* 184:7–158. Albany.

—— 1916a The Origin of the Iroquois as Suggested by Their Archaeology. *American Anthropologist*, n.s., 18(4): 479–507.

—— 1918 The Constitution of the Five Nations: A Reply. *American Anthropologist* 20(1):120–24.

—— 1922 The Archaeological History of New York State. 2 Pts. *New York State Museum Bulletins* 235–238. Albany.

—— 1926 An Analytical History of the Seneca Indians. *Researches and Transactions of the New York State Archaeological Association* 6(1–5). Rochester. (Reprinted: I.J. Friedman, Port Washington, Long Island, N.Y., 1967.)

—— 1936 A Museum Sponsors an Indian Arts Project. *Social Welfare Bulletin* 7:12–14.

Parkman, Francis 1867 The Jesuits in North America in the Seventeenth Century. Boston: Little, Brown.

Parman, Donald L. 1976 The Navajos and the New Deal. New Haven: Yale University Press.

Pearce, R.H. 1965 The Savages of America. Baltimore: Johns Hopkins University Press.

Penacock Papers 1832 *Collections of the New Hampshire Historical Society* 2:212–24. Concord, New Hampshire.

Pendergast, James F. 1966 Three Prehistoric Iroquois Components in Eastern Ontario: The Salem, Grays Creek, and Beckstead Sites. *Anthropological Series 73, National Museum of Canada Bulletin* 208. Ottawa.

Pfeiffer, Susan 1977 The Skeletal Biology of Archaic Populations of the Grant Lakes Region. *Canada. National Museum of Man, Mercury Series* 64. Ottawa.

Philp, Kenneth R. 1977 John Collier's Crusade for Indian Reform, 1920–1954. Tucson: University of Arizona Press.

Pickering Papers 1791 Papers of Timothy Pickering. *Massachusetts Historical Society* 60.

Pilling, James 1888 Bibliography of the Iroquoian Languages. *Bureau of American Ethnology Bulletin* 6. Washington.

Potts, Robert 1855 Liber Cantabrigiensis: An Account of the Aids Afforded to Poor Students, The Encouragements Offered to Diligent Students, and the Rewards Conferred on Successful Students, in the University of Cambridge; To Which is Prefixed a Collection of Maxims, Aphorisms, and Designed for the Use of Learners. Cambridge, Eng.: University Press.

Pound, Cuthbert W. 1922 Nationals Without a Nation: The New York State Tribal Indians. *Columbia Law Review* 22(2):97–102.

Pratt, Peter P. 1976 Archaeology of the Oneida Iroquois. *Occasional Publications in Northeastern Anthropology* 1. George's Mills, N.H.

Price, Monroe 1973 Law and the American Indian: Readings, Notes and Cases. New York: Bobbs-Merrill Company, Inc.

Provincial Papers of New Hampshire 1891 [Isaac Bradley Deposition 1737.] 19:319–20.

Quain, Buell 1937 The Iroquois. Pp. 240–81 in Cooperation and Competition Among Primitive Peoples. Margaret Mead, ed. New York: McGraw-Hill.

RIC = Records of the Indian Committee. Haviland Records Room, Society of Friends Record Committee, New York.

Radisson, Pierre E. 1967 The Explorations of Pierre Esprit Radisson. Arthur T. Adams, ed. Minneapolis: Ross and Haines.

Ramsden, Peter 1976 Rocky Ridge: A Stratified Archaic Site Near Inverhuron, Ontario. *Ontario Ministry of Culture and Recreation, Historical Planning and Research Branch* 7.

——— 1977 A Refinement of Some Aspects of Huron Ceramic Analysis. *Canada.National Museum of Man, Mercury Series, Archaeological Survey of Canada Paper.* 63. Ottawa.

Randle, Martha C. 1951 Iroquois Women, Then and Now. Pp. 167–80 in Symposium on Local Diversity in Iroquois Culture. William N. Fenton, ed. *Bureau of American Ethnology Bulletin* 149. Washington.

——— 1952 Psychological Types from Iroquois Folktales. *Journal of American Folk-Lore* 65(255):13–22.

Reid, C.S. 1975 The Boys Site and the Early Ontario Iroquois Tradition. *Canada. National Museum of Man, Mercury Series* 42. Ottawa.

Ricciardelli, Alex F. 1961 Factionalism at Oneida, An Iroquois Indian Community. (Unpublished Ph.D. Dissertation in Anthropology, University of Pennsylvania, Philadelphia.)

Richards, Cara E. 1957 Matriarchy or Mistake: The Role of Iroquois Women Through Time. Pp. 36–45 in Cultural Stability and Cultural Change. Verne F. Ray, ed. *Proceedings of the 1957 Annual Meeting of the American Ethnology Society.*

—— 1967 Huron and Iroquois Residence Patterns, 1600–1650. Pp. 51–56 in Iroquois Culture, History and Prehistory: Proceedings of the 1965 Conference on Iroquois Research. Elisabeth Tooker, ed. Albany: New York State Museum and Science Service.

—— 1974 Onondaga Women: Among the Liberated. Pp. 401–19 in Many Sisters: Women in Cross-Cultural Perspective. Carolyn J. Matthiasson, ed. New York: Free Press.

Rickard, Clinton 1973 Fighting Tuscarora: The Autobiography of Chief Clinton Rickard. Barbara Graymont, ed. Syracuse: Syracuse University Press.

Ridley, Frank 1954 The Frank Bay Site, Lake Nipissing, Ontario. *American Antiquity* 20(1):40–50.

—— 1958 The Boys and Barrie Sites. *Ontario Archaeological Association Publication* 4. Toronto.

Ritchie, William A. 1944 The Pre-Iroquoian Occupations of New York State. *Rochester Museum of Arts and Sciences Memoir* 1. Rochester, N.Y.

—— 1949 An Archaeological Survey of the Trent Waterway in Ontario, Canada and its Significance for New York State Prehistory. *Researches and Transactions of the New York State Archaeological Association* 12(1). Rochester, N.Y.

—— 1949a The Bell-Philhower Site, Sussex County, New Jersey. *Indian Historical Society, Prehistory Research Series* 3(2). Indianapolis.

—— 1952 The Chance Horizon: An Early Stage of Mohawk Iroquois Cultural Development. *New York State Museum and Science Service Circular* 29. Albany.

—— 1955 The Northeastern Archaic—A Review. mimeo.

—— 1965 The Archaeology of New York State. Garden City, N.Y.: Natural History Press.

—— 1969 The Archaeology of Martha's Vineyard: A Framework for the Prehistory of Southern New England; A Study in Coastal Ecology and Adaptation. Garden City, N.Y.: Natural History Press.

—— 1971 A Typology and Nomenclature for New York Projectile Points. *New York State Museum and Science Service Bulletin* 384 (revised edition). Albany

Ritchie, William A., and Don W. Dragoo 1960 The Eastern Dispersal of Adena. *New York State Museum and Science Service Bulletin* 379. Albany.

Ritchie, William A. and Robert E. Funk 1973 Aboriginal Settlement Patterns in the Northeast. *New York State Museum and Science Service Memoir* 20. Albany.

Ritzenthaler, Robert E. 1950 The Oneida Indians of Wisconsin. *Bulletin of the Public Museum of the City of Milwaukee* 19(1). Milwaukee.

Robinson, W. Stitt 1951 A Method for Chronologically Ordering Archaeological Deposits. *American Antiquity* 16(4): 293–301.

Rouse, Irving 1958 The Inference of Migrations from Anthropological Evidence. Pp. 63–68 in Migrations in New World Culture History. Raymond H. Thompson, ed. *University of Arizona Social Science Bulletin* 27.

SNAM = Six Nations Agency Minutes 1847–1924 Minutes of the Six Nations Councils. Six Nations Indian Agency Archives, Brantford, Ontario.

SNCM = Six Nations Chiefs Minutes 1880–1924 Minutes of the Six Nations Councils. Ohsweken, Ontario.

SNIO = Six Nations Indian Office Archives Chisholm File, New England Company Reports, Six Nations v. New England Company File, Brantford, Ontario.

SNRC = Seneca Nation, Records of Council. Allegany and Cattaraugus Reservations, New York.

Sagard-Théodat, Gabriel 1866 Histoire du Canada et voyages que les Frères Mineurs recollects y ont faicts pour la conversion des infidèles depuis l'an 1615. Avec un dictionnaire de la langue huronne. 4 vols. Paris: E. Tross.

Salisbury, Richard F. 1973 Economic Anthropology. *Annual Review of Anthropology* 2: 85–94.

Sanger, David 1975 Culture Change as an Adaptive Process in the Maine-Maritimes Region. *Arctic Anthropology* 12(2):60–75.

Schoolcraft, Henry R., comp. 1851–1857 Historical and Statistical Information Respecting the History, Condition, and Prospects of the Indian Tribes of the United States. 6 vols. Philadelphia: Lippincott, Grambo.

Scott, Duncan C., ed. 1912 Traditional History of the Confederacy of the Six Nations, Prepared by a Committee of the Chiefs. *Transactions of the Royal Society of Canada*, 3d ser., Vol. 5(2):195–246. Ottawa.

Sheldon, George 1895 Pocumtuck, 1636–1886. A History of Deerfield, Massachusetts: The Times When the People by Whom it was Settled, Unsettled, and Resettled: With a Special Study of the Indian Wars in the Connecticut Valley. 2 vols. Deerfield, Mass.

Shimony, Annemarie A. 1961 Conservatism Among the Iroquois at the Six Nations Reserve. *Yale University Publications in Anthropology* 65. New Haven, Conn.

Shurtleff, Nathaniel B., ed. 1853–1854 Records of the Governor and Company of the Massachusetts Bay in New England. 5 vols. Printed by Order of the Legislature. Boston: W. White, Printer to the Commonwealth.

Smith, Wallis M. 1970 A Re-appraisal of the Huron Kinship System. *Anthropologica*, n.s., 12(2):191–206.

——— 1973 The Fur Trade and the Frontier: A Study of an Intercultural Alliance. *Anthropologica*, n.s., 15 (1): 21–35.

Snow, Dean R. 1973 A Model for the Reconstruction of Late Eastern Algonquian Prehistory. *Studies in Linguistics* 23:77–85.

——— 1975 The Passadumkeag Sequence. *Arctic Anthropology* 12(2):46–59.

——— 1977 Archaeology and Ethnohistory in Eastern New York. Pp. 107–12 in Current Perspectives in Northeastern Archaeology. *Researches and Transactions of the New York State Archeological Association* 17(1):107–112.

—— 1978 Shaking Down the New Paradigm. *Archaeology of Eastern North America* 6:87–91.

Snyderman, George S. 1948 Behind the Tree of Peace: A Sociological Analysis of Iroquois Warfare. *Pennsylvania Archaeologist* 18(3–4):3–93.

—— 1951 Concepts of Land Ownership Among the Iroquois and Their Neighbors. *Bureau of American Ethnology Bulletin* 149(6):15–34.

Speck, Frank G. 1945 The Iroquois: A Study in Cultural Evolution. *Cranbrook Institute of Science Bulletin* 23. Bloomfield Hills, Mich.

—— 1949 Midwinter Rites of the Cayuga Long House. Philadelphia: University of Pennsylvania Press.

Speck, Frank G., and Claude E. Schaeffer 1945 The Mutual-aid and Volunteer Company of the Eastern Cherokee: as Recorded in a Book of Minutes in the Sequoyah Syllabary, Compared with the Mutual-aid Societies of the Northern Iroquois. *Journal of the Washington Academy of Sciences* 35:169–79.

Spence, Michael W. and J. Russell Harper 1968 The Cameron's Point Site. *Royal Ontario Museum, Art and Archaeology Occasional Paper* 12. Toronto.

Spicer, Edward H. 1962 Cycles of Conquest: The Impact of Spain, Mexico and the United States on the Indians of the Southwest, 1533–1960. Tucson, Ariz.: University of Arizona Press.

Stern, Bernhard J. 1933 The Letters of Asher Wright to Lewis H. Morgan. *American Anthropologist* 35:138–45.

Stewart, Alexander M. 1970 French Pioneers in the Eastern Great Lakes Area: 1609–1791. *New York State Archaeological Association Occasional Paper* 3. Rochester Museum and Science Center.

Stewart, W.A.C. 1972 Progressives and Radicals in English Education, 1750–1970. London: MacMillan.

Stites, Sara H. 1905 Economics of the Iroquois. Lancaster, Pennsylvania: New Era Printing Co.

Stone, William L. 1838 Life of Joseph Brant-Thayendanegea: Including the Border Wars of the American Revolution and Sketches of the Indian Campaigns of Generals Harmar, St. Clair and Wayne; and Other Matters Connected with the Indian Relations of the United States and Great Britain from the Peace of 1783 to the Indian Peace of 1795. 2 vols. New York: A.V. Blake, G. Dearborn and Company. (Reprinted: Kraus Reprint, New York, 1969.)

—— 1841 The Life and Times of Red Jacket, or Sa-go-ye-wat-ha; Being the Sequel to the History of the Six Nations. New York and London: Wiley and Putnam.

Stothers, D.M. 1977 The Princess Point Complex. *Canada. National Museum of Man, Mercury Series, Archaeological Survey of Canada Paper* 58. Ottawa.

Sturtevant, William C. 1952–1961 [Ethnographic Fieldnotes from about 15 Weeks at Cattaraugus and Allegany Reservations.] (Manuscripts in Sturtevant's possession.)

—— 1961–1962 [Notes From About 5½ Weeks Ethnographic Field Work Among Oklahoma Seneca-Cayuga.] (Manuscripts in Sturtevant's possession.)

—— 1961 Comment on Gertrude P. Kurath's Effects of Environment on Cherokee-Iroquois Ceremonialism, Music and Dance. *Bureau of American Ethnology Bulletin* 180 (19):199–204.

—— 1962 [Ethnographic Fieldnotes from Attendance at Code Recitation at Seneca Longhouse, Six Nations Reserve.] (Manuscripts in Sturtevant's possession.)

—— 1978 Oklahoma Seneca-Cayuga. Pp. 537–43 in Northeast. Bruce G. Trigger, vol. ed. Handbook of North American Indians, Vol. 15. William C. Sturtevant, gen. ed. Washington: Smithsonian Institution.

—— 1983 Seneca Masks. Pp. 39–47 in The Power of Symbols: Masks and Masquerade in the Americas. N. Ross Crumrine and Marjorie Halpin, eds. Vancouver: University of British Columbia Press.

Swanton, John R. 1938 John Napoleon Brinton Hewitt. *American Anthropologist* 40(2):286–90.

Talbot, Francis X. 1956 Saint Among the Savages: The Life of Jean de Brébeuf. Garden City, N.Y.: Image Books.

Taylor, Graham D. 1975 Anthropologists, Reformers and the Indian New Deal. *Prologue* 7:151–62.

Teggart, Frederick J. 1960 Theory and Process of History. Berkeley: University of California Press.

Thomas, Jacob E. 1975 The Friendship Treaty Belt Between the Oh-kwe-hon-weh and the Dutch. (2-page manuscript in Thomas's possession.)

1975a The Two Row Wampum Treaty Belt Between the Oh-kwe-hon-weh and the Dutch, the French, the English and George Washington. (5-page manuscript in Thomas's possession.)

Thomas, Peter A. 1973 Squakheag Ethnohistory: A Preliminary Study of Culture Conflict on the Seventeenth Century Frontier. *Man in the Northeast* 5:27–36.

—— 1979 In the Maelstrom of Change: A Systematic Look at the Indian Trade and Cultural Process in the Middle Connecticut River Valley, 1635–1672. (Unpublished Ph.D. Dissertation in Anthropology, University of Massachusetts Amherst.)

Thwaites, Reuben G. *see* JR

Tooker, Elisabeth 1960 Three Aspects of Northern Iroquoian Culture Change. *Pennsylvania Archaeologist* 30(2): 65–71.

—— 1963 The Iroquois Defeat of the Huron: A Review of Causes. *Pennsylvania Archaeologist* 33(1–2):11–123.

—— 1964 An Ethnography of the Huron Indians, 1615–1649. *Bureau of American Ethnology Bulletin* 190. Washington. (Reprinted: The Huronia Historical Development Council, Midland, Ontario, 1967.)

—— ed. 1967 Iroquois Culture, History, and Prehistory: Proceedings of the 1965 Conference on Iroquois Research. Albany: New York State Museum and Science Service.

—— 1970 The Iroquois Ceremonial of Midwinter. Syracuse, N.Y.: Syracuse University Press.

—— 1971 Clans and Moieties in North America. *Current Anthropology* 12(3):357–76.

—— 1978 The League of the Iroquois: Its History, Politics, and Ritual. Pp. 418–41 in Northeast. Bruce G. Trigger, vol. ed. Handbook of North American Indians, Vol. 15. William C. Sturtevant, gen. ed. Washington: Smithsonian Institution.

—— 1978a Iroquois Since 1820. Pp. 449–65 in Northeast. Bruce G. Trigger, vol. ed. Handbook of North American Indians, Vol. 15. William C. Sturtevant, gen. ed. Washington: Smithsonian Institution.

Torok, Charles H. 1967 Tyendinaga Acculturation. Pp. 31–33 in Iroquois Culture, History, and Prehistory: Proceedings of the 1965 Conference on Iroquois Research. Elisabeth Tooker, ed. Albany: New York State Museum and Science Service.

Trelease, Allen W. 1960 Indian Affairs in Colonial New York: The Seventeenth Century. Ithaca, N.Y.: Cornell University Press.

Trigger, Bruce G. 1960 The Destruction of Huronia: A Study in Economic and Cultural Change, 1609–1650. *Transactions of the Royal Canadian Institute* 33(1):14–45. Ottawa.

—— 1963 Order and Freedom in Huron Society. *Anthropologica*, n.s., 5:151–69. Ottawa.

—— 1963a Settlement as an Aspect of Iroquoian Adaptation at the Time of Contact. *American Anthropologist* 65(1):86–101.

—— 1969 The Huron: Farmers of the North. New York: Holt, Rinehart and Winston.

—— 1970 The Strategy of Iroquoian Prehistory. *Ontario Archaeology* 14:3–48.

—— 1971 Champlain Judged by His Indian Policy: A Different View of Early Canadian History. *Anthropologica*, n.s., 13(1–2):85–114. Ottawa.

—— 1971a The Mohawk-Mahican War (1624–1628): The Establishment of a Pattern. *Canadian Historical Review* 52(3):276–86.

—— 1976 The Children of Aataentsic: A History of the Huron People to 1660. 2 vols. Montreal: McGill-Queen's University Press.

—— 1978 Iroquoian Matriliny. *Pennsylvania Archaeologist* 48(1–2):55–65.

Trudel, Marcel 1963–1966 Histoire de la Nouvelle-France. 2 vols. Montreal: Fides.

—— 1966 Samuel de Champlain. Pp. 186–99 in Dictionary of Canadian Biography, Vol. 1. Toronto: University of Toronto Press.

Tuck, James A. 1971 Onondaga Iroquois Prehistory: A Study in Settlement Archaeology. Syracuse, N.Y.: Syracuse University Press.

—— 1975 Prehistory of Saglek Bay, Labrador: Archaic and Paleo-Eskimo Occupations. *Canada. National Museum of Man, Mercury Series Archaeological Survey of Canada Paper* 32. Ottawa.

—— 1976 Paleoeskimo Cultures of Northern Labrador. *Society for American Archaeology Memoir* 31. Washington.

—— 1976a Newfoundland and Labrador Prehistory. *Canada. National Museum of Man, Canadian Prehistory Series*. Ottawa.

—— 1977 A Look at Laurentian. Current Perspectives in Northeastern Archeology. *New York State Archeological Association Researches and Transactions* 17(1):31–40.

—— 1978 Regional Cultural Development, 3000 to 300 B.C. Pp. 28–43 in Northeast. Bruce G. Trigger, vol. ed. Handbook of North American

Indians, Vol. 15. William C. Sturtevant, gen. ed. Washington: Smithsonian Institution.

—— 1978a Northern Iroquoian Prehistory. Pp. 322–33 in Northeast. Bruce G. Trigger, vol. ed. Handbook of North American Indians, Vol. 15. William C. Sturtevant, gen. ed. Washington: Smithsonian Institution.

Tylor, Edward B. 1889 On a Method of Investigating the Development of Institutions: Applied to Laws of Marriage and Descent. *Journal of the Royal Anthropological Institute* 18:245–69.

USPG = United Society for the Propagation of the Gospel in Foreign Parts. London, Eng.

Underwood, William D. 1977 A Determination of Provenience of Potsherds by Heavy Mineral Analysis. (Unpublished M.A. Thesis in Anthropology, State University of New York, Buffalo.)

U.S. Census Office. 11th Census 1892 . . . Indians. The Six Nations of New York, Cayugas, Mohawks (Saint Regis), Oneidas, Onondagas, Senecas, Tuscaroras, by Thomas C. Donaldson. Extra Census Bulletin. Washington: U.S. Government Printing Office.

U.S. Statutes at Large 1934 Vol. 48. Washington: U.S. Government Printing Office.

Venn, John, and J.A. Venn, comp. 1952–1954 Alumni Cantabrigiensis: A Biographical List of All Known Students, Graduates and Holders of Office at the University of Cambridge, From the Earliest Times to 1900. Cambridge, Eng.: Cambridge University Press.

Voget, Fred W. 1951 Acculturatation at Caughnawaga: A Note on the Native-modified Group. *American Anthropologist* 53(2):220–31.

—— 1953 Kinship Changes at Caughnawaga. *American Anthropologist* 55(3):385–94.

—— 1975 A History of Ethnology. New York: Holt, Rinehart and Winston.

WP = Wheelock Papers 1728–1779 Papers of Eleazar Wheelock. Dartmouth College Library, Hanover, New Hampshire. (Calendar numbers as given in A Guide to the Microfilm Edition of the Papers of Eleazar Wheelock, 1971.)

Wallace, Anthony F. C. 1949 King of the Delawares: Teedyuscung, 1700–1763. Philadelphia: University of Pennsylvania Press.

—— 1951 Some Psychological Determinants of Culture Change in an Iroquoian Community. Pp. 55–76 in Symposium on Local Diversity in Iroquois Culture. William N. Fenton, ed. *Bureau of American Ethnology Bulletin* 149(4). Washington.

—— 1952 The Modal Personality Structure of the Tuscarora Indians as Revealed by the Rorschach Test. *Bureau of American Ethnology Bulletin* 150. Washington.

—— 1956 Revitalization Movements: Some Theoretical Considerations for Their Comparative Study. *American Anthropologist* 58(2):264–81.

—— 1957 Political Organization and Land Tenure Among the Northeastern Indians, 1600–1830. *Southwestern Journal of Anthropology* 13(4):301–21.

—— 1958 The Dekanawideh Myth Analyzed as the Record of a Revitalization Movement. *Ethnohistory* 5(2):118–30.

———— 1958a Dreams and the Wishes of the Soul: A Type of Psychoanalytic Theory Among the Seventeenth Century Iroquois. *American Anthropologist* 60(2):234–48.

———— 1961 Cultural Composition of the Handsome Lake Religion. Pp. 143–51 in Symposium on Cherokee and Iroquois Culture. William N. Fenton and John Gulick, eds. *Bureau of American Ethnology Bulletin* 180(14). Washington.

———— 1969 The Death and Rebirth of the Seneca. New York: Alfred A. Knopf.

———— 1978 Origins of the Longhouse Religion. Pp. 442–48 in Northeast. Bruce G. Trigger, vol. ed. Handbook of North American Indians, Vol. 15. William C. Sturtevant, gen. ed. Washington: Smithsonian Institution.

Wallace, Paul A. W. 1945 Conrad Weiser, 1696–1760, Friend of Colonist and Mohawk. Philadelphia: University of Pennsylvania Press.

Warre Cornish, Francis 1910 The English Church in the Nineteenth Century. 2 vols. London: Macmillan and Co.

Watson, G. D. 1972 A Woodland Indian Site at Constance Bay, Ontario. *Ontario Archaeology* 18. Toronto.

Waugh, Frederick W. 1916 Iroquois Foods and Food Preparation. *Anthropological Series 12, Memoirs of the Canadian Geological Survey 86.* Ottawa. (Reprinted: National Museum of Man, Ottawa, 1973.)

Weaver, Sally M. 1972 Medicine and Politics Among the Grand River Iroquois: A Study of the Non-conservatives. *Canada. National Museum of Man, Publications in Ethnology* 4. Ottawa.

———— 1978 Six Nations of the Grand River, Ontario. Pp. 525–36 in Northeast. Bruce G. Trigger, vol. ed. Handbook of North American Indians, Vol. 15. William C. Sturtevant, gen. ed. Washington: Smithsonian Institution.

Weinreich, Uriel 1967 Lexicographic Definition in Descriptive Semantics (1962). Pp. 25–44 in Problems in Lexicography. F. W. Householder and S. Saporta, eds. The Hague: Mouton.

———— 1974 Languages in Contact (1953). The Hague: Mouton.

West, John 1827 A Journal of a Mission to the Indians of the British Provinces of New Brunswick, and Nova Scotia, and the Mohawks, on the Ouse, or Grand River, Upper Canada. London: L. B. Sealy and Son.

Whallon, Robert, Jr. 1968 Investigations of Late Prehistoric Social Organization in New York State. Pp. 223–44 in Perspectives in Archeology. New York: Aldine.

Wheelock, Eleazar 1763 A Plain and Faithful Narrative of the Original Design, Rise, Progress, and Present State of the Indian Charity-School at Lebanon in Connecticut. Boston: Richard and Samuel Draper.

———— 1765–1775 A Continuation of the Narrative of the Indian Charity-School, Begun in Lebanon, Connecticut; Now Incorporated with Dartmouth-College, in Hanover, in the Province of New Hampshire. Hartford, Conn.: E. Watson.

White, Marian E. 1961 Iroquois Culture History in the Niagara Frontier Area of New York State. *University of Michigan Museum of Anthropology, Anthropological Papers* 16. Ann Arbor.

—— 1971 Ethnic Identification and Iroquois Groups in Western New York and Ontario. *Ethnohistory* 18(1):19–38.

—— 1976 Late Woodland Archaeology in the Niagara Frontier of New York and Ontario. Pp. 110–36 in The Late Prehistory of Lake Erie Drainage Basin: A 1972 Symposium Revised. David Brose, ed. Cleveland Museum of Natural History.

—— 1977 The Shelby Site Reexamined. Pp. 85–91 in Essays in Honor of William A. Ritchie. Robert E. Funk and Charles F. Hayes III, eds. New York State Archaeological Association.

Wilkinson, Charles F., and John M. Volkman 1975 Judicial Review of Indian Treaty Abrogation: "As Long as Water Flows, or Grass Grows Upon the Earth"—How Long a Time Is That? *California Law Review* 63:601–66.

Wilson, Edmund 1960 Apologies to the Iroquois, with a Study of the Mohawks in High Steel, by Joseph Mitchell. New York: Farrar, Strauss, and Cudahy.

Wilson, J. D. 1974 No Blanket to be Worn in School: The Education of Indians in Early Nineteenth Century Ontario. *Social History* 7:293–305.

Wintemberg, W. J. 1931 Distinguishing Characteristics of Algonkian and Iroquoian Cultures. *Canada. National Museum of Canada Bulletin* 67:65–125. Ottawa.

Winthrop, John 1825–1826 The History of New England from 1630 to 1649. James Savage, ed. 2 vols. Boston: Phelps and Farnham; Thomas B. Wait and Son.

Winthrop Papers. Papers of John Winthrop, Jr. Massachusetts Historical Society, Boston.

Witthoft, John 1953 Broad Spearpoints and the Transitional Period Cultures. *Pennsylvania Archaeologist* 23(1):4–31.

Wood, William 1634 Nevv England's Prospect: A True, Lively and Experimentall Description of That Part of America, Commonly Called Nevv England: Discovering the State of That Countrie, Both as it Stands to Our New-Come English Planters; and to the Old Native Inhabitants. London: Tho. Cotes.

Woodbury, Hanni 1975 Noun Incorporation in Onondaga. (Unpublished Ph.D. Dissertation in Anthropology, Yale University, New Haven, Conn.)

—— 1976 The Semi-reflexive in Onondaga. (Paper Read at the 75th Annual Meeting of the American Anthropological Association.)

Wray, Charles F. and Harry L. Schoff 1953 A Preliminary Report on the Seneca Sequence in Western New York, 1550–1687. *Pennsylvania Archaeologist* 23(2):53–63.

Wright, Gary 1972 Ohio Hopewell Trade. *The Explorer* 14(4):4–11.

Wright, James V. 1962 A Distributional Study of Some Archaic Traits in Southern Ontario. *Canada. National Museum of Canada Bulletin* 180. Ottawa.

—— 1965 A Regional Examination of Ojibwa Culture History. *Anthropologica* n.s. 7(2):189–227. Ottawa.

—— 1966 The Ontario Iroquois Tradition. *Canada. Anthropological Series* 75, *National Museum of Canada Bulletin* 210. Ottawa.

—— 1967 The Laurel Tradition and the Middle Woodland Period. *Canada. Anthropological Series* 79, *National Museum of Canada Bulletin* 217. Ottawa.

—— 1969 The Michipicoten Site. Pp. 1–85 in Contributions to Anthropology, VI: Archaelogy and Physical Anthropology. *Canada. Anthropological Series* 82. *National Museum of Canada Bulletin* 224. Ottawa.

—— 1972 Ontario Prehistory: An Eleven-thousand Year Archaeological Outline. *Canada. National Museum of Man, Canadian Prehistory Series.* Ottawa.

—— 1972a The Aberdeen Site, Keewatin District, NWT. *Canada. National Museum of Man, Mercury Series Archaeological Survey of Canada* 2. Ottawa.

—— 1972b The Knechtel I Site, Bruce County, Ontario. *Canada. National Museum of Man, Mercury Series Archaeological Survey of Canada* 4. Ottawa.

—— 1974 The Nodwell Site. *Canada. National Museum of Man, Mercury Series Archaeological Survey of Canada Paper* 22. Ottawa.

—— 1978 The Implications of Probable Early and Middle Archaic Projectile Points from Southern Ontario. *Canadian Journal of Archaeology,* 2:59–78.

—— 1981 Prehistory of the Canadian Shield. Pp. 86–96 in Subarctic. June Helm vol. ed. Handbook of North American Indians, Vol. 6. William C. Sturtevant, gen. ed. Washington: Smithsonian Institution.

Wright, James V. and J. E. Anderson 1963 The Donaldson Site. *Canada. Anthropological Series 58, National Museum of Canada Bulletin* 184. Ottawa.

—— 1969 The Bennett Site. *Canada. Anthropological Series 85 National Museum of Canada Bulletin* 229. Ottawa.

Wright, Roy A. 1974 The People of the Panther—A Long Erie Tale. Pp. 47–118 in Papers in Linguistics from the 1972 Conference on Iroquoian Research. Michael K. Foster, ed. *Canada. National Museum of Man, Ethnology Division, Mercury Series Paper* 10. Ottawa.

Zoltvany, Ives 1973 Three Recent Books on New France. *Acadiensis* 3(1): 97–102.

A Bibliography of William N. Fenton's Publications to 1982

COMPILED BY MICHAEL K. FOSTER
AND DORIS E. FOSTER

Two series of items are listed separately at the head of the bibliography: first, Fenton's contributions to the Annual Reports of the Bureau of American Ethnology, signed by the Bureau Chief, M. W. Stirling, for the twelve years Fenton was on staff (1939–1951); second, Fenton's "General Statements" in the Annual Reports of the New York State Museum and Science Service, signed by him as Assistant Commissioner, for the thirteen and a half years of his tenure (1954–1968). Among other things, these reports cover field and archival work underlying many of Fenton's publications between 1939 and the mid-1960s.

BUREAU OF AMERICAN ETHNOLOGY, ANNUAL REPORTS

1940 Fifty-sixth (1938–1939), pp. 5–6.
1941 Fifty-seventh (1939–1940), pp. 6–7.
1942 Fifty-eighth (1940–1941), pp. 7–8.
1943 Fifty-ninth (1941–1942), pp. 5–7.
1944 Sixtieth (1942–1943), pp. 5–6.
1945 Sixty-first (1943–1944), pp. 3–4.
1946 Sixty-second (1944–1945), pp. 3–4.
1947 Sixty-third (1945–1946), pp. 4–5.
1948 Sixty-fourth (1946–1947), pp. 5–7.
1949 Sixty-fifth (1947–1948), pp. 3–4.
1950 Sixty-sixth (1948–1949), pp. 3–4.
1951 Sixty-seventh (1949–1950), p. 4.
1952 Sixty-eighth (1950–1951), p. 4.
1953 Sixty-ninth (1951–1952), pp. 3–4.

NEW YORK STATE MUSEUM AND SCIENCE SERVICE, ANNUAL REPORTS

1958 119th (1 July 1956–30 June 1957), Bulletin 370, pp. 7–12.
1959 120th (1 July 1957–30 June 1958), Bulletin 374, pp. 7–15.

1960 121st (1 July 1958–30 June 1959), Bulletin 381, pp. 7–13.
1961 122nd (1 July 1959–30 June 1960), Bulletin 385, pp. 7–12.
1962 123rd (1 July 1960–30 June 1961), Bulletin 387, pp. 1–21.
1963 124th (1 July 1961–30 June 1962), Bulletin 393, pp. 1–5.
1964 125th (1 July 1962–30 June 1963), Bulletin 395, pp. 1–4.
1965 126th (1 July 1963–30 June 1964), Bulletin 401, pp. 1–7.
1966 127th (1 July 1964–30 June 1965), Bulletin 407, pp. 1–8.
1967 128th (1 July 1965–30 June 1966), Bulletin 409, pp. 1–6.

1931

Outdoor Wisdom. [Review of] The Boy Campers, by William Hillcourt. *The Saturday Review of Literature* 8(17): 282.

1934

[Review of] Bulletin of the Society for Pennsylvania Archaeology. *American Anthropologist*, n.s., 36(3): 464–65.

1935

(with Cephas D. Hill) Reviving Indian Arts Among the Senecas. *Indians at Work* 2(21): 13–15.
The Tonawanda Indian Community Library. *Indians at Work* 3(5): 46–48.

1936

Guide Posts on Tonawanda Reservation. *Indians at Work* 3(10): 31–32.
Some Social Customs of the Modern Senecas. *Social Welfare Bulletin* 7(1–2): 4–7. (Also in *Indians at Work* 3(21): 10–14; 4(6): 41–42.)
An Outline of Seneca Ceremonies at Coldspring Longhouse. *Yale University Publications in Anthropology* 9. New Haven, Conn. (Reprinted: Human Relations Area Files Press, New Haven, Conn., 1970.)

1937

The Seneca Society of Faces. *Scientific Monthly* 44(March): 215–38.

1938

Reviews:
   Oklahoma Delaware Ceremonies, Feasts and Dances, by Frank G. Speck. *American Anthropologist*, n.s., 40(2): 304–5.
   Legends of the Longhouse, by Jesse J. Cornplanter. *New York Herald Tribune Books*, March 20, p. 11.

1939

Native Culture. [Review of] Indian Arts in North America, by George C. Vaillant. *New York Herald Tribune Books*, November 26, p. 10.

1940

A Further Quest for Iroquois Medicines. Pp. 93–96 in *Explorations and Fieldwork of the Smithsonian Institution in 1939*. Washington.
Problems Arising from the Historic Northeastern Position of the Iroquois. Pp. 159–251 in Essays in Historical Anthropology of North America. *Smithsonian Miscellaneous Collections* 100. Washington.

An Herbarium from the Allegany Senecas. Pp. 787–96 in The Historic Annals of Southwestern New York. William J. Doty and others, eds. 3 vols. New York: Lewis Historical Publishing Company.

Reviews:

The Wars of the Iroquois: A Study in Intertribal Relations, by George T. Hunt. *American Anthropologist*, n.s., 42(4): 662–64.

More Books About the Indians. [Review of] We Called Them Indians, by Flora W. Seymour; and Border Captives, by Carl C. Rister. *The Washington Post*, June 2.

Speaking of Indians. [Review of] Hear Me, My Chiefs! by Herbert R. Sass. *The Washington Post*, December 11.

1941

Masked Medicine Societies of the Iroquois. Pp. 397–429 in *Annual Report of the Smithsonian Institution for 1940*. Washington.

Iroquois Suicide: A Study in the Stability of a Culture Pattern. *Bureau of American Ethnology Bulletin* 128(14): 80–137.

Tonawanda Longhouse Ceremonies: Ninety Years After Lewis Henry Morgan. *Bureau of American Ethnology Bulletin* 128(15): 140–65. Washington.

Museum and Field Studies of Iroquois Masks and Ritualism. Pp. 95–100 in *Explorations and Field-work of the Smithsonian Institution in 1940*. Washington.

Reviews:

Roebuck Prehistoric Village Site, Grenville County, Ontario, by William J. Wintemberg. *American Antiquity* 6(3): 290–94.

Indians of the United States, by Clark Wissler. *The American Historical Review* 46(2): 413–15.

Council Fires on the Upper Ohio: A Narrative of Indian Affairs in the Upper Ohio Valley Until 1795, by Randolph C. Downes. *New York Herald Tribune Books*, January 12, p. 15.

1942

Contacts Between Iroquois Herbalism and Colonial Medicine. Pp. 503–26 in *Annual Report of the Smithsonian Institution for 1941*. Washington.

Fish Drives Among the Cornplanter Senecas. *Pennsylvania Archaeologist* 12(3): 48–52.

Last Seneca Pigeon Hunts. Pp. 4–5, 38 in Warren County Pennsylvania Almanac, 1943. Warren, Pennsylvania.

Songs from the Iroquois Longhouse. Program Notes for an Album of American Indian Music from the Eastern Woodlands. Smithsonian Institution Publication 3691. Washington.

(Recorder and Editor) Songs from the Iroquois Longhouse. Folk Music of the United States, Archive of Folk Song, Album 6. Washington: Library of Congress.

[Review of] Comments on Certain Iroquois Masks, by Joseph Keppler. *American Anthropologist*, n.s.,44(1): 118–19.

1943

(with Merle H. Deardorff) The Last Passenger Pigeon Hunts of the Cornplanter Senecas. *Journal of the Washington Academy of Sciences* 33(10): 289–315.

Reviews:

The Tutelo Spirit Adoption Ceremony, by Frank G. Speck. *Journal of American Folklore* 56(222): 304–6.

The Indian's Last Stand. [Review of] Indian Experiences, by DeCost Smith. *New York Herald Tribune Weekly Book Review*, May 2, p. 17.

The Indian in the Brave New World. [Review of] The Changing Indian. Oliver LaFarge, ed. *The Washington Post*, January 10.

1944

(Editor) The Requickening Address of the Iroquois Condolence Council, by J. N. B. Hewitt. *Journal of the Washington Academy of Sciences* 34(3): 65–85.

Samuel Crowell's Account of a Seneca Dog Sacrifice near Lower Sandusky, Ohio, in 1830: A Commentary. *Northwest Ohio Quarterly* 16(3–4): 158–63.

Obituaries:

Simeon Gibson: Iroquois Informant, 1889–1943. *American Anthropologist*, n.s., 46(2): 231–34.

Simeon Gibson (1889–1943), Informant in the Iroquois Ritual of Condolence. *Cranbrook Institute of Science News Letter* 13(6): 5–7.

Reviews:

Delaware's Forgotten Folk: The Story of the Moors and Nanticokes, by Clinton A. Weslager. *American Anthropologist*, n.s., 46(2): 245–48.

Flintlocks of the Iroquois, 1620–1687, by Joseph R. Mayer. *American Antiquity* 9(4): 459–60.

1945

(with J. N. B. Hewitt) Some Mnemonic Pictographs Relating to the Iroquois Condolence Council. *Journal of the Washington Academy of Sciences* 35(10): 301–15.

A Day on the Allegheny Ox-Bow. *The Living Wilderness* 10(13): 1–8.

Place Names and Related Activities of the Cornplanter Senecas: I. State Line to Cornplanter Grant: Northern Approaches. *Pennsylvania Archaeologist* 15(1): 25–29.

Place Names and Related Activities of the Cornplanter Senecas: II. Cornplanter Grant: The Place Where Handsome Lake Rose to Preach. *Pennsylvania Archaeologist* 15(2): 42–50.

Place Names and Related Activities of the Cornplanter Senecas: III. Burnthouse at Cornplanter Grant. *Pennsylvania Archaeologist* 15(3): 88–96.

Place Names and Related Activities of the Cornplanter Senecas: IV. Cornplanter Peak to Warren. *Pennsylvania Archaeologist* 15(4): 108–18.

Pennsylvania's Remaining Indian Settlement. *Pennsylvania Park News* 44(October), 2 pp.

Reports on Area Studies in American Universities. (Six reports prepared for the Ethnogeographic Board, Washington, D. C., Mimeographed.)
Reviews:
Trivia Iroquoia. [Review of] The Long House of the Iroquois, by Spencer L. Adams; and Seneca Indians, Home Life and Culture, by Spencer L. Adams. *Pennsylvania Archaeologist* 15(1): 33–35.
Anthropology as an Integrating Science. [Review of] The Science of Man in the World Crisis, by Ralph Linton. *The Scientific Monthly* 61(5): 386–89.

1946

Integration of Geography and Anthropology in Army Area Study Curricula. *Bulletin of the American Association of University Professors* 32(4): 696–706.
An Iroquois Condolence Council for Installing Cayuga Chiefs in 1945. *Journal of the Washington Academy of Sciences* 36(4): 110–27.
Place Names and Related Activities of the Cornplanter Senecas: V. The Path to Conewango. *Pennsylvania Archaeologist* 16(2): 42–57.
The Six Nations of Canada. *Proceedings of the Royal Canadian Institute* 11 (Series IIIA): 27–28.
[Obituary] Twí-yendagon' (Woodeater) Takes the Heavenly Path: On the Death of Henry Redeye (1864?–1946), Speaker of the Coldspring Seneca Longhouse. *The American Indian* 3(3): 11–15.
Reviews:
The Celestial Bear Comes Down to Earth: The Bear Sacrifice Ceremony of the Munsee-Mahican in Canada as Related by Nekatcit, by Frank G. Speck and Jessee Moses. *American Anthropologist*, n.s., 48(3): 423–27.
Towards an Iroquois Material Culture. [Review of] The Iroquois: A Study in Cultural Evolution, by Frank G. Speck; and Iroquois Crafts, by Carrie A. Lyford. *American Anthropologist*, n.s., 48(3): 427–30.
A Study of the Pine Ridge Sioux. [Review of] Warriors Without Weapons, by Gordon Macgregor and others. *The Scientific Monthly* 62(June): 565–68.

1947

Anthropology During the War. VII: The Arab World. *American Anthropologist*, n.s., 49(2): 342–43.
Iroquois Indian Folklore. In Folklore Research in North America. Reports of the Committee on Research in Folklore 1945 and 1946. *Journal of American Folklore* 60(October–December): 383–97.
(with Martha Champion Huot) Seneca Songs from Coldspring Longhouse, by Chauncey Johnny John and Albert Jones [Program Notes]. *Library of Congress, Archives of American Folksong*, Album 17. Washington.
(Recorder and Editor) Seneca Songs from Coldspring Longhouse, by Chauncey Johnny John and Albert Jones. *Library of Congress, Archives of American Folksong*, Album 17. Washington: Library of Congress.

Area Studies in American Universities. The Commission on Implications of Armed Services Educational Programs of the American Council on Education. Washington.

Reviews:

The New World. Stefan Lorant, ed. *American Antiquity* 13(2): 189. (Also in *United States Quarterly Book List* 3(1): 5–6.)

The Last Trek of the Indians, by Grant Foreman. *The Scientific Monthly* 64(June): 529–30.

The Cherokee Nation, by Marion L. Starkey. *United States Quarterly Book List* 3(1): 64.

Indians Before Columbus: Twenty Thousand Years of North American History Revealed by Archeology, by Paul S. Martin, George I. Quimby, and Donald Collier. *United States Quarterly Book List* 3(3): 224.

Pontiac and the Indian Uprising, by Howard H. Peckham. *United States Quarterly Book List* 4(1): 82.

1948

The Present Status of Anthropology in Northeastern North America: A Review Article. *American Anthropologist* 50(3): 494–515.

The Fourth Conference on Iroquois Research. *Science* 108: 611–12. (Also in *American Antiquity* 14(2): 159–60.)

Letters to an Ethnologist's Children. *New York Folklore Quarterly* 4(2): 109–20.

Reviews:

Historical Ethnology. [Review of] Chippewa Village: The Story of Katikitegon, by W. Vernon Kinietz. *Scientific Monthly* 66(3): 263–64.

Pontiac and the Indian Uprising, by H. H. Peckham. *United States Quarterly Book List* 4(1): 62.

Childhood and Youth Among the Jicarilla Apache Society, by M.E. Opler. *United States Quarterly Book List* 4(1): 82.

The Journals of Francis Parkman. Mason Wade, ed. *United States Quarterly Book List* 4(2): 181–82.

The Heathens, by William W. Howells. *United States Quarterly Book List* 4(3): 283.

Naskapi Law, by Julius E. Lips. *United States Quarterly Book List* 4(3): 295–96.

Winnebago Hero Cycles: A Study in Aboriginal Literature, by Paul Radin. *United States Quarterly Book List* 4(4): 441–42.

An Analysis of Coeur d'Alene Indian Myths, by Gladys A. Reichard. *United States Quarterly Book List* 4(4): 442.

1949

(with Ernest S. Dodge) An Elmbark Canoe in the Peabody Museum of Salem. *The American Neptune* 9(3): 185–206.

(with the Seneca of Coldspring Longhouse) Another Eagle Dance for Gahéhdagowa (F[rank] G. S[peck]). *Primitive Man* 22(3–4): 60–64.

Seth Newhouse's Traditional History and Constitution of the Iroquois Confederacy. *Proceedings of the American Philosophical Society* 93(2): 141–58. Philadelphia.

Collecting Materials for a Political History of the Six Nations. *Proceedings of the American Philosophical Society* 93(3): 233–38. Philadelphia.

Medicinal Plant Lore of the Iroquois. *The University of the State of New York, Bulletin to the Schools* 35(7): 233–37.

Report on Grants. Pp. 155–57 in The American Philosophical Society Year Book 1948. Philadelphia.

Racism as a Barrier to Research and Economic Development: Indians of the United States. Pp. 1–5 in Proceedings of the Second Inter-American Conference on Indian Life, Cuzco, Peru, October 10–20. Mexico City: Instituto Indigenista Interamericano.

Reviews:

An Anthropological Bibliography of the Eastern Seaboard. Irving Rouse and John M. Goggin, eds. *American Anthropologist* 51(3): 497.

Mirror for Man, by Clyde K. Kluckhohn. *United States Quarterly Book List* 5(2): 189–90.

Law and Government of the Grand River Iroquois, by John A. Noon. *United States Quarterly Book List* 5(4): 472.

1950

Second Progress Report: Political History of the Six Nations. Pp. 186–88 in The American Philosophical Society Year Book 1949. Philadelphia.

The Roll Call of the Iroquois Chiefs: A Study of a Mnemonic Cane from the Six Nations Reserve. *Smithsonian Miscellaneous Collections* 111(15): 1–73. Washington.

[Obituary] John Montgomery Cooper. *Journal of the Washington Academy of Sciences* 40(2): 64.

Reviews:

Primitive Warfare, by H. H. Turney-High. *American Anthropologist* 52(2): 246–47.

Excavation of Ste. Marie I, by Kenneth E. Kidd. *American Anthropologist* 52(2): 265.

Midwinter Rites of the Cayuga Long House, by Frank G. Speck. *American Anthropologist* 52(4): 521–23.

They Came Here First: The Epic of the American Indian, by D'Arcy McNickle. *American Anthropologist* 52(4): 546–47.

Dark Trees to the Wind, by Carl Carmer. *United States Quarterly Book List* 6(1): 87.

Selected Writings of Edward Sapir [in Language, Culture, and Personality]. David G. Mandelbaum, ed. *United States Quarterly Book List* 6(2): 155–56.

1951

(Editor) Symposium on Local Diversity in Iroquois Culture. *Bureau of American Ethnology Bulletin* 149. Washington.

Introduction: The Concept of Locality and the Program of Iroquois Research. Pp. 3–12 in Symposium on Local Diversity in Iroquois Culture. William N. Fenton, ed. *Bureau of American Ethnology Bulletin* 149(1). Washington.

Locality as a Basic Factor in the Development of Iroquois Social Structure. Pp. 39–54 in Symposium on Local Diversity in Iroquois Culture. William N. Fenton, ed. *Bureau of American Ethnology Bulletin* 149(3). Washington.

(with Gertrude P. Kurath) The Feast of the Dead, or Ghost Dance, at Six Nations Reserve, Canada. Pp. 143–65 in Symposium on Local Diversity in Iroquois Culture. William N. Fenton, ed. *Bureau of American Ethnology Bulletin* 149(7). Washington.

Iroquois Studies at the Mid-Century. *Proceedings of the American Philosophical Society* 95(3): 296–310. Philadelphia.

Seventh Conference on Iroquois Research. *Science* 114(2970): 588–89.

Reviews:

The Voice of the Old Frontier, by R. W. G. Vail. *American Anthropologist* 53(1): 126.

Law and Government of the Grand River Iroquois, by John A. Noon. *The Quarterly Review of Biology* 26(2): 239–40.

Midwinter Rites of the Cayuga Long House, by Frank G. Speck. *The Quarterly Review of Biology* 26(2): 240.

Hollywood, the Dream Factory, by Hortense Powdermaker. *United States Quarterly Book Review* 7(1): 81–82.

The Sky Clears; Poetry of the American Indian, by Arthur Grove Day. *United States Quarterly Book Review* 7(2): 183.

Cherokee Dance and Drama, by Frank G. Speck and Leonard Broom. *United States Quarterly Book Review* 7(3): 255–56.

1952

The Training of Historical Ethnologists in America. *American Anthropologist* 54(3): 328–39.

Research on National Disasters. *News Report, National Academy of Sciences, National Research Council* 2(1): 3–5.

Reviews:

Diplomacy and Indian Gifts, by Wilbur R. Jacobs. *American Anthropologist* 54(1): 103–4.

Notes and Queries on Anthropology [1951 revision]. *American Anthropologist* 54(3): 417–18.

A History of Medicine. Vol. 1: Primitive and Archaic Medicine, by Henry E. Sigerist. *Bulletin of the Medical Library Association* 40(1): 80–81.

1953

The Iroquois Eagle Dance: An Offshoot of the Calumet Dance; with an Analysis of the Iroquois Eagle Dance and Songs, by Gertrude P. Kurath. *Bureau of American Ethnology Bulletin* 156. Washington.

Cultural Stability and Change in American Indian Societies. *Journal of the Royal Anthropological Institute of Great Britain and Ireland* 83(2): 169–74.

A Calendar of Manuscript Materials Relating to the History of the Six Nations or Iroquois Indians in Depositories Outside of Philadelphia, 1750–1850. *Proceedings of the American Philosophical Society* 97(5): 578–95. Philadelphia.

Reviews:
The California Indians. R. F. Heizer and M. A. Whipple, eds. *Quarterly Review of Biology* 28: 112.
Menomini Peyotism, by James S. Slotkin. *United States Quarterly Book Review* 9(3): 313–14.
The Savages of America, by Roy H. Pearce. *William and Mary Quarterly*, 3d ser., 10(4): 650–52.

1954

Anthropology. Pp. 47–49 in Britannica Book of the Year 1954. Chicago: Encyclopaedia Britannica.
The Hyde de Neuville Portraits of New York Savages in 1807–1808. *The New-York Historical Society Quarterly* 38(2): 118–37.
[Review of] Culture Change, by Felix M. Keesing. *United States Quarterly Book Review* 10(1): 72.

1955

Factionalism in American Indian Society. *Actes du IVe Congrès International des Sciences Anthropologiques et Ethnologiques* 2: 330–40. Vienna.
Anthropology. Pp. 108–10 in Britannica Book of the Year 1955. Chicago: Encyclopaedia Britannica.
The Maple and the Passenger Pigeon in Iroquois Indian Life. *The University of the State of New York, Bulletin to the Schools* 41(March): 253–59.
Reviews:
Index to the Proceedings (1–13) and to the Journal (1–40) of the Washington Academy of Sciences. Mary A. Bradley, compiler. *American Anthropologist* 57(4): 918.
Walam Olum or Red Score: The Migration Legend of the Lenni Lenape or Delaware Indians, by Eli Lilly. *The New York Historical Society* 39(2–3): 338–41.
Joseph Henry: His Life and Work, by Thomas Coulson. *New York History* 36(1): 93–95.
Indians of the Plains, by Robert H. Lowie. *United States Quarterly Book Review* 11(1): 81.
Changing Navaho Religious Values, by Robert N. Rapoport. *United States Quarterly Book Review* 11(1): 82.

1956

The Science of Anthropology and the Iroquois Indians. *New York State Archeological Association Bulletin* 6(March): 10–14.
Toward the Gradual Civilization of the Indian Natives: The Missionary and Linguistic Work of Asher Wright (1803–1875) Among the Senecas of Western New York. *Proceedings of the American Philosophical Society* 100(6): 567–81. Philadelphia. (Also in Library Bulletin of the American Philosophical Society for 1956.)
A Request from Scientist to Farmers. *Rural New Yorker*, April 7, p. 280.
Iroquois Research [the Ninth Conference on Iroquois Research]. *Science* 123(3185): 69.

A Century of Natural History Research in Albany. *Times-Union* (Albany, New York) Centennial Edition, April 22.

Some Questions of Classification, Typology, and Style Raised by Iroquois Masks. *Transactions of the New York Academy of Sciences*, 2nd ser., 18(4): 347–57. New York.

Reviews:

Powell of the Colorado, by William Culp Darrah. *American Anthropologist* 58(2): 403–4.

American Indians Dispossessed, by Walter H. Blumenthal; Wilderness Messiah, by Thomas R. Henry; Indians of the Southern Colonial Frontier [by Edmond Atkin], Wilbur R. Jacobs, ed. *William and Mary Quarterly*, 3d ser., 13(2): 293–95.

1957

American Indian and White Relations to 1830: Needs and Opportunities for Study. Chapel Hill: University of North Carolina Press.

Factionalism at Taos Pueblo, New Mexico. *Bureau of American Ethnology Bulletin* 164(56): 297–344.

(Editor) Seneca Indians by Asher Wright (1859). *Ethnohistory* 4(3): 302–21.

Long-term Trends of Change Among the Iroquois. Pp. 30–35 in Cultural Stability and Cultural Change. Verne F. Ray, ed. *Proceedings of the 1957 Annual Spring Meeting of the American Ethnological Society.* Seattle.

Reviews:

League of the Ho-Dé-No-Sau-Nee or Iroquois, by Lewis H. Morgan [reprinting of the Lloyd 1901 edition]. *American Anthropologist* 59(1): 169–70.

A Survey of Aboriginal Populations of Quebec and Labrador. Jacob Fried, ed. *American Anthropologist* 59(3): 553–54.

The Livingston Indian Records, 1666–1723. Lawrence H. Leder, ed. *The New-York Historical Society Quarterly* 41(1): 83–84. (Also in *The American Historical Review* 62[2]: 487.)

1958

Preface. P. v in Systems of Political Control. Verne F. Ray, ed. *Proceedings of the 1958 Annual Spring Meeting of the American Ethnological Society.* Seattle.

1959

[Obituary] John Reed Swanton (1873–1958). *American Anthropologist* 61(4): 663–68.

Reviews:

An Anthropologist at Work: Writings of Ruth Benedict, by Margaret Mead. *Journal of American Folklore* 72(286): 349–50.

Big Chief Johnson. [Review of] Mohawk Baronet: Sir William Johnson of New York, by James T. Flexner. *New York Times Book Review*, November 22.

1960

The Museum and Anthropological Research. *Curator* 3(4): 327–55.

The Hiawatha Wampum Belt of the Iroquois League for Peace: A Symbol for the International Congress of Anthropology. Pp. 3–7 in Men and Cultures, Selected Papers of the Fifth International Congress of Anthropological and Ethnological Sciences. Philadelphia, September 1–9, 1956. Anthony F. C. Wallace, ed. Philadelphia: University of Pennsylvania Press.

Reviews:

The Primordia of Bishop White Kennett, the First English Bibliography on America. *American Anthropologist* 62(5): 912–13.

Mohawk Baronet: Sir William Johnson of New York, by James T. Flexner. *Ethnohistory* 7(3): 311–17.

Lewis Henry Morgan: American Scholar, by Carl Resek. *New York History* 41(3): 333–35.

Susquehannock Miscellany. John Witthoft and W. Fred Kinsey III, eds. *The Pennsylvania Magazine of History and Biography* 84(April): 257–58.

Lewis Henry Morgan: The Indian Journals, 1859–1862. Leslie A. White, ed. *Science* 131(3398): 404.

1961

(with John Gulick, ed.) Symposium on Cherokee and Iroquois Culture. *Bureau of American Ethnology Bulletin* 180. Washington.

(with John Gulick) Foreword by the Editors. Pp. 3–8 in Symposium on Cherokee and Iroquois Culture. William N. Fenton and John Gulick, eds. *Bureau of American Ethnology Bulletin* 180(1). Washington.

Iroquoian Culture History: A General Evaluation. Pp. 257–77 in Symposium on Cherokee and Iroquois Culture. William N. Fenton and John Gulick, eds. *Bureau of American Ethnology Bulletin* 180(25). Washington.

Folklore (American Indian). Pp. 441–42 in Encyclopaedia Britannica. Vol. 9. Chicago: Encyclopaedia Britannica.

[Comment on] Method of Studying Ethnological Art, by Herta Haselberger. *Current Anthropology* 2(4): 367.

Reviews:

Indian Affairs in Colonial New York: The Seventeenth Century, by Allen W. Trelease. *American Anthropologist* 63(2): 416–18.

Letters of Francis Parkman. Wilbur R. Jacobs, ed. *American Anthropologist* 63(4): 849–50.

Anthropology and the Public: The Role of Museums, by H. H. Frese. *American Antiquity* 27(2): 246–47.

Selected Papers from the American Anthropologist, 1889–1920. Frederica de Laguna, ed. *Journal of American Folklore* 74(292): 169–71.

1962

Ethnohistory and Its Problems. *Ethnohistory* 9(1): 1–23.

"This Island, the World on the Turtle's Back." *Journal of American Folklore* 75(298): 283–300.

Introduction: Lewis Henry Morgan (1818–1881), Pioneer Ethnologist. Pp. v–xviii in League of the Iroquois, by Lewis Henry Morgan. New York: Corinth Books.
Reviews:
  Seneca Thanksgiving Rituals, by Wallace L. Chafe. *American Anthropologist* 64(5): 1124–26.
  Indians of North America, by Harold E. Driver. *American Antiquity* 27(4): 590–91.

1963

The Seneca Green Corn Ceremony. *The New York State Conservationist* 18(October-November): 20–22, 27–28.
Horatio Hale (1817–1896). Pp. vii–xvii in The Iroquois Book of Rites. Horatio Hale, ed. 2d ed. Toronto: University of Toronto Press. (Reprinted: 1965).
Reviews:
  Conservatism Among the Iroquois at the Six Nations Reserve, by Annemarie Anrod Shimony. *American Anthropologist* 65(2): 444–47.
  Francis Parkman, by Howard N. Doughty. *American Anthropologist* 65(2): 488–89.
  Indians of the Woodlands, from Prehistoric Times to 1725, by George E. Hyde. *American Anthropologist* 65(6): 1391–92.

1964

(with Stanley Diamond and William C. Sturtevant) Memorandum Submitted to Subcommittees on Indian Affairs of the Senate and House of Representatives. *American Anthropologist* 66(3) Pt. 1: 631–33.
[Review of] The Indian and the White Man. Wilcomb E. Washburn, ed. *American Anthropologist* 66(4): 918.

1965

American Participation in VIIth International Congress of Anthropological and Ethnological Sciences, Moscow, August 3–10, 1964. *American Anthropologist* 67(3): 771–73.
(Editor) Captain Hyde's Observations on the Five Nations of Indians at New-Yorke, 1698. *American Scene Magazine.* Tulsa, Oklahoma: Gilcrease Institute of American History and Art.
(Editor) The Journal of James Emlen Kept on a Trip to Canandaigua, New York, September 15 to October 30, 1794, to Attend the Treaty Between the United States and the Six Nations. *Ethnohistory* 12(4): 279–342.
The Iroquois Confederacy in the Twentieth Century: A Case Study of the Theory of Lewis H. Morgan in "Ancient Society." *Ethnology* 4(3): 251–65. (Reprinted: pp. 471–84 in The Emergent Native Americans: A Reader in Culture Contact. Deward E. Walker, Jr., ed. Little, Brown, Boston, 1972.)
(with Donald Collier) Problems of Ethnological Research in North American Museums. *Man* 65(100): 111–12.

Reviews:
The American Drawings of John White 1577–1590, by Paul Hulton and David Beers Quinn. *American Anthropologist* 67(1): 200–201.
Francis Parkman, by Howard N. Doughty. *American Anthropologist* 67(2): 488–89.
Iroquois Music and Dance: Ceremonial Arts of Two Seneca Longhouses, by Gertrude P. Kurath. *American Anthropologist* 67(3): 808–9.
Ancient Society, by Lewis H. Morgan. Leslie A. White, ed. *American Anthropologist* 67(4): 1025–26.
The Bark Canoes and Skin Boats of North America, by Edwin T. Adney and Howard I. Chappelle. *American Neptune* 25(4): 295–97.
The Valley of the Six Nations. Charles M. Johnston, ed. *The Canadian Historical Review* 46(December): 355–56.

1966

Field Work, Museum Studies, and Ethnohistorical Research. *Ethnohistory* 13(1–2): 71–85.
(with Donald Collier) Problems in Ethnological Research in North American Museums. *Museologist* 99: 12–16.
Reviews:
The Paths of Culture: A General Ethnology, by Kaj Birket-Smith. *American Anthropologist* 68(2): 530–32.
The Native Americans. Robert F. Spencer and Jesse D. Jennings, eds. *Ethnohistory* 13(3–4): 197–98.

1967

La théorie de L. H. Morgan de périodisation de l'histoire de société primitive et l'ethnographie modern. *Actes du VIIe Congrès International des Sciences Anthropologiques et Ethnologiques*, 4: 461–74. Moscow.
History and Purposes of the Conference on Iroquois Research. Pp. 3–4 in Iroquois Culture, History and Prehistory: Proceedings of the 1965 Conference on Iroquois Research. Elisabeth Tooker, ed. Albany: New York State Museum and Science Service.
From Longhouse to Ranch-type House: The Second Housing Revolution of the Seneca Nation. Pp. 7–22 in Iroquois Culture, History and Prehistory: Proceedings of the 1965 Conference on Iroquois Research. Elisabeth Tooker, ed. Albany: New York State Museum and Science Service.
Reviews:
Dictionary of Canadian Biography, Volume I: 1000–1700. George W. Brown, gen. ed. *American Anthropologist* 69(2): 269–70.
The American Indian: Perspectives for the Study of Social Change, by Fred Eggan. *American Anthropologist* 69(6): 748–49.
The Catawba Indians, by Douglas S. Brown. *American Historical Review* 42(July): 1477–78.
Houses and House-Life of the American Aboriginals, by Lewis H. Morgan. With an introduction by Paul Bohannan. *New Mexico Historical Review* 42(3): 237–39.
Red Man's Religion, by Ruth Underhill. *Pennsylvania History* 34(2): 211–13.

1968

(Editor) Parker on the Iroquois. Syracuse, N. Y.: Syracuse University Press.
Introduction. Pp. 1–47 in Parker on the Iroquois. William N. Fenton, ed.
Syracuse, N. Y.: Syracuse University Press.

[Obituary] MacEdward Leach, 1892–1967. *Journal of American Folklore* 81(320):
104–5.

1969

Kondiaronk. Pp. 320–23 in Dictionary of Canadian Biography. Vol. 2. David
M. Hayne, gen. ed. Toronto: University of Toronto Press.

(Editor) Answers to Governor Cass's Questions by Jacob Jameson, a Seneca
(ca. 1821–1825). *Ethnohistory* 16(2): 113–39.

Conference on Iroquois Research 1969: Iroquois Research After 25 Years.
Newsletter of the American Anthropological Association 10(10): 9.

J.-F. Lafitau (1681–1746), Precursor of Scientific Anthropology. *Southwestern
Journal of Anthropology* 25(2): 173–87.

Anthropology and the University: An Inaugural Lecture. State University of
New York, Albany.

1970

A Further Note on Jacob Jameson's Answers to the Lewis Cass Questionnaire.
Ethnohistory 17(1–2): 91–92.

The Funeral of Tadodáho: Onondaga of Today. *The Indian Historian* 3(2):
43–47, 66.

Reviews:

Museum and Research, by Jiři Neustupný. *American Anthropologist* 72(4):
967–68.

Fraud, Politics, and the Dispossession of the Indians: The Iroquois Land
Frontier in the Colonial Period, by Georgiana C. Nammack. *American
Anthropologist* 72(5): 1141–42.

The Death and Rebirth of the Seneca, by Anthony F. C. Wallace. *Chicago
Sun-Times Book Week*, January 18, p. 7.

Indian Place Names: Their Origin, Evolution, and Meanings, Collected in
Kansas, by John Rydjord. *Pacific Historical Review* 39(1): 108–9.

1971

The Iroquois in History. Pp. 129–68 in North American Indians in Historical
Perspective. Eleanor B. Leacock and Nancy O. Lurie, eds. New York:
Random House.

Converse, Harriet Maxwell (1836–1903). Pp. 375–77 in Vol. 1 of Notable
American Women, 1607–1950: A Biographical Dictionary. Edward T.
James, ed. Cambridge: Harvard University Press.

Wright, Laura Maria Sheldon (1809–1886). Pp. 680–81 in Vol. 3 of Notable
American Women, 1607–1950: A Biographical Dictionary. Edward T.
James, ed. Cambridge: Harvard University Press.

The New York State Wampum Collection: The Case for the Integrity of
Cultural Treasures. *Proceedings of the American Philosophical Society*
115(6): 437–61. Philadelphia.

[Review of] The Colonial Records of South Carolina: Documents Relating to Indian Affairs, 1754–1765. William L. McDowell, Jr., ed. *William and Mary Quarterly* 28(April): 344–45.

1972

Iroquois Masks: A Living Tradition in the Northeast. Pp. 42–47 in American Indian Art: Form and Tradition. An Exhibition Organized by the Walker Art Center, the Indian Art Association, and the Minneapolis Institute of Arts, 22 October–31 December, 1972. Minneapolis.

Return to the Longhouse. Pp. 102–18 in Crossing Cultural Boundaries: The Anthropological Experience. Solon T. Kimball and James B. Watson, eds. San Francisco: Chandler Publishing Co.

[Obituary] Howard Sky, 1900–1971: Cayuga Faith-Keeper, Gentleman, and Interpreter of Iroquois Culture. *American Anthropologist* 74(3): 758–62.

Foreword. Pp. xiii–xxi in Cartier's Hochelaga and the Dawson Site, by James F. Pendergast and Bruce G. Trigger. Montreal and London: McGill-Queen's University Press.

1973

An Instructor's Librarian [Andy Peters]. *Bulletin of the Friends of the Owen D. Young Library, St. Lawrence University* 3(2): 5–6.

Ethnology and Ethnohistory as Tools for Interpreting the Past: The Case of the Iroquois. Pp. 111–16 in Clash of Cultures: The American Indian Student in Higher Education, a Report. Roy H. Sansdstrom, ed. St. Lawrence University, July 10–28, 1972. Canton, New York.

Folklore (American Indian). Pp. 520–22 in Encyclopaedia Britannica. Vol. 9. Chicago: Encyclopaedia Britannica.

B. B. Thatcher's Indian Biography (1832). [Introduction to] Indian Biography or, An Historical Account, by B. B. Thatcher. Vol. 1. Glorieta, New Mexico: The Rio Grande Press.

[Review of] Red Man's Land—White Man's Law: A Study of the Past and Present Status of the American Indian, by Wilcomb E. Washburn. *Terrae Incognitae* 5: 83–84.

1974

(Editor and translator with Elizabeth L. Moore) Customs of the American Indians Compared with the Customs of Primitive Times, by Father Joseph François Lafitau. Vol. 1. Toronto: The Champlain Society.

(With Elizabeth L. Moore) Preface, Bibliographic Note, and Introduction. Pp. ix–cxix in Customs of the American Indians Compared with the Customs of Primitive Times, by Father Joseph François Lafitau. William N. Fenton and Elizabeth L. Moore, eds. and trans. Vol. 1. Toronto: The Champlain Society.

Lafitau, Joseph-François. Pp. 334–38 in Dictionary of Canadian Biography, Vol. 3. Francess G. Halpenny, gen. ed. Toronto: University of Toronto Press.

The Advancement of Material Culture Studies in Modern Anthropological Research. Pp. 15–36 in The Human Mirror: Material and Spatial Images of Man. Miles Richardson, ed. Baton Rouge: Louisiana State University Press.

[Review of] White Savage, by Richard Drinnon; White into Red, by J. Norman Heard; and The Journal of Major John Norton, 1816, by Carl F. Klinck and James J. Talman. *The American Historical Review* 79(4): 1258–60.

1975

The Lore of the Longhouse: Myth, Ritual and Red Power. *Anthropological Quarterly* 48(3): 131–47.

1976

[Obituary] Marian E. White (1921–1975). *American Anthropologist* 78(4): 891–92.

1977

(Editor and translator with Elizabeth L. Moore) Customs of the American Indians Compared with the Customs of Primitive Times, by Father Joseph François Lafitau. Vol. 2. Toronto: The Champlain Society.

(with Elizabeth L. Moore) Lafitau et la pensée ethnologique de son temps. *Études littéraires* 10(1–2): 19–47.

1978

"Aboriginally Yours," Jesse J. Cornplanter, Hah-Yonh-Wonh-Ish, The Snipe, Seneca, 1889–1957. Pp. 177–95 in American Indian Intellectuals. Margot Liberty, ed. 1976 Proceedings of the American Ethnological Society. Robert F. Spencer, gen. ed. St. Paul: West Publishing Co.

Problems in the Authentication of the League of the Iroquois. Pp. 261–68 in Neighbors and Intruders: An Ethnohistorical Exploration of Hudson's River. Laurence M. Hauptman and Jack Campisi, eds. *Canada. National Museum of Man, Canadian Ethnology Service, Mercury Series Paper* 39. Ottawa.

Northern Iroquoian Culture Patterns. Pp. 296–321 in Northeast. Bruce G. Trigger, vol. ed. Handbook of North American Indians, Vol. 15. William C. Sturtevant, gen. ed. Washington: Smithsonian Institution.

(with Elisabeth Tooker) Mohawk. Pp. 466–80 in Northeast. Bruce G. Trigger, vol. ed. Handbook of North American Indians, Vol. 15. William C. Sturtevant, gen. ed. Washington: Smithsonian Institution.

Cherokee and Iroquois Connections Revisited. *Journal of Cherokee Studies* 3(4): 239–49.

Reviews:

Huronia: An Essay in Proper Ethnohistory. [Review of] The Children of Aataentsic: A History of the Huron People to 1660, by Bruce G. Trigger. *American Anthropologist* 80(4): 923–35.

Cherokees in Transition: A Study of Changing Culture and the Environment Prior to 1775, by Gary C. Goodwin. *The Journal of American History* (September): 421.

1979

The Great Good Medicine. *New York State Journal of Medicine* 79(10): 1603–9.
[Review of] The Delaware Indian Westward Migration, by Clinton A. Weslager. *The New-York Historical Society Quarterly* 63(2): 171–72.

1980

Gayë'göthwë:' Hadihadi:ya's Yí:'do:s [Tobacco Burning Invocation, they cross the forest, the Yí:'do:s Ceremony]. Wallace L. Chafe, ed. Pp. 3–8 in Northern Iroquoian Texts. Marianne Mithun and Hanni Woodbury, eds. *International Journal of American Linguistics, Native American Texts Series* 4. Chicago: University of Chicago Press.
Frederick Starr, Jesse Cornplanter and the Cornplanter Medal for Iroquois Research. *New York History* 61(2): 187–99.

1981

The Iroquois in the Grand Tradition of American Letters: The Works of Walter D. Edmonds, Carl Carmer, and Edmund Wilson. *American Indian Culture and Research Journal* 5(4): 21–39.

1982

[Review of] Savages and Scientists: The Smithsonian Institution and the Development of American Anthropology 1846–1910, by Curtis M. Hinsley, Jr. *American Anthropologist* 84(3): 650–53.
John Canfield Ewers and the Great Tradition of Artists and Ethnologists of the West. Pp. 11–17 in Plains Indian Studies: A Collection of Essays in Honor of John C. Ewers and Waldo R. Wedel. Douglas H. Ubelaker and Herman J. Viola, eds. *Smithsonian Contributions to Anthropology* 30. Washington.

In Press

Structure, Continuity, and Change in the Process of Iroquois Treaty Making. To appear in Reference Guide to the Iroquois Nations and Their League. Francis Jennings, ed. Syracuse University Press.
Frank G. Speck's Anthropology (1881–1950). To appear in Frank G. Speck, The Last Magician, 1881–1950. Roy Blankenship, ed. University of Pennsylvania Press.
Morgan's Legacy to Iroquois Studies and to American Ethnology. Symposium on Lewis Henry Morgan and Anthropology: A Centennial Evaluation. Symposium on Kin and Communities, Smithsonian Institution, June 14–17, 1977. Morton H. Fried, ed.

Index